ハワイ作戦部隊(機動部隊・充[追]部隊)行動図

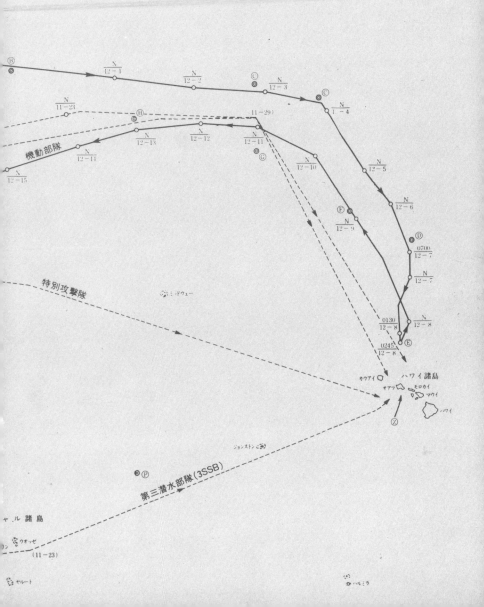

A BATTLE HISTORY OF
THE
IMPERIAL
JAPANESE
NAVY
(1941–1945)

NAVAL INSTITUTE PRESS • ANNAPOLIS • MARYLAND

大日本帝國海軍

A BATTLE HISTORY OF
THE
IMPERIAL
JAPANESE
NAVY
(1941–1945)

BY PAUL S. DULL

All photographs courtesy of U. S. Navy, with the following exceptions:
Courtesy of Captain Roger Pineau, USNR: photograph
numbers 1, 13, 17, 24 and 45.
Courtesy of Japan Defense Agency, War History Section, photograph
numbers 5, 6, 7, 12, 38, 39 and 40; and all official portraits
of Japanese officers.
Japanese calligraphy by Tai Falconeri

Printed in the United States of America

To *all* the brave sailors who have lost their lives in warships

CONTENTS

MAPS AND
TRACK CHARTS

FOREWORD

When Paul Dull contacted the U. S. Naval History Division in 1973 to arrange for the use of our collection of microfilmed Japanese naval records, we were especially pleased to offer assistance. These records had been selected and prepared for microfilming in the late 1950s by Mrs. Lily Y. Tanaka, a member of the staff assisting Samuel E. Morison in the preparation of his classic *History of United States Naval Operations in World War II*. Upon the return of the original documents to Japan in 1958, the more than 200 microfilm reels resulting from Mrs. Tanaka's efforts represented the only sizeable group of Imperial Japanese Navy documents remaining in the United States. Yet, despite the numerous students of World War II naval history, the collection had seen virtually no use for a number of years, due to the formidable problems involved in using Japanese-language materials.

Professor Dull was in an ideal position to write a history based almost exclusively upon Japanese sources. Having recently retired from the history department of the University of Oregon, he could concentrate on a lengthy research project. Further, his interest in Japanese history was a long-standing one, dating from his World War II service as a Japanese language specialist and intelligence officer with the United States Marine Corps, as well as his many years of postwar experience as an academic specialist in Asian history.

In addition to using contemporary Japanese documents, Professor Dull also consulted the official Japanese history currently under preparation by the Japanese Defense Agency's War History Section (Boeicho Kenshujo Senshishitsu). It seems unlikely that this extensive series, already numbering more than ninety volumes, will appear in English translation. Hence, as with the case of the original documents, this history serves to introduce into Western literature little-used data from Japanese sources.

Professor Dull has elected to concentrate on the principal surface and carrier engagements of the war, between the Pearl Harbor raid and the disastrous sortie of the super-battleship *Yamato* almost four years later. He also provides Western readers with an appreciation of these battles as seen through the eyes of Japanese commanders. In both respects the author deepens and sometimes corrects the coverage offered by previous histories.

Paul Dull's work is testimony to the keen interest in the great Pacific War and to the existence of new materials that remain to be fully exploited by historians. His tenacity in pursuing this major work and the decision of the United States Naval Institute to publish it for American readers will be welcomed by all who are interested in the role played by navies in World War II.

DEAN C. ALLARD
U. S. Naval History Division

PREFACE

This book is a battle history of the Imperial Japanese Navy in World War II, and is, to the best of my knowledge, the first book written in a non-Japanese language to tell the Imperial Japanese Navy's story by relying primarily on the relevant official Japanese records. It has thus been my aim to tell the story just as the Japanese saw and recorded it. Because of the vastness of the subject, the book's scope has deliberately been limited to surface naval engagements in World War II; this has meant that certain important subjects could be dealt with only in passing—Japanese naval doctrine, submarine warfare, antisubmarine strategy, amphibious landings, mine warfare, and shore-based air forces.

The Japanese source material falls into two categories: microfilmed material, and the monumental history of World War II being written by the Japan Defense Agency, War History Section (Boeicho Kenshujo Senshishitsu, abbreviated BKS), a project which has already produced some ninety volumes. The 260 microfilmed reels contain the day-by-day history and battle data of individual ships, divisions, squadrons, and fleets; there are also special reels concerning major battles, like Midway. Only one microfilm reel (JT 1) is in English; all the others are in handwritten Japanese (often in execrable penmanship). The microfilm reels have some gaps from lost or misplaced records, but what could not be found on microfilm could usually be found in the Japan Defense Agency volumes. All track charts and line drawings have been derived from the BKS volumes or the microfilmed material, sometimes used in conjunction with Western sources. In the selection of photographs to accompany the text, I have tried as much as possible to use Japanese photography—some photos obtained through the Japan Defense Agency, War History Section, and others through the U. S. National Archives and the Naval Historical Center, and the personal collection of Captain Roger Pineau.

Data on the U. S. Navy and the other Allied navies involved in the battles described were taken from standard national naval sources written in English. These accounts, which rarely use Japanese sources, sometimes differ from the official Japanese versions. When such variances or errors are pointed out in the text or footnotes of this book, I have done so in the spirit expressed by the doyen of U.S. naval historians, Samuel Eliot Morison, in the preface of his *History of United States Naval Operations in World War II*, Volume IV (Boston: Little, Brown and Co., 1951), pp. ix–x:

> I have simply gone ahead and told the story as it happened, to the best of my knowledge and ability. I do not claim omniscience. As fresh data appear, mistakes will be found and later writers will make new interpretations. It is the fate of all historians, especially those who take the risk of writing shortly after the event, to be superseded. Far safer to write about an era long past, in which all the actors are long since dead! But my warm contact with the United States Navy in action has given me the opportunity to see events for myself, to obtain oral information while men's memories are still fresh, and to correct mistakes in the written record. I hope that naval officers and others will not hesitate to point out errors and take issue about conclusions, as they have done generously in the past.

It is my sincere hope that future authors on this subject will show equal generosity toward the present work.

To some degree, the idea for this book was engendered by my personal experience. I was a captain in the U. S. Marine Corps Reserve and was at Pearl Harbor on 7 December 1941. After that I did a tour of duty in Fleet Intelligence and then, with Captain John Merrill (USMCR), founded a Japanese language school, for the purpose of teaching front-line combat Japanese to enlisted Marines. In 1944 I also gave a month's instruction in military Japanese to Marine Corps graduates of the U. S. Navy's language school at Boulder, Colorado. I was given a medical discharge in September 1944, and was then employed by the Office of War Information, Psychological Warfare Division, Japanese Section, in charge of daily estimates of Japanese domestic and military conditions, and of editing the material that was sent by radio from Saipan to Japan.

This book is the result of a long ambition to give the account from the Japanese side, and thus to make available in English both sides of the naval war in the Pacific. It is my hope that by doing so, the war may be seen in a new perspective, possibly strengthening the cultural ties between the Western world and Japan.

Japanese military and political thought is heavily influenced by the Japanese language. Language is not merely a tool for human communication; language is itself a means by which the realities of the world are divided and viewed. Even among Western languages each national language expresses different concepts of these realities. They are all, however, heavily influenced by Hebrew/Christian culture and Aristotelian logic. The Japanese language, however, owes many of its characteristics to the culture and values of Shinto, Bushido, and Buddhism. The fact that the written language uses ideographic symbols also heavily influences the form and content of Japanese thought.

I have tried to construct the Tables of Organization for Japanese naval forces, which appear at the end of chapters, so that the reader will understand relationships which are not actually expressed in unit titles. The Japanese, despite their strong sense of hierarchy, do not indicate the precise relationship among different units. This is a result of the unique character of the Japanese language, whose nature is often difficult for the Westerner to grasp. Almost always, a unit of ships will be designated only as *tai* or *butai*, which I have usually translated as "force." The Japanese had no equivalent to the U. S. Navy's operational system of Task Forces, Task Groups, and Task Units. My Japanese Tables of Organization, therefore, do not show the administrative or tactical chains of command, despite the way in which I have arranged the various units. In most cases, it is simply impossible to *find* a clear hierarchy of command, when the words *tai* and *butai* are used over and over, to designate any and all levels of command. (To give an example, the force that raided Pearl Harbor was called "Hawaii Operation *Butai*, Mobile *Butai*, Advance *Butai*.")

So many kind people gave of their time and knowledge to supply me with answers and assistance that it is almost impossible to note them all. Dr. D. C. Allard, Head, Operational Archives Branch, Department of the Navy, Naval Historical Center, at the Washington Navy Yard, deserves special thanks for his valuable advice and encouragement on the project, and for his helpfulness in finding the microfilm records I needed. Great appreciation is also due to Dr. Kengo Tominaga, former Chief Consultant of the War History Section, Japan Defense Agency, and to Mr. Seiichiro Ohnishi, President of the National Defense College, who graciously gave me permission to use certain parts of the section's war history volumes, and supplied me with photographs and encouragement.

Thanks and credit are due Ms. Ryoko Toyama of the Orientalia Collection of the University of Oregon library; Professor G. Ralph Falconeri, professor of Japanese history, University of Oregon; Professor John Perrin, who did a professional job of editing the first draft; Captain Roger Pineau, USNR, Director of the U. S. Navy Memorial Museum at the Washington Navy Yard, who gave me valuable direction and encouragement; Mr. Donald Hoegsburg of the Department of Geography, the University of Oregon, the cartographer and track-chart composer, who did a difficult task so well; Lieutenant Colonel Otis W. Bauske, USAF (Ret.), who gave me valuable technical advice; and to Ms. Kasey Arceneaux (my daughter), Ms. Erma Robbins, and my wife Ruth, for typing and proofreading the manuscript. Without Ruth's patience, encouragement, and help, this book could not have been written.

A note on times used in this book: the Imperial Japanese Navy always kept its ships' chronometers on Tokyo time, but I have instead followed the Standard Time Zone Chart of the World, prepared by the Hydrographic Office under the authority of the Secretary of the Navy. An exception was made in the case of the Pearl Harbor attack, which is given in Hawaiian time.

Japanese names are rendered in English order.

ABBREVIATIONS

AA Antiaircraft (gun)

AACL Antiaircraft light cruiser

ABD A unified command of the United States, Great Britain, the Netherlands

ABDA A unified command of the United States, Great Britain, the Netherlands, Australia

Air Desron A Japanese destroyer squadron assigned to operate with one or more aircraft carriers

Airflot A Japanese air flotilla (squadron)

Airsol Aircraft Solomons Command

ANZAC Australia, New Zealand area command

AO Fleet tanker, oiler

AP Armor-piercing (shell)

APD Destroyer converted to transport

APHE Anti-personnel high-explosive shell

AR Japanese action report of a warship

ASW Antisubmarine warfare

BB Battleship

Batdiv A division of battleships

BKS Boeicho Kenshujo Senshishitsu; Japan Defense Agency, War History Section

CA Heavy cruiser

CAP Combat air patrol. Fighter planes, generally over aircraft carriers, for protection against enemy planes

Cardiv A division of aircraft carriers or seaplane tenders

CINC Commander in Chief

CINCPAC Commander in Chief U. S. Pacific Fleet

CL Light cruiser

CM Minelayer

COMSOPAC Commander in Chief South Pacific

Crudiv A division of cruisers (heavy or light)

CV Large aircraft carrier

CVE Escort aircraft carrier

CVL Light aircraft carrier

CVS Seaplane tender

DAR Japanese Detailed Action Report. Kept by units of ships up through larger echelons to fleets

DD Destroyer

Desdiv Destroyer division

Desron Destroyer squadron, generally led by a light cruiser or minelayer

HA High-angle (antiaircraft) gun

HF/DF High-frequency direction finder, to pinpoint enemy radio transmissions

HMNZS His Majesty's New Zealand ship

HMS His Majesty's ship (British)

IJA Imperial Japanese Army

IJN Imperial Japanese Navy

JCS Joint Chiefs of Staff

JOMS Japanese Operational Monograph Series, No. 116. Prepared by U. S. Army, Far East Command, *A Graphic Presentation of the Japanese Naval Organization and List of Combatant and Non-Combatant Vessels Lost or Damaged in the War*

LST Amphibious landing ship, tanks (also used to transport troops)

MTB Motor torpedo boat

NEI Netherlands East Indies

OTC Officer in Tactical Command

PT Motor torpedo boat

Patwing U.S. naval wing of aircraft: amphibious

RAAF Royal Australian Air Force

RAF Royal Air Force (British)

RAN Royal Australian Navy

RN Royal Navy (British)

RNN Royal Netherlands Navy

RNZAF Royal New Zealand Air Force

SNLF Japanese Special Naval Landing Force

Soex Fleet Japanese Southern Expeditionary Fleet—Operated off Malaga to Burma

Subron Submarine squadron

TBS Talk between ships (by low frequency radio)

TF Task Force

TG Task Group

TO Table of Organization

TROM (Japanese) Tabular Records of Movement (kept by each ship) showing administrative and tactical command and a complete daily record of activities

TU Task Unit

VAAF Fifth Army Air Force under General MacArthur's administrative command

USA United States Army

USAAF United States Army Air Force

USAAFFE United States Army Air Force Far East. Based in Philippine Islands 1941

USMC United States Marine Corps

USN United States Navy

USS United States ship

WD (Japanese) War Diary. A daily diary of all operations kept by units of ships

XCV (Japanese) hybrid battleship/carrier

section 1

JAPAN GOES TO WAR

chapter 1

THE ATTACK
ON PEARL HARBOR

On Sunday morning, 7 December 1941, with a devastating surprise attack on the U. S. Pacific Fleet at Pearl Harbor by Vice Admiral Chuichi Nagumo's carrier-based planes, Japan began her war against the United States. This operation was only one of more than a score of roughly simultaneous naval and land operations by the Japanese, in a coordinated assault on American and British forces throughout the vast Pacific theater. Western naval historians have called Japan's plunge into war "insane," "imbecilic," or "ultimately disastrous." But to understand why Japan went to war, one must take into account the profound cultural differences between the West and Japan.

Although Japan was a modern industrial nation, its people were often strongly motivated by the primitive mythology of Shinto. They believed that they were ruled by a semi-divine emperor, a direct descendant of Emperor Jimmu, who was said to have come down from the Plains of Heaven in 660 B.C. to rule the Japanese people (who were themselves descendants of lesser gods). Between the twelfth and nineteenth centuries, Japan evolved from a collection of proto-feudal manors into a true (although uniquely Japanese) feudal state. During these centuries, militarism was highly esteemed, and action was preferred to words. This strong sense of militarism blended well with the beliefs underlying the Japanese national state, which was instituted in 1868. Under this form of government, a Japanese was thought to owe a debt to the Emperor that even death could not repay.

The Japanese, then, believed that their country was unique because of its origins and political organization. They had never lost a war, and even when the Mongols established a beachhead in Kyushu in the thirteenth century, a typhoon wrecked the Mongol fleet and the survivors withdrew; that typhoon was called "Kamikaze," which means "divine wind." The belief in "Nihon Seishin," the Japanese spirit that could prevail over any foe, evolved from such tales. The influence of such beliefs was strongest among the military men, especially the junior officers whose limited military education had not yet exposed them to the larger world. But it affected the behavior of almost all of the Japanese people.

Despite the tremendous strides Japan had made as a modern state by 1941, her leaders felt that she still was not accepted as an equal by the Western world. Relations with the United States, Japan's ocean neighbor, had been deterioriating since 1907. Even when moderates were in power in Japan in the 1920s, the U. S. Congress passed the Immigration Act of 1924, which barred Orientals from immigrating to the United States—a gratuitous insult, since in the Gentleman's Agreement with President Theodore Roosevelt, made in 1907, the Japanese had imposed such a ban on themselves.

After World War I, in order to head off a naval arms race, the Five Power Naval Armaments Treaty of 1922 was signed by the United States, Great Britain, Japan, France, and Italy. This agreement fixed the tonnage of capital ships at a ratio of 5(United States)—5(Britain)—3(Japan)—1.67(France)—1.67(Italy). Although under the 5-5-3 ratio the Imperial Japanese Navy was certainly strong enough to protect Japan in Empire waters, the agreement only intensified Japanese resentment of the supposed superiority of the West. The ratio was kept at the London Naval Conference in 1930, but the days of the moderate in Japan were over; when the more militant Japanese came to power, they planned to end Japanese participation in the treaty.

When the Japanese Army, spurred on by both military and civilian ultra-militarists, invaded Manchuria in 1931 (without the consent of the Japanese Diet), relations with the United States, which had denounced the aggression most emphatically, deteriorated even more.

In the 1930s, it became apparent that another era of militarism in the world was approaching. Alarmed at Japan's foreign policy, the United States began to enlarge its navy, which had been allowed to deteriorate since 1922, and in 1934 Congress provided funds for the navy to build itself up to treaty limits. Then in 1936, Japan formally pulled out of the London Naval Conference treaty. In 1937 two further events exacerbated the fear and hostility between the two countries: U. S. President Franklin Roosevelt authorized the building of two powerful battleships, the *Washington* and the *North Carolina*;

and Japan invaded North China—the United States again being the most vocal critic of her aggression.

When war broke out in Europe in 1939, the United States rapidly began to increase its naval military strength. In 1940, authorization was given for the construction of 6 *Iowa*-class battleships (45,000 tons); 5 *Montana*-class battleships (58,000 tons; these were never constructed); 6 *Alaska*-class large cruisers (27,000 tons; only two of these were completed); 11 *Essex*-class aircraft carriers (27,000 tons); 40 cruisers; 115 destroyers; and 67 submarines. This huge building program forced Japan to reassess her military situation, for she had neither the shipbuilding capacity nor the oil reserves to match such naval strength. It was predicted that her oil reserves could sustain her navy for only two years in a war with the United States. Plans began to be made to establish, by conquest, the Greater East Asia Co-Prosperity Sphere, a strategy long advocated by Japanese right-wing and military pamphleteers. The territory thus acquired could provide the oil and other raw materials needed by Japan to continue her deepening involvement in China. Such aggression, however, would probably mean war with the United States, Great Britain (along with Australia and New Zealand), and the Netherlands.[1] Nevertheless, because of the extremists' strong influence over the Army, Japan occupied southern French Indochina, in July 1941. At once, the United States, Great Britain, and the Netherlands embargoed oil supplies to Japan.

The Japanese were now faced with a real crisis. Most responsible Japanese wanted the embargo issue settled by diplomacy; but many of the military people felt that war was the only solution. The Liaison Council agreed, on 3 September, that if the embargo was not lifted by early October, Japan would go to war to gain the South Seas territory that she needed. This decision locked the Japanese government into an either/or policy, since President Roosevelt would agree to lift the oil embargo only if the Japanese Army would leave French Indochina and China. The impasse became intensified after General Hideki Tojo became prime minister in October, because Tojo would never agree to the Americans' demand for withdrawal. Therefore, the decision was made to prepare for war, although the diplomatic talks were to be continued, with little hope for their success.

To further understand this decision, one must consider the peculiar structure of the Japanese government and military. The War and Navy ministries could both function independently of the parliamentary branch of government, even though they were ostensibly part of it. Also, in the Army and Navy during the 1930s a peculiar system had evolved, whereby junior officers and staff members could and did override the recommendations of admirals and generals. The real decisions were often made by lower-level officials, and if a top official disagreed with them, he might be assassinated. Many senior officers in the Navy, including Admiral Isoroku Yamamoto, strongly opposed a war with the United States, but found themselves overridden by war-thirsty subordinates.

With the United States adamant, the debate in the Imperial General Headquarters (composed of the chiefs of Army and Navy General Staffs, Army and Navy ministers, and selected high-ranking officers) became long and complicated. Their preliminary decision to pursue a southern policy, even if it meant war, was finally agreed to by the chief of the Naval General Staff, Admiral Osami Nagano. The possibility of avoiding war by withdrawing from China was not considered, since it would mean a "loss of face."

Admiral Nagano argued that control of the South Seas region was indispensable, and that to obtain this objective, Japan should not hesitate to engage in war with England and the United States. He further stated that his decision was not based on the assumption that Japan would necessarily win the war. As Nagano explained to the Emperor: "The government has decided that if there were no war, the fate of the nation was sealed. Even if there is war, the country may be ruined. Nevertheless a nation which does not fight in this plight has lost its spirit and is already a doomed nation."[2]

It was the combination of the Japanese way of thinking, Japan's past history, her pride, and the peculiar nature of her political process, which produced the decision for war—the decision was not made by any one man, or caused by any one event. It was left up to the armed forces to continue to make plans which would increase the chances for victory. If Germany prevailed in Europe, Japan's only enemy would be the United States, where public opinion was bitterly divided on the question of involvement in a foreign war. Therefore, the Japanese believed an early and decisive destruction of the U. S. Pacific Fleet would end a war with the United States with an early peace on Japan's terms, and the Greater East Asia Co-Prosperity Sphere would thus become a reality.

The duty of successfully protecting the Army's push to the South Seas had been given to the Navy, without consideration being given to alternate plans. Therefore, if a major catastrophe had befallen Admiral Nagumo's fleet, a chaotic alternate-planning period would have confronted the Imperial General Headquarters. The Pearl Harbor raid was a massive gamble that had to be won, for the sake of all the other operations already set in motion. Guam was to be rapidly overwhelmed, and Wake Island was to be attacked. The Philippines would be combed by land- and carrier-based planes, and shelled by warships, in order to neutralize American air power there. The Japanese Army was to land in Malaya, with the Navy giving close support and providing protection against Force Z of the British Eastern Fleet, based at Singapore, and against the Royal Air Force (RAF), stationed throughout Malaya. Enemy ships in Hong Kong and Shanghai were also to be immediately attacked.

This coordinated and complex naval strike and support strategy had all been put together under the guidance of Admiral Yamamoto, the commander-in-chief of the Imperial Japanese Navy—a man fascinated by gambling in private life, but one who never gambled until he felt that he had mastered the odds of the game. Yamamoto was a patriotic Japanese who revered his emperor and his country, and whose sole preoccupation was his career as a Japanese naval officer. He was well informed about Great Britain and the United States, and he never underestimated the industrial capacity of the latter. In the years preceding Pearl Harbor, he had risked assassination by stubbornly opposing a war against the United States, a war which he feared Japan could not win. When, however, it was decided to attempt such a war, his sense of duty led him to plan how to strike the United States with the most devastating blow possible. He hoped to defeat and destroy as much of American naval power as possible, by at once seeking a decisive battle with the U. S. Pacific Fleet.

Admiral Yamamoto, however, did not entirely control Japanese military planning. His strategy had to accommodate the aims of the Japanese Army (with which he often disagreed), and the opposing views of those in higher administrative positions within the Navy. Although he was commander-in-chief of the Combined Fleet, he was subordinate to the Navy Department and Imperial General Headquarters, the latter being army-dominated, for the most part, on matters of major strategic planning.

The basic outline of American naval strategy in case of war against Japan—"Orange," then "Rainbow Five"—was partially known to Imperial General Headquarters. It projected an American advance through the islands of the Central Pacific (the Marshalls, Carolines, and Marianas), with an eventual defeat of the Japanese

Navy near Japan's home waters.[3] It would not be a rapid advance, but while it was taking place, American industry could easily outproduce the Japanese in military hardware, especially ships.

The Japanese strategy for the first stage of the East Asian War was set, then, by 7 December 1941: first, Japan would acquire the resources of an enlarged empire, so that she could continue to build up her military forces and supply them adequately; and then establish a perimeter defense, to protect the empire against counterattack. To Yamamoto, it was absolutely essential to destroy the U. S. Pacific Fleet at the very outset, so that the Navy would be unimpeded in protecting the Army's southern advances. He firmly believed that a short war was the only kind of war that Japan could hope to win—a stunning initial victory which would lead a divided and discouraged United States, faced with a two-ocean war, to negotiate a peace settlement on terms that would preserve Japan's newly won territories. It was from this premise that Yamamoto conceived the surprise attack on Pearl Harbor (but, as he was led to understand, the attack was to occur thirty minutes to an hour after a formal declaration of war). If Japan were to win the war, the Navy had to make Pearl Harbor the decisive battle that would destroy American sea power in the Pacific. It was a gambler's decision, but the gambler hoped to alter the odds with a bold plan and new naval concepts.

The possibility of war with the United States had long occupied the attention of the Japanese Naval Staff. The two most apparent choices open to them were either to assist the Army in its southern advance and await an American counterattack (possibly with British support), preferably in home waters; or to devise a surprise attack on the U. S. Pacific Fleet at the very outset. The proponents of the first measure cited the success at the battle of Tsushima Strait in the Russo-Japanese war. From what the Japanese knew of the Rainbow Five plan, however, it was clear that the United States would probably first seek the conquest of the Marshall Islands and the establishment of forward bases there, and then leapfrog through the Carolines and Marianas. If the Americans proceeded thus, an early decisive battle in Japan's home waters would not occur; instead, the war would be prolonged, and the industrial capacity of the United States would prevail. Since a long war was what most Japanese naval men feared, they came to favor the idea of a decisive surprise attack, if an effective operation could be conceived.

Yamamoto had to devise an operation that would insure success with a minimum of risk. It was standard naval doctrine at that time that a fleet could not operate successfully more than two thousand miles from its base (and the Marshalls, which did not have a major naval base, were outside that range), and that a navy lost 10 percent of its fighting capability for every thousand miles it operated from its base. These were, however, battleship doctrines arising out of World War I, and Yamamoto's attack would not be by battleships, but by carrier-based planes, armed with torpedoes and heavy bombs, and covered by fighter planes. His task force would be accompanied by oilers, so that refueling could take place at sea.

The effectiveness of a carrier-based torpedo-plane raid against warships at anchor in a harbor was tested in the Japanese naval war games in April and May, 1940. As in most war games, there were disagreements in part with referees' arbitrary decisions. But Rear Admiral Shigeru Fukudome, a senior naval aviation officer and Yamamoto's chief of staff, concluded that the games had proved that such an engagement would be a decisive victory, because the surface vessels would have no means of evading the torpedo planes. Admiral Yamamoto also concluded that a massed torpedo-plane attack, if it were a surprise, would be successful. When a similar attack was actually carried out in the British naval air raid on the Italian fleet at Taranto on 12 November 1940, the results confirmed the evidence of the Japanese war games, since twenty-one planes sank three Italian ships, with only two planes lost. Yamamoto ordered detailed studies of the Taranto raid to be made by Japanese naval attachés in London and in Rome.

After receiving these analyses, Yamamoto ordered Fukudome to begin study of such an attack with planes carrying specially constructed shallow-running torpedoes, which could be launched at short range. Rear Admiral Takijiro Onishi and Commander Minoru Genda, one of Japan's top airmen, were brought into the study. By January 1941, the finished report was available to Yamamoto, and he decided that, if war came, this would be the first blow struck by the Navy. After vigorous debate, Yamamoto was able to overcome the objections of Admiral Nagano, chief of naval staff.

Because most of the U. S. Pacific Fleet was constantly at anchor at Pearl Harbor, plans for the surprise attack could begin immediately. A close surveillance of the U. S. Pacific Fleet at Pearl Harbor was begun by personnel attached to the Japanese consulate in Honolulu, and weekly summaries of ships at anchor and at sea, and their schedules, were sent back to naval intelligence in Tokyo. In September, Kagoshima Bay was chosen as the secret site for practicing a

Pearl Harbor attack, and realistic training began. Production of torpedoes with wooden fins, designed to run in Pearl Harbor's shallow waters, was undertaken.

By 3 November Yamamoto had overcome all opposition within the Navy; there would be a surprise attack on Pearl Harbor, if the politicians and diplomats could not reach a peace settlement. Operation Order #1 was issued secretly to senior officers on 5 November; it read, "To the east, the American fleet will be destroyed. The American lines of operation and supply to the Far East will be severed. Enemy forces will be intercepted and annihilated. Victories will be exploited to smash the enemy's will to fight." Vice Admiral Nagumo, commander-in-chief of the First Air Fleet and overall commander of the Pearl Harbor Strike Force, on board his flagship, the heavy carrier *Akagi*, received specific and detailed orders on 11 November concerning the strike. Then on 25 November he received an order to sail the next day. Neither the original order nor the fragmentary order #9, issued to each unit of Nagumo's strike force, even mentioned an attack on the oil storage tanks or machine shops at Pearl Harbor[4]—a fact which proved to be of no small importance.

Admiral Nagumo, who was regarded as a gruff and uncommunicative officer, was Japan's top carrier commander. He did not believe in the Pearl Harbor raid, emphasizing to Yamamoto (with whom he was not on good personal terms) that carriers were very vulnerable ships; although their planes could inflict damage, enemy planes could sink a carrier by scoring with only one or two well-placed bombs or torpedoes. Nagumo would have preferred to cover the southern push, but, late in the summer of 1941, he reluctantly accepted the idea of a Pearl Harbor strike.

On 22 November the task force began to assemble at Tankan Bay (also called Hitokappu) in the Kurile chain, north of Hokkaido. The raid was to hit Pearl Harbor at 0830 Sunday, 7 December. The Japanese had undertaken their vast preparations with the utmost secrecy; in order to hide the assembling of the Strike Force, warships in the Inland Sea had been generating false radio traffic, to lead American intelligence to believe that the Japanese carriers were still in home waters. Actually, American intelligence, after having lost track of the carriers, deduced that they were on the move, but Pearl Harbor was never seriously considered as their destination.

Admiral Yamamoto issued the Strike Force's sailing orders on 25 November: to sail on the following morning; to refuel at sea at a predetermined site on 3 December; and, if they were not recalled, to launch an attack to hit Pearl Harbor as scheduled; and then to retire west in order to prevent a counterattack, returning to Japan.

Admiral Nagumo's force sailed from Tankan Bay in extremely foggy weather, the carriers leaving at 0900 on 26 November. Their course took them through the deserted region of the North Pacific, south of the Great Northern Circle and north of the rhumb-line navigational routes between the Hawaiian Islands and Japan. The force was under orders to return to base, if detected. The weather, however, was foul, with fog at times interspersed with winter gales— difficult weather for sailing on schedule in formation, but excellent

Table of Organization, Pearl Harbor Strike Force

(an asterisk indicates a flagship):

First Air Fleet

Heavy Carriers: *Akagi**, *Kaga, Hiryu, Soryu, Shokaku, Zuikaku*
Light Cruiser: *Abukuma*⁵*
Destroyers: *Isokaze, Urakaze, Tanikaze, Hamakaze, Arare, Kasumi, Kagero, Shiranuhi, Akigumo*

Support Force

Battleships: *Hiei, Kirishima*
Heavy Cruisers: *Tone, Chikuma*

Ship Lane Reconnaissance Units

Submarines: *I-19, I-21, I-23*

Midway Destruction Unit

Destroyers: *Ushio, Sazanami*

Fleet Train

Eight Tankers and Supply Ships⁶

weather for escaping detection. In the van, acting as a screen were the destroyers and light cruiser; next came the heavy cruisers, steaming abreast the six heavy carriers, which were in parallel columns of three each; last came the two battleships.⁷

The decision to carry out the attack came on 1 December, and the code message—"Niitaka yama nobore," ("Climb Mount Niitaka")—was sent to Admiral Nagumo on 2 December. Now only pre-mature detection could prevent the launching of the raid. On 3 December the wind abated, which allowed refueling to go ahead without difficulty. With the smoother seas, the force, which had been sailing at an economical speed of 13 knots, increased its speed to 26 knots in order to reach the launch site on schedule. The fog, however, continued.

On board the *Akagi*, Admiral Nagumo was worried about pre-strike detection, and about how much of the U. S. Pacific Fleet would be in the harbor at the time of the attack. Constant surveillance of Pearl Harbor by Japanese consulate staff in Honolulu kept Tokyo and Nagumo's strike force informed of U.S. ship dispositions. Nagumo hoped to find carriers anchored with the rest of the fleet, and when he sailed from Tankan Bay, he had been led to believe that there might be six carriers at Pearl Harbor. Subsequently, he was informed that the heavy carrier *Saratoga* was at San Diego. Japanese intelligence had not yet discovered that the carriers *Hornet* and *Yorktown* were both stationed in the Atlantic.

By the evening of 6 December he knew the worst: according to the latest radio message from Tokyo, there were no carriers at Pearl Harbor. For a commander making an air assault which was based upon the assumption that carriers were superior to battleships, this was discouraging news. It would not affect the outcome of the impending attack, but it did affect the attack's strategic value to Japan. On the other hand, constant monitoring of American aerial patrols showed that their routine reconnaissance was directed to the southwest, leaving Nagumo's launch point unobserved. As he neared Oahu, the commercial radio stations were broadcasting only normal programming, with no hint of an alert. He was still undetected.

The weather worsened during the afternoon and early evening of 6 December, raising concern that the planes could not be launched at the appointed time. At 2100, with the force still some 400 miles north of Oahu, Admiral Nagumo called all hands on deck throughout the fleet, and Admiral Yamamoto's battle order was read: "The rise or fall of the Empire depends upon this battle. Everyone will do his duty to the utmost"—a reiteration of Admiral Togo's Nelsonian order before the battle of Tsushima Strait. In an emotional scene, the flag that Admiral Togo had raised on his flagship *Mikasa*, thirty-six years before, was raised on the *Akagi*. Then the force turned south at 26 knots. The launching point was to be 26° North, 158° West; Pearl Harbor would be 275 miles away, due south.

The Strike Force was by no means the only element in the Pearl Harbor attack plan. An advance force of twenty-seven submarines, most of them *I*-class, left the Yokosuka and Kure naval bases, beginning on 10 November. Eleven of the *I*-class submarines carried small reconnaissance floatplanes. Five more submarines, the *I-16*, *I-18*, *I-20*, *I-22*, and *I-24*, left on 18 November, each carrying a secret weapon: a midget two-man submarine, designated Special Attack Unit, that could be launched from a mother ship near the attack area. Of the original twenty-seven, the *I-26* went to the Aleutians and the *I-10* to Samoa and the Fijis; the remaining twenty-five went to Kwajalein in the Marshall Islands, refueled there during 18–20 November, and then sailed to take up their war positions. They were to deploy around Oahu to furnish reconnaissance detail on the location, number, and kind of naval units in Pearl Harbor, to sink any ships escaping from the Strike Force's attack, and to disrupt shipping between the United States mainland and the Hawaiian Islands.[8] The five midget submarines were launched at 0100 on 7 December; a rendezvous for their recovery, never kept by the five, was designated off Lanai.

On 6 December, an *I*-class submarine scouted Lahaina Roads, an alternate anchorage used by the American fleet when it was not in Pearl Harbor. She signalled Admiral Nagumo via Tokyo that the

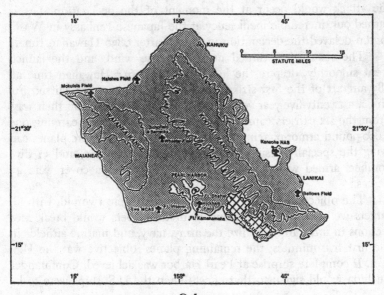

Oahu

U.S. fleet was not there. Nagumo knew, then, that most of the fleet was at anchor in the shallow waters of Pearl Harbor, at last report unprotected by any sort of torpedo nets. His unanswered questions, however, were still with him: would any carriers join the main fleet during the night, and if not, where would they be? He now definitely knew that the heavy carriers *Enterprise* and *Lexington* were at sea.

During the Strike Force's run south, because of the rough seas, it was still not known whether the planes could be launched on schedule. At 0500, reconnaissance floatplanes were catapulted from the heavy cruisers *Tone* and *Chikuma* to determine whether conditions were still favorable for the raid. (Reports were, in fact, received from them just prior to the attack, marking ship targets.) An hour later, it was decided to launch the first strike at once, because it was feared that the pitching carrier decks would make the launching operation take longer than planned. Yamamoto believed that the formal declaration of war would be delivered to U. S. Secretary of State Cordell Hull by Ambassador Kichisaburo Nomura and Special Envoy Saburo Kurusu, at 0800 Hawaiian time; he had issued strict orders that the raid should not take place until after war had been declared—preferably at least thirty minutes afterward. He could not afford a much longer wait, because then the secrecy of the air assault would be endangered. If Nagumo began to launch at 0530 instead of 0600, and if the launch were executed in an ordinary amount of time, the attack would occur at the moment of the declaration. (As it turned out, incredible inefficiency at the Japanese Embassy in Washington delayed the declaration until well after 0830 Hawaiian time.)

The six carriers turned north into the wind, and the launch went smoothly, despite the heavy seas. By 0615 Hawaiian time all 183 aircraft of the first strike wave, led by Commander Mitsuo Fuchida, a twenty-five-year veteran of naval aviation, were on their way. From the six carriers came 49 high-level bombers, each carrying one 1,600-pound armor-piercing modified naval shell, 40 more planes carrying the specially designed shallow-running torpedoes, and 51 dive bombers armed with 500-pound bombs. Flying as a cover were 43 Zeroes.[9]

The objectives of the combined air fleet were twofold, with all targets well-assigned. One group of dive bombers would break into sections in order to neutralize the army, navy, and marine airfields in the first five minutes; the remaining planes' objective was the U.S. fleet. If complete surprise at Pearl Harbor was achieved, Commander Fuchida would signal to that effect. Then the U.S. ships were to be destroyed as follows: first, the torpedo planes would attack, with battleships and carriers as primary targets, and then high-level and dive bombers would attack other targets of opportunity among the fleet. If complete surprise had not been achieved, Fuchida would give a different signal, and the attack would proceed in reverse order: the Japanese would send their bombers in first, hoping that, in the confusion of the attack, American gunners would be so preoccupied that the torpedo planes could slip in unnoticed, at water level. Hickam, Wheeler, Kaneohe, Ewa, Bellows, and Ford Island fields were dive-bombed at 0755. At 0800, Zeroes strafed these fields to destroy undamaged planes remaining on the ground or to shoot down any planes managing to get aloft.

The sight that met the eyes of those flyers ordered to make the direct attack on the American naval units in Pearl Harbor was awe-inspiring, despite the hours of drill at the mock-up tables and at Kagoshima Bay. Lying below them in the early morning sunlight, only partially obscured here and there by shreds of clouds from an earlier light rainfall, the Japanese saw some ninety ships of the U.S. fleet spread out before them. Seven battleships were moored close together in battleship row, and the *Pennsylvania* was in No. 1 drydock. Scattered at their various berths were the other ships of the fleet: two heavy cruisers, six light cruisers, twenty-nine destroyers, three seaplane tenders, five submarines, ten minesweepers, nine minelayers, and various auxiliary craft. But in that instant before attack, the Japanese saw that there were indeed no aircraft carriers present; although the flyers were disappointed, they did not yet know how fateful to the Japanese war effort this turn of events would be.

As so often happens in the excitement of battle, the agreed-upon order of attack fell into shambles. The "complete surprise" signal of Fuchida was virtually ignored. At 0755, the torpedo planes and the high-level and dive bombers all went in together, neither group waiting for the other. Having achieved complete surprise, they met no initial antiaircraft fire; it then built up only to a negligible response. For the first fifteen minutes, Pearl Harbor was an arena of wave-skimming torpedo planes, plunging dive bombers, and high-level bombers, small specks in the sky—all discharging their lethal cargoes. At 0810, an enormous explosion in the *Arizona* sent a column of red-cored black smoke hurtling into the sky. One of eight hits by 1,600-pound bombs had penetrated her forward powder magazine. She rose from the water, broke in half, and settled back—in an instant, she had become a total wreck. Other warships were sinking,

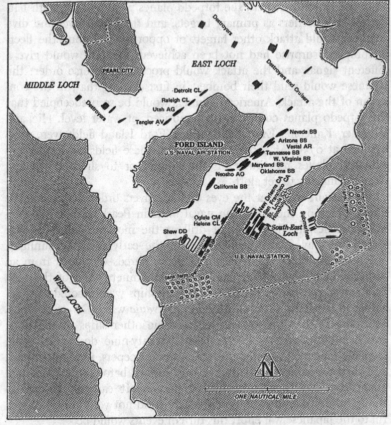

Pearl Harbor, 7 December 1941

capsizing, or afire. Similar success was achieved in attacks on the airfields, so that American air power was almost completely neutralized within a few minutes.

Slowly, American counterfire, at first wildly inaccurate, began to score. But the first wave of attack continued, with planes seeking new targets of opportunity or rebombing ships that had already been crippled. At 0830, a lull developed, but Fuchida rallied his planes and the attack regained its intensity, until the planes' ammunition started to give out and their gas began to run low. The first strike, although out of formation, then began to return to the carriers.

The carriers had already launched the second strike of 167 planes at 0715, with the same mixture of plane types and tactical assignments as before. This wave hit Pearl Harbor at 0915. It met a greater amount of hostile fire, and, while the attack was pressed home against fleet ships with the same intensity, it did little additional damage. Further attacks were made on Hickam Field, Ford Island, and Kaneohe air base, also with only minor results. By 1000, the second wave withdrew. The attack was over, although neither side yet realized it.

The damage was finally officially tabulated as follows:

Battleships

the *Arizona* blown up with a loss of more than 1,000 lives.
the *Oklahoma* capsized with a small part of her hull above water.
the *California* "sank gradually for about three or four days" and came to rest rather solidly on a mud bottom, with her mainmasts and the upper parts of her main batteries above water. "The quarterdeck [was] under about twelve feet of water. . . ."
the *Nevada*, which had got under way, beached in the narrow channel opposite Hospital Point in a wrecked condition.
the *West Virginia* sunk at her berth.
the *Maryland* moderately damaged but not needing to go into drydock.
the *Tennessee*, seriously damaged aft in the officers' quarters from fire and otherwise moderately damaged.
the *Pennsylvania*, in drydock, with considerable damages, "but not of vital nature."
the *Utah*, then used as a target ship, capsized, having been at the *Saratoga*'s regular berth.

Light cruisers

the *Raleigh, Helena,* and *Honolulu* moderately damaged.

Destroyers

the *Cassin* and *Downes*, in drydock No. 1, severely damaged.
the *Shaw*'s bow blown off while in floating drydock, severely damaged.

Others

the repair ship *Vestal* was alongside the *Arizona* when the raid commenced and was beached at Aeia to prevent further sinkage.
the seaplane tender *Curtiss* badly damaged by a crashing plane and one 500-lb. bomb.
the minelayer *Oglala* capsized.[10]

Strangely enough, three tempting and strategic targets were left untouched. The first of these was the machine shops, principally those around 10-10 dock. The second was the oil tank farms (holding 4,500,000 barrels) scattered around the Navy Yard. Because the former were spared, repair work could be undertaken immediately; if the latter had not been spared, so much fuel oil would have been lost that the Navy Yard probably could not have continued to function as a major naval base. The third target neglected was a group of nine submarines at the submarine base, which were not in submarine bunkers. The U. S. Pacific Fleet, minus its carriers, had sustained a devastating blow—but Pearl Harbor, as a naval base, had not.

American losses of military aircraft were also staggering: 188 planes were destroyed, equally divided between the army and the navy, and 159 additional aircraft were badly damaged. After the attack, only forty-three planes were still operational. American casualties were 2,403 killed and 1,178 wounded.

In proportion to the damage inflicted, Japanese losses were minimal. Twenty-nine planes did not return: fifteen dive bombers and high-level bombers, five torpedo planes, and nine fighter escorts. The midget submarines inflicted no damage, and none returned to their mother ships; four were sunk and one was wrecked on a reef, its captain captured. One *I*-class submarine was also sunk.

Despite the feeling of jubilation on the Japanese carriers, a difference of opinion immediately developed regarding an additional strike. Planes had been refueled and rearmed and were available for further strikes, but it was finally decided not to take the risk. Nagumo had discussed the question with his chief of staff, Rear Admiral Ryunosuke Kusaka, who inferred from intercepted radio traffic that a fairly large number of land-based bombers were still operational (his estimate was fifty), and that the Strike Force should quickly sail out of their range. The Japanese reconnaissance planes could cover only a 250-mile protective arc, and what lay beyond that was unknown. Information was also lacking from the *I*-class submarines, which could have furnished further details. Returning flyers reported that smoke over Pearl Harbor was dense, making target selection difficult for flyers in a third attack. The most telling argument, however, was the fact that the American carriers had not been in Pearl Harbor, had not been neutralized, and that their whereabouts were unknown. A withdrawal toward the Marshalls, at top speed, was signalled at 1335.[11]

By the next day, the Strike Force was out of American bomber range, and it slowed to 15 knots, keeping well out of range of Midway patrol planes. The *Soryu* and *Hiryu*, and the heavy cruisers *Tone* and *Chikuma*, and the destroyers *Urakaze* and *Tanikaze* were detached to support the Wake Island Invasion Force, while the rest of the Strike Force sailed directly back to the Inland Sea.

What did the attack on Pearl Harbor accomplish? For Japan to go to war with the United States, Great Britain, and the Netherlands, the Japanese Navy had to keep the U. S. Pacific Fleet neutralized for a long period of time, and had to sever the Wake–Guam–Philippines line of communications. The attack on Pearl Harbor did indeed neutralize the U.S. fleet, but the absence of carriers in the harbor shortened that period of neutralization. An attack by American carrier planes against Japanese warships was still a cause for concern.

In retrospect, the Japanese choices of targets reflected the illogical excitement of battle—in this case, an initial battle employing new tactics against an enemy always envied as "big league." Destruction of ships became the overwhelming urge of excited flyers; the destruction of oil tanks, machine shops, and submarines must have appeared prosaic by comparison. Admiral Nagumo could defend his failure to launch a third attack with more logic, though. While a third attack could have concentrated on machine shops and oil tanks, the presence of almost fifty flyable American land-based planes, the heavy smoke obscuring the target, the readiness of the American antiaircraft batteries, and the unknown location of the American carriers—all placed his precious fleet in very real jeopardy. A brilliant Japanese success could have been diminished, or even negated, by any serious damage to the Japanese fleet. At any rate, a death struggle between Imperial Japan and the United States had been insured by the Pearl Harbor attack—an attack which angered the Americans all the more because it had (unintentionally) been carried out before a formal declaration of war was made.

chapter 2

FURTHER
ATTACKS AGAINST
THE UNITED STATES

1941

7 December	Two Japanese destroyers shell Midway Island
8 December	Japanese planes attack military airfields in the Philippines: decimation of U. S. Army Air Force, Far East
8 December	Japanese carrier planes raid Davao, Philippine Islands
10 December	Japanese capture Guam
10 December	Japanese Army lands at Aparri, Philippine Islands
11 December	Japanese make first attempt to occupy Wake Island
12 December	Japanese Army lands at Legaspi, Philippine Islands
20 December	Japanese Army lands at Davao
22 December	Japanese Army lands at Lingayen (main landing for capture of Manila)
23 December	Japanese capture Wake Island
24 December	Japanese Army lands at Lamon Bay, Philippine Islands
25 December	Japanese Army lands at Jolo, Philippine Islands

Midway

The Midway Destruction Unit, composed of the destroyers *Ushio* and *Sazanami*, staged a nuisance raid on Midway Island on 7 December. Firing commenced at 2131, with the *Ushio* firing 108 rounds from her main batteries, and the *Sazanami*, 193 rounds. The destroyers retired after 54 minutes of action, recording hits on oil tanks and other installations.[1] The U. S. Marine command on Midway, however, reported only a few sporadic rounds and no damage suffered.

Guam

Guam was potentially troublesome to the Japanese, because it is situated in the Marianas some 100 miles from Saipan, which was under Japanese mandate at the time. Actually, in December 1941 Guam could be had for practically nothing, because fortification of the island had been forbidden by the 1922 Five Power Treaty, and even with the lapse of the treaty in 1936, nothing had been done by the United States to strengthen the island's defenses. At the outbreak of the war it had a garrison of fewer than 500 men, and 246 native Insular Force men. The heaviest weapons on the island were .30-caliber machine guns and .45-caliber automatics.

The Japanese forces detailed to take the island were large, in relation to the task: 5,000 landing-force troops, including an elite Special Naval Landing Force (SNLF). The ships assigned to escort duty and possible bombardment of the island were the heavy cruisers *Kako, Furutaka, Aoba,* and *Kinugasa,* with the minelayer *Tsugaru.*[2] These were under the administrative control of the First Fleet, but had been transferred to the Fourth Fleet under the tactical command of Vice Admiral Shigeyoshi Inouye, whose headquarters was at Truk. Also transferred to the tactical command of Inouye were the destroyers *Kikuzuki, Yuzuki, Uzuki,* and *Oboro,* administratively assigned to the First Air Fleet. This group had sailed directly for the Guam invasion from Hahajima on 4 December. The duty of softening the island's defenses, however, was assigned to naval bombers stationed at Saipan. The first air attack was made on 8 December at 0927, and the raids continued for two days. Landing craft with the invasion force came ashore on 10 December at 0625, and the U.S. garrison surrendered at 0645, making it unnecessary for the units of the Fourth Fleet to lay down a bombardment. The Japanese forces had lost ten men, the defenders, seventeen. The first cut into the U.S. line of supply from Hawaii to the Philippines had thus been made without major resistance.[3]

Wake

What is called Wake is actually a group of three islands: Peale, Wilkes, and Wake islands, the last being a low-ground atoll formed by a volcano with all but its top submerged. The circumference of Wake (the three-island group) is less than three miles. The Japanese wanted Wake so that it could not serve as a base for American air attacks on the Japanese-held Marshall Islands. Furthermore, the capture of Wake, along with Guam, would block the United States' mid-Pacific line of supply to the Philippines. In addition, possession of Wake would give the Japanese another link in their defense perimeter, and would provide a base for air reconnaissance and a possible steppingstone in an invasion of Midway Island.

The inhabitants of Wake on 8 December were the 447 Marines of the First Defense Battalion and a Marine Air Unit, 68 sailors, 5 army postal service men, 70 Pan American Airways employees, and 1,146 unarmed civilians of the Contractors Pacific Naval Air Bases, who were engaged in developing the atoll's air and submarine bases. Armament included six 5-inch coast defense guns, twelve 3-inch antiaircraft guns (some without fire-control equipment), twenty-four

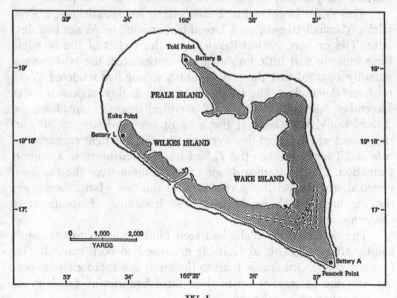

Wake

.50-caliber machine guns, and a smaller number of .30-caliber machine guns. The air defenses for the island consisted of one fighter squadron, made up of twelve old Grumman Wildcats.

Flying thirty-six of its twin-engined bombers, the 24th Air Flotilla attacked Wake at midday on 8 December, destroying seven planes, severely damaging another, damaging the Pan American facilities, and cratering the airstrip. Not a single Japanese plane was lost. Bombing raids continued through 10 December, exploding ready ammunition and damaging some of the 5-inch guns.

While the Guam Invasion Force had been a massive one, pitted against opposition known to be minor, the Wake Invasion Force was dangerously weak against a force known to be potentially strong. The Fourth Fleet at Truk assigned the following ships to the Wake Island invasion: the light cruiser *Yubari* (flagship of Rear Admiral Sadamichi Kajioka), the destroyers *Mutsuki, Kisaragi, Yayoi, Mochizuki, Oite*, and *Hayate*, escorting two transports (converted destroyers) with 450 SNLF troops and two *Maru* transports carrying garrison troops. (*Maru* is a term attached to a Japanese merchant ship, and the title was retained when the ship was impressed into naval service.) The light cruisers *Tenryu* and *Tatsuta*, old cruisers commissioned in 1919, would act as a support group. This definitely was not the Japanese first team, as events were soon to prove.

The Wake Invasion Force sailed from Ruotta anchorage, Kwajalein, Marshall Islands, on 8 December, arriving off Wake two days later. The cruisers' Action Reports and the tactics of the invading force indicate that little resistance was anticipated; the Japanese apparently assumed that the two days of bombing had rendered Wake relatively defenseless. The Japanese ships began their approach on 11 December shortly before 0500. In a typical destroyer squadron, the *Yubari* would have been at the head of her six destroyers; this arrangement was modified, however, by situating the light cruisers *Tatsuta* and *Tenryu* between the *Yubari* and the destroyers, in a column formation. On the starboard side of the column were the two converted destroyers, on the port side were the two *Marus*. Seas were running high, which would make the launching of assault craft slower and more difficult.

The defenders at Wake had seen blinking lights to the south shortly after midnight, so available defenses had been readied. The four remaining Grummans took to the air as the approach was spotted, and the Marines stood to their three batteries of 5-inch guns, one battery on each of the three islands.

The Japanese column opened fire at 0522, after having turned to port to make its firing run, paralleling Wake's southern perimeter at 6,000 yards from shore. The Marines on Wake held their fire, and the records of the *Tenryu* indicate that the Japanese bombardment target was the "Wake residential area" and "housing in the West area." At any rate, their target was definitely not the defense batteries. Oil tanks at the southwest end of Wake Island were hit, however, and set afire. As the column advanced to the west, the transports began to prepare to land their troops. After twenty minutes, having reached the west edge of Wilkes Island, the *Yubari* closed the range to 4,500 yards and reversed for another firing run. The Marine defenders still held their fire. At 0600 the *Yubari* reversed again, once more closing range for a third firing run, and at 0610, the islands' batteries opened fire. Battery A, at the southeast tip of Wake Island, claimed to have hit the *Yubari* with its second salvo, although the *Yubari's* Action Report makes no mention of any damage. One of the converted destroyers, carrying half of the SNLF troops, received a fatal hit from Battery A, at about the same time, and eventually drifted ashore at Wake Island.

Rear Admiral Kajioka immediately retired his command ship to the southwest, escorting the remaining converted destroyer. The transports came under the fire of Battery L on Wilkes Island, and one of the *Marus* was hit. The destroyers *Hayate*, *Oite*, and *Mochizuki*, in order to screen the transports and to deliver counterbattery fire, charged directly toward Battery L and thus proved anew the truth of an old naval dictum: fixed ground defense guns can usually outshoot attacking ships. The *Hayate*, in the lead, was hit squarely by three salvos and blew up, with no survivors: 168 men were killed. The *Oite* was hit, with nineteen men wounded; along with the *Mochizuki*, she turned south-southwest of Wilkes Island. Meanwhile, a reconstructed column made up of the *Yayoi*, *Mutsuki*, and *Kisaragi*, backed up by the *Tatsuta* and *Tenryu*, got into a fire fight with Battery B on Peale Island. The *Yayoi* was hit (one man killed, seventeen wounded), but she returned fire and did considerable damage to Battery B.

A new element was added to the battle when the four Grumman Wildcats attacked. At 0724, they made a strafing run on the starboard bow of the *Tenryu*. The forward section of the cruiser was raked in the vicinity of her No. 1 torpedo tube, wounding five, disabling three of her torpedoes, and puncturing the hull. With this, the remaining ships made smoke and also retired to the southwest.

But the Wildcats were not through; the *Kisaragi* came under attack about 30 miles southwest of Wake. Hits on her depth charges set off a huge explosion, and the *Kisaragi* went down at once with all hands (her normal complement was 150 men) at 0731.

The *Yubari*'s Action Report sums up the battle succinctly. "Although the enemy sustained heavy damage from the numerous attacks by the medium-attack bombers of the 24th Air Flotilla, he still retained intact several fighters, ground batteries, etc.—he fiercely counterattacked and we were temporarily forced to retire." The total Japanese casualty list was 340 killed, 65 wounded, and 2 missing. The Wake Invasion Force, now missing two destroyers and one converted destroyer transport, returned to Ruotta anchorage to repair its damages and to await reinforcements before a new effort. On Wake, the defense batteries were still mainly intact, but there were only two planes left. Amazingly, only one U. S. Marine was killed. This battle certainly showed that warships should not charge into the point-blank range of fixed 5-inch guns.

In the interval between the first and second invasion operations, the Americans wanted to reinforce the Wake garrison. But confusion in the command echelons, caused by the Pearl Harbor debacle, and the lack of hard intelligence on the whereabouts of the Japanese Combined Fleet or on the nature of Japanese naval installations in the Marshalls, caused the Americans to fail to reinforce Wake or engage new invading enemy forces in battle. Although three fleet carriers with cruiser and destroyer screens were then available, it was feared that Wake was the bait in a Japanese trap, and the risk of losing three fleet carriers on top of the battleship losses at Pearl Harbor seemed too great.

The Japanese continued a daily air bombardment by the 24th Air Flotilla, augmented by planes from the heavy carriers *Hiryu* and *Soryu* and from the seaplane tender *Chitose*. They set no ambush, however, between 11 and 23 December, even though they realized that Wake could have been reinforced in that time. Although they made an efficient and successful invasion in the predawn of 23 December, the Japanese invasion force was inferior in all its elements to what the United States could have mustered. Thus, the Americans had been timid and cautious, while the Japanese showed an almost rash lack of caution or preparation for a battle that might have proved decisive. The Japanese Navy provided only a token sort of covering force which an American fleet, acting with initiative, might have easily overwhelmed.

The Second Wake Invasion Force mustered at Ruotta anchorage. It included the quickly repaired original ships: the light cruisers *Yubari, Tatsuta, Tenryu*; the destroyers *Mutsuki, Yayoi, Oite, Mochizuki*; two *Maru* transports; and one converted-destroyer transport. Rear Admiral Kajioka in the *Yubari* was still in overall command. The force also gained two destroyers, the *Asanagi* and the *Yunagi* (which had helped to capture Makin Island and had been raiding elsewhere in the Gilbert Islands), one converted-destroyer transport, another *Maru* transport, a minelayer, and a troop-carrying seaplane tender. The original SNLF troops were reinforced by some of the troops that had captured Guam. The combined strength of the SNLF forces, then at Ruotta, was nearly 2,000. The heavy cruisers *Kinugasa, Aoba, Kako,* and *Furutaka* of the Guam Invasion Force were, on 13 December, designated the Marshall Area Operation Support Unit for the second Wake invasion. The 24th Air Flotilla was augmented by the seaplane tender *Chitose*'s twenty-eight seaplanes. The *Hiryu* and *Soryu*, with 108 planes, the heavy cruisers *Tone* and *Chikuma,* and the destroyers *Urakaze* and *Tanikaze,* had split off from the retiring Pearl Harbor Strike Force to support the second Wake invasion attempt, passing under the tactical command of the Fourth Fleet.

The Second Wake Invasion Force left Ruotta at 0545 on 21 December. The *Hiryu* and *Soryu* were already positioned about 200 miles north-northwest of Wake, and carrier-plane strikes on 21 December were added to the 24th Air Flotilla's continuous raids. Rear Admiral Kajioka's forces did not storm in on Wake as on 11 December, and there was no sustained preinvasion bombardment. Instead, the SNLF men were put into assault boats in the dark at 0220 on 23 December, some two miles from their objective. Despite fierce resistance, beachheads were soon secured. At 0600, carrier planes joined in the attack, and by 0630, the overwhelmed garrison surrendered. The SNLF and Army landing forces had lost 140 men; the ships lost 4 men. Ten Japanese planes were lost. Wake's three islands became part of the Japanese empire and a link in the Japanese Navy's perimeter defense, the Philippines' lifeline had been severed, without damage to any naval units, and the Japanese had learned a lesson in amphibious tactics.[4]

Philippine Islands

The tactical plan for the Imperial Japanese Army's invasion of the Philippines called for the conquest of certain key areas to provide air-

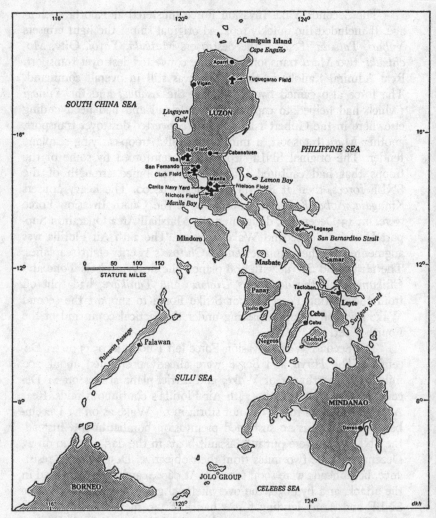

The Philippines

strips, so that the Army would always be under air cover. Thus Batan Island, a small island lying 125 miles north of Luzon, would be invaded on 8 December, so that planes flying from there could cover landings at Aparri, scheduled for 10 December. The plan also called for the invasion of Camiguin Island, about 30 miles north of Luzon, on the same date, and for its immediate use as a base for seaplanes covering the Aparri landings. Aparri itself was important only for the establishment of air bases; Lingayen Gulf would be the site of the main landings, which would provide the northern jaw of a pincers on Manila. Vigan was to be occupied on 11 December, also to provide air cover for the later Lingayen invasion.

But the U. S. Navy had strength to the south to be reckoned with; Davao had a naval base that had to be neutralized, and American air power from the south had to be eliminated. Thus, a carrier-plane raid was planned for 8 December, to be followed a few days later by landings at Legaspi. To provide the southern jaw to the pincers on Manila, landings were scheduled on 23 December at Lamon Bay. On 20 December Davao was to be captured by Japanese troops escorted from Palau and covered by the Southern Fleet's Davao Attack Force under the command of Rear Admiral Raizo Tanaka. The Davao Attack Force would then occupy Jolo, a small island just northeast of Borneo. The Philippines would thus be isolated, and Davao and Jolo would also provide bases and air cover for the scheduled attacks on Borneo.

The Imperial Japanese Navy's role in the invasion of the Philippines would be threefold: to neutralize, destroy, or disperse American naval and air power; to cover and support the Japanese Army's landings; and, once the invasion targets were secured, to protect the Army's lines of supply and reinforcement. The occupation of the Philippines was a necessary step in Japan's drive into the South Seas in search of raw materials, and for that reason, American military power in the Philippines had to be eliminated. However, the Philippines themselves did not possess any strategic resources (with the possible exception of copper) in the quantities needed by wartime Japan.

Admiral Yamamoto assumed that American naval and air power, relatively inferior though it was, would be used to its fullest extent. On 8 December 1941, the U. S. Navy had on station in Philippine waters one heavy cruiser, one light cruiser, four destroyers, twenty-nine submarines, six gunboats, two seaplane tenders, and various auxiliary craft. In aircraft, the Navy had thirty-two PBYs (Catalina flying boats), four Grumman Ducks (general amphibious transports), and five Kingfishers (ship-based reconnaissance float planes). Additional American naval forces were close by at Tarakan and Balikpapan in Borneo, including one light cruiser and nine destroyers. The United States Army Air Force, Far East (USAAFFE) stationed in the Philippines had about thirty-four B-17s (Boeing Flying

Fortresses) and seventy P-40s (Curtiss Warhawks) on hand on 8 December.

News of the attack on Pearl Harbor reached Manila at 0300, thirty minutes after the event, and American army and naval forces were alerted within the hour. Meanwhile, the Japanese at army and naval air bases at Taiwan were in a state of anxiety; their original plans had called for a dawn launching for raids against air bases at Luzon, but, since the skies provided a two-way road, Taiwan's airfields would be just as vulnerable to attack as those on the Philippines. Foggy weather forced the Japanese Navy's 11th Air Fleet to postpone its takeoff. However, thirty-two Army bombers did fly on schedule, striking military sites at Baguio airfield at 0930 and Tuguegarao airfield in northern Luzon shortly thereafter. The Taiwan naval air armada from Taichu, Tainan, and Takao, consisting of 192 planes, was finally airborne at 0915, its targets being three major air bases near Manila. Ninety planes attacked Clark Field; the rest, Iba and Nichols fields.[5] Despite the length of time elapsed since American air forces had been alerted, the Japanese attack, at 1135, caught the USAAFFE with most of its planes on the ground, and destroyed half of its bombers and more than a third of its fighters in a few minutes. Thereafter, the Americans could offer little effective resistance against air attacks or invasion forces, and could no longer pose a threat to the Taiwanese airfields.

Two days later, Japanese planes continued their attack on the Philippines. Fifty-two protecting Zeroes put down minor U.S. fighter opposition. Bombing targets for the day were Cavite Navy Yard in Manila Bay, and Nielson and Nichols airfields; the former was utterly destroyed by more than eighty unopposed bombers, while the two airfields suffered extensive damage. By evening, USAAFFE had only thirty-three operational fighter planes left. The U. S. Navy recognized that, with the loss of control of the air, it had lost control of the seas around the Philippines; so rather than sending additional naval units to reinforce the north, which had been the original war plan, most operational vessels (but not all submarines) were ordered south.

Davao, on Mindanao, the large southernmost island of the Philippines, was regarded by the Japanese Navy with anxiety, for it was the site of an American naval base and was only about 500 miles from the Japanese naval base at Palau. Therefore, the Japanese wanted to neutralize it on the first day of the war. As it turned out, however, the only major U.S. vessel in Davao Harbor on 8 December was the seaplane tender *William B. Preston*, with three operational PBYs.

The Fourth Surprise Attack Force, Legaspi Operation, under Rear Admiral Kyuji Kubo, steamed from Palau between 1330 and 1600 on 6 December, keeping a sharp lookout for American submarines, which were thought to be in the area in force. At a point 50 miles east of Cape San Augustin and 100 miles east of Davao, between 0400 and 0445 on 8 December, the *Ryujo* launched thirteen dive bombers, with nine fighters as cover. (Captain Tameichi Hara has written, contrary to Japanese official records, that only twenty planes took part in the raid.)⁶ The destroyers *Hayashio*, *Kuroshio*, *Natsushio*, and *Oyashio* broke from the formation to make a high-speed run toward Davao, in order to attack any American vessels escaping the *Ryujo*'s planes. The remaining destroyers took up a line formation centered on the *Ryujo*. This raid was an overreaction to the supposed American threat, and turned out to be something of a fiasco. The *Ryujo*'s planes did not recognize the *William B. Preston* as a seaplane tender, and she thus escaped serious damage and subsequently sailed south. Two of her PBYs were destroyed on the water. (The third was on patrol.) The U.S. forces offered no air resistance; one of the *Ryujo*'s planes had to ditch because of engine trouble, but the destroyer *Kuroshio* rescued the pilot. After the raid, Davao could no longer function as an American naval base. On 12 December, American air power was further diminished when the seven PBYs of Patrol Wing 10, stationed at Olongapo, were destroyed on the water by strafing Zeroes.

The Japanese Navy had not based its strategy in the invasion of the Philippines upon such an easy mastery of the skies and of the surrounding seas. Instead, the initial plans dictated a slow and cautious approach, designed first to establish air bases close to the Philippines. At dawn on 8 December the Third Surprise Attack Force of Rear Admiral Sueto Hirose, led by the destroyer *Yamagumo*, covered the landing of 490 troops on Batan Island from two *Maru* transports. The island was taken without resistance, but an airstrip was never constructed there. On 10 December, part of the same invasion force occupied Camiguin Island.

The Aparri landings by the Japanese Army began at dawn on 10 December. The First Surprise Attack Force, under Rear Admiral Kenzaburo Hara, consisted of the light cruiser *Natori* (flagship), the destroyers *Fumizuki*, *Nagatsuki*, *Satsuki*, *Minazuki*, *Harukaze*, and *Hatakaze*, three minesweepers, nine antisubmarine craft, and six

Maru transports. Heavy seas and poorly designed landing craft, rather than effective American opposition, impeded the landing operations, and the beachheads were eventually shifted to the east. Air opposition was relatively light but determined—one minesweeper was sunk by air attack, the *Harukaze* was slightly damaged by a bomb, and the *Natori* suffered near-misses. Uneasiness about the danger from the air made the landings less than efficient.[7] Because they were under bombing attack, Admiral Hara's forces retired earlier than scheduled, so that they were forced to throw some supplies overboard and allow them to drift ashore. The Japanese Navy on this occasion showed a healthy respect for the capabilities of air power against surface units (even if that air power was now becoming minimal). The Aparri landings were so lightly opposed by U.S. infantry that the landing troops, whose mission was to capture areas for airfield construction, could also act as an invasion force, pushing southward into Luzon.

A second invasion force was planned for Vigan, also on 10 December. This group, designated the Second Surprise Attack Force, was under Rear Admiral Shoji Nishimura in the light cruiser *Naka*, accompanied by the destroyers *Murasame, Yudachi, Harusame, Samidare, Asagumo, Minegumo, Natsugumo*, six minesweepers, nine antisubmarine craft, and six *Maru* transports holding 4,400 troops. It met difficulties on the first day; weather and the USAAFFE caused a twenty-four-hour postponement and a shift in the landing site, several miles to the south. The landing took place on 11 December. The *Naka* had been strafed several times by American planes and suffered fourteen damaged areas in the skin of her hull, three men killed, and one wounded. A minesweeper was sunk, and two transports were so damaged that they were beached; thirty men in the *Hawaii Maru* were wounded. Nevertheless, the Vigan landings had been successfully completed by the evening of 11 December.[8]

A third invasion force, the Second Fleet, which was under the tactical command of the Third Fleet, was designated the Fourth Surprise Attack Force, under Rear Admiral Kyuji Kubo. It was to land at Legaspi in southeast Luzon, and protect the rear of the Lingayen Gulf invasion against southern-based air attacks. It was made up of the light cruiser *Nagara* (flagship), the destroyers *Yamakaze, Suzukaze, Kawakaze, Umikaze, Yukikaze*, and *Tokitsukaze*; the seaplane tenders *Chitose* and *Mizuho*, two minesweepers, two patrol ships, and seven transports. It was given support by the Davao and Legaspi Cover Force, consisting of the following: the heavy cruisers

Haguro, Myoko, and *Nachi,* the light carrier *Ryujo* with the destroyer *Shiokaze* attached, and a portion of Destroyer Squadron 2—the light cruiser *Jintsu* and the destroyers *Amatsukaze, Hayashio, Kuroshio, Hatsukaze, Natsushio,* and *Oyashio.* To further protect the Legaspi invasion, which would be undertaken on 12 December, the *Jintsu,* along with two destroyers, had laid mines on the previous day in Surigao and San Bernardino straits.[9] The Legaspi invasion met only a token defense and one regiment was put ashore.

The Japanese invasions had met only scattered resistance. In the Aparri landing, U.S. planes had forced the Japanese to hurry their unloading operation, and had destroyed a Japanese minesweeper. A B-17, piloted by Captain Colin Kelly, attacked the heavy cruiser *Ashigara* of the Northern Cover Force on 10 December. Captain Kelly, who did not survive the mission, reported by radio before his plane went down that he had hit and set afire a *Kongo*-class battleship (later claimed by the USAAFFE to be the *Haruna*), but the *Ashigara* was not hit. At Vigan there had been only minor damage. At Aparri, on 14 December, the submarine USS *Seawolf* fired four torpedoes at the merchant seaplane tender *Sanyo Maru,* but the one torpedo that hit its target did not explode. On 14 December the USAAFFE had launched five B-17s for an attack on the Legaspi invasion force. Although the Japanese naval units in the other invasion actions had been vigilantly guarding against air raids, the Legaspi group was caught at anchor in crowded Legaspi Harbor; still, the only damage was to a minesweeper which was strafed.

The stage was now set for the main effort: an invasion force to be set ashore in Lingayen Gulf for the early capture of Manila. The Japanese Navy had to escort transports from three staging areas in Taiwan and the Pescadores, and cover the troops against any counterattacking enemy fleet. The Northern Cover Force of Vice Admiral Takahashi, combined with Admiral Nobutake Kondo's Distant Cover Force, now released from its role in the Malaya invasion (see Chapter 3), could provide further protection against enemy counterattack.

The Lingayen Force, which was carrying the 48th Division of the Japanese Army and a variety of special units, in seventy-three transports, was divided into three elements. The invading force lay off Lingayen, beginning at 0010 on 22 December. Coastal defenses there had already been attacked by bombers and fighters, starting on 18 December. U. S. General Douglas MacArthur, in overall command of the defense of the Philippines, had guessed correctly the beachheads that would be invaded, but he had not anticipated that this main invasion attempt would come so early. Consequently, U.S. submarines had not yet been placed in defensive positions. This was fortunate for the Lingayen Force, because the weather was foul and the amphibious landing was chaotic and confused; the fleet and transports created a twenty-mile scene of disarray, at dawn on 22 December. Nevertheless, because of the softness of defense and the strength of the covering naval bombardment, the troops were well-established ashore on the same day.

Japanese naval losses were minimal. The destroyer *Nagatsuki* was strafed, with one man killed, and five wounded.[10] The U.S. submarine *S-38* sank a small transport on the morning of 22 December. The following day, the U.S. submarine *Seal* sank another small transport. The merchant seaplane tender *Sanuki Maru* was also hit, but not seriously damaged, by coastal defense guns. Some warships, making a preinvasion bombardment, were strafed in the early morning by the few American planes still left, but no appreciable damage was done.

On 24 December, Lamon Bay, southeast of Manila, was invaded. The Lamon Bay Attack Force, under the protection of former elements of the Legaspi Support Force, landed unopposed. This force provided the Japanese with the southern jaw to their pincers on Manila.

Davao was invaded by the Davao Attack Force under Rear Admiral Raizo Tanaka on 20 December. The heavy cruisers *Nachi*, *Haguro*, *Myoko*, the light carrier *Ryujo*, and the seaplane tender *Chitose*, returning from delivering planes to the Marshalls, provided support, while the light cruiser *Jintsu*, with destroyers *Amatsukaze*, *Hatsukaze*, *Kuroshio*, *Oyashio*, *Hayashio*, and *Natsushio*, escorted the five transports from Palau to Davao. No organized resistance was met and part of the landing force was put ashore. A raid by B-17s on 23 December, however, did damage the *Kuroshio*, wounding four.[11] The remainder of the troops, covered and escorted by the *Ryujo*, *Chitose*, and four destroyers, were put ashore on 25 December at Jolo.

Japan had thus secured, in only three weeks, the means to an early conquest of the Philippines. Also, in establishing bases and airfields in Mindanao and Jolo, she had taken the first step in providing air cover for an invasion of Borneo. The Navy's duty of escorting and covering the invasion of the Philippine Islands had been carried out efficiently. Of course, the convoy and escort operations would continue, and some additional fire cover would be provided until all of the islands were occupied. But the main job had been completed, and the Japanese had achieved a brilliant success, much more easily than Admiral Yamamoto and his planners had reason to anticipate. The swiftness of their conquest of the Philippines convinced the Japanese that they could win in the "big leagues." The scene was now set for the capture of the outer Netherlands East Indies, and for an eventual invasion of the most sought-after island of all—Java.

chapter 3

ATTACKS AGAINST GREAT BRITAIN AND THE NETHERLANDS

1941

8 December	Japanese Army lands at Kota Bharu, Malaya. (Attack starts one hour before attack on Pearl Harbor.)
8 December	Japanese Army lands at Singora and Patani, Thailand
8 December	Japanese Navy sinks or captures British and American warships at Hong Kong and Shanghai
9 December	Thailand surrenders
10 December	Japanese land-based planes sink the British ships *Prince of Wales* and *Repulse*
16 December	Japanese Army lands at Miri, British Borneo

1942

10 January	ABDA Command established
19 January	British Borneo surrenders
27 January	Naval battle off Endau, Malaya

Hong Kong

Because the main assault on Hong Kong was overland by Japanese troops, the Navy's role in the city's capture was slight. The light cruiser *Isuzu* of the Second China Expeditionary Fleet and two destroyers, the *Ikazuchi* and *Inazuma,* in the initial phase of the attack upon the Crown Colony, sank the gunboats HMS *Cicada* and HMS *Robin* and a number of junks of British registry, and captured enemy merchant ships in the harbor. They did not, however, assist the Army to any appreciable degree.

Malaya

On the first day of the East Asian war, the Japanese Navy took three major risks. Disaster in any one of these operations would at least have forced an immediate change in the strategy of the war, and might, at the worst, have produced a terrible debacle. First, in the Pearl Harbor attack, they risked early detection and the possible presence of American carriers nearby, which could have severely damaged Admiral Nagumo's strike force. They took a second risk, when the launch of the Japanese Navy's air fleets at Taiwan was delayed by fog, for the USAAFFE could have struck a first and possibly devastating blow against these grounded planes. If this had happened, the Philippine landings would have lacked air cover, would have been met by an intact American air fleet, and American ships in the Philippines and Borneo would have been able to remain in Philippine waters. They took a third risk when the Japanese Army made landings in Malaya (and Thailand), protected by a Japanese naval force inferior in capital-ship fire power to what the British had in the battleship *Prince of Wales* and the battle cruiser *Repulse*. But again the Japanese were depending on naval air power (land-based this time) to counter and destroy British naval strength. They were throwing the dice for the third time.[1]

Although Great Britain was hard-pressed by conditions in Europe and North Africa, she had gathered ships at Singapore and formed them into Force Z. The *Prince of Wales*, one of Britain's newest and most powerful battleships, fresh from participating in the successful hunt for Germany's battleship the *Bismarck*, had been so dispatched, joined by the *Repulse*. The remainder of Force Z consisted of the destroyers *Electra, Express, Vampire,* and *Tenedos*. Force Z's ships could not depend on the Royal Air Force (RAF), which was pitifully weak in Malaya and which, in the first days of the invasion, would be committed to the defense of the Malayan beachheads; they were supposed to get air support from a first-class carrier, the *Indomitable,* but that carrier unfortunately had run aground at Kingston, Jamaica on 3 November, and was not yet repaired.

The Japanese Navy could not depend upon the planes of Admiral Nagumo's strike force to counter Force Z; but since Yamamoto was committed to the use of planes to destroy warships, he resorted to the use of land-based naval planes to attack Force Z. The Japanese

Navy had constructed three airfields in French Indochina in November 1941, and had placed an air fleet there, composed of six reconnaissance planes, thirty-nine fighters, and ninety-nine bomber and torpedo planes—a formidable group.[2] At the same time, as a backup force, a Japanese fleet was sailing south to engage Force Z in battle, if necessary.

The Japanese Army made extensive preparations for the conquest of the Malay Peninsula and the capture of Singapore. The major elements in the initial landings were the 15th Army and the 25th Army. The troops had gathered at Samah Bay, Hainan, and embarked on 4 December, carried by nineteen transports. Since war had not been declared, the ultimate destination of the expedition was unknown to the Americans, British, or Dutch. They hoped that an invasion of Thailand was the objective, which was exactly what the Japanese wanted them to believe. The convoy rounded Cape Camao on the 6th of December and changed course toward Bangkok, where it proceeded to a point "C" in the Gulf of Siam. Course was again changed on 7 December at 0830 toward Singora and Patani, Thailand.

The initial invasion, however, was made at Kota Bharu, Malaya, from three transports on 8 December, more than an hour before the attack on Pearl Harbor. The landings, again, did not get off to a good start: seas were rough, landing craft capsized, the British army had artillery batteries firing in defense, and there were sporadic British air attacks. Japanese casualties were moderate. The landing was backed by the *Sendai* and her destroyers, the *Isonami*, *Uranami*, *Shikinami*, and *Ayanami*, which delivered covering and counterbattery fire from two miles offshore.[3] Conversely, at Singora, there was no resistance met by the troops disembarking from the eleven transports. The operation was covered by the destroyers *Asagiri*, *Amagiri*, *Sagiri*, and *Yugiri*. (The *Sagiri* acted as headquarters ship for all invasion points.) By midnight all eleven troopships were heading north, thus allowing the destroyer group to reinforce the warships at Kota Bharu. The second beachhead in Thailand was at Patani (sixty-five miles south of Singora); troops from five transports began landing on 8 December, again meeting no resistance. This landing was covered by the destroyers *Shinonome* and *Shirakumo*, which then also raced south to Kota Bharu. The *Murakumo*, who had been off Tepoh, nine miles to the south of Patani, also joined the other ships, gathered around the flagship *Sendai*. (Four other landings were made on 8 December against no resistance, farther north on the Kra

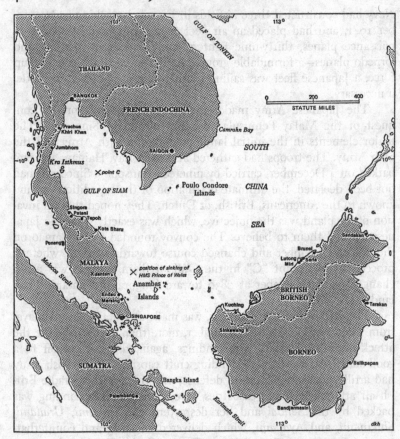

The Malay Campaign

Isthmus in Thailand: a transport of troops landed at Prachuab, two transports at Jumbhorn, one transport near Bandon, and three transports near Nakhorn. These landings did not require destroyer support.) When British resistance at Kota Bharu crumbled on 9 December, the *Sendai* with eleven destroyers could join the Southern Force heading south, possibly to meet Force Z. Because a considerable portion of the Japanese Army was then ashore in Thailand and Malaya, their lines of supply had to be open, and the destruction of Force Z therefore became an urgent priority.

The invasion did not catch the British entirely by surprise; indeed, they had held out little hope that Malaya would be spared. But the locations of the landings did surprise them, for they had expected an invasion farther north, on the narrow Kra Isthmus. The three major beachheads, however, were about halfway between the Kra Isthmus and Singapore. Thailand surrendered on 9 December. From the very first moments of invasion, Japanese air raids fully occupied the attention of the small Malayan-based Royal Air Force.

The officer in command of Force Z, Admiral Sir Thomas Phillips, faced a dilemma. His air forces on the heavy carrier *Indomitable* were unavailable, and the hard-pressed RAF could promise him no air cover. But, at the same time, British naval tradition would have been violated if the British fleet were to remain at anchor in Singapore while enemy landings were taking place within its striking distance. Furthermore, there was always the chance that he might catch loaded or unloading transports at a beachhead. In the end, Phillips had no choice, for, although Force Z sailed from Singapore on 8 December at 1705, the invasions had been carried out too rapidly and too efficiently—Singora and Patani were occupied, the troop transports had been withdrawn, and by the time Force Z could reach Kota Bharu, the transports there would also have departed.

Without adequate air reconnaissance or other reliable information, Admiral Phillips was unaware of these events. All that he knew was that the Japanese were invading to the north—so he sailed north, between the mainland and the Anambas Islands. By 0559 on 9 December he knew that Force Z had been detected, for the destroyer *Vampire* had seen a Japanese reconnaissance plane. Phillips could expect an air attack, and he knew that he would have little or no air protection. Still hoping, however, to get at the Singora transports, he took the force north, to a point 150 miles south of French Indochina and 250 miles east of the Malayan Peninsula. From there, his tactical position began to worsen rapidly, and at 1800, Japanese planes were once again spotted. He then turned south, toward Singora; but at 2330, receiving false intelligence that landings were being made at Kuantan (between Kota Bharu and Singapore), he headed Force Z there, at top speed. At daybreak, when it was still sixty miles from Kuantan, Force Z was again spotted by a Japanese reconnaissance plane. After Admiral Phillips' own observation planes reported that there were no landings at Kuantan, he then steamed first north and then east, stubbornly searching for Japanese ships. His luck, however, had finally run out, and on 10 December at 1000, Force Z came under concentrated Japanese air attack.

The Japanese Navy, for its part, had a healthy respect for the potential threat posed by Force Z's foray north. Carrier planes from

Admiral Ozawa's Third Fleet had spotted an RAF "snooper" on 6 December, so the Japanese knew that their huge southward movement had been discovered. Although war had not yet been declared and Admiral Nagumo's success depended on a surprise attack at Pearl Harbor, Vice Admiral Jisaburo Ozawa nevertheless recklessly ordered his carrier pilots to shoot down any further British reconnaissance planes.[4]

To counter Force Z, the Japanese had Vice Admiral Nobutake Kondo's Malay Force. When, at 1315 on 9 December, the submarine I-65 sighted the northbound Force Z, south of Poulo Condore Island, Admiral Kondo ordered all transports to return to the Gulf of Siam and ordered his air fleet in French Indochina to begin shadowing the British force. (Submarine I-58 also tracked Force Z.)[5] Kondo ordered his own warships to close on the British to offer battle. First his heavy cruisers, the *Mogami*, *Mikuma*, *Suzuya*, and *Kumano*, screened by the destroyers *Fubuki*, *Hatsuyuki*, *Shirayuki*, and by the *Sendai* and her destroyers, would launch a night attack if Force Z were discovered.[6] Meanwhile, Kondo would bring up his two battleships, the *Haruna* and *Kongo*, and the heavy cruisers *Atago*, *Takao*, and *Chokai*, and all ships would then launch a daylight attack. Admiral Kondo was kept informed of the location of Force Z by the *Kumano*'s floatplane, and by reports from submarines. The surface engagement never took place, but Force Z, with its larger naval rifles, could certainly have given a worthy account of itself.

The Japanese bases in Indochina were also kept informed of the various courses taken by Force Z. On 9 December observation and attack units were sent out, but they found nothing. During the night, however, it was concluded that an air attack on Force Z, early on 10 December, would be possible, and at 0220, five Japanese planes left Camranh Bay, refueling at Poulo Condore Island and taking off again at 0430. From Saigon a nine-plane formation was sent out at 0525 to search a 40° arc up to 600 miles. Also from Saigon's airfields, from 0614 to 0730, thirty-four bombers and fifty torpedo planes took off. When Force Z was sighted at 1120, the location was passed to all units in the air.

Although the Japanese planes were almost at the limit of their fuel supply, they made an attack, beginning at 1148, with eighty-four planes taking part in the assault. Despite heavy antiaircraft fire from the five ships of Force Z (the destroyer *Tenedos* had been ordered back to Singapore at 1805 on 9 December), the *Repulse* received ten torpedo hits on her port side, almost evenly spaced from bow to stern, four forward on the starboard side, and a 550-pound bomb amidships. Unable to withstand such a pounding, she sank at 1203. The *Prince of Wales* received one torpedo forward, one aft on her port side, and five evenly spaced along the starboard side. She was hit twice aft by 1,100-pound bombs, was damaged in her starboard quarter by a near-miss, and finally sank at 1250.[7] No British destroyers were sunk, but the *Tenedos* underwent a thirty-minute air attack during midmorning 10 December. In all, three Japanese planes had been shot down, and twenty-eight of the returning planes had been damaged.

Force Z had been crushed, and British power to defend Malaya at sea had been destroyed, without any intervention by Admiral Kondo's surface fleet. Most remaining British naval units either went south to the Netherlands East Indies or retired to their Indian Ocean bases. The lack of British warships or planes gave Japan freedom of the sea; thus the Japanese Army could bypass strong British land positions by using barges for transports. The Japanese had taken the state of Penang on the west coast by overland march on December the 19th.[8] The Malay Force could then be released for the successful invasions of Borneo, which were taking place at the same time.

The last effort of the Royal Navy to intervene in the rapid advance on Singapore came at Endau, a small town on the east side of the Malay Peninsula. If the Japanese could come ashore in sufficient strength at Mersing, a few miles to the south of Endau, a considerable portion of the British army's strength would be cut off from Singapore, 100 miles to the south. The Japanese Army, believing that the defenses at Mersing would be formidable, bypassed it in favor of Endau, which was invaded and captured on 21 January—but not in enough strength to break through the British Sungei–Mersing barrier. British Command at Singapore fully expected that the Japanese effort at Endau would soon be strengthened by a large convoy, a suspicion confirmed on 26 January when, at 0715, a large armada was sighted by plane, 20 miles north of Endau. Some of the group were headed for the invasion of the Anambas Islands; others served as a cover force for both operations.[9] The RAF threw many of its operational planes into counterattack, flying from Sumatra and Singapore. (There had been some crated RAF planes on Singapore's piers.) By the time the air attacks could begin, the beachhead had been widened. Despite heavy antiaircraft fire and fighter-plane opposition by the Japanese, their transports, fuel dumps, and landing troops were bombed. The attacks continued until dark, with the British losing half of their attacking planes.

The Royal Navy then took up the task of breaking up the Endau landing by sending north from Singapore two old destroyers built in World War I: the *Vampire* and the *Thanet*. The *Vampire* had only six torpedoes, and the *Thanet*, four. The Japanese overestimated the actual British naval strength, for the departure of the two destroyers was reported by Japanese naval intelligence as a departure of two cruisers. Moreover, British submarines were reported to be in the area. Therefore, a relatively large attack group, made up of the light cruiser *Sendai* and the destroyers *Fubuki*, *Hatsuyuki*, *Shirayuki*, *Yugiri*, and *Amagiri*, was sent to intercept the British ships.

There ensued an unequal but fierce little sea battle off Endau, in the darkness of early 27 January. In the exchange of gunfire and torpedoes, the *Thanet* was hit several times; she was then illuminated by the *Shirayuki*'s searchlights, and the *Amagiri* and *Hatsuyuki* finished her off at 0348. Fifty-seven of her sailors were rescued and became prisoners of war. The *Vampire* retired under smoke and returned to Singapore.[10]

The end of the Malayan campaign was near, and thousands of people, including important officials, began to flee Singapore through the Malacca and Bangka straits, bound for Sumatra, Java, or even Australia, using anything that would float. Few ships found any refuge, though. Admiral Ozawa's Mobile Force, in the course of three days, sank more than forty ships, with gunfire and bombs.

With South Sumatra, Borneo, and Celebes (discussed in Chapter 4) in Japanese hands by the time of the fall of Singapore, the Malaya boundary of the Netherlands East Indies had been broken. The surprisingly rapid capture of the Malayan peninsula, in a little more than two months of war against major powers, caused Japanese "Victory Fever" to shoot up several degrees.

Japanese naval losses were minimal in the Malayan campaign. An Australian bomber sank a Japanese transport in the Gulf of Siam. A Dutch submarine, *O-XVI*, attacked four loaded transports off Patani on 11 December but failed to sink any of them, and was herself lost when she hit a British mine. Another Dutch submarine sank a loaded transport, while the submarine USS *Swordfish* sank an 8,600-ton Japanese merchant ship off Hainan on 16 December.

British Borneo

The Japanese drive to occupy all of Malaya, and destroy all British military power there, was intended to establish a protective right flank for a major thrust into the South Seas. To the east lay Borneo, Celebes, and the rest of the Netherlands East Indies. The military forces available to protect either British or Dutch territory were so pitifully inadequate that Japan could choose the time and place of her next offensives—a tremendous advantage, given the vastness of the region to be defended.

Borneo, the third largest island in the world, with an area of just under 260,000 square miles, but with a population of only three million and only a dozen towns, was rich in oil and other vital raw materials. By its location, Borneo could threaten the sea route to a Japanese-held Malaya, and form a barrier to an east-to-west Japanese offensive. The island was at that time a Dutch possession, except for a small northern portion owned by Great Britain.

With Malaya hard-pressed from the beginning, the British Command at Singapore could never spare forces to defend British Borneo. The Japanese wasted little time in exploiting this weakness, making the occupation of Borneo an integral part of the Malayan campaign. The oil fields at Miri in northern Sarawak and at Seria in Brunei were Japan's first objectives. On 13 December a convoy carrying forces for the occupation of Miri and Seria left Camranh Bay at 0530. The group was composed of the destroyers *Shinonome, Shirakumo,* and *Murakumo* as close escort, a small subchaser, and ten transports. For further support, they were joined by the light cruiser *Yura* and the seaplane tender *Kamikawa Maru,* and at 0900 by the heavy cruisers *Kumano* and *Suzuya,* and the destroyers *Fubuki* and *Sagiri.* The landings were made on 16 December with minor opposition. The immediate prize, however, had already been destroyed by the evacuating British; on 8 December, the Lutong refinery had been blown up and the Miri and Seria oil fields sabotaged.[11]

The convoy lay off Miri until 22 December, and was subjected to occasional air attacks by the few planes the Dutch and British could get in the air, from Singkawang II, on the Sarawak border, and from Singapore. No transports were damaged, but on 18 December at 0650 the destroyer *Shinonome,* on patrol off Lutong, about nine miles to the north of Miri, was sunk by a mysterious explosion, with her entire crew of 228 men killed. The Dutch air force claimed responsibility for the sinking.[12] The conquest of British Borneo on the ground was almost uncontested. An airfield, being hastily constructed by the British at Kuching in Sarawak, fell on 24 December. British forces then retreated into Dutch Borneo on Christmas Day.

Since 15 December, the Japanese forces had been subject to sporadic air and submarine attacks. Further losses were incurred when the destroyer *Sagiri*, on 24 December, was torpedoed twice and sunk, with 121 men killed, by the Dutch submarine *K-XVI*. At Kuching one transport was sunk by planes, and one by the *K-XVI*. Three transports were also damaged by the *K-XVI*.[13]

British Borneo formally surrendered to the Japanese Army on 19 January at Sandakan. The resource-rich islands of the Netherlands East Indies were next on the conquerors' list. The government of the Netherlands had participated, starting in 1940, in preliminary talks

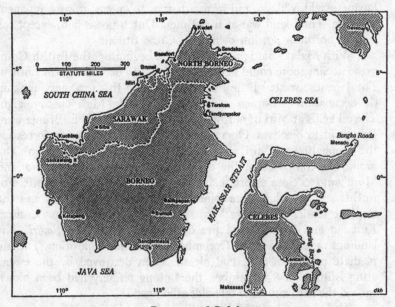

Borneo and Celebes

with Great Britain and the United States about the defense of Southeast Asia, should Japan go to war against the three allies. Consequently, the Netherlands declared war on Japan on the same day that the United States and Great Britain did. (Japan declared war against the Netherlands on 11 January 1942.) General Sir Archibald

Wavell was in Batavia (now called Djakarta) on 10 January, at which time the American-British-Dutch-Australian (ABDA) organization was established, with General Wavell as Supreme Commander.

ABDA began to function too late, with too few ships, troops, or planes, and extremely poor organization. Wavell soon found that he had too much to cope with in Malaya alone, and delegated the administration of ABDA to Admiral Conrad Helfrich of the Netherlands. However, he left operational command with the national officers of the naval, land, and air forces encompassed by the organization. Because Helfrich was also commander-in-chief of the Royal Netherlands Navy, his headquarters was in Batavia, while Army, Navy, and Air ABDA headquarters were located first in Lembang and then Bandung. (See map of Netherlands East Indies, p. 54.) These three organizations were not organized to cooperate with each other, or with Helfrich; in fact, Helfrich's only knowledge of ABDA's operational plans was through a Dutch officer on the Air ABDA staff. The confusion was further compounded when the command of Dutch land-based planes was placed under the RAF, while all naval planes were under Navy ABDA. This meant that in naval battles, the Allied warships could not direct the ABDA air cover and were deprived of reconnaissance and combat air patrol protection.

The Dutch felt that, given the fact that almost all of the threatened area was under Dutch rule, they were underrepresented and almost ignored by ABDA Command. Who knew the vast region of the Netherlands East Indies better than the Dutch? Helfrich soon found, too, that his military and naval forces were being depleted, as Wavell desperately called them in for Singapore's defense. Finally a strike cruiser force was established under Dutch Rear Admiral Karel Doorman on 3 February, but it was still without adequate cooperation from the ABDA headquarters ashore. Although the defense of the Netherlands East Indies was impossible, the Dutch were doggedly determined at least to save Java, and to meet the Japanese naval forces when and where they could.[14]

Table of Organization for the Invasion and Conquest of the Malay Peninsula

Second Fleet, Southern Force, Malay Force

Battleships: *Haruna, Kongo*

Heavy cruisers: *Atago, Takao, Chokai, Mogami, Mikuma, Kumano, Suzuya*
Light cruiser: *Sendai**
Destroyers: *Fubuki, Hatsuyuki, Shirayuki, Murakumo, Shinonome, Shirakumo, Isonami, Uranami, Shikinami, Ayanami, Amagiri, Asagiri, Yugiri, Sagiri*

Southern Expeditionary Fleet
(escort for Army troopships)

Light cruiser: *Kashii*
Destroyers: from Second Fleet, above[15]

section 2

ESTABLISHMENT OF THE ORIGINAL DEFENSE PERIMETER

chapter 4

ISOLATION OF JAVA

1942

4 January	USAAF raids Japanese warships at Malalag Bay, Davao
11 January	Japan declares war on the Netherlands East Indies
11 January	Japan occupies Menado, Kema, Bangka Roads (Celebes)
12 January	Japan occupies Tarakan, Dutch Borneo
23–24 January	Japan occupies Balikpapan, Dutch Borneo
24 January	U.S. destroyers raid Admiral Takahashi's Central Force at Balikpapan
24 January	Japan occupies Kendari, Celebes
31 January	Japanese land on Ambon Island
2 February	Sea ABDA Strike Force created
4 February	Battle of Makassar Strait
14–17 February	Melee in Bangka Strait
15 February	Singapore surrenders
15 February	Japan occupies Bangka Island and Palembang, Sumatra
16 February	Japan occupies Bandjarmasin, Dutch Borneo
18–19 February	Japan occupies Bali-Lombok
19–20 February	Battle of Badung Strait
19 February	Nagumo's Carrier Strike Force raids Port Darwin, Australia
20 February	Japan occupies Timor

The Japanese planned to conquer the outlying islands of the Netherlands East Indies as a prelude to their final assault on Java. They had selected invasion targets which were rich in raw materials, and could provide airfields to cover future advances. They needed powerful fleets to escort them to beachheads, giving covering fire as needed, protecting them against aggressive moves by ABDA's Combined Fleet. At the same time, these fleets were themselves a strike threat to ABDA.

The operation to be employed in capturing Java was a double envelopment. On the eastern flank, two invasion forces were created, commanded by Vice Admiral Ibo Takahashi in the heavy cruiser *Ashigara* at Davao. The invasion forces were called the Eastern Invasion Force and Central Invasion Force, and were deployed to give each other mutual aid, if needed. Until the fall of Bandjarmasin on 16 February, their invasions went on almost simultaneously. The Eastern Force was to lock in Java on the east, taking: Bangka Roads (in Celebes; not to be confused with Bangka Island, near Sumatra), Kema, Menado, and Kendari, Ambon Island, Makassar, Bali-Lombok, and Dutch and Portuguese Timor. To aid the Eastern Invasion Force, Admiral Nagumo used his carrier fleet, usually stationed south of Java, to knock out Port Darwin, Australia as a military staging base, and to present a constant threat to ABDA forces. The Central Invasion Force was to take Tarakan, Balikpapan, and Bandjarmasin (all in Dutch Borneo), and after the fall of Singapore, it was to launch an attack on west Java.

On the western flank, staging from Camranh Bay in French Indochina, would be Admiral Nobutake Kondo's Distant Cover Force and Vice Admiral Jisaburo Ozawa's Southern Expeditionary Fleet, which would capture Anambas Island and aid the Army's conquest of Malaya and Singapore. After Singapore fell, this fleet would then assist in the capture of Bangka Island and Palembang, and the rest of southeast Sumatra. It then would undertake the invasion of Java from the west. In the east, Vice Admiral Ibo Takahashi had a Support Force, under Rear Admiral Takeo Takagi, which provided close cover.

As the various Japanese invasion forces were gathering in French Indochina and the Philippine Islands, the Japanese Navy suffered its first serious loss. At Malalag Bay, Davao, the major elements of the eastern invasion forces were crowded together at anchor. Suddenly, at 1100 on 4 January, ten B-17s of the U. S. Army Air Force (USAAF), flying at an altitude of 30,000 feet made an attack on the crowded and immobilized Japanese fleet. No advance air-raid warning had been signalled. The heavy cruiser *Myoko* was hit with a 250-pound bomb on her No. 2 turret; thirty-five men were killed, and twenty-nine wounded. Splinters hit various other ships, and damaged four planes on the deck of the seaplane tender *Chitose*, 545 yards away. The heavy cruiser *Nachi* was also sprayed with bomb fragments. The *Myoko* had to go to Sasebo for repairs and did not return to action until 26 February.[1] No Japanese planes intercepted the raiders, and antiaircraft fire was weak, so that the B-17s returned to base undamaged. Negligence, perhaps bred by the easy successes already attained, had made the Japanese unprepared. The damage to the *Myoko* did not weaken the Cover Force, nor did it teach the Japanese a lesson; there would be many more incidents where the destructive power of U.S. planes against anchored Japanese ships would be demonstrated.

The next target for the Japanese was Celebes, a large island (70,000 square miles) lying east of Borneo and forming the western boundary to the Molucca Sea. It consists mainly of four long, twisting peninsulas, separated by three deep gulfs. Because its elevation is much higher than Borneo, its vegetation is not as lush. It contains no rich oil fields, but instead is noted for its spices, coffee, and a fair amount of gold, copper, tin, and diamonds. It became a target for occupation, not so much for any materials it could provide, but rather to clear the way for Japanese expansion into the Molucca Sea area, and to provide air and naval bases to aid further occupation of the Netherlands East Indies.

Menado, Kema, Bangka Roads

Admiral Takahashi's First Eastern Invasion Force left Davao in the southern Philippines on 9 January for Menado, Kema, and Bangka Roads, at the northern tip of Celebes. Opposing a powerful landing force of eleven transports, Menado had a garrison of only 1,500 men, fewer than 400 of them regular army troops. A few ABDA planes tried unsuccessfully to bomb the Japanese ships as they came to anchor. The landings were started at 0300 on 11 January and the Dutch were overwhelmed. There had been no need for the 334 Japanese naval paratroopers (in twenty-seven planes) flown from Davao, who confused the operation more than they helped it. (It was the first time the Japanese had used paratroopers, the winds were strong, and the drops were made from much too high an altitude. Equipment and men were scattered all over the end of the peninsula.) The regular landings, however, were made swiftly and the transports quickly left the area. The Menado airfield was in operation for the 21st Air Flotilla by 24 January.[2]

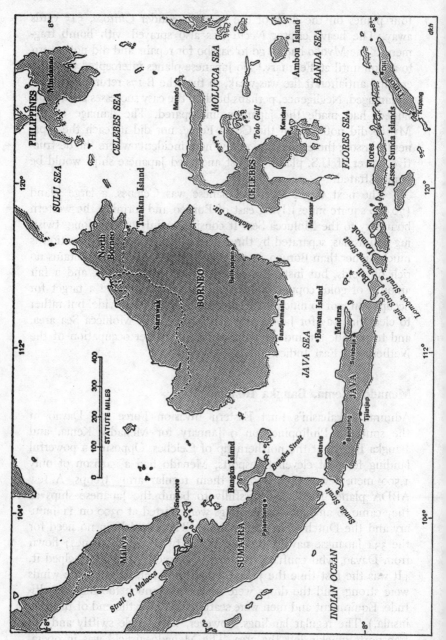

The Netherlands East Indies

Kendari

The Eastern Invasion Force soon was on the move again, staging at Menado on 21 January and appearing off Kendari in southeast Celebes on 24 January. An American seaplane tender, the *Childs*, upon leaving Kendari harbor, spotted the Japanese. A rain squall obscured the *Childs* for a while, allowing her to avoid two Japanese destroyers. She then suffered a bombing attack by six Japanese planes at 0800, but was unhit, and escaped to the south.[3]

Kendari could not be given enough military support to stop the invasion, and little resistance was offered. There were only two men wounded in the Japanese landing force, and Kendari was fully occupied by the evening of 24 January.[4] It was indeed a prize for the Japanese; its air base was considered the best in the Dutch Indies, and was immediately put into operation by the 21st Air Flotilla. The new base put Japanese bombers within range of Surabaja, Java, with its naval base, and enabled them to disrupt air reinforcements being sent to the Dutch Indies from Australia. Furthermore, the sea road had been opened to Ambon Island to the east and Makassar to the west. A primary naval base was established at Staring Bay, just to the south of Kendari.

Ambon Island

Although ABDA command's intelligence had no way of knowing so, the Japanese wanted an early occupation of Ambon Island. Because its regular garrison of 2,600 Australian, British, Dutch, and American troops had been reinforced in December by an Australian battalion and a Royal Australian Air Force (RAAF) squadron of 13 Hudsons, Ambon Island posed an air threat to Kendari and blocked a Japanese advance to the Timors. The Japanese Imperial General Headquarters regarded an early Ambon Island invasion as dangerous but urgent. More than fifty planes from the carriers *Hiryu* and *Soryu* began air raids on 24 January, the day Kendari fell, and were soon joined by other carrier- and land-based aircraft.

In the face of the superiority of Japanese air power, the RAAF squadron had been withdrawn from Ambon, leaving it without air defense. The Japanese force of eleven transports anchored off the island on the night of 30 January. Predawn landings were made 31 January, covered by planes from the *Chitose* and the *Mizuho*, at

Bangka Roads, Celebes. The garrison put up stiff resistance, in a hopeless fight; the last ABDA troops surrendered on 3 February, and the complete occupation of the island was accomplished by the next day. The Japanese moved closer to establishing the eastern jaw of their pincers on Java.[5]

Battle of Makassar Strait

Makassar, on the southern tip of Celebes, was the next Japanese objective. ABDA Command knew that a new Japanese invasion force was gathering, but it could not pinpoint where the force would strike; the guess was, however, that the target would be Bandjermasin, inland on the southeast end of Borneo. Wherever the target, Admiral Doorman was determined to try to stop the Japanese force moving south. Doorman's Combined Fleet sailed from Bunda Roads (between Madura Island and Surabaja) at 0000 on 4 February.

ABDA intelligence had reported that the Japanese convoy was supported by three cruisers and several destroyers, so that the ABDA force was roughly equal to the Japanese force in surface strength. However, the Japanese controlled the air; Admiral Doorman could not get Air ABDA support, even though Air ABDA included the Dutch navy's planes. Nevertheless, Doorman resolved to deny freedom of Makassar Strait to the convoy. In the morning of 4 February, as the Combined Fleet approached the strait, the inevitable Japanese air attacks began, with the planes having excellent visibility. The *Marblehead* came under continuous attack by two-engined bombers from Kendari; one plane was shot down by antiaircraft fire, while other planes managed six or seven hits or near-misses. Consequently, she suffered severe damage and lost steering control. The *Houston* also met with considerable damage, losing her after gun turret, with forty-eight men killed and more than fifty wounded. The *De Ruyter* was also attacked, but Doorman's flagship maneuvered well and escaped with only minor damage. The *Marblehead* dropped out of line and slowly headed for Bali Strait, with Doorman's force forming a protective ring around her. The task force retired through Lombok Strait to Tjilatjap, arriving about midnight.[6]

Thus the first genuine attempt to resist the Japanese Navy in the Netherlands East Indies resulted in the loss of more ABDA naval power. The Japanese Makassar Occupation Force (without the destroyer *Suzukaze*, which was torpedoed by a submarine, with nine men killed),[7] sailing from Staring Bay, easily took Makassar on 8

February, with only five men killed and five wounded. Dutch defenses had been softened by constant air attacks, staged from Kendari. However, at 2115 on 8 February a torpedo from the U.S. submarine S-37 penetrated the forward engine room of the destroyer *Natsushio*. Her crew was rescued by the destroyer *Kuroshio* at 0245, but a strong wind arose, and, despite efforts of the *Kuroshio* to tow her, the *Natsushio* sank at 0743 on 9 February, twenty miles from Makassar. She had suffered eight men killed and two wounded.[8]

Port Darwin Raid

The hit-and-run raid on Port Darwin by Nagumo's carrier fleet on 19 February 1942 was an important element in Japanese naval strategy regarding Java. Along with the invasion of Bali and Timor, it provided a way to interdict plane reinforcements to Java.

Admiral Nagumo's First Carrier Fleet was often stationed south of Java, to keep ABDA guessing as to where the next unexpected blow would fall. Port Darwin had become an important (albeit inadequate) ABDA staging area for the aircraft and troops sent to the Netherlands East Indies, and it was the closest port to imperiled Java. The Japanese felt that a destructive air raid on Port Darwin would not only disrupt aid being sent north, but also would have a demoralizing effect on Australia—a partner in ABDA, and fast becoming the rallying point for Japan's adversaries.

Consequently, a Port Darwin Task Force was assembled, its composition slightly different from that of Nagumo's Pearl Harbor Strike Force. It still had four heavy carriers, the *Kaga*, *Akagi*, *Hiryu*, and *Soryu*, but it had no battleships. Its heavy cruisers were still the *Tone* and the *Chikuma*, and the screen was still the light cruiser *Abukuma* with the destroyers *Urakaze*, *Isokaze*, *Tanikaze*, *Hamakaze*, *Kasumi*, *Shiranuhi*, and *Ariake*.[9]

Admiral Nagumo's fleet left Davao on 15 February, refueled at Staring Bay, and passed through the Flores Sea into the Timor Sea, making directly for Port Darwin. The four carriers, northwest by north of their target, began their launch at 0615 on the 19th. Each sent off nine Zero fighters. The *Akagi*, *Hiryu*, and *Soryu* each launched eighteen attack planes, and the *Kaga* launched twenty-seven; the *Kaga*, *Akagi*, and *Soryu* launched eighteen bombers and the *Hiryu* seventeen bombers, for a total of 188 Japanese planes.[10] Coordinated with the carrier-plane strike were land-based bombers flying from Kendari and Ambon.

At 1010 waves of planes descended without warning on ships in the harbor, and on the airfields, military installations, and the town itself. Port Darwin's harbor was filled with ships; two transports returned by the *Houston* were crowded together with three other transports, the destroyer *Peary*, the seaplane tender *William B. Preston*, tankers, freighters, and an Australian hospital ship. The raid caused heavy damage; in all, eight ships were sunk, including the *Peary*; two transports, and two freighters, and nine ships were seriously damaged, including the *William B. Preston*. Eighteen planes were destroyed, thus eliminating air opposition. The town, which was made up of wooden buildings, was strafed and set afire. Civilians, fearing an invasion, evacuated the town for some days. The airfield had been made inoperable and stockpiles of military equipment had been destroyed. Darwin was thus put out of business as a port of supply for Java. The Japanese carriers recovered their planes at 1200, the *Kaga* and *Hiryu* losing one plane each, and the task force returned to Staring Bay on 21 February.[11]

Bali—Lombok

In the meantime, Japanese transports were loading and task forces were assembling for the next thrust toward Java. Bali was the target, along with its larger sister island, Lombok, from which it is separated only by the narrow Lombok Strait. Bali, only a few miles across Bali Strait from Java, is part of the Lesser Sunda Islands, the last land barrier to the northeastern part of the Indian Ocean. To the north is the Flores Sea, which separates the Lesser Sundas from the Celebes. Aside from its strategic location in relation to both Java and Australia, Bali had little to offer the Japanese, for it is volcanic and mountainous, and has none of the resources vital to Japan's economy. The occupation of Bali, however, would place the naval base at Surabaja within a hundred miles of Bali's airfields. The Japanese were finding that the airfields in Borneo and Celebes, although often useful, were also often shut down by bad weather. Since Bali's climate was drier, weather would be less of a hindrance there.

Battle off Bali (ABDA Title: Battle of Badung Strait)

On 19 February ABDA Command knew that a Japanese occupation force was at sea, because an invasion armada had left Ambon on 18 February, backed by the seaplane tender *Mizuho*, sailing from

Kendari to provide air cover over the Banda Sea. ABDA Command felt (wrongly) that Timor would be the objective of the next invasion, and had tried desperately to reinforce the island's defenses with a convoy of troops, escorted by the heavy cruiser *Houston*, which had sailed from Port Darwin on 15 February. This convoy had come under bomber attack, however, as it neared Timor the following day, and consequently was recalled.

Admiral Doorman could have taken on the Bali Occupation Force successfully, if his forces had been concentrated. His one task force, however, was just disengaging itself at the eastern end of Java, while four American destroyers were refueling at Ratai Bay, in south Sumatra. British ships were escorting a convoy of troopships through the Sunda Strait, and the heavy cruiser *Houston* was returning to Java from Port Darwin. Still, while he could not gather all his naval forces, Admiral Doorman used whatever he could to fight it out with the Bali Occupation Force. Late on 18 February, coming from Tjilatjap, he took to Sanur Roads his two light cruisers, the *De Ruyter* and *Java*, the destroyer *Piet Hein* (the destroyer *Kortenaer* was unavailable, after running aground in the treacherous entrance at Tjilatjap harbor during the sortie) and the American destroyers *Pope* and *John D. Ford*. A second group, formed at Surabaja, contained the Dutch light cruiser *Tromp* and the American destroyers *Stewart*, *Parrott*, *John D. Edwards*, and *Pillsbury*. This group was due to arrive at Badung Strait shortly after Admiral Doorman's force had made a first attack and retired to the north. A third group of eight Dutch motor torpedo boats (MTBs) would attack last.

Doorman's battle plan was for his group to attack Japanese escort warships and transports which were involved in a reported landing at Sanur Roads, on the southeast coast of Bali, a little before midnight 19 February. The group would make its approach through Badung Strait, a narrow channel only fifteen miles wide, separating Bali and the island of Nusa Besar. After a strike and the partial destruction of the Japanese force, the second wave would arrive several hours later. Finally, the MTBs would arrive in the confusion of battle to create further havoc.

Admiral K. Kubo in the light cruiser *Nagara* had reason, then, to move his occupation force swiftly as he reached the perimeter of ABDA's remaining strength. The convoy made the voyage in one day, 18 February, arriving at Sanur Roads shortly before midnight. There was no effective opposition to the landing, and the transports were unloaded quickly. Admiral Kubo wanted to leave this advanced and exposed position as soon as possible. On the next day, his force was harassed by sporadic B-17 raids; one transport, the *Sagami Maru*, received a serious hit but was able to get underway homeward that afternoon, protected by the destroyers *Arashio* and *Michishio*. The other transport, the *Sasago Maru*, was leaving for Makassar, escorted by the *Asashio* and *Oshio*, when Doorman's first wave arrived. The Battle off Bali Island was about to begin.[12]

The Bali Invasion Force was scattered by now. The *Arashio* and *Michishio* were escorting the damaged *Sagami Maru* to a safe port, and the *Nagara* and her destroyers were bound for Makassar. At 2300, just as the *Asashio* and *Oshio* were weighing anchor, the enemy ships were spotted to the south, headed on a northerly course. The light cruisers *De Ruyter* and *Java*, in column, led their three destroyers, with the *Piet Hein* 5,500 yards astern, and the *Pope* and *Ford* the same distance behind the *Piet Hein*.

At once the *Asashio* and then the *Oshio* left their transport, turned on searchlights and illuminated the area with star shells, and headed east. This course closed range and put them in the position of crossing the British light cruisers' "T." The *Java* immediately fired on the *Asashio*, and the *De Ruyter* on the *Oshio*, at a range of 2,200 yards. The fire was returned by the Japanese ships; however, neither side scored.[13] After the initial salvos, the two light cruisers turned northeast and retired from the battle, finally heading north. The *Asashio* steamed east for several minutes and then turned south-southeast. The *Oshio* followed a parallel course but went farther east before taking a southeasterly course, which put her on the *Asashio*'s port beam.

At 2305, the *Piet Hein*, still coming north, made smoke which obscured the *Pope* and *Ford*, but which also hid the two Japanese destroyers from the two American destroyers. It was a dark, cloudy night, and, as so often happens in night battles, it became difficult to tell foe from friend. Finally, the *Piet Hein*, turning south, fired torpedoes at the *Asashio* and opened gunfire at 2310. Within a minute the *Asashio* returned fire, as the two antagonists closed range. At 2316, the *Piet Hein* was torpedoed, and sank at once.

The *Pope* and *Ford* had also turned south, away from the battle, and were also paralleling the *Asashio*. (The *Oshio* was screened by the *Piet Hein*'s smoke, and had not yet entered the fight.) At 2324 the *Asashio* opened fire on the two U.S. destroyers, which then made smoke and continued south. The *Asashio* followed them, ex-

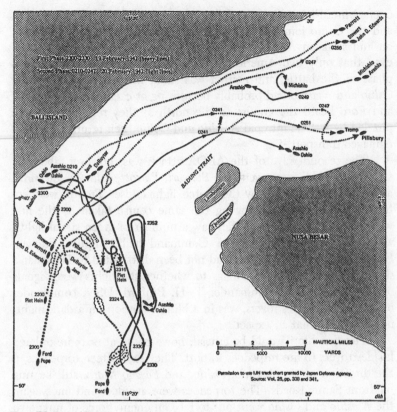

Two Phases of Battle off Bali Island, 19–20 February 1942
IJN ships indicated by solid lines, ABDA ships by dotted lines.

changing torpedoes with the *Pope* and *Ford*, and firing at the *Ford*. To avoid the *Asashio's* fire, the two American destroyers began to circle, first heading south and then, in accordance with Admiral Doorman's prebattle orders, trying to exit to the north. There ensued another brief but brisk engagement, as the two Japanese and two American destroyers followed parallel courses. The *Asashio* and *Oshio* continued firing, while dodging five torpedoes launched by the *Pope*. The American destroyers, temporarily screened from the *Asashio* and *Oshio* by smoke made by the *Ford*, then retired to the southeast.

As the *Oshio* reversed from the retiring American destroyers, she sighted still another ship, thought to be an American destroyer, and opened fire. Fire was returned, but after a few minutes it died down, and the *Oshio* joined the *Asashio*. Each ship claimed she had fired on and sunk an American destroyer. It was later determined, however, that only two American destroyers had been involved in this phase of the battle, and neither was sunk, which suggests that the *Oshio* and *Asashio* had probably been firing at each other. The *Pope* and *Ford* heard the gunfire to the north as they retired, and were puzzled by it. The intrepid *Asashio* and *Oshio* then returned to their damaged transport.[14]

The second wave of the ABDA attack was, however, about to strike. Four U.S. destroyers, the *Stewart*, *Parrott*, *John D. Edwards*, and *Pillsbury*, followed by the Dutch light cruiser *Tromp*, were entering Badung Strait, following the same course taken by the first wave. Sailing up the strait, they saw a number of green signal lights, which confused them. (ABDA Command had compiled French/ English code books, but they had not been distributed to Doorman's ships, so there was confusion as to whether the lights were signals of a friend or foe.) Commander T. H. Binford, USN, commander of the American destroyers, was in a blind situation on a dark night, not knowing what to expect.

The first blow would be crucial, however, so at 0045 he ordered his destroyers to fire torpedoes to port. They sent fifteen torpedoes in the direction of the *Asashio*, *Oshio*, and *Sasago Maru*, still bearing off from Sanur Roads. The torpedoes were avoided, and once again the *Asashio* and *Oshio* went out to face an enemy force of unknown strength.

The two were then spotted by the *Stewart* off her port beam. The *Stewart* illuminated the area, and began firing at 0215. The *John D. Edwards* also attempted a torpedo launch at the same time, but was able to launch only two. The *Oshio* and *Asashio* answered with rapid and accurate fire, and the *Stewart* received a direct hit, knocking out the steering engine room. The *John D. Edwards* had to veer hard to starboard to avoid a collision with the *Parrott*. The *Pillsbury* had left the column formation early, following a course parallel to the other ships on their starboard side. The fire of the *Oshio* and *Asashio* was so effective that the American destroyers never did charge, as was their assignment, into the transport anchorage site, and were instead forced to the northeast.

The light cruiser *Tromp* brought up the rear. The course of the *Asashio* and *Oshio* cut the wakes of the *John D. Edwards*, *Parrott*, and *Stewart*, placing the Japanese destroyers between the three-destroyer column and the *Pillsbury*. The *Tromp* found herself farthest to the west, acting as a rear guard against the aggressive *Asashio* and *Oshio*. The two opposing forces followed roughly parallel courses, bearing to the northeast. Little gunfire was exchanged until the ABDA force turned east; then, at 0241, the *Tromp* was hit eleven times on her superstructure by gunfire from the *Asashio*. At the same time, she managed to avoid torpedoes launched by the *Oshio*. (Her damage, however, was sufficient that she was later sent to Australia for repairs.) The *Oshio* was hit forward, with seven men killed. Finally, the *Oshio* and *Asashio*, like good shepherds, circled to starboard and again returned to their transport.

By this time ABDA forces were considerably scattered. The *Parrott*, then the ship closest to Bali, ran aground briefly but was able to get away again. She did not reenter the battle, however. At 0241, the *John D. Edwards* and *Stewart* were still in column, steaming northeast. The *Tromp* was on an easterly course, 8,000 yards off the starboard quarter of the two U.S. destroyers. The *Pillsbury*, on a northeasterly course, was 3,000 yards away on the *Tromp*'s starboard beam, on an intersecting course. At that moment, destroyers *Michishio* and *Arashio*, which had left the damaged transport *Sagami Maru* and returned to aid the Japanese ships still at Bali, came rushing in on a southwest-by-west course; they soon found themselves at close quarters, between the *John D. Edwards* and the *Stewart* on their starboard beam and the *Tromp* and *Pillsbury* on their port beam. The *Stewart* turned on her searchlights, and both sides began firing and launching torpedoes at 0247. The *Michishio* could not withstand the concentrated attack from both flanks, so she veered to the north to avoid the *Stewart*'s searchlights, only to be hit repeatedly by fire from the *John D. Edwards*. The *Michishio* went dead in the water, out of the fight, with thirteen men killed and eighty-three wounded. (She survived, was repaired, and eventually returned to duty.) The battle was over, for the opposing columns had closed at high speed, and, after passing in their firefight, neither reversed course. It is understandable that they felt confused and uncertain at this point; because this was a night engagement, neither side knew the size or position of its opposition.

The planned strike by eight Dutch MTBs went through the strait on schedule, in two waves of four.[15] Originally nine were sent, but on leaving Surabaja one hit a lightbuoy and retired, so the formation was revised. The first wave spotted some ships at a distance, but fired no torpedoes, while the second group saw nothing. (Because an MTB lies so low in the water, her crew has a short field of vision.)

The box score of the battle was unimpressive, given the number of ships involved and the disparity in numbers. One Japanese destroyer was severely damaged, two were lightly damaged, and two transports were damaged; but the entire Bali Occupation Force returned safely to port. On ABDA's side, the light cruiser *Tromp* was badly damaged, and the destroyer *Piet Hein* was sunk.[16]

The ABDA fleet has frequently been criticized for fighting the Battle of Badung Strait ineptly. True, its ships were not so concentrated as they would have been, had time allowed; and the cruisers, their crews desperately tired, met only two destroyers, when they were looking for larger ships to engage. These factors contributed to the ABDA force's inept fighting. However, it must be noted that, while it is true that the Japanese destroyers were newer, stronger, and more heavily armed than the Allied destroyers, it was the two destroyers *Oshio* and *Asashio* that waged efficiently and audaciously fought battles that, in the end, negated Doorman's battle plan.[17]

Throughout the war, the Japanese warships showed remarkable skill in night fighting, caused by several factors. They practiced night-fighting training in maneuvers more than the Allied fleets did. Their 24-inch torpedoes, besides having almost no wake, had a tremendous range (over three times the range of U. S. Navy torpedoes, even after they were improved in 1942). It was a standard Japanese night-battle doctrine to use torpedoes first, not to use gunfire unless necessary (although their powder had relatively little flash), and to use searchlights as little as possible. They continued to carry torpedoes on their heavy cruisers even after the U. S. Navy removed theirs. (Both sides had unproven myths about the other's visual ability: the Allies believed that most Japanese had poor eyesight; the Japanese believed that brown eyes could see better in the dark. Battle records do show the work of Japanese lookouts was phenomenal. They could often spot American ships before U. S. Navy radar could detect Japanese ships. See the incident of the destroyer *Blue* in Chapter 13, p. 206.) In addition, Japanese optical equipment was of a superior quality. One weakness of Japanese torpedo attacks was, however, that their torpedo spreads were not selective.

Comparative Table: Torpedoes[18]

	Size (Torpedo tubes)	Speed (Knots)	Range (Yards)	Powder charge (Pounds)
Japan	24-inch	49	24,000	225
		36	43,600	225
U.S.	21-inch	48	4,360	135
		32	8,720	135
G.B.	21-inch	46	3,270	144
		30	10,900	144

Bali and Lombok fell to Japanese force on 19 February, and the Bali airfield was receiving Japanese planes the next day. No place in Java was then out of reach of Japanese power, and no ABDA reinforcements, air, naval, or army, could now be provided to the forces there.

Timor

Timor, the largest and most southeasterly of the Lesser Sunda Islands, belonged partly to Portugal and partly to the Dutch. The Portuguese capital was Dili, and the Dutch capital was Kupang. Most of the population was primitive, and Timor contained little in the way of needed resources; but, just as Bali had been a staging area for large ABDA plane reinforcements to Java, Timor was the only staging area for short-range ABDA fighter planes. Although a flight from Timor to Java was longer than one from Bali, Timor was the only place in the Lesser Sunda Islands within fighter-plane range of Australia. That marked it for Japanese invasion, because its possession would destroy the fighter-plane support for Java's defenders.

The troops, carried in fourteen transports, one carrying paratroopers, landed on 20 February. The paratroopers were landed, and after the airfield was captured, they were picked up by land planes and dropped over Kupang. Both jurisdictions of the island were fully under Japanese control by 24 February, despite fierce resistance by the ABDA forces. The Portuguese had some troops en route to defend Dili, but the Japanese arrived before them. Cut off effectively from Australia at all points, Java was about to be forced to fight alone for its existence—the eastern pincer on Java had been established.[19]

Dutch Borneo

Simultaneously with the Eastern Force's southward sweep Admiral Takahashi sent his Central Invasion Force from Davao to capture Dutch Borneo, to assist his Eastern Force if necessary, and then to wait to invade east Java—the invasion timed to take place when Admiral Ozawa would be able to cover the invasion of west Java.

Tarakan Island is located on the east coast of Borneo, just south of what was British Borneo. The Japanese wanted it because of its rich oil fields, and because its capture would provide a base and airfield from which Japanese forces could be covered in their next advance. Tarakan was defended by a Dutch garrison of 1,300 men.

The Tarakan Invasion Force sailed from Davao on 7 January 1942. En route, it was bombed without result by three of Air ABDA's B-17s, based in Java. The speed of Japanese operations had made it impossible for ABDA Command to position any intercepting submarines. By the afternoon of 10 January the convoy, with fourteen transports carrying Army and Marine troops, was just off Tarakan Island. The Dutch garrison commander, on his own initiative, immediately set fire to Tarakan's oil fields and sabotaged its airfield. At 2400, the landing troops began a double envelopment, and on the morning of 12 January the small Dutch garrison at Tarakan surrendered, facing overwhelming odds, without any hope of reinforcement. Dutch planes attacked the invaders on 13 and 14 January, further damaging Tarakan's airfield. But by 17 January, the Japanese Navy's 23rd Air Flotilla was using a repaired Tarakan airfield as its headquarters.[20]

Balikpapan—Bandjarmasin

The next targets, which would put all of Borneo in Japanese hands, were the port of Balikpapan and the inland settlement of Bandjarmasin, both of which had oil fields. The Japanese had begun gathering a Balikpapan Occupation Force at Tarakan, and had ordered the Balikpapan authorities to surrender their oil fields and installations, unsabotaged. The invasion ships had only intermittent air cover because of foul weather; however, because of the weather, and the scarcity of ABDA planes, they were not attacked until they arrived off Balikpapan. As fifteen transports prepared to anchor on 23 January, great columns of fire and smoke covered the Balikpapan oil fields. The local Dutch commander had not heeded the Japanese order.

Admiral Shoji Nishimura, the escort commander, was to have a busy afternoon and night. First, beginning at 1525, the convoy was attacked by three B-17s flying from Surabaja; the transports *Tatsugami Maru* and *Nana Maru* were hit and damaged. Nevertheless, anchorage was made at 1945 on 23 January, and the troops were landed, screened by the light cruiser *Naka* and her squadron's destroyers. Despite Nishimura's screen, the Dutch submarine *K-XVIII* torpedoed and sank the transport *Tsuruga Maru*, around 2400. The night was dark with thunderclouds, and Nishimura's primary concern was additional submarine attacks; he certainly was not expecting an attack by ABDA ships.[21]

The threat to Balikpapan, however, had caused considerable anxiety at ABDA Command. The American naval force at Timor, under Vice Admiral W. A. Glassford, was available to contest the landings. It consisted of the light cruisers *Boise* and *Marblehead*, and the destroyers *Pope* (flagship), *Parrott, John D. Ford*, and *Paul Jones*. When ABDA Command first heard of the convoy headed south on 20 January, it ordered the American ships to sail at once to intercept and destroy the transports. But on the next day, the *Boise* hit an uncharted reef and had to retire, while the *Marblehead* developed engine trouble and could make only 15 knots; she continued north, however, in order to provide a rendezvous point for the returning destroyers. The four destroyers, making 27 knots, headed for Balikpapan on a course which would bring them into the area at about midnight, on a north-northwesterly course. The burning oil fields would silhouette a relatively unguarded transport force.

The American force, holding course in column, made a parallel attacking run. In the first attack, from 0316 to 0325, three destroyers fired ten torpedoes at close range. None found a mark. The Americans had attacked quickly and boldly, and a more stealthy and calculated approach would probably have yielded better results. They were unaware, however, of the precise location of Nishimura's protecting force.

The destroyers reversed course to the south in a second more deliberate attack. At 0330, the *Pope* torpedoed the *Sumanoura Maru*, which immediately exploded and sank. The *Ford* used main batteries at close range on transports, and at 0345 she torpedoed and sank the *Kuretake Maru*. The last two destroyers, in column, torpedoed and sank the *Tatsugami Maru* at 0335, and continuing south, they exchanged fire with two patrol boats. The Battle off Balikpapan was over at 0350.[22]

With the first intimation of enemy action, Admiral Nishimura in the *Naka* had taken his destroyers even farther away from the transports, to the east in an antisubmarine sweep. Such a move was understandable, for it must have seemed inconceivable to him that a hard-pressed ABDA navy would attack his large force with surface ships. His transports had already been attacked by at least two submarines, and he knew that ABDA had about forty, so his movement to the east was a proper antisubmarine tactic. This course, however, allowed the American force to slip in between Nishimura's force and the transports. Such are the gambles of war.

The Japanese troops landed at Balikpapan in the early morning of 24 January. They were resisted by the Dutch garrison until the Dutch commanding officer received permission to withdraw his 200 men to an airfield at Ulin, 120 miles west of Samarinda. Realizing the Japanese would soon discover the new Dutch position, the Dutch commanding officer had already destroyed the nearby oil fields on 20 January, and withdrawn his troops, this time to Muaranmuntai. The Balikpapan garrison was finally trapped there by the Japanese Army, and it surrendered on 8 March.[23]

The Japanese troops, taken by barges from Balikpapan, disembarked 50 miles south-southeast of Bandjarmasin. From this point they marched overland to Bandjarmasin. Another column marched 160 miles overland, directly from Balikpapan. Bandjarmasin was captured on 16 February; by 28 January Air Flotilla 23 was operating from the Balikpapan airfield and by 23 February also from the Bandjarmasin field.[24] The arc of air protection available to the Japanese Navy had been expanded by the occupation of Borneo. The sea lanes for the Japanese attack on Singapore, Sumatra, and west Java were now protected by the occupation of Borneo and Malaya. The line of advance for the attack on east Java was secured by the seizure of the Celebes and the key islands in the Molucca Sea and Flores Sea.

The Fall of Singapore and Bangka, Palembang, and Southeast Sumatra

The fall of Singapore, a city of more than 500,000, on 15 February, to a Japanese force half the size of that defending Malaya, drove the British back into Burma and into Ceylon and the Indian Ocean. Singapore, an island connected to Johore, Malaya, by a short causeway, had been the symbol of British authority in Malaya and Malaya's administrative, political, and economic center. Now, however, it was made part of the Greater East Asia Co-Prosperity Sphere.

Bangka, an island 138 miles long and 62 miles wide, then supplied over ten percent of the world's tin. Lying as it does a short distance northeast of the south tip of Sumatra, its occupation was essential both for the attack on Batavia and for an invasion of Palembang and southeast Sumatra.

Sumatra was a prize because of its rich oil fields. It is a long, rather narrow island, covered with lush jungle and infested with disease—an inhospitable land. The Japanese made their initial assault on Palembang, the center of one of the world's richest oil deposits, in order to obtain desperately needed oil and drive the Allied forces out of southeast Sumatra, from which the Japanese could invade west Java unimpeded. There was oil also in the northwest part of the island, but it was still relatively unexploited. Northeast Sumatra, separated from the west coast of Malaya by the Malacca Strait, would be a buffer to Malaya if the English ever tried to return, and it lay along most of the sea route to Burma.

The four days 12–15 February saw as wild a scene of confusion as war can bring, in the area of Singapore through the Bangka Strait to Palembang, Sumatra. The orderly Japanese naval table of organization for the occupation of Bangka–Palembang went to pieces, as a variety of factors left every ship and squadron on its own. ABDA intelligence reported that the first convoy in a new Japanese occupation force had left Camranh Bay on 9 February. Admiral Ozawa's powerful Southern Expeditionary Fleet followed the next day, and on 11 February an even larger convoy of transports sailed under escort. Obviously the attack would be directed at Palembang, Sumatra, since it held over half of the Netherlands East Indies' oil reserves.

General Wavell, as defender of Singapore and the ABDA region, was in a desperate plight, for Singapore was falling, and Sumatra was threatened. On 11 February, he ordered Admiral Doorman's strike force to assemble west of Java. When these orders were received, the strike force was south of Bali, some 800 miles away. Doorman, however, at once ordered his ships to assemble north of Sunda Strait; he would try with his small force to save Palembang.

In Singapore, thousands of people finally realized that the impossible was going to happen—the city was about to fall to the Japanese. Fleeing civilians and high-ranking civil and military authorities all crowded onto almost anything that could float. If they could not go directly to Java and then to Australia, they headed instead for Sumatra, hoping that by an overland journey they could find unoccupied ports from which they could reach Australia. Bangka Strait, the main route to Sumatra or Java, became crowded with fleeing ships for the next three days. But Admiral Ozawa's force was also in Bangka Strait, and the air was filled with Japanese planes. To add to the confusion, the Bangka–Palembang Occupation Force was coming through this melee. Thus, most of the ships trying to escape Singapore were brutally massacred.[25]

Admiral Doorman sailed into this confusion on 14 February, from a rendezvous north of Sunda Strait. His hastily gathered force contained the light cruiser *De Ruyter* (flagship), his other two light cruisers, the *Java* and the *Tromp*; the British heavy cruiser *Exeter* and the light cruiser *Hobart*; the Dutch destroyers *Banckert, Kortenaer, Van Nes, Van Ghent*; and the American destroyers *Bulmer, Barker, Parrott, Stewart, Pope,* and *John D. Ford.* Misfortune struck almost at once, when the *Van Ghent* hit an uncharted reef at Stolze Strait, off Bangka, and sank. The *Banckert* was detached from the force to rescue survivors.

Admiral Ozawa knew by dawn of 15 February that the ABDA force was approaching. He ordered his main convoys dispersed, and ordered continuous strikes by planes from the *Ryujo* and from the well-stocked Japanese airfields. He then prepared for an engagement with any remaining ABDA Command ships. Japanese high-level bombing of Doorman's fleet was ineffective, with only slight damage inflicted on two American destroyers by near-misses, despite continuous bombing, during the entire day.

Admiral Doorman, however, was realistic, and in the afternoon he ordered a retirement, preferring not to risk an encounter with Ozawa's dangerous force in the Bangka Strait. However, the *Van Nes,* still in the area picking up surviving escapees, was sunk off Bangka Strait on 17 February by Japanese bombers. The retirement of Doorman's strike force meant the loss of Bangka and Palembang;

both fell on 15 February, and the Dutch and British defenders retreated to Java, without fully demolishing their oilfields and refineries. There was no opposition left in southeast Sumatra; thus, Java was locked in from the west.[26]

Table of Organization for the Isolation of Java; Second Fleet, Southern Force, Netherlands East Indies Force (Vice Admiral Ibo Takahashi)

Eastern Invasion Support Force, Main Body (Vice Admiral Takeo Takagi)

Light carrier: *Zuiho*
Seaplane tenders: *Chitose, Mizuho*
Heavy cruisers: *Nachi*, Haguro, Myoko* (after 26 February)
Destroyers: *Ikazuchi, Inazuma, Ushio, Sazanami, Akebono, Yama-kaze, Kawakaze*

Eastern Distant Support Force

Heavy carriers: *Hiryu, Soryu*
Light carrier: *Zuiho*
Seaplane tender: *Chitose*
Heavy cruiser: *Maya*
Destroyers: *Akebono, Ushio, Ariake, Sazanami, Ikazuchi*

FIRST EASTERN INVASION FORCE (Invasion of Bangka Roads, Kema, Menado, and Kendari)

Seaplane tenders: *Chitose, Mizuho*
Light cruisers: *Jintsu*, Nagara*
Destroyers: *Yukikaze, Amatsukaze, Tokitsukaze, Hatsukaze, Ikazu-chi, Kuroshio, Oyashio, Natsushio, Hayashio, Inazuma*

INVASION OF AMBON ISLAND

See Eastern Distant Support Force, above

SECOND INVASION FORCE

Light cruiser: *Jintsu**
Destroyers: *Hatsukaze, Yukikaze, Amatsukaze, Tokitsukaze, Kuro-shio, Oyashio, Hayashio, Natsushio, Arashio, Oshio, Michishio, Asashio*

INVASION OF MAKASSAR

Seaplane tenders: *Chitose, Mizuho*

Light carrier: *Zuiho*
Light cruiser: *Nagara**
Destroyers: *Asagumo, Natsugumo, Minegumo, Kuroshio, Oyashio, Hayashio, Natsushio, Arashio, Oshio, Nenohi, Michishio, Hatsuharu, Suzukaze, Kawakaze, Umikaze, Hatsushimo*

INVASION OF BALI–LOMBOK

Light cruiser: *Nagara**
Destroyers: *Hatsushimo, Nenohi, Wakaba, Michishio, Oshio, Arashio, Asashio*

TIMOR INVASION FORCE

Seaplane tender: *Mizuho*
Light cruiser: *Jintsu**
Destroyers: *Kuroshio, Oyashio, Hayashio, Hatsukaze, Yukikaze, Amatsukaze, Tokitsukaze, Sazanami, Ushio*

CENTRAL INVASION FORCE (Tarakan)

Seaplane tenders: *Sanyo Maru, Sanuki Maru*
Light cruiser: *Naka**
Destroyers: *Umikaze, Kawakaze, Yamakaze, Suzukaze, Natsugumo, Yudachi, Samidare, Harusame, Asagumo, Minegumo*

Second Fleet, Southern Force, Malay Force, Main Body, Distant Cover (Vice Admiral Nobutake Kondo)

Battleships: *Kongo, Haruna*
Heavy cruisers: *Atago**, *Takao, Maya*
Destroyers: *Arashi, Hagikaze, Akatsuki, Hatakaze, Nowaki, Hibiki*

Second Fleet, Southern Force, Malay Force, Main Body (Also called First Southern Expeditionary Fleet) (Vice Admiral Jisaburo Ozawa)

Light carrier: *Ryujo*
Heavy cruisers: *Chokai**, *Mikuma, Mogami, Suzuya, Kumano*
Light cruiser: *Yura*
Destroyers: *Shirakumo, Ayanami, Isonami, Shikinami, Murakumo, Shirayuki, Hatsuyuki*[27]

Major Allied Warships for the Defense of the Netherlands East Indies

Dutch

Light cruisers: *De Ruyter, Java, Tromp*

Destroyers: *Witte de With, Evertsen, Kortenaer, Van Nes, Van Ghent, Piet Hein, Banckert*

Submarines: twelve K-type, four O-type

American

Seaplane tenders: *Langley, Childs, William B. Preston, Heron*

Heavy cruiser: *Houston*

Light cruisers: *Marblehead, Boise*

Destroyers: *Barker, Bulmer, Edsall, John D. Edwards, John D. Ford, Parrott, Paul Jones, Peary, Pillsbury, Pope, Stewart, Whipple, Alden*

Submarines: six S-type, twenty-two modern

Australian

Light cruisers: *Perth, Hobart*

British

Heavy cruiser: *Exeter*

Light cruisers: *Danae, Dragon*

Destroyers: *Tenedos, Scout, Stronghold, Electra, Encounter, Jupiter*

Submarines: two modern submarines

ABDA Strike Force (formed on 2 February)

Heavy cruiser: *Houston* (USN)

Light cruisers: *De Ruyter* (RNN)*, *Tromp* (RNN)

Destroyers: *Van Ghent, Piet Hein, Banckert*—(RNN); *Stewart, Bulmer, Barker, Edwards*—(USN)[28]

chapter 5

FROM THE FALL
OF JAVA TO THE
INVASION OF BURMA

1942

27 February–1 March	Battle of the Java Sea
28 February–1 March	Battle of the Sunda Strait
8 March	Netherlands East Indies surrenders
8 March	Japanese capture Rangoon, Burma
23 March	Japanese occupy Andaman and Nicobar Islands
28 March	Japanese occupy all of Sumatra

The diminution of the ABDA naval forces was caused by more than just battle damage; ironically, there was then a fuel shortage in Java's ports. Java had large oil deposits, but not in the quantity that Borneo and Sumatra did. It did have large storage facilities, but these were inland, and the Javanese who operated the oil facilities at the ports refused to work after the Japanese air raids began. Oil, then, was not readily available to warships needing to refuel. Likewise, munitions were running low; the destroyer tender *Black Hawk* issued her last torpedoes on 21 February, which meant that the destroyers *Pillsbury* and *Parrott* were eliminated from the ABDA naval force, since they had no torpedoes in their magazines.

The repair facilities in Java, which had always been inadequate for a large naval force, also had suffered from the bombing. Since such facilities could not accomplish necessary repair and overhaul, the number of warships available and ready for action was further diminished. The *Stewart*, which was damaged in the Battle of Badung Strait, was placed in drydock at Surabaja, only to have the drydock collapse. The light cruiser *Tromp*, having been hit eleven times on her bridge and control tower in the Battle of Badung Strait, had to be sent to Australia for repairs, because there were no facilities in Java which were not already in use. The destroyer *Banckert* was knocked out of the war, severely damaged by a bombing raid on Surabaja on 24 February. The destroyer *Whipple* had collided with the *De Ruyter* and was inoperative; she was temporarily given a "soft" bow but was still unfit for inclusion in the Combined Fleet. The destroyer *Edsall* had been damaged when depth charges were incorrectly set and exploded too near her stern. She, too, could perform only limited escort duty. The *Marblehead* could not be repaired in Java and was sent to Ceylon. The *Black Hawk* was sent to Australia, escorted by the destroyers *Bulmer* and *Barker*, which were in a sorry state of disrepair, with their torpedo supplies almost exhausted.

Even among those left in the ABDA force, the heavy cruiser *Houston*'s after turrets were still inoperable, although her forward guns were still working. Indeed, all of the ships left to Admiral Doorman were in need of overhaul; the force that was to face Japan in a last effort to stop the invasion of east Java was simply inadequate. So desperate was the situation that General Wavell, after consultation with Washington, dissolved ABDA Command on 25 February and placed the defense of Java under the operational command of Admiral Helfrich. All army, naval, and air forces were now commanded by Dutch officers.[1]

In contrast, the Japanese Imperial General Headquarters, with the richest prize now locked in, prepared a massive assault with both army and naval units. Their plan called for three landings on the western end of Java, in Sunda Strait—at Bantam Bay, Merak, and Eretenwetan—for the capture of the capital at Batavia. An eastern wing was to land at Kragan, 100 miles west of Surabaja. Preliminary to the landing, Bawean Island, 80 miles north of Surabaja, was to be invaded to set up a radio station.

Two covering forces hovered south of Java. These were Admiral Nobutake Kondo's Southern Force, Main Body, and Admiral Nagumo's First Mobile Fleet, Carrier Strike Force, the latter still constituted as it had been for the Pearl Harbor raid. They were so placed as to cut off Australia from Java and India. Nagumo's planes thus interdicted and sank the seaplane tender *Langley*, with thirty-two desperately needed P-40s, near Tjilatjap.

Java was important to the Japanese, for it had considerable oil deposits and it also had a number of important refineries. The island, the most densely populated region in the world (50 million inhabitants), was the administrative, industrial, and vital working center for

1. *Admiral Isoroku Yamamoto, commander-in-chief, Combined Fleet*

2. *The Pearl Harbor Strike Force, en route to its target. In the foreground is a dive-bomber squadron aboard the carrier Soryu, steaming behind her is the Hiryu*

3. Vice Admiral Chuichi Nagumo, commander of the Pearl Harbor Strike Force

. *Photograph taken from an attacking plane, early in the Pearl Harbor raid. The* akes of two torpedoes, one of which is just striking the battleship West Virginia (*in* he center foreground) *are clearly visible. In the background, Hickam Field is being* ombarded.

5. *Rear Admiral Sadamichi Kajioka*

6. *Vice Admiral Nobutake Kondo, com-
    mander of Malay Force*

7. *The destroyer Umikaze, of the Fourth Surprise Attack Force, Philippines invasio*

8. The Dutch submarine K-XVI, which sank the destroyer Sagiri of the Miri convoy support force, shown with her sister boat, the K-XV.   (International News Photo)

9.   Rear Admiral Shoji Nishimura, commander of the escort group for the Balikpapan invasion.

10.   Vice Admiral Jisaburo Ozawa, commander of Southern Expeditionary Force

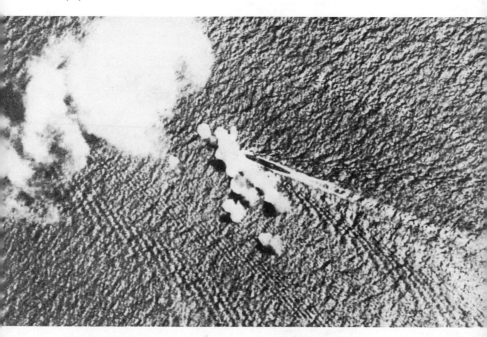

11.   The Dutch destroyer Van Nes in her last moments, under attack by Japanese bombers in Bangka Strait, 17 February 1942.

12. *The light cruiser* Jintsu, *flagship, Destroyer Squadron* 2.

13. *The destroyer* Amatsukaze *of Destroyer Division 16, commanded by Lieutenant Commander Tameichi Hara.*

14. *The British cruiser* Exeter *sinks, after being hit by gunfire from the heavy cruiser* Nachi, *and by torpedoes from Japanese destroyers and cruisers, 1 March 1942.*

15. *The U. S. destroyer* Pope *being sunk by gunfire from Japanese heavy cruisers, 1 March 1942.*

the 3,000-mile-long chain of the Netherlands East Indies. It was the heart of the Dutch possessions in the South Seas.

The responsibility for the capture of Surabaja was given to the Imperial Japanese Army's 48th Division, which had been fighting in the Philippines. It was brought to Jolo and embarked on transports, sailing on 19 February as the First Escort Force. The convoy put in at Balikpapan to take on the 56th Regiment (without the detachment at Bandjarmasin), and sailed again on 23 February. On 25 February, it was joined by the Second Escort Force, led by the *Jintsu* and her nine destroyers.

For the invasion of Batavia in the west, the Japanese Army combined the headquarters of the 16th Army, 2nd Division, and the 230th Regiment of the 38th Division. The convoy of fifty-six transports left Camranh Bay on 18 February. On the first leg of its journey, this Third Escort Force was screened by the *Natori* and her eight destroyers. As it neared its three beachheads, it was further backed up by the West Support Force of four cruisers and three destroyers, the *Yura* and her eight destroyers, and by the light carrier *Ryujo* and the seaplane tenders *Chitose* and *Mizuho*.

ABDA Command knew of the concentration of ships at Jolo and received correct information on 24 February that several invasion armadas were headed south. It had guessed correctly that the invasion would be a two-pronged one. There was little that could be done about it, besides awaiting the appearance of Japanese ships and attacking them as the situation developed. ABDA naval forces had been under constant attack by land-based planes, from the east, north, and west; its retaliatory force was thus being reduced daily. Nevertheless, ABDA Command planned to use its remaining bombers on the first warships that appeared, and then to throw its Combined Strike Force at the convoy.

It was the Eastern Force that appeared first, when destroyers from the First Escort Force backed the occupation of Bawean Island on 25 February. At once Admiral Helfrich, commander-in-chief of all naval forces in Java, ordered Admiral Doorman to concentrate his fleet at Surabaja, thus bringing in the heavy cruiser *Exeter*, the light cruiser *Perth*, and the destroyers *Jupiter*, *Electra*, and *Encounter* from Batavia. (The light cruiser *Hobart* was also at Batavia but was low on fuel, because the tanker that could have refueled her was put out of action by an air raid on the morning of 25 February.) Admiral Doorman did not await the arrival of the ships from Batavia, however. On 25 February, he used his ships at Surabaja in a dusk-to-dawn sweep along the coast westward toward Madura, hoping to intercept transports. He was joined by the Batavian contingent upon his return to Surabaja. By then reports of large convoys, headed for both east and west Java, were coming in. Doorman ordered the remaining ships at Batavia—the Australian light cruiser *Hobart*, two old Royal Navy light cruisers, the *Dragon* and the *Danae*, two Royal Navy destroyers, the *Tenedos* and the *Scout*, and the Dutch destroyer *Evertsen*—all now mobile, to intercept a Japanese convoy, reported to be nearing Muntok. They sortied at 2200, but were back in port by 0100 on 26 February.

On 27 February, the same force was ordered to make another sweep to the north from Batavia; if no enemy were sighted by 0430 on 28 February, the force was to escape through the Sunda Strait to the British naval base at Trincomalee, Ceylon. All but the Dutch destroyer *Evertsen* went to Ceylon. The *Evertsen*, however, lost contact with her sister ships, because of a squall. She then tried to join the *Houston* and *Perth*, which were in action at Bantam Bay. Engaged in a fire fight with the destroyers *Murakumo* and *Shirakumo*, she received hits, caught fire, and was beached.[2]

The Second Escort Force, leading the armada bound for Kragan, was disorganized as it neared Java. Lieutenant Commander Tameichi Hara (later to be a captain), skipper of the destroyer *Amatsukaze*, felt that Admiral Yamamoto, who was convinced that air power in Java had been eliminated, was unwise in sending the Carrier Strike Force to make a raid in the Indian Ocean, while cancelling air cover from land-based planes. "This audacity resulted in jeopardizing the operation of at least the convoy which I escorted."[3]

The convoy of forty-one transports was disposed in two columns, with 650 yards between ships and about 2,000 yards between columns, sailing slowly at 10 knots and zigzagging in what Hara thought was a disgraceful manner. Many of the transports were requisitioned merchant ships, whose captains were inexperienced in this kind of operation. The convoy straggled over a length of 20 miles. At its head were four minesweepers, in line abreast at 3,300 yards, followed by three destroyers with a similar spacing. Behind this double advance line came the light cruiser *Naka* with a small patrol ship on either side. The middle section of the transports had one destroyer on each side. Much farther away to port came the light cruiser *Jintsu* with the four destroyers of Destroyer Division 16 (of which the *Amatsukaze* was a part). The Eastern Region Support Force of the heavy cruisers *Nachi* and *Haguro* was 200 miles astern.

Hara's fears might well have been realized if the Dutch had had more planes, or if Admiral Doorman had attacked the convoy when its exact position had been given him, at 1357 on 27 February. A PBY had attacked the *Amatsukaze* at 0600 on 26 February, its bomb dropping, however, 300 yards ahead of the destroyer. A few fighter planes flying from Balikpapan were giving afternoon cover for the Japanese ships on that day. At 1748, two American B-17s flying from Malang broke through a low ceiling, this time dropping six 500-lb. bombs. The bombs were poorly aimed, however; four hit about 1,500 yards from the *Amatsukaze* and two about 500 yards from the *Hatsukaze*.

Admiral Doorman's strike force did not make an immediate assault on the reported invasion fleet—probably out of weariness and fear of enemy planes, rather than command indecision. His fleet had spent the night of 26 February on a searching sweep that took him to Bawean Island shortly before the Japanese occupied it. Luck was against Doorman, for the Bawean Island occupation force had only a light naval escort. He turned back toward Surabaja at 0900 on 27 February. Although Admiral Helfrich had asked him to immediately attack the convoys now being constantly reported by air reconnaissance, Doorman nevertheless returned to Surabaja at about 1400. But again Helfrich ordered him to turn and fight, so he once more reversed course to seek the enemy.

A scout plane from Balikpapan had reported the morning movement of Doorman's force. Its proximity to the advance echelons of the eastern convoy now began to alarm the Japanese naval command. The *Nachi* catapulted a plane which was to keep Doorman's force in sight, and both heavy cruisers, the *Nachi* and *Haguro*, with the destroyers *Ikazuchi* and *Akebono*, went to top speed in order to be in position when Admiral Doorman finally made his sortie from outer Surabaja harbor toward the convoy. The Battle of the Java Sea was about to begin.[4]

First Phase: 1525–1650——27 February

The Japanese were not caught by surprise, for the *Nachi*'s scout plane had been radioing accurate ships' positions. Doorman's strike force had its cruisers in column led by the light cruiser *De Ruyter* (flagship), followed by the heavy cruisers *Exeter* and *Houston* (the latter could fire only her forward turrets), and the light cruisers *Perth* and *Java*. On the column's port beam were the two Dutch destroyers *Witte de With* and *Kortenaer*.

On the port quarter of the cruiser column came the U.S. destroyers *John D. Edwards*, *Alden*, *John D. Ford*, and *Paul Jones*. (The *Pope* was in Surabaja harbor but could not catch up with Doorman's force.) Three miles from the main column's starboard bow were the English destroyers *Electra*, *Jupiter*, and *Encounter*. The group set a course northwest by west, almost crossing, at first, the Japanese convoy column's escorts heading south.

The Japanese had, in column, the light cruiser *Jintsu* (flagship, Destroyer Squadron 2) with four destroyers: the *Yukikaze* (with Rear Admiral Tanaka on board), and the *Tokitsukaze*, *Amatsukaze*, and *Hatsukaze*. These ships had been sailing northwest, but on sighting Doorman's fleet they turned toward it, and headed due south, still in single column. The time was 1521. The *Jintsu's* group maintained this course for nine minutes, until, again in column, it turned due west for nine more minutes, paralleling Doorman at a distance of 30,500 yards.[5]

Coming up fast, on a southerly course, were the heavy cruisers *Nachi* and *Haguro*, screened on their port side by the destroyers *Ushio*, *Sazanami*, *Yamakaze*, and *Kawakaze*. At 1525 they were still some 13,000 yards north of the *Jintsu's* destroyers. As they gained ground, they, too, swung westward but were 10,000 yards north of Destroyer Squadron 2, which was making a deep south-to-west loop. Japanese heavy cruisers fired their first salvos at the *Houston* and the *Exeter* at 1547, and kept up their fire until 1650.

Another 13,000 yards to the west, and nearly parallel to the heavy cruisers, a third column was sailing south, preparing for battle: Destroyer Squadron 4, with the light cruiser *Naka* and the destroyers *Asagumo*, *Minegumo*, *Murasame*, *Samidare*, *Harukaze*, and *Yudachi*. They went the farthest south of the three groups, not turning southwest until 1557. Thus three separate groups of ships were roughly paralleling Doorman's columns.[6]

At this point, the Japanese began using their favorite weapons—the "long lances," their 24-inch torpedoes, which because they were oxygen-propelled, made almost no wake. The *Naka* and her destroyers made torpedo launches at 1603, 1610, and 1615, at distances of between 13,000 and 15,000 yards. They were also involved in a fire fight with the outranged British destroyers *Electra*, *Jupiter*, and *Encounter*, and with Doorman's cruisers; no real damage was suffered by either side.

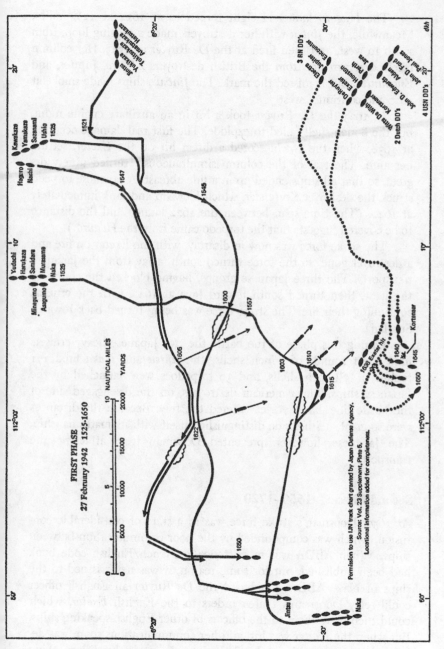

FIRST PHASE
27 February 1942 1525-1650

Jintu
Amatsukaze
Hatsukaze
Yukikaze
Tokitsukaze
1521

Kawakaze
Yamakaze
Sazanami
Ushio
1525

Haguro
Nachi
1547
1545

Yudachi
Harukaze
Samidare
Murasame
1525

Minegumo
Asagumo
Naka

1600
1557

1605
1603
1610
1615

1622

1650

Jintsu
Naka

3 RN DD's
Electra
Encounter
Jupiter

De Ruyter
Exeter
Perth
Houston
Java

Kortenaer

White De With
John D. Edwards

2 Dutch DD's

4 USN DD's
Alden
John D. Ford
Paul Jones

1638 Exeter hit
1640
1645
1650

Kortenaer

NAUTICAL MILES
0   5   10
YARDS
0   5000 10000 15000 20000

Permission to use IJN track chart granted by Japan Defense Agency.
Source: Vol. 23 Supplement, Plate 5.
Locational information added for completeness.

First Phase of Battle of the Java Sea, 27 February 1942

The *Haguro* launched eight torpedoes at 1622 at 12½ miles. Meanwhile, the *Jintsu* with her destroyers made a sagging loop, from south to west, and then fired at the *De Ruyter* at 1545. Her column received return fire from the British destroyers *Electra, Jupiter,* and *Encounter,* but it missed the mark. The *Jintsu*'s ships made smoke at 1600 and continued west.

At 1623 the *De Ruyter* took a hit in an auxiliary engine room, but the 8-inch shell failed to explode. The first real damage occurred at 1638, when the *Nachi* scored a direct hit on the *Exeter,* setting her afire. The rest of the column simultaneously turned ninety degrees, so that all ships ended up in a line abreast. A Japanese torpedo struck the destroyer *Kortenaer,* which blew up and sank immediately at 1640. (The time span between the 1622 launch and the distance to be covered suggests that the torpedo came from the *Haguro.*)

The strike force was now in disarray, with the *Exeter* on fire and a destroyer gone, so the force turned south, away from the Japanese transports. The three Japanese groups, having blocked the course to the west, then turned south toward Java at 1640, with the cruisers continuing their fire. The strike force was being turned back towards Surabaja.

During this phase of the battle the two Japanese heavy cruisers fired 1,271 rounds of 8-inch shells, the *Jintsu* and *Naka* fired 171 rounds of 5½-inch shells, and 39 torpedoes were launched by the Japanese ships. The American destroyers, on the disengaged side of the battle line, had not yet entered the fray. Because the distances were so great, neither side distinguished itself with its marksmanship. The Japanese, however, prevented Doorman from attacking the transports.

Second Phase: 1650–1720

At 1650, Doorman's strike force was in a state of considerable confusion, which was compounded by the poor communication between ships. When ABDA was in existence, a French/English code book had been published, but for some reason, it was never issued to the ships of Navy ABDA. On board the *De Ruyter* an English officer could relay Doorman's Dutch orders to the English *Exeter,* which could then relay them to the officers of other English-speaking ships. But when the *Exeter* was hit, and her communications room was destroyed, orders could not be flashed to the other English-speaking

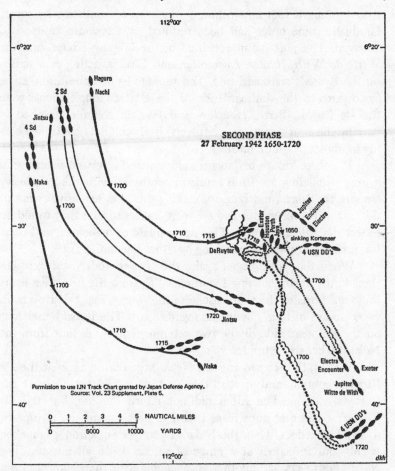

Second Phase of Battle of the Java Sea, 27 February 1942

ships by blinker lights or semaphores, because those ships did not have the code book.

The *Exeter*, still in flames, headed on a nearly straight course, steaming southeast by south; shortly before 1700 she had become the outermost ship on the port side of the force. As she slowly pursued this course, the four American destroyers cut her wake, and formed a screen for the main column of cruisers. Farther south, the *Perth* and *Java* turned ninety degrees to the west, and then, having arranged themselves in column, reversed their course. The *Houston* and *De Ruyter*, after making a complete circle, joined the *Perth* and *Java*, thus forming a four-ship column, which sailed southeast by south. Gradually some order had been restored; two separate groups had emerged. The port group consisted of the limping *Exeter*, and the *Witte de With, Jupiter, Encounter,* and *Electra,* acting as a screen on the *Exeter*'s starboard side. Ten thousand yards ahead and some 6,000 yards to the starboard side of the *Exeter* group's course were the *De Ruyter, Perth, Houston,* and *Java,* in column, screened to port by the four American destroyers. Both columns continued sailing southeast by south, until 1713.

The three groups of Japanese ships were in pursuit, sweeping in a long paralleling arc from south to southeast, with the two heavy cruisers, the *Nachi* and *Haguro,* making the most extensive swing to the east. All three groups had set their courses so that they would intersect the Allied columns. This was a phase of maneuver, and there was no firing or torpedo launching by either side until 1715.

When the battle began again, the *Haguro* and *Nachi* were farthest to the north, crossing Doorman's "T" from the rear. Five to six thousand yards to the southeast were the *Jintsu*'s eight destroyers, in two columns of four, about 2,000 yards apart. The *Jintsu* herself was on the starboard side of the two columns, equally distant from the *Naka* and her six destroyers.

At 1715, the *Haguro* and the *Nachi* began firing again at the *De Ruyter*'s column, and at 1718 the *Nachi* launched torpedoes at the *Exeter*'s column. The Allies did not return the fire, but the *De Ruyter*'s column at once turned hard to port toward the transports, to avoid torpedoes. Then the *Naka*'s Destroyer Squadron 4 launched twenty-four torpedoes at a range of 21,000 yards; all missed.[7] The *Naka*'s destroyers had another engagement with the *Exeter* and her screen, at 18,000 yards. The *Houston,* now in position to use her undamaged forward turrets, returned the *Naka*'s fire. The Combined Strike Force, however, was headed for new trouble, for its two groups were on a collision course when the *De Ruyter*'s column turned northeast toward the *Exeter*'s column, which was still southbound. A second melee, with ships falling out of formation, was in the making. Furthermore, the force was being squeezed together from the north and the west, as the Japanese began to sense Doorman's predicament. Rear Admiral Takeo Takagi, commander-in-chief of the Eastern Support Force, ordered the transports to reverse course and head again for their beachheads.

Third Phase: 1720–1750

A new Japanese attack was forming up. The heavy cruisers *Nachi*
and *Haguro* continued east at a distance of about 19,000 yards from
Doorman's force, which, after its unavoidable confusion, had gathered itself and started south again. The two heavy cruisers kept up a
long-distance barrage from their twenty 8-inch guns, and at 1724,
they launched more torpedoes. Finally at 1726 they reversed course
and headed southwest by west, ceasing fire. About 12,000 yards

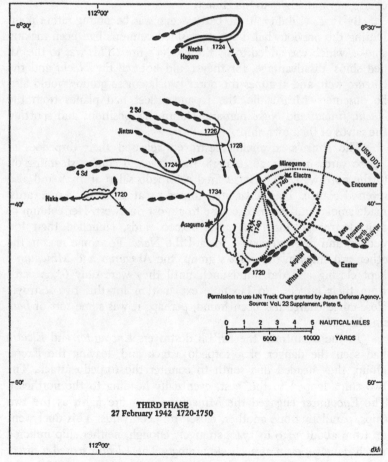

Permission to use IJN Track Chart granted by Japan Defense Agency.
Source: Vol. 23 Supplement, Plate 5.

THIRD PHASE
27 February 1942 1720–1750

Third Phase of Battle of the Java Sea, 27 February 1942

northwest of the reconstructed *Exeter* column, the *Jintsu* and her eight destroyers, steaming southeast by east, were readying a torpedo attack against the *Exeter* group. South and slightly west of the *Jintsu*, the *Naka* was forming up her destroyers into two columns (of four and two) on her starboard quarter, also to attack the crippled *Exeter*.

On the Allied side, the *Exeter* was screened to starboard by the destroyers *Jupiter, Witte de With, Encounter,* and *Electra.* The group moved slowly, since the *Exeter* could make only five knots. The *De Ruyter* column, now ahead of the *Exeter* and screened on its port side by the four American destroyers, had set a northeasterly course, at right angles to the *Exeter.*

By 1720, visibility at the battle scene was becoming rather poor. During the previous half hour, the Allied columns had been making smoke, which was added to by the *Exeter's* fires. This was to the Allied ships' disadvantage, for they could not see the *Nachi* and the *Haguro* well, and at times the other two Japanese groups would also be obscured. Meanwhile, the Japanese fleet had planes from the *Nachi, Jintsu,* and *Naka* marking Doorman's positions and spotting the salvos of their own ships.

The *Jintsu's* advancing destroyers released their torpedoes at 15,000 yards, from 1726 to 1728, then reversed course, steaming off to the northwest. The *Jintsu* fired a torpedo salvo at 1728 and also reversed course. The *Naka* fired torpedoes at 1720 at 18,500 yards, made smoke, and reversed course to almost due west. Her column of four destroyers closed to under 10,000 yards, launched their torpedoes, and reversed course, toward the *Naka.* For some reason, the other two ships in the *Naka's* group, the *Asagumo* and *Minegumo,* kept closing and did not launch until they were only 6,500 yards from their targets. No Japanese explanation for this two-destroyer close-range charge has been found; perhaps it was some sort of *banzai* charge.

In the meantime, the British destroyers *Encounter* and *Electra* had seen the danger of a torpedo attack and, leaving the *Exeter* group, they headed due south to counter the torpedo attack. The two ships looped to the west, eventually heading to the northeast. The *Encounter* engaged the *Minegumo* in a fire fight, as the two ships, paralleling one another, closed to 3,000 yards. This duel went on from about 1730 to 1740; strangely enough, neither ship inflicted much damage, even at such close range. The *Electra* scored a direct hit on the *Asagumo* at 5,000 yards, causing her to go dead in the

water for a few minutes, with four of her men killed.[8] She made it
back to Balikpapan, however, the next day. At the same time, the
Asagumo made two direct hits on the *Electra*; she limped along,
tried to continue her circle to the east, but finally went down at
1746. Nevertheless, the bravery shown by the two British destroyers
in countercharging a superior force (at the start of the charge, they
faced two light cruisers and fourteen destroyers) exemplified the British style of destroyer training, in the best tradition of the Royal
Navy.[9]

Meanwhile, Admiral Doorman was determined to have another
try at the transports, which he knew were close by. At 1720, the *De
Ruyter* column began swinging to the northeast, and since all the
Japanese ships appeared to be retiring (except the *Asagumo* and the
Minegumo), it continued to circle. The four American destroyers,
however, struck out on their own transport hunt, sailing almost due
north. Admiral Doorman temporarily gave up on the transports
shortly thereafter, and the column, completing its circle, headed toward the southeast, on the port side of the *Exeter* and her two escorts. The American destroyers, 10,000 yards north-northeast of the
De Ruyter group, also turned. The crews of the strike force were
exhausted and frustrated, and the ships were low on fuel and ammunition. For the moment it looked as if the battle was over. Doorman's force had been weakened, with one heavy cruiser afire and another destroyer lost.

Fourth Phase: 1850–1910

After sailing east for a few minutes and seeing no Japanese ships,
Admiral Doorman decided to make another try for the transports,
and headed almost due north, directly for the convoys. His counterpart, Admiral Takagi in the *Nachi*, did not know whether the Allied
force had returned to Surabaja to refuel, whether it knew of the presence of Admiral Takahashi's Main Force led by the heavy cruiser
Ashigara, east of Madura Island, or whether Admiral Doorman
would make still another try for the transports. Since Admiral Takagi's biggest responsibility was the protection of the transports, he
set a course which would block Doorman's group if it came from the
south. He guessed correctly, for, at 1850, they sighted each other
again.

The Allied column was still led by the *De Ruyter*, followed by
the *Perth*, *Houston*, and *Java*. One British destroyer, the *Jupiter*,

screened the port van and the four American destroyers protected the starboard rear.

The Japanese had the *Jintsu* and her eight destroyers headed north on an exactly parallel course, 17,500 yards away, on the port beam of Doorman's column. The *Nachi* and the *Haguro* were also on the port side at 16,000 yards, slightly north of the Allied ships. They turned on searchlights briefly and opened fire at 1855, then turned to the northwest, making smoke. The Allied cruisers returned the fire from 1855 to 1910 and then, again heading away from the transports, began a slow turn to the east. The *Jintsu's* group continued north until 1907, when they fired torpedoes at the turning Allied

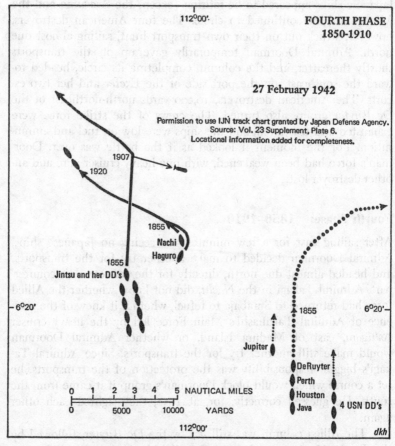

112°00′.

FOURTH PHASE
1850-1910

27 February 1942

Permission to use IJN track chart granted by Japan Defense Agency.
Source: Vol. 23 Supplement, Plate 6.
Locational information added for completeness.

1907

1920

1855

Nachi
Haguro

1855

Jintsu and her DD's

1855

Jupiter

DeRuyter
Perth
Houston
Java

4 USN DD's

6°20′

6°20′

0 1 2 3 4 5 NAUTICAL MILES

0   5000   10000   YARDS

112°00′.

dkh

Fourth Phase of Battle of the Java Sea, 27 February 1942

column, at a range of slightly under 21,000 yards. The *Jintsu* and her two destroyer columns turned to the northwest. No damage was sustained by either side in the long-range skirmish, but once again the transports had been protected from attack.

Fifth Phase: 2230–2300

After losing contact with the enemy, Doorman again tried a northern thrust. But by this time his force had been further diminished. Although she had been clearly informed of a minefield in the area, the destroyer *Jupiter* suffered a huge explosion, probably from a

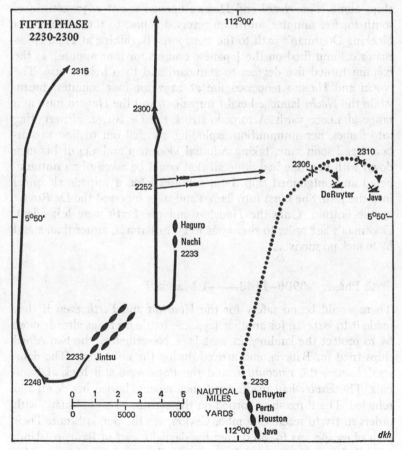

Fifth Phase of Battle of the Java Sea, 27 February 1942

mine, and sank. Doorman had also sent the four American destroyers (the old four-pipers simply could not make the speed necessary) back to Surabaja to refuel, and then to Tanjong Priak, to pick up torpedoes. His column of cruisers, now stripped of destroyers, remained in the same order as before, heading north. It was spotted at 16,000 yards by a lookout on the *Nachi* at 2233. At that time the *Nachi* and the *Haguro* were headed due south, with Doorman's column on their port bow. The ever-present *Jintsu* with her eight destroyers, steaming on a southwesterly course, was 16,000 yards north-northwest of Doorman. She slowly turned to starboard, until she was on a northeasterly course, protecting the transports.

The two Japanese heavy cruisers, then, took on the four Allied ships alone. The *Nachi* and *Haguro* opened fire at 2237, continued south for five minutes, and then reversed course to the north, again blocking Doorman's path to the transports. Beginning at 2240, Doorman's column fired on the Japanese cruisers for four minutes, as the column turned five degrees to starboard and then held course. The *Nachi* and *Haguro* reopened fire at 2252 for four minutes; meanwhile the *Nachi* launched eight torpedoes, and the *Haguro* four, at a range of 14,000 yards. A torpedo struck the *De Ruyter* aft; erupting into flames, her ammunition exploding, she fell out of line to starboard and soon sank, taking Admiral Doorman and 344 of his men down with her. She had done all that could be asked of an outnumbered and outgunned ship. Four minutes later, a torpedo slammed into the *Java*. She burst into flames and soon followed the *De Ruyter* to the bottom. Only the *Houston* and the *Perth* were left afloat. Doorman's last order to them was to go to Batavia, rather than stand by to pick up survivors.

Sixth Phase: 0900–1140——1 March

There would be no safety for the *Houston* and *Perth* even if they made it to Batavia, for another Japanese battle fleet was already close by to protect the landings in west Java. Nevertheless, the two Allied ships tried for Batavia, and arrived during the mid-watch. The damaged *Exeter*, the *Encounter*, and the *Pope* were still back at Surabaja. The *Exeter* had made emergency repairs, buried her dead, and refueled. The three ships sortied on the evening of 28 February, with orders to try to reach Colombo, Ceylon, via the Sunda Strait. Their plan of escape was to sail during the daylight, east of Bawean Island, toward the south coast of Borneo, and then make a night run for

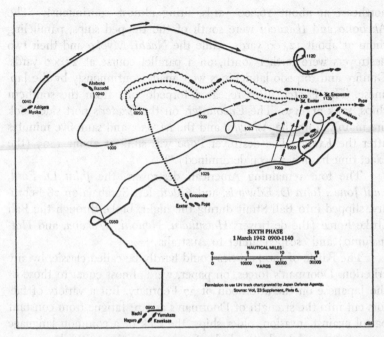

Sixth Phase of Battle of the Java Sea, 1 March 1942

Sunda Strait. Their hopes, which were slim to begin with, vanished altogether on 1 March, when they were spotted by Japanese aircraft as they left Surabaja. Admiral Takagi was ready and waiting for them.

The *Nachi* and *Haguro* and their two destroyers, the *Yamakaze* and *Kawakaze*, sighted the three Allied ships to the northeast, at about 33,000 yards. For about an hour, the Japanese ships steamed northwest and then at 0950 they turned to the northeast, thus cutting the Allied ships off from a retreat to Surabaja. Admiral Takahashi had arrived from the west with the *Ashigara* and *Myoko*, which, at 0940, were due west of the *Exeter*, at 33,750 yards. Nearer, to the east, were the *Akebono* and *Ikazuchi*. Although trapped, the three Allied ships nevertheless continued sailing on a northwesterly course. The battle began at around 0940, with the Allied ships firing at the *Akebono* and *Ikazuchi*, which returned fire, along with the *Ashigara* and *Myoko*. The three escaping ships immediately made smoke and turned to starboard; by 1000, they were headed due east. The Japanese heavy cruisers *Ashigara* and *Myoko* paralleled them to the northeast at about 16,000 yards, firing almost continuously. The *Akebono* and *Ikazuchi* were south of the trapped ships, paralleling them at about 12,000 yards, while the *Nachi, Myoko* and their two destroyers were farther south, on a parallel course at 27,000 yards. Gunfire and torpedo launchings were made continuously by the Japanese. The *Exeter*, after repeated torpedo hits from the southern ships, sank at 1130. The *Encounter*, on the *Exeter*'s port side, took fire mainly from the *Ashigara* and the *Myoko*, and sank five minutes after the *Exeter*. The destroyer *Pope* was sunk at about 1205 (the exact time has never been determined).[10]

The four remaining American destroyers, the *John D. Ford, Paul Jones, John D. Edwards,* and *Alden,* left Surabaja on 28 February, slipped into Bali Strait during the night, broke through the Bali Strike Force (the destroyers *Hatsuharu, Nenohi, Wakaba,* and *Hatsushimo*) and escaped intact to Australia.[11]

The Battle of the Java Sea could hardly be called classic, by any criterion. Doorman's forces, on paper, were almost equal to those of the Japanese on the afternoon of 27 February. But a variety of factors cut into the strength of Doorman's group: fatigue from constant patrol against invasion, older ships, the lack of a common language or common codebook, the lack of communication with shore commanders, and a command and force which were composed of men of different nationalities, who therefore lacked training in common tactics. It has also been claimed that loss of the air contributed to the Allied defeat; yet this battle was fought almost exclusively by ships. (Australian Buffalo aircraft did attack Japanese ships, but without result.) Still, the Japanese planes, from both heavy and light cruisers, which acted as spotters, gave the Japanese a great advantage. In addition, Japanese aviation was wreaking havoc with Java's naval facilities ashore, thus adding to Helfrich's difficulties.

All this expenditure of energy and equipment, and loss of life (almost all from the Allied side), delayed the invasion of east Java by less than twenty-four hours. Whatever the size, quality, and quantity of Japanese naval strength, the Japanese warships executed their assigned tasks. They had displayed an extraordinary skill in night fighting that would work to their advantage again and again. The eastern Java invasion transports were completely untouched.

Battle of Sunda Strait

The action off Surabaja did not interfere with the scheduled invasion of west Java on the three beachheads at Merak, Bantam Bay, and Eretenwetan. Landings began on the evening of 28 February.

The *Houston* and the *Perth* refueled at Batavia, which was under constant air attack, and sortied at 1900, heading for Tjilatjap by way of Sunda Strait. Forty miles to the west, Japanese troops were coming ashore at Bantam Bay. In the immediate vicinity of the beachhead were the heavy cruisers *Mikuma* and *Mogami*, the light cruiser *Natori*, and the destroyers *Shirakumo*, *Murakumo*, *Fubuki*, *Shirayuki*, *Hatsuyuki*, *Asakaze*, and *Shikinami*.

The *Houston* and the *Perth*, heading south and then southwest together, saw lines of transports twelve miles directly ahead as they rounded Babi Island at about 2215 on 28 February. There were only two destroyers, the *Harukaze* and *Hatakaze*, then screening the transports. The *Houston* and *Perth* had been sighted, however, at the same time that they spotted the transports, by the destroyer *Fubuki*, which was alone far to the west on their starboard beam. A chaotic series of maneuvers by the Japanese ships farther to the west ensued. As the *Houston* and *Perth* charged down onto the transports with their guns blazing, the *Harukaze* got under way at 2231 on a northwest course making smoke to hide the vulnerable troop ships. The *Hatakaze*, which was only a few yards behind the transports, took a more northerly course, disappearing in the smoke screen and heading for the main portion of the Third Escort Force. This left the *Fubuki* as the only warship charging the two cruisers. To add to the confusion, the transports were attacked by some of the few planes left on Java's airfield.

The main force of Japanese ships were widely dispersed to the west and northwest. Destroyer Division 12 was sixteen miles to the west, and the heavy cruisers *Mikuma* and *Mogami* and the destroyer *Shikinami* were fourteen miles to the northwest. Other units were somewhat nearer but still could not give immediate relief to the transports. They all steamed at flank speed towards the unexpected intruders. Naturally the course of the *Houston* and *Perth* was a straight line, aimed at the transport group. Their only anatagonist at that moment was the *Fubuki*, which rounded the east corner of Babi Island and then followed directly in the wake of the cruisers. It had taken her almost twenty minutes to get into a position where she had a line of fire.

The *Houston* and *Perth* were now doomed to pay the price, as three Japanese cruisers and nine destroyers converged on them. The *Fubuki* chased the two ships for fourteen minutes, taking fire from the after guns of the *Perth*. At 2244, the *Fubuki* turned to starboard, launched torpedoes, and then disappeared to the north in her own smoke. The launch was a dangerous tactic, for if the torpedoes missed the Allied cruisers, they would be directly on course for the transports.

To avoid the *Fubuki*'s torpedoes, the two cruisers made a tight full circle and then, heading west, continued on a course which paralleled the transports. But the Western Support Force and Third Escort Force were closing fast; and the destroyer *Hatakaze* began firing at the cruisers at 2252. It seemed as if all the Japanese ships arrived in the small area at once, with all columns going in different directions, while firing rapidly and launching torpedoes. Under this attack, the *Houston* and *Perth* turned south at 2300, then northeast at 2308. At about this time, Japanese torpedoes struck the *Houston* and *Perth* (and some of their own transports). Hit by gunfire and two torpedoes, the *Perth* circled to the northeast, and sank at 2342.

The *Houston* turned back to the east, but, having also been hit repeatedly by shells and three torpedoes, she went under an hour later. In all, eighty-seven torpedoes were launched at the *Houston* and *Perth*. Given the melee of Japanese ships, all firing, it seems extremely likely that friendly ships were hitting one another, and that torpedoes were missing their marks but finding other targets.

Meanwhile, explosions began taking place among the transports. Minesweeper No. 2, part of the transports' screen, received a torpedo hit from the *Fubuki*, and capsized. The *Sakura Maru*, at about the same time, also caught one of the *Fubuki*'s torpedoes and sank. Three other transports, including the *Ryujo Maru*, were hit and severely damaged. General Imamura, commander-in-chief of the 16th Army, was on board the *Ryujo Maru* directing the second wave of landing craft, when an explosion threw him into the oil-coated water. It took him about three hours to get ashore; he arrived there covered with oil and exhausted. The destroyers *Shirakumo* and *Harukaze* suffered battle damage, and the latter had three men killed and five wounded.[12]

The battle for Java was over. The destroyer *Edsall* and the oiler *Pecos* were picked off and sunk on 1 March while fleeing Java for

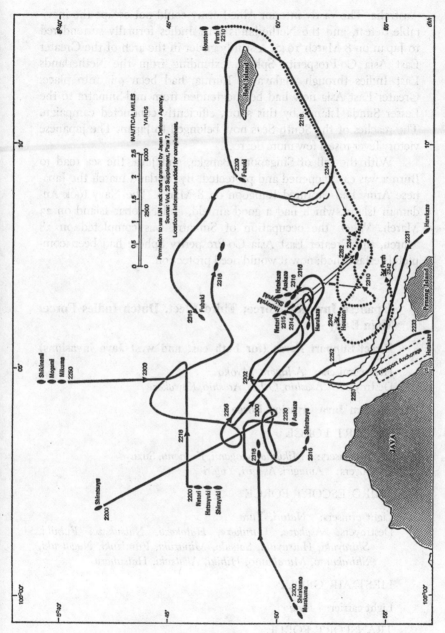

Battle of Sunda Strait, 1 March 1942

Australia. The vastly inferior Allied army could not escape the inevitable defeat, and the Netherlands East Indies formally surrendered to Japan on 8 March 1942. A sturdy girder in the arch of the Greater East Asia Co-Prosperity Sphere, extending from the Netherlands East Indies through Malaya to Burma, had been put into place. Greater East Asia now had been extended from mid-Sumatra to the Lesser Sunda Islands by this short, efficiently conducted campaign. The reaches of the South Seas now belonged to Japan. The Japanese victory fever rose a few more degrees.

With the fall of Singapore, Bangka, and Java, the sea road to Burma was easily opened and protected. By overland march the Japanese Army had captured Rangoon on 8 March. The Navy took Andaman Island, which had a good airfield, and Nicobar Island on 23 March. When the occupation of Sumatra was completed on 28 March, the Greater East Asia Co-Prosperity Sphere had been completely established; now it would need protection.

Japanese Invasion Force; Third Fleet, Dutch Indies Force, Main Body

Direct Support Force (for both east and west Java invasions)

Heavy cruisers: *Ashigara, Myoko*
Destroyers: *Asashio, Oshio, Arashio, Kawakaze*

Western Java Invasion Force

SUPPORT FORCE

Heavy cruisers: *Mikuma, Mogami, Kumano, Suzuya*
Destroyers: *Amagiri, Asagiri, Yugiri*

THIRD ESCORT FORCE

Light cruisers: *Natori, Yura*
Destroyers: *Asakaze, Harukaze, Hatakaze, Natsukaze, Fubuki, Shirayuki, Hatsuyuki, Satsuki, Minazuki, Fumizuki, Nagatsuki, Shirakumo, Murakumo, Hibiki, Akatsuki, Hatsuharu*

FIRST AIR GROUP

Light carrier: *Ryujo*

TRANSPORT FORCE

Fifty-six transports

Eastern Java Invasion Force

SUPPORT GROUP

Heavy cruisers: *Nachi, Haguro*
Destroyers: *Ikazuchi, Akebono*

FIRST ESCORT FORCE

Light cruiser: *Naka**
Destroyers: *Murasame, Harusame, Yudachi, Samidare, Asagumo, Natsugumo, Minegumo, Yamakaze*

SECOND ESCORT FORCE

Light cruiser: *Jintsu*
Destroyers: *Kuroshio, Oyashio, Hayashio, Hatsukaze, Yukikaze, Amatsukaze, Sazanami, Ushio, Tokitsukaze*

FIRST BASE FORCE

Light cruiser: *Nagara*
Destroyers: *Hatsuharu, Nenohi, Wakaba*

SECOND BASE FORCE

Seaplane tenders: *Chitose, Mizuho*

TRANSPORT FORCE

Forty-one transports[13]

ABDA Combined Strike Force for the Defense of East Java

Heavy cruisers: *Houston* (USN), *Exeter* (RN)
Light cruisers: *Java* (RNN), *De Ruyter* (RNN), *Perth* (RAN)
Destroyers: *John D. Edwards, Paul Jones, John D. Ford, Alden, Pope*—(USN); *Electra, Jupiter, Encounter*—(RN); *Witte de With, Kortenaer*—(RNN)[14]

chapter 6

FROM THE GILBERT ISLANDS TO NEW GUINEA

1941

9 December	Japanese occupy Makin Island, Gilbert Islands
10 December	Japanese temporarily occupy Tarawa Island (permanent occupation in September 1942)

1942

23 January	Japanese occupy Rabaul, New Britain, and Kavieng, New Ireland
19 February	Nagumo's Carrier Strike Force raids Port Darwin, Australia
8 March	Japanese occupy Lae and Salamaua, New Guinea
10 March	U. S. Navy carrier planes raid Lae, Salamaua convoy
March	Japanese occupy key points of northern New Guinea to Huon Peninsula
March–April	Japanese occupy Admiralty Islands and other key islands in Bismarck Sea, and Halmahera

The original Japanese war plan had envisaged a defense perimeter to protect the newly conquered empire. The perimeter would guard the Marshall Islands by occupation of strategic points in the Gilbert and Ellice islands—Tarawa, Makin, Nauru, and Ocean Islands. The ring would then extend to protect the Carolines, where Japan had established at Truk an excellent naval base. In order to block an American counteroffensive in the gap between Truk and the naval and air bases at Palau in the southern Marianas, or a coun-

Japan's Defense Perimeter

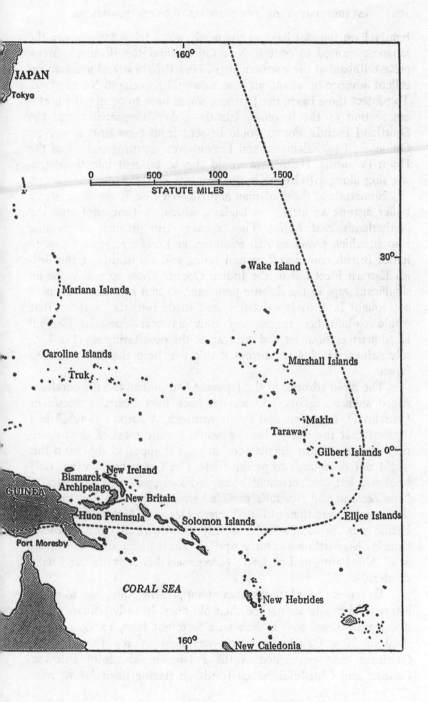

terattack on the east flank of the newly won Malay Archipelago, the Japanese wanted to control New Guinea and the Bismarck Archipelago. Rabaul at the northern tip of New Britain would make an excellent advance naval and air base, as would Kavieng in New Ireland. To protect these bases, the Japanese would have to occupy the northern section of the Solomon Islands—Buka, Bougainville, and the Shortland Islands. Forces would be sent from New Britain to New Guinea at Lae, Salamaua, and Finschhaven, insuring control of the Huon Peninsula. Halmahera would also be brought into the defensive ring, along with Manus in the Bismarck Sea.

Sumatra and the Andaman and Nicobar islands would serve as a buffer against an attack on Malaya, which, in turn, protected the Netherlands East Indies. The Japanese also planned to conquer Burma, which possessed rich resources, and could serve as a base to harass British convoys off eastern India, and aid in driving the British Eastern Fleet out of the Indian Ocean. There seemed to be no significant gaps in the defense perimeter, so that raw materials could be brought back to Japan safely, and made into the weapons that would sustain her against any counterattacks. Imperial General Headquarters, however, did not foresee the devastating effect of U.S. submarines, which later disrupted shipping from the South Seas to Japan.

The rapid advance of the Japanese had pushed the few surviving Allied soldiers, sailors, and airmen back into Australia. President Franklin D. Roosevelt and Prime Minister Winston Churchill had decided that the war in Europe would require most of their countries' troops and armaments (and in 1942 it appeared that even this might not be enough to prevent defeat by Germany), so that only what was left over, or could be cajoled away, was sent to Australia. New Zealand and Australia provided what they could, but most of their armies were then in the Western Desert in Africa. Because the Pacific war, then, would be mainly an American effort, General Douglas MacArthur was on 2 April appointed supreme commander of all Allied army and air forces (except naval aircraft) in the Pacific theater.

To protect MacArthur's lines of supply, the Allies had to establish new bases and strengthen their old ones. In early January a Marine regiment was sent to Samoa; a fortnight later, 17,000 men arrived at New Caledonia, which was held by the Free French. Garrisons were established at the Polynesian islands of Palmyra, Canton, and Christmas, which furnished staging fields for air reinforcements to Australia. Construction workers began building a naval fueling base at Bora-Bora in the Society Islands, and in March, Tongabatu in the Friendly Isles and Efate in the New Hebrides were made into naval bases. Garrisons at the Fijis and Port Moresby were increased to brigade strength, and in May work began on a naval and air base at Espiritu Santo in the New Hebrides.

With Australia's lines of supply securely established, a difference of opinion over the conduct of the war developed between Admiral Nimitz, commander-in-chief of the Pacific Fleet, and General Mac-Arthur. Nimitz favored the "Rainbow Five" plan, which called for a drive through the Central Pacific islands—the Marshalls, the Carolines, and the Marianas. On the other hand, General MacArthur wanted to drive on New Guinea directly, and retake the Philippines on the way to Taiwan and Japan. In the end, both routes were used.

There were also areas of strong disagreement among the Japanese leaders. Although not always backed by his superiors, Admiral Yamamoto stubbornly held to his belief that Japan would eventually lose the war if she did not secure an early decisive victory over the U. S. Pacific Fleet. But, because the victories so far had been so easily won, some of Yamamoto's staff proposed an invasion of Ceylon. At the same time, Admiral Nagano, chief of the Naval Staff, proposed an offensive which would cut Australia's line of supply by taking Samoa. Nevertheless, Yamamoto maintained that the Japanese had to undertake an operation to bring about the decisive battle; the Doolittle Tokyo raid on 18 April helped decide the issue in Yamamoto's favor. The Japanese would first expand the defense perimeter by occupying the southern Solomon Islands at Tulagi and south New Guinea; then they would precipitate the decisive battle by invading Midway and the Aleutian Islands. They also kept a task force at Truk to repel an American attack on the Marshalls.[1]

Gilbert, Ellice, and Ocean Island Groups

Until the war began, the Marshall Islands had been Japan's easternmost defense frontier. For her wartime defense perimeter, though, she wished to control the islands in the Gilbert and Ellice groups, which were then under British mandate. These islands could provide airstrips for American attacks on the Marshalls, or for Japanese attacks on the American supply lines to Australia.

The Japanese planned to occupy three islands: Makin, Tarawa, and Howland islands. Although possession of Howland would threaten the expanding Allied supply base at Canton Island, control of Makin and Tarawa in the Gilberts was considered more important, for if the Rainbow Five plan were to become operative, the Marshalls would need all the defense they could get.

Preparations for attacks on these two islands had been made long before 7 December. A small attack force, divided into three parts, was assembled at Jaluit, in the Marshalls. The flagship was the minelayer *Okinoshima*, which would accompany four transports carrying garrison troops. Labor troops, which would build an airfield and seaplane base, were taken directly to Makin, for there was no British garrison there. The destroyers *Yunagi* and *Asanagi* would first go to Tarawa and then back to Makin to supply any support needed. Air cover was assigned to a unit of Air Flotilla 24 and the seaplane tender *Chitose*.[2]

The destroyers put ashore a landing party at Tarawa on 10 December at 0100. The party discovered a small generator, a radio shack, a warehouse, and one white man and five hundred natives. After destroying the material installations and releasing all Tarawa's inhabitants, the ships set a course for Makin, which had been occupied on 9 December.[3] Tarawa was reoccupied in September 1942 by Special Naval Landing Force troops, and a large airfield was then built. The failure of the first Wake invasion attempt later drew the Makin/Tarawa force back to Ruotta anchorage, to supply replacements for Destroyer Squadron 6.

The Japanese Navy had planned to occupy Ocean and Nauru islands in the Ocean Island chain, so that they could disrupt the American lines of communication with Australia and could screen the western flank of the Japanese in the Solomon Islands. One exigency after another, however, delayed the execution of the operation.

Admiral Yamamoto was right in thinking that the U. S. Navy would eventually attack the Marshalls, because it had to eliminate the advance bases of the Japanese defense perimeter. The battle at Tarawa would be one of the bloodiest of the war.

Rabaul, Kavieng, New Guinea, and the Admiralties

The Japanese next prepared to take Rabaul, Kavieng, north New Guinea, and the Admiralties. Rabaul, at the northern end of New Britain, and Kavieng in New Ireland, lay along the best route to the Philippines available to the Allies without their having first to recapture the Malay Archipelago. Rabaul had something the Japanese wanted: an excellent landlocked harbor which would serve as an advance base and would protect Truk to the east. It was the key to their strategy for blocking the northward advance of MacArthur's armies and for controlling the Bismarck Sea and New Guinea, and it was regarded as a vital link in the original defense perimeter. Kavieng's harbor was inferior to Rabaul's, but it easily fit into the occupation plans.

Early plans were made for the capture of Rabaul and Kavieng, which was to be called R Operation. (The Japanese often used Roman letters to designate their operations.) In September 1941, Imperial General Headquarters of the Japanese Army had stated: "The capture of Rabaul is a necessity. Because it is, there must be intensive cooperation (with the Navy)."[4] Operational plans called for Rabaul's capture in mid-January.

As usual, the Japanese Navy's preparation for the invasion of Rabaul and Kavieng was thorough. Rabaul's defenses had been softened by prior air raids from Truk and by air support covering the invasion. Little resistance was met, and Kavieng and Rabaul were both captured on 23 January. In a very short time Rabaul had been converted into a valuable naval base; it was surrounded by airfields, and in many ways was stronger than Truk, which became the rear headquarters for the Combined Fleet. The Japanese had a virtual free hand in this region for the next three months. The new command of General MacArthur had not yet been established, so there was nothing to stop the Japanese from carrying out their plans.

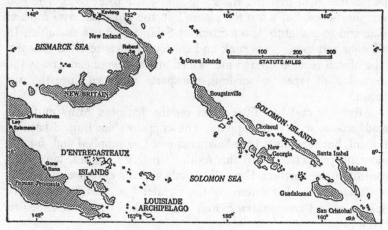

From Kavieng to the Louisiades

There were only four American heavy carriers in the Pacific during the first three months of the war; only three were operational after a Japanese submarine torpedoed the *Saratoga* near Johnston Island south of Hawaii, on 11 January, forcing her to return to Pearl Harbor. That left only the *Yorktown, Enterprise,* and *Lexington.* Admiral Halsey made a raid on the Marshalls in February that did little damage. On 20 February, planes from the *Lexington* on a raid on Rabaul were intercepted by twin-engine bombers; in the ensuing dogfights the Japanese lost a number of planes, but the American planes used up so much fuel that the strike on Rabaul was recalled.

In this period of relatively unhindered movement, the Japanese began their SR Operation (code name for Salamaua and Lae) in New Guinea. The landings at Lae and Salamaua were made on 8 March, facing no resistance. Finschhaven to the north fell two days later. An airfield and radio station were quickly established at Salamaua and Lae.[5] The naval escort for the invasion of Lae and Salamaua was the light cruiser *Yubari* acting as cover and the destroyers *Mutsuki, Yayoi, Mochizuki, Oite, Asanagi,* and *Yunagi* escorting the transports, with the minelayer *Tsugaru* as flagship.[6] The only opposition came from the air. The *Enterprise* and *Yorktown* had been near Port Moresby headed north when they heard of SR Operation. Being too far away for an interception by sea, on 10 March they launched planes, which flew over the 7,000-foot Owen Stanley Mountains to raid both Lae and Salamaua.

The occupation force was caught by surprise when some ninety planes roared in over the transports and warships at 0820. The raid was short-lived, but when the planes left, the Japanese naval force at Lae, and to a slightly lesser extent at Salamaua, was a shambles. In all, four transports were sunk and thirteen vessels received damage. The official records list 130 men killed and 145 wounded. It was the worst loss of Japanese warships, transports, and men since the war began.[7]

But the raid had little effect on the Japanese Army units, already ashore with their supplies. The crippled ships limped back to Rabaul, but new units kept Salamaua and Lae supplied and, for the moment, protected. With this foothold in New Guinea, Japan had control of the northern Huon Peninsula and the entrance to the Sea of Bismarck, and her defense of the Greater East Asia Co-Prosperity Sphere against counterattack from Australia had been established in this region.

In March, the Japanese continued to expand their southern defenses, by occupying Buka, Bougainville, and the Shortland Islands, and constructing airfields in each place. To the north, Manus Island in the Admiralties was similarly exploited.[8] Halmahera, a large island west of New Ireland, was occupied on 29 March.

Rabaul was secured, developed, and encircled with a protective ring of air bases and naval facilities. The Bismarck Sea barrier, as well, had been constructed. Thus, General MacArthur's forces had no direct path from Australia north to the Philippines. Japan had constructed a strong defense, beyond the range of retaliatory land-based air raids, to protect her empire, which now spread from the Marshalls to Burma.

Table of Organization for Japanese Occupation of Rabaul and Kavieng (under tactical command of Fourth Fleet, South Seas Force)

Distant Cooperating Force

Heavy carriers: *Kaga, Akagi, Shokaku, Zuikaku*
Battleships: *Hiei, Kirishima*
Heavy cruisers: *Tone, Chikuma*
Light cruiser: *Abukuma*
Destroyers: *Isokaze, Urakaze, Tanikaze, Hamakaze, Akigumo, Arare, Kasumi, Kagero, Shiranuhi*

Invasion Screening Force

Heavy cruisers: *Aoba, Kako, Kinugasa, Furutaka*
Seaplane tender: *Chitose*

Invasion Force, Main Body, Screening Force

Light cruisers: *Tenryu, Tatsuta, Yubari*
Minelayers: *Okinoshima, Tsugaru*
Destroyers: *Mikazuki, Uzuki, Yuzuki, Oite, Asanagi, Yunagi, Mutsuki, Yayoi, Mochizuki*[9]

chapter 7

RAIDS IN
THE INDIAN OCEAN

1942

31 March	Japanese temporarily occupy Christmas Island (Indian Ocean)
5 April	Nagumo's Carrier Strike Force raids Colombo, Ceylon
6 April	Japanese Southern Expeditionary Fleet raids convoys, and bombards coastal installations south of Calcutta, east coast of India
9 April	Nagumo's Carrier Strike Force raids Trincomalee, Ceylon

Christmas Island (X Operation)

Christmas Island (not to be confused with the Christmas Island in the Pacific) lies some 190 miles south of western Java. Eleven by nine miles in area, it contains large deposits of calcium phosphate rock. In 1942, Christmas was a British possession, worked for its minerals by a few Englishmen and a labor force of about a thousand Indians, Malays, and Chinese. The island also had a garrison of 100 British troops.

After Java fell, Christmas Island drew the attention of Imperial General Headquarters. On 7 March 1942 the battleships *Haruna* and *Kongo* bombarded the island to destroy its commercial installations. The island was then marked for possible occupation, and a small occupation force set sail from Makassar on 25 March. Japan was interested in the island as a source of phosphate resources, and as a possible site for an airstrip or emergency supply base. The small task force consisted of the light cruisers *Natori*, *Nagara* and *Naka*, accompanied by the destroyers *Natsugumo* and *Minegumo* (joined on 28

March by the *Amatsukaze*) plus the usual antisubmarine forces and transports.[1]

After preinvasion air bombings, on 31 March the occupation force began to bombard the island, and the British garrison surrendered almost immediately. The transports, along with some warships, including the *Naka*, moved in shortly thereafter, and the town was quickly secured. The garrison troops were made prisoners and forced to load the transports with refined phosphate ore, while Japanese troops moved inland to occupy and explore the entire island.

The naval commander of the task force, Rear Admiral Kyuji Kubo, knew there was an enemy submarine in the vicinity, for three torpedoes had narrowly missed his flagship, the *Naka*. After vigorous antisubmarine measures, including use of planes, a large quantity of oil appeared on the water; the USS *Seawolf* had not been sunk, however, and she finally scored a torpedo hit, starboard amidships on the *Naka*, on 1 April. The explosion shook the light cruiser, breaking off her foremast, and she began flooding. The *Naka*'s Tabular Records of Movement stated: "Sustained hit on starboard beam, Nos. 1 and 2 boiler rooms completely flooded, seepage into No. 5 crew space, forward wiring and passageways." Despite additional antisubmarine measures, the submarine escaped.[2]

After emergency measures, the *Naka*'s flooding was stopped, and she was taken in tow by the *Natori*. To help protect the crippled cruiser, Combined Fleet Headquarters sent the destroyers *Satsuki*, *Minazuki*, *Fumizuki*, and *Nagatsuki* as the escort. The *Naka* made Shonan Island (Singapore) on 6 April, and two months later, after repairs, left for Yokosuka. Meanwhile, the *Natori* returned to Christmas Island on 3 April and gathered up the troops and remaining ships. The island was not occupied because it was considered unsuitable for an airstrip. All that the Japanese had gained was the phosphate rock which was loaded on the transports.

C Operation—The Indian Ocean Raids

The operations in the Indian Ocean during the first part of April 1942 were essential to the establishment of the defense perimeter. Imperial Naval Headquarters planned to send Nagumo's First Carrier Fleet on a strike against Ceylon, the heart of British naval power in the East. Making Pearl Harbor-style raids on Colombo and Trincomalee, the Japanese would drive the British Eastern Fleet out of the Indian Ocean, thus protecting the defense perimeter from Burma to Singapore against British naval power.

Acting toward the same end, the Second Southern Expeditionary Fleet carried out a three-pronged attack to destroy British merchant shipping in the Bay of Bengal. Beyond the practical objective of stopping, at least for a time, seaborne commerce from the east-coast ports of India, there was a psychological element involved. At a time when all British military strength was committed to saving Burma, there might be a general panic if India itself were also threatened with invasion.

The British Admiralty was all too aware of the danger to its British Eastern Fleet as the collapse of Burma continued. It was also aware that Nagumo might make another carrier raid. Recognition of the danger, however, provided no solution, for the Royal Navy was already so hard-pressed on so many fronts that it did not have enough ships for any of them. Nevertheless, the British chiefs of staff wanted to strengthen the British Eastern Force at Ceylon so that it could hold that base. Without control of Ceylon, essential convoys from India to Europe and the Western Desert in Africa would be in constant danger.

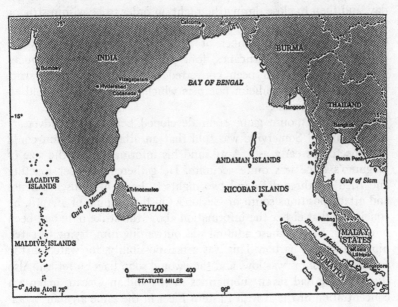

The Eastern Indian Ocean

The first step was to appoint one of Britain's top admirals, Sir James Somerville, as commander-in-chief of the British Eastern Fleet; he assumed command on 26 March. Admiral Somerville's intelligence officers guessed that raids on Colombo and Trincomalee were very likely. The British also had a third naval base at Addu Atoll, 600 miles southwest of Ceylon, the southernmost of the Maldive Islands. Constructed as an anchorage and fueling base, it lacked antisubmarine and antiaircraft defenses, but could still be used in prebattle maneuvering. (The Japanese were unaware of the naval base on Addu Atoll until after the war.) The British admiral had no illusions about his Force B. The old R-class battleships were slow and short-ranged, and the cruisers and destroyers were a hodgepodge collection which had never practiced together and were badly in need of repairs and refits. The admiral knew that since they would be of no help against a carrier raid, it would be best to keep them in reserve for other work, especially to act as cover for convoys in the Indian Ocean. Therefore, the task of repulsing the anticipated raids would fall on Force A. (For composition of Forces A and B, see Table of Organization, p. 117.)

Somerville's battle plan was standard: he intended to keep his fleet beyond the range of Japanese reconnaissance planes during the day, and then to close during the night, in order to be within striking distance for his own planes at daybreak. The airfields of Ceylon contained a respectable number of aircraft; Colombo had forty-two planes: twenty-two Hurricanes, fourteen Spitfires, and six Fulmers. Also, a racetrack had been converted into an additional airstrip. Trincomalee had Blenheim bombers which, it was hoped, could attack Japanese carriers.

A cat-and-mouse game soon developed between the adversary fleets. Admiral Somerville was told that an attack on Ceylon could be expected as early as 1 April, and his information on the size of Nagumo's force was quite accurate. He gathered his fleet together and tried for three days and two nights to be in his chosen defense and attack positions south of Ceylon.[3] On the evening of 2 April, he concluded that either the information about the strike date had been in error, or the Japanese admiral was outwaiting him, trying to catch him at night in harbor. This was a real possibility, for water on the British battleships was low, and they would soon have to return. Also the Japanese had seven submarines in the Indian Ocean, making a concentration of the British Eastern Fleet in the same area an invitation to disaster. As it turned out, Admiral Nagumo was not outwaiting Admiral Somerville, but was making his approach, as planned, to the south of Ceylon on a westerly course. Thus, Somerville's staff had merely placed the raid date several days too early.

Somerville then made a costly error. At 2100 on 2 April he sent the bulk of his fleet toward Addu Atoll for supplies. The next morning he again split his force and sent two cruisers, the *Dorsetshire* and the *Cornwall*, back to Colombo: the first to resume refitting, and the second to escort a convoy. The light carrier *Hermes* and the destroyer *Vampire* were sent to Trincomalce to resume preparations for the upcoming British invasion of Madagascar. No sooner had the British forces reached Addu Atoll than a British reconnaissance plane reported, in the late afternoon of 4 April, that the Japanese carrier fleet had been sighted 360 miles south of Dondra Head, the southernmost part of Ceylon. Now Admiral Somerville realized that there would indeed be a Japanese raid, and it was certain the strike would come the following morning, 5 April, while he was 600 miles from Colombo and in no position to interfere.

Measures were taken at once to correct the British errors. Admiral Layton, at Colombo, ordered all defenses to be at general quarters, starting at 0300 on 5 April. After 28 March, most of the ships in the harbor had already been sent to sea; now the rest were dispatched. The cruisers *Dorsetshire* and *Cornwall* sortied at 2200 for Addu Atoll, and at Trincomalee, the *Hermes* and the *Vampire* were also ordered to Addu Atoll as soon as they had refueled.

Colombo's radar gave early warning of the first waves of Japanese planes but the message was not delivered until 0740. Just before 0800 on Easter Sunday 5 April, Nagumo's flyers struck again, with a force of 315 fighters, bombers, and attack planes involved in the raid. (Forty-five planes were kept in reserve.)[4]

This time, Admiral Nagumo emphasized to his airmen that they were not to make the mistake made at Pearl Harbor, but were to go after naval harbor installations and oil-tank farms, as well as ships. This raid, however, was to be no repetition of Pearl Harbor or Port Darwin. The attacking Japanese planes were met first by twenty-eight British fighters. The Japanese carrier fighters engaged them, and a brief but intense dogfight took place. Meanwhile the bombers and attack planes, seeking out their targets, were attacked by fourteen Hurricanes which had taken off from the converted racecourse. They, too, were at once engaged by the Japanese fighter protection. Blundering into the fight were six slow Swordfish, armed with torpedoes, on their way to Colombo from Trincomalee; they were all shot down.

One formation of Japanese planes bombed the shipping in and around the harbor. A second formation, coming in low and using machine guns as well as bombs, attacked the railyards, shops, and the known airfield. Next came high-altitude bombers, which aimed for ships. They sank the destroyer *Tenedos* and an armed cruiser, severely damaged a submarine tender, the *Lucia*, and slightly damaged a freighter. The naval repair shops were destroyed. By 0835 the raid was over; the British immediately sent up Blenheim bombers to counterattack the carriers, but the effort failed.

The British lost two Catalinas, four Fulmers, fifteen Hurricanes, and the six Swordfish. Japanese records show the loss of seven planes.[5]

Upon recovery of its planes, the Strike Force retreated to the southeast. Meanwhile, Force A had left Addu Atoll at around midday on 5 April, steaming on a course that would bring it 250 miles south of Ceylon at daybreak on 6 April. Somerville also ordered his two heavy cruisers from Colombo to try to join him on 5 April at 1600. The orders were received and the ships' courses reset for the rendezvous. At 0648 on 5 April, however, the *Dorsetshire* learned that there were Japanese ships 150 miles to her east. Both cruisers went to flank speed (27½ knots for the *Cornwall*), but their luck had run out. Visibility was good, and shortly after noon they were spotted by a float plane from the *Tone*. Eighty-eight planes were then launched from the *Akagi*, the *Hiryu*, and the *Soryu*; neither cruiser had a chance. The *Dorsetshire* was attacked at 1338, and after repeated hits, sank at 1348; she was followed by the *Cornwall* at about 1400.[6]

Somerville had changed course to the south when he heard of the threat to his two cruisers. When confirmation of their sinking was received at 1817 he reversed course, in pursuit of the Japanese fleet. Search planes from the *Indomitable* had failed to locate any enemy ships. Somerville wanted to be in position for an attack at daybreak if the carriers were located, but all the night plane searches proved negative. In the early morning of 6 April, Force B joined Somerville's force.

After sinking the two British cruisers, Admiral Nagumo's force continued in a southeasterly direction until shortly after 0500 on 6 April, when it reversed course. By 0600 on 8 April it was on a northwesterly course, about 450 miles due east of its next target, Trincomalee, on the east coast of Ceylon.[7]

Again Admiral Somerville guessed wrong about the intentions of his rival. He expected an attack on Addu Atoll, assuming that Admiral Nagumo would expect the British fleet to return there. Therefore, the British admiral maneuvered his ships so that he could catch the Japanese carrier fleet with a dawn strike when it neared Addu Atoll. This maneuver, however, placed the British fleet almost 600 miles from Trincomalee and almost 1,000 miles from the Japanese force. It had thus lost its last chance to engage Admiral Nagumo's fleet.

The British Admiralty, realizing that Force B was a liability, had advised Admiral Somerville on 9 April to send it to Mombasa Island, Kenya, which he did. With Nagumo still on the loose, the east coast of India itself under bombardment, and with scores of freighters being sunk in the Bay of Bengal, the British Admiralty had decided for the moment to concede the eastern part of the Indian Ocean to the Japanese. At 0600, Admiral Somerville ordered Force A to make for Bombay, on India's west coast.

The *Hermes* and her escorts, in the harbor at Trincomalee, were ordered to sortie during the night of 8 April on a southerly course, keeping close to Ceylon's coastline. The *Hermes*, the destroyer *Vampire*, the oiler *British Sergeant*, the corvette *Hollyhock*, and the depot ship *Athelstane* were all clear of the harbor by 9 April.

At 0600 the Japanese began to launch their attack planes, about 150 miles east of Trincomalee. Eighty-five planes made the initial launch. The attack hit the naval base at 0725, and it was met in the air by all the planes available: seventeen Hurricanes and six Fulmers. Since the harbor was empty of ships, the main targets were the naval installations, dockyard, and airfield; eight Hurricanes and one Fulmer were shot down.[8]

The naval authorities at Trincomalee were warned at daybreak of the location and number of the raiding ships, and they countered by sending nine Blenheim bombers against Nagumo's fleet. The British planes spotted their targets at 1025, but immediately the carrier fleet's Zero fighters tangled with them. The Blenheims did no damage, claiming only three near-misses, while five of them were shot down, and the remaining four were badly damaged.

At the time of the raid the *Hermes* and *Vampire* were 65 miles south of Trincomalee. Believing that, once the raid was over, they could return to Trincomalee, they reversed course at 0900. The other ships that had fled the naval base also began to come back. But the *Hermes* had been sighted even before her reverse turn, and at 0900, Nagumo launched ninety planes against the British group.[9]

The *Hermes* was attacked by dive bombers at 1035, and was pounded for ten minutes. By 1050 she was dead in the water, and five minutes later, she capsized and sank. It was then the *Vampire's* turn; she lasted ten minutes, broke in two, and sank. The *British Sergeant*, the *Hollyhock*, and the *Athelstane* all suffered the same fate.[10]

Admiral Nagumo now turned his fleet toward home, for his carriers had been at sea constantly since 26 November 1941, and were badly in need of a thorough overhaul. His crews needed rest, and he needed new pilots, with additional training. At the moment, also, Imperial General Headquarters had no assignment for them. Thus, Nagumo returned, having won spectacular victories at Pearl Harbor, Rabaul, Port Darwin, and now Colombo and Trincomalee, all at the cost of only a few planes. Not one of his ships in four months of raiding had even been hit. The British Eastern Fleet had been driven from the Indian Ocean to East Africa; and Burma, the Andamans, and Sumatra were protected from British naval raids. It is little wonder that most of the Japanese, both military and civilian, began to regard themselves as invincible. With this kind of "Victory Fever" running rampant, many Japanese began to advocate the acquisition of more territory (and resources) to protect what was already won, and won so easily.

In coordination with Nagumo's Ceylon raid, Admiral Ozawa had a Second Expeditionary Fleet, Malay Force, which was to give distant support to Nagumo, raid India's east-coast shipping, and bombard India's east-coast installations. Its Main Body had three elements: a Central Force of one heavy cruiser, one light cruiser, one light carrier (the *Ryujo*), and two destroyers; a Southern Force with two heavy cruisers and a destroyer; and a Northern Force of two heavy cruisers and a destroyer, with the specific duties of bombarding enemy installations south of Calcutta and attacking any British shipping that might be found. A Supply Force of two destroyers was attached to the Second Expeditionary Fleet, Malay Force. Also protecting Ozawa's fleet was a Strike Force, Main Body, acting as a Cover Force. A Screening Force containing the light cruiser *Kashii*, the minelayer *Hatsutaka*, and nine destroyers had the duty of watching for enemy ships to the north of Andaman Island and protecting the withdrawal of Nagumo's carrier fleet.

Ozawa's forces sortied from Mergui, Burma, 200 miles south of

Rangoon, at 1100 on 1 April. The fleet maneuvered between the Andaman and Nicobar islands from 2 to 4 April, to match Nagumo's attack schedule, then turned to the northeast. Then at 1730, the fleet split up into its three forces.

The Northern Force found ships to sink, despite attempts by the British to halt east-coast convoys. It patrolled the northern Indian coast for 200 miles, south from Calcutta. The Central Force also scoured the coast, from Vizagapatam north, on 6 April and victimized British ships, some of them sunk by the *Ryujo*'s planes. The Southern Force worked the area off Cocanada, with the same results. The *Ryujo*'s planes also bombed Vizagapatam and Cocanada on 6 April, causing the civilians to panic. The raid ended, however, on 6 April and most of the raiding force then withdrew to Singapore.[11] According to the British records, from 4 April to 9 April the Japanese sank twenty-three freighters, with a total tonnage of 32,404.[12] This naturally cut down on the flow of ships in unprotected convoys for some months. At the same time, Japan had given the westernmost portion of her defense perimeter, from Burma to Singapore, additional strength against a counterattack.

Japanese Carrier Strike Force (Admiral Chuichi Nagumo)

Heavy carriers: *Kaga†, Akagi, Hiryu, Soryu, Shokaku, Zuikaku*
Battleships: *Haruna, Kirishima, Hiei, Kongo*
Heavy cruisers: *Tone, Chikuma*
Light cruiser: *Abukuma*
Destroyers: *Tanikaze, Urakaze, Isokaze, Hamakaze, Arare, Shiranuhi, Kasumi, Kagero, Maikaze, Hagikaze, Akigumo*[13]

British Eastern Fleet, 26 March 1942

Force A (Fast class)

Heavy carriers: *Indomitable, Formidable*
Battleship: *Warspite*
Heavy cruisers: *Dorsetshire, Cornwall*
Light cruisers: *Enterprise, Emerald*
Destroyers: *Napier, Nestor, Paladin, Panther, Hotspur, Foxhound*

Force B (Slow class)

Light carrier: *Hermes*

† Returned to base with engine trouble, 2 March.

Battleships: *Resolution, Ramillies, Royal Sovereign, Revenge*
Light cruisers: *Caledon, Dragon, Heemskerk* (RNN)
Destroyers: *Griffin, Norman, Arrow, Decoy, Fortune, Scout, Vampire* (RAN), *Isaac Sweers* (RNN) [14]

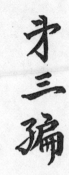

section 3

CORAL SEA, MIDWAY, AND THE ALEUTIANS

chapter 8

BATTLE OF
THE CORAL SEA

1942

April   Imperial General Headquarters decides to capture Port Moresby, southwest tip of New Guinea, by direct assault from the sea. The establishment of a seaplane base at Tulagi, southern part of Solomon chain (MO Operation)

18 April   Doolittle air raid on Japan

30 April   Japanese occupy Tulagi

1–4 May   Sorties of various Port Moresby invasion forces

4 May   Heavy carrier *Yorktown*'s planes raid convoy at Tulagi

7 May   U. S. Navy carrier planes attack Close Support Force of Port Moresby invasion fleet, sink the light carrier *Shoho*

8 May   Carrier battle of the Coral Sea. The heavy carrier *Lexington* sunk, the heavy carrier *Shokaku* moderately damaged

8 May   MO Operation suspended

The Greater East Asia empire had been won by the time that Admiral Nagumo's First Carrier Fleet Mobile Force returned to bases in Japan in mid-April. But there were still some trouble spots; it was not until the fall of Corregidor on 6 May that the U. S. Army, commanded by General Wainwright, surrendered the Philippine Islands. (The Japanese Navy was later called upon to aid in putting down pockets of resistance near Cebu and Zamboanga.) Nauru and Ocean islands had not yet been taken, and the Japanese Army in New Guinea at Lae and Salamaua found it difficult to maintain its bases, because of the horrendous climate and lack of land communication, other than trails running through thick jungles and swamplands.

Despite Japan's spectacular achievement in creating a new empire, establishing a strong defense perimeter, and acquiring the resources for Japan's war and industrial needs, Admiral Yamamoto was not satisfied. After four months of war, the decisive battle had not been fought, and he well knew American industrial power could quickly produce a navy far superior to what Japan possessed or could produce. Military strength, drawn from the United States, Australia, and New Zealand, was even then beginning to grow in Australia. Doolittle's Tokyo raid on 18 April, while inflicting little damage, gave further urgency to Yamamoto's plans, as did other hit-and-run raids by American carriers. Therefore, Yamamoto began to think about a Japanese operation to precipitate the decisive battle: the occupation of Midway, along with diversionary raids on Dutch Harbor and the occupation of Kiska and Attu, in the Aleutians.

War situations, however, do not remain static, and the Japanese Army wanted at that time to strengthen the defense perimeter against the growing forces of the enemy in Australia. Thus, a new offensive would be initiated, even as the Japanese prepared for the battle at Midway, for it was becoming evident that the Australia-based forces would have to be reckoned with. The Japanese, who had always advanced under cover of land-based planes and had selected new targets for occupation by this criterion, saw the Solomon Islands chain as a two-way street, for the Allies could by the same technique come island-hopping northward against Rabaul.

Their problem would be solved by taking the southernmost of the Solomons, along with Nauru and Ocean islands. They would then have a means of interdicting American military movement along the line of bases which had been won in the early months of 1942. Victory fever made such steps seem not only possible, but inevitable. Thus, the Japanese were going to expand beyond their original basic war plans. In planning an advance beyond land-based air cover, the Japanese were forgetting a basic military maxim: a defense perimeter can be weakened by extending it too far from its strongest bases. The farther the Japanese Army went from Rabaul, the northern Solomons, and New Guinea, the weaker its forces became and the greater the opposition's strength became.

So, at a time when the Japanese Navy should have been gathering its maximum strength for the battle at Midway, the Army was asking it for naval forces to support the Southwest Pacific operations (called MO Operation). Admiral Yamamoto certainly did not believe that the Southwest Pacific was the place for the decisive battle. Nevertheless, he exposed his naval forces to a diminution of strength by allowing them to support the capture of Port Moresby and the occupation of Tulagi. Yamamoto was becoming desperately anxious for the crucial battle with the U. S. Pacific Fleet to take place; but this operation looked so easy that he allowed it to go forward. Besides, it was usually the Army that decided which operations would be undertaken; the Navy would then be expected to support the operation. However anxious Yamamoto might have been, morale among the Japanese naval officers had never been higher; perhaps they, too, were beginning to believe in their invincibility.

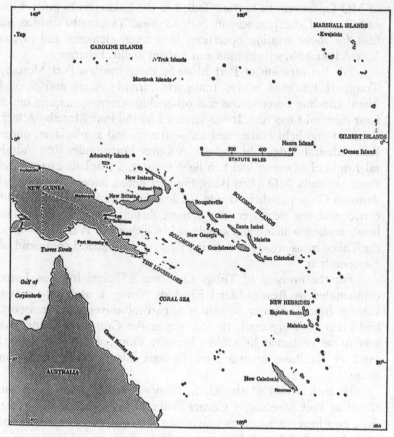

From Truk to New Caledonia

These days were not easy ones for the U. S. Navy. Cryptographers had broken the Japanese code and Admiral Nimitz was quite aware that his counterpart was planning for a battle in the Central Pacific, probably at Midway. Yet he could not ignore intelligence reports of new activity in the Southwest Pacific. He had to meet each threat as it materialized; none could be ignored. It was apparent that Japan planned to move into the south Solomons—so apparent that the Australians withdrew their meager garrison from Tulagi on 1 May.

Admiral Yamamoto still followed the Japanese naval doctrine of diminution of forces as he planned MO Operation—to invade Port Moresby by the sea, to meet and destroy any U. S. Navy ships which would respond to the Port Moresby threat, and, as a subsidiary part of MO Operation, to capture Tulagi in the Solomons to protect the east flank of the Japanese in New Guinea. Yamamoto divided his fleet for these invasion operations into seven elements and placed Vice Admiral Shigeyoshi Inouye at Rabaul in direct charge.

For the invasion of Port Moresby there was the Port Moresby Transport Force of twelve transports carrying Army and Special Naval Landing Force troops and other ships carrying supplies under Rear Admiral Koso Abe. It was screened by the Port Moresby Attack Force of one light cruiser and six destroyers and a minelayer, under Rear Admiral Sadamichi Kajioka. A Cover Force under Rear Admiral Kuninori Marumo had two light cruisers, a seaplane carrier, and three gunboats. MO Main Body, Support Force, under Rear Admiral Aritomo Goto was divided into a Close Support Force with a light carrier and one destroyer, and a more distant Cover Force of four heavy cruisers which could supply aid to either the Port Moresby or the Tulagi invasions. Rear Admiral Goto was in tactical command of the operation.

For the invasion of Tulagi there was a Tulagi Invasion Force commanded by Rear Admiral Kiyohide Shima, containing two destroyers from Destroyer Squadron 6, two minelayers, one transport, and other auxiliary craft. It, too, was under Goto's command and was to be protected by Goto's Support Force, which was located most of the time around New Georgia Island, in the Solomon chain.

In anticipation of the U. S. Navy's expected reaction to the threat at Port Moresby, a Carrier Strike Force with two heavy carriers, two heavy cruisers, and six destroyers, under the command of Vice Admiral Takeo Takagi, was to leave Truk on 1 May to arrive east of any intruding American warships, forcing them into battle and preventing an eastward retreat by any surviving ships.

MO Operation had several objectives. Tulagi, a small island in the southern part of the Solomon chain, across a narrow strait from the larger Guadalcanal, was to be occupied and used as a seaplane base. Such a base would extend the defense barrier against air attacks on Rabaul. Once Tulagi was secured, the same forces would then invade Nauru and Ocean islands. A large occupation force would be taken to Port Moresby, which was within aircraft range of northern Australia. (Indeed, the possibility of landings in northern Australia was already being discussed by the Japanese military leaders.) Port Moresby would also be valuable as a springboard for operations against New Caledonia, which in turn could serve as a base for operations against Samoa and the Fijis, to cut the life line connecting Australia with the United States. Of more immediate consequence, the capture of Port Moresby would help secure the Lae and Salamaua beachheads from air attack. Finally, Japanese naval headquarters believed that the American fleet would have to respond to the Port Moresby occupation; so a trap for the destruction of the Pacific Fleet would thus be set.

The Tulagi Invasion Force, under Admiral Kiyohide Shima, a small force in both ships and troops, sortied from Rabaul at 0830 on 30 April. The Distant Cover Force of the MO Main Body, Support Force, under Admiral Aritomo Goto, which had to cover the Port Moresby Transport Force and the Tulagi Occupation Force, stayed in the region just south of New Georgia Island, having left Truk on 28 April. The lighter Support Force of Admiral Kuninori Marumo was some 60 miles west of Tulagi, having sailed from Rabaul on 29 April. The Port Moresby Transport Force, with twelve transports, was relatively large. It left Rabaul on 4 May and was joined the following day by Kajioka's Attack Force. Its route would take it through Jomard Passage in the Louisiades, to the east of Milne Bay, at the southern tip of New Guinea.[1]

Takagi's formidable Carrier Strike Force left Truk on the morning of 1 May. Its course was almost due south until the afternoon watch the next day, when it went into a box course. It came out at 0600 on the 3rd, on a long looping movement to the southeast, that left it, by the afternoon of 5 May, east of San Cristobal Island. It then turned southwest by west.[2] It was now positioned to strike any American fleet going after the Port Moresby group. If the Japanese had any great disadvantage in this upcoming Battle of the Coral Sea, it was the relative inferiority of their intelligence about the size and numbers of U.S. and Australian ships in the area. They knew, of course, about the air strike against Tulagi on 4 May, so it could be presumed that at least one carrier was in the vicinity. In addition, they knew from their own air reconnaissance that naval forces were approaching from Australia.

U.S. intelligence was far superior, and after the Japanese code was broken, Nimitz knew what to expect and where to expect it. Also throughout the war, Australians living in the Solomon Islands, who had even before the war kept in touch with the outside world by powerful receiving and transmitting radio sets, kept the Allied forces informed of Japanese naval activities in their midst. They were known as the "coast watchers." But knowledge of Japanese intentions and dispositions did not guarantee an Allied victory. All Admiral Nimitz could do was to muster all his available forces for a counterattack.[3]

To meet the Japanese Carrier Strike Force, Task Force 17, with the *Lexington* under Rear Admiral Aubrey W. Fitch, and the *Yorktown* under Rear Admiral Frank Jack Fletcher, was ordered to meet and assume an attack position. On 1 May, the two forces joined, about 250 miles west of Espiritu Santo. All of 3 May, the *Lexington* group refueled from the *Tippecanoe*, while one hundred miles away, the *Yorktown* finished refueling from the *Neosho*. Both then set course for their point of rendezvous, scheduled for 0800 on 4 May. They were also expected to meet British Admiral J. G. Crace with his three cruisers and two destroyers, coming from Australia. All this changed, however, when aircraft flying from Australia reported that a Japanese air invasion group was disembarking in Tulagi Harbor. Admiral Fletcher at once sent the *Neosho* and the destroyer *Russell* back to the *Lexington* force, set a new rendezvous point for the morning of 5 May, and ordered the *Yorktown* to steam toward Tulagi. The task groups of Admirals Crace and Fitch were now at least 250 miles to the *Yorktown*'s rear. The *Lexington* did not learn of the *Yorktown*'s solitary charge until the morning of 4 May, when the *Neosho* and the *Russell* arrived. Fletcher intended, however, to launch his planes at dawn on 4 May.

All of these activities were unknown to the Japanese officers involved in MO Operation. They did not know the whereabouts, number, or kind of U.S. and Australian warships in the MO operational area. But Operation MO was proceeding exactly as planned; Goto's Distant Cover Force was headed northeast, the Port Moresby Invasion Force was still at anchor at Rabaul, and the Japanese carrier fleet was still north of Bougainville.

For some unexplained reason, Admiral Fitch, having joined up with the Australian ships, set a course for the 5 May rendezvous that took him an additional 50 miles away from the *Yorktown;* so the *Yorktown* would be acting alone. There were only a few Japanese ships to oppose an attack on Tulagi, although Admiral Fletcher could not be completely certain of this, and he had no immediately available backup support. The *Yorktown* launched her first wave of planes on 4 May at 0630, under cloudy skies—ideal weather conditions for a carrier to strike and yet remain unobserved. (A weather front created a 100-mile band of cloud cover for the next five days, which alternately gave cover to one side and then the other.) The first wave had twelve torpedo planes, twenty-eight dive bombers, and six fighters.

At 0730 at Tulagi, the minelayer *Okinoshima* and the destroyers *Kikuzuki* and *Yuzuki* formed a protective barrier for the harbor, while the unloading for the day began. Suddenly at 0820 the *Yorktown's* torpedo planes swept in, surrounding the harbor. At 0822 the *Kikuzuki* was hit by a 500-pound bomb that penetrated her starboard engine room. With the sudden inrush of water, the destroyer, unable to move, began to list badly. One of the supply ships took her in tow and beached her on nearby Gavutu Island; however, on the next tide she slipped back into the sea and sank.[4]

In all, the first air strike succeeded only in sinking the *Kikuzuki* and damaging the *Okinoshima*. The transports, minelayers, and the remaining destroyer immediately left Tulagi Harbor. Upon recovery of her planes, the *Yorktown* launched a second strike which arrived at Tulagi at 1210, sank two patrol ships, and damaged an escaping transport, the *Tama Maru*, which sank two days later. The *Yuzuki* was strafed and set afire near Savo Island, losing her captain and nine other men, while twenty were wounded. Still believing there were good targets around Tulagi, a third strike arrived at 1500 and found a transport to attack. In all, the Japanese lost one destroyer, two patrol boats, and a transport; a transport was badly damaged with twenty Japanese troops on board seriously wounded and one destroyer and one minelayer were damaged.[5]

The damage may have been slight, but the shock felt by the Japanese at the sudden appearance of U.S. carrier planes was not. The shock was felt throughout all of MO Operation's units, but particularly by the Carrier Strike Force. Now the game was serious; the carrier force knew that it had to contend with one or more U.S. carriers, and the Americans knew that Japanese carriers were at sea covering MO. Thus, two carrier strike forces were to meet in the first carrier-to-carrier battle—but no one had written any rules for the correct conduct of such a battle, other than to "get in the first strike." After recovering her last planes, the *Yorktown* turned south to rendezvous with the rest of Task Force 17, and made contact on the morning of 5 May.

For the next two days the rival carrier forces groped about, in search of each other. The Japanese sent out long-range four-engine search seaplanes from Rabaul; planes from the *Yorktown* shot one down around noon of 5 May. When the plane failed to return to base, the Japanese felt certain that a U.S. carrier (or carriers) was somewhere in the Coral Sea, but its location could not be pinpointed. Admiral Inouye, in command of the entire MO Operation, was handicapped in his air reconnaissance because most of his Air Flotilla 25 from Rabaul was bombing Port Moresby. Apparently Admiral Takagi did not use his carrier planes for long-range search missions, depending instead on his battleship and cruiser float planes for such duty. On 6 May in mid-morning a Japanese flying boat from Rabaul found the American task force and accurately reported its position; but Admiral Takagi did not receive this intelligence until 7 May.[6] By that time, however, he thought he had located Task Force 17 himself.

Unfortunately for Task Force 17, the air searches left an unsearched gap. The responsibility for air operations in the Coral Sea area had been allotted to General MacArthur, but he did not have enough long-range planes to make a thorough search of the Coral Sea area. Admiral Nimitz was forbidden, by the terms of the official division of air operations set up by the U. S. Joint Chiefs of Staff, to intrude into MacArthur's zone. If one drew an almost 45-degree angle from south latitude 10°, east longitude 165° down through the South Pacific, the zone to the northeast of the line was General MacArthur's Southwest Pacific area and opposite it was Admiral Nimitz's South Pacific area.[7] The twelve seaplanes at Nouméa did not have the range capacity to search the Solomon Islands and were, moreover, banned from entering MacArthur's zone. This left areas not fully searched by either MacArthur's B-17s or the PBYs. Air reconnaissance was thus left in the hands of Task Force 17 itself.

But while the two carrier forces groped for knowledge of each other's position, MO Operation in its other aspects was right on

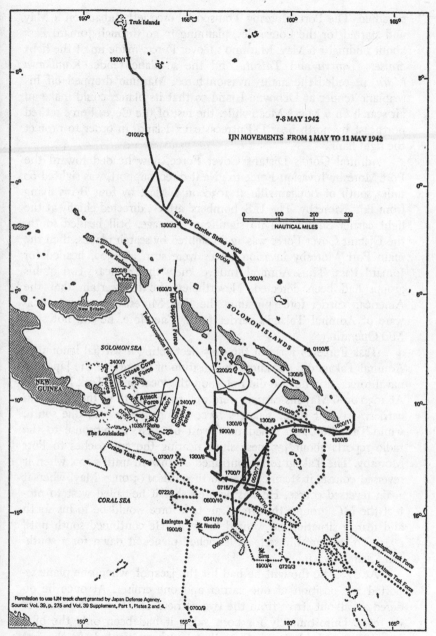

Battle of the Coral Sea, 7–8 May 1942, and IJN movements from 1–11 May 1942.

schedule. The Port Moresby Transport Force left Rabaul on 4 May and started for the Louisiades, planning to go through Jomard Pass about midnight 6 May. Marumo's Cover Force, made up of the light cruisers *Tenryu* and *Tatsuta* and the seaplane tender *Kamikawa Maru*, preceded the main invasion force. Marumo dropped off his seaplane tender at Deboyne Island so that its planes could make an air search on 7 May.[8] Meanwhile, the rest of the Cover Force retired northeast by north near D'Entrecasteaux Island, in order to protect the right flank.

Admiral Goto's Distant Cover Force, now headed toward the Port Moresby Invasion Force to give it direct support, was sighted 60 miles south of Bougainville at 1030 on 6 May, by four B-17s flying from Port Moresby. The U.S. bombers' attack, directed chiefly at the light carrier *Shoho*, did no significant damage. Still headed south, the Distant Cover Force was again sighted by search planes; then the main Port Moresby invasion forces were seen at 1300, headed for Jomard Pass. Thus Admiral Inouye knew that at least two of his groups had been detected. Nevertheless, he felt certain that the American carrier force pursuing the Port Moresby group was unaware of Admiral Takagi's carrier force. Therefore, he did not stop MO Operation.

Task Force 17 was not the only fleet acting in virtual ignorance. Admiral Takagi did not know the position of the rest of the Japanese naval forces, and he also did not know the location of Task Force 17. At 1030 on 6 May his carriers were well to the north of the American carriers. At that time, Takagi's force changed course to due south, while Task Force 17 sailed northwest by west, in response to the radio reports about Japanese ships nearing the approaches to Port Moresby. The Takagi force continued southward until 2000, when it reversed course; it steamed due north until 0115 on 7 May, when it again reversed course. He was worried that if he sailed west to protect the MO groups, the American task force would be to his south and rear, a situation he wanted to avoid. He continued south until 0740. To reassure himself, he launched planes at dawn for a southward search sweep.

At 0730, he thought he had hit the jackpot, when one plane reported the position of one carrier and one cruiser. At once he ordered an all-out strike from the two carriers, and turned his ships to the east. Unfortunately for both sides, it had been only the oiler *Neosho* and the destroyer *Sims* that had been sighted. As the first wave came in, the *Sims* put up a good defense for the *Neosho* and herself; but after two and one-half hours, an attack by dive bombers hit the destroyer with three bombs, sinking her almost immediately. The *Neosho* was hit directly seven times and sustained damage from eight near-misses.[9] When she was found four days later by U.S. ships, her suffering crew was rescued, and the crippled ship was torpedoed and sunk. Their mistake proved costly to the Japanese, for while their carrier-force planes were engaging the oiler and destroyer, they missed the chance to find Task Force 17, which, in the meantime, had found Goto's Distant Cover Force, now aiding the Close Support Force with the light carrier *Shoho*.

The *Yorktown* had rejoined the *Lexington* in the early morning of 5 May. Task Force 17 had been sailing northwest by west, from 2000 on 5 May to 0725 on 7 May, ending up about 100 miles south of Rossel Island, the farthest east of the Louisiades. At sunrise, Admiral Fletcher ordered Admiral Crace's force to continue northwest, to prevent the Port Moresby Invasion Force from turning the corner of southeastern New Guinea. Crace ran into continuous air attacks from Japanese land-based planes (and a few from the USAAF), but his ships were untouched. During the night of 7 May, when he heard that the Port Moresby force had turned back, he returned to Australia.

On the morning of 7 May, this was the situation: Kajioka's Attack Force was escorting Abe's MO invasion force toward Jomard Pass. The *Shoho* launched four fighter planes and one attack plane at 0630 as protection for the invasion fleet. The cover force was about 35 miles east of Woodlark Island and 30 miles northwest of the convoy. The *Zuikaku* and the *Shokaku*, then attacking the *Neosho* and the *Sims*, were about 175 miles to the east of Task Force 17, and just then becoming aware of the American carriers' real position.

At 0625, Task Force 17 turned north-northwest and launched reconnaissance planes. At 0815, a plane from the *Yorktown* sighted two carriers and four cruisers, 225 miles northwest of Task Force 17. Admiral Fletcher decided to launch an all-out attack; the *Lexington* began launching at 0826 and the *Yorktown* at about 0900, so that all ninety-three planes had started for the target by 0930. The Americans had the good fortune of running into a cold front, which provided the U.S. carriers with cloud cover, while Goto's Close Support Force was in bright sunlight. Once the U.S. planes were on their strike mission, it was discovered that it was not Takagi's carrier fleet that had been spotted, but rather the Close Cover Force. The Japanese began to transmit Task Force 17's position to all forces. At 0700 Admiral Inouye ordered the MO Invasion Force not to enter Jomard Pass, but to retire for the moment. Admiral Goto ordered the *Shoho* to launch what planes she could spare, to attack the American carrier fleet.

Fortune smiled on the *Lexington*'s planes, for at 0950 they spotted the *Shoho*, only 90 miles to the northwest, and they went in against almost no air resistance. The *Yorktown*'s planes followed at 1025. Despite the evasive action and antiaircraft fire of the Close Support Force, the light carrier had no chance. Thirteen bombs and seven torpedoes found their mark, and she burst into flames. The order to abandon ship was given at 1031, and she sank at 1035; only 255 men, out of a crew of about 800, were saved.[10] Goto's Cover Force, now containing four heavy cruisers and one destroyer, retired to the northeast, launching float planes to join the *Kamikawa Maru*'s seaplane force at Deboyne Island.

Task Force 17 had scored a triumph, the first sinking of a Japanese carrier (albeit an almost undefended light carrier). But the Americans were in for a worrisome night; Admiral Fletcher realized that Takagi now knew his location, and he did not know where Takagi was. To avert impending disaster, and yet accomplish his mission of interception and destruction, he had to make an educated guess at the position of the carriers. He set course to the west, in order to be within striking range of the invasion fleet going through Jomard Pass. (Of course, he had no way of knowing it had been recalled.)[11] Takagi also had to make some choices. He sent out search planes all day on 7 May, but since Task Force 17 was still in foul weather, the plane reports were incomplete and contradictory.

At any rate, both admirals could assume that their forces were close together, so that in the morning, it would only be a question of who got in the first blow. At 2200, the two Japanese carriers were about 100 miles east of the two American carriers. Both admirals toyed with the idea of a night attack, but both abandoned the idea. Task Force 17 continued west through the later part of the night, while Takagi's force went north. Task Force 17's course, however, took it out of the cloud cover, so at dawn on 8 May it was clearly visible. At daylight both sides began to look for each other. The *Lexington*, sailing west, launched an eighteen-plane search group at 0625 (Time Zone −10).[12] At 0722, the Japanese Carrier Strike Force was spotted. The *Lexington*, by intercepted radio messages, knew that her force had also been located. Acting on the 0722 sighting, Admiral Fletcher projected where the Japanese carriers would be when Task Force 17's planes were launched and had covered the distance between the two fleets. Then, at 0738, both the Lexington and the Yorktown were given the launch order. The Yorktown dispatched thirty-nine aircraft, starting at 0815, while the Lexington launched forty-three.

The Yorktown's planes struck the first blow. Their pilots saw the Zuikaku and the Shokaku, about eight miles apart, each with a heavy cruiser and destroyer screen, just as the Zuikaku was slipping under a cloud cover. The dive bombers circled to allow the torpedo planes the opportunity to get into position, while below them the Shokaku turned into the wind to launch more fighters. The Yorktown's attack planes finally went in at 1000. The attack, understandably, was not as successful as it might have been: the rules of carrier-to-carrier warfare had yet to be learned, and this battle was Lesson 1. The torpedo planes released their torpedoes at too great a distance and failed to score a hit. The dive bombers scored twice, however, starting gasoline fires and damaging the flight deck. The Shokaku lost her launch capability for an hour; she could still recover planes, however.

The Lexington's planes did even less damage. At first, they could not find the Japanese carriers, and many had to return because of low fuel. At 1040 what planes were left—eleven torpedo planes, four dive bombers, and six fighter escorts—made their attack on the Shokaku. No torpedoes found their mark, and only one bomb scored. In all, the Shokaku suffered three bomb hits, one on the forward port side of the flight deck, one on the after starboard side of the flight deck, and one to the starboard side of the bridge. She was in no danger of sinking, but she had 109 men killed and 114 wounded. After her fires were extinguished, she started home for repairs under her own power, while forty-six of her planes landed on the Zuikaku.

While Task Force 17's aviators were having a go at the Shokaku, Admiral Takagi's planes were attacking the Lexington and Yorktown. Despite their fewer planes (sixty-nine) the Japanese had the advantage, since their air strike force had a good balance of plane types and a clear idea of where the American ships were. They also had experience in battle. The American carriers' fighter protection was inadequate and poorly placed. At about 1010, Japanese torpedo planes made a scissors attack on the Lexington, approaching simultaneously at 45 degrees on both bows, holding their run to a short one-half-mile range. Thus the Lexington could not evade one group of planes without turning into another torpedo spread. She was hit to starboard at 1020, closely followed by another starboard hit, abaft the island. While maneuvering to avoid torpedoes, she was also being dive-bombed. Because of the lack of American fighter-plane and antiaircraft resistance, the Japanese dive bombers were able to hold their dives to an altitude of 2,500 feet before releasing, and their bombs were deadly accurate. One bomb hit a ready-ammunition box on the *Lexington*'s port bow, while another hit her smoke funnel, and near-misses loosened her plates.

Meanwhile, the *Yorktown* was not being neglected. She was able to evade the first three torpedoes, all launched at her port bow, but when the dive bombers made their run, she was hit by a 750-pound bomb on the flight deck, at the base of her island. Fires broke out, but were quickly brought under control, and her launch and retrieval capabilities had not been impaired.

Although it looked for a while as if the *Lexington* had survived the attack, at 1247 she was shaken by a huge explosion, caused by a spark which had ignited the gasoline fumes from her ruptured fuel-storage tanks. More explosions followed; although she was still making 25 knots, she was being torn apart internally. At 1345 another explosion wrecked her ventilating system. Finally the "Abandon Ship" order was given at 1607, and, torpedoed by the destroyer *Phelps*, she sank at 2000. The *Yorktown* then retired to Nouméa, and thence to Pearl Harbor; Task Force 17 had been broken up.

The returning Japanese aviators reported that both American carriers had been sunk. Admiral Inouye, at Rabaul with the *Shokaku* on her way home, ordered the *Zuikaku* to Truk. Later on 8 May he ordered MO Operation postponed until 3 July. Although he believed that Task Force 17 had been destroyed, he did not want his Port Moresby Invasion Force to proceed without carrier protection, because of the intensity and number of the land-based USAAF attacks on 7 May.

Admiral Yamamoto, however, countermanded Inouye's order. At 0000 on 8 May, he directly ordered Takagi to utterly destroy all remaining enemy forces. In spite of attempts to get Goto's forces and the *Zuikaku* back into action, though, it was too late; it was 10 May before Goto could join his force together with the large carrier. On 11 May, Admiral Takagi was again ordered to take the *Zuikaku* to Truk.

It is difficult to say who won the Battle of the Coral Sea. American losses were greater: the *Neosho*, the *Sims*, and the *Lexington* lost, compared to the Japanese loss of only the *Shoho*, with damage to the *Shokaku*. But the *Zuikaku* lost planes and aviators, and did not get back into action until 12 June. Thus, with their decisive battle at Midway impending, the Japanese had lost the services of Carrier Division 5's two heavy carriers. That loss alone might very possibly have denied the Japanese a smashing victory at Midway. The Japanese were more efficient in their attacks, but efficiency is bred of experience, which the Japanese carrier pilots had, and the American pilots did not. The Japanese lost opportunities and made mistakes because of poor communications—so poor that admirals did not inform other admirals of essential facts, and there were day-long delays in transmitting vital information. The Japanese at this time had better plotting techniques and plotting officers to direct their planes to their targets. The U. S. Navy needed to improve its methods, as was demonstrated by the difficulty that most of the *Lexington*'s planes had in finding the two Japanese carriers. It would not be until after the Battle of Midway that they became proficient at this crucial task.

Japanese Forces at the Battle of Coral Sea

(The Japanese Navy did not use anything similar to the TF, TG, TU designations used by the U. S. Navy; rather, they used the ideograph "Tai" or sometimes "Butai", which could be any group of ships—except for "Combined Fleet", which was "Rengo Kantai." "Tai" has been translated as "Force", "Body", etc.)

Carrier Strike Force (Vice Admiral Takagi)

Heavy carriers: *Zuikaku, Shokaku*
Destroyer screen: *Ariake, Yugure, Shigure, Shiratsuyu*
Heavy cruisers: *Myoko, Haguro*
Destroyers: *Ushio, Akebono*

Port Moresby Invasion Force

TRANSPORT FORCE (Rear Admiral Koso Abe)

Minelayer: *Tsugaru*
Twelve transports
Auxiliary craft

ATTACK FORCE (Rear Admiral Sadamichi Kajioka)

Light cruiser: *Yubari*
Destroyers: *Oite, Asanagi, Mutsuki, Mochizuki, Yayoi*

One patrol boat
Auxiliary craft

CLOSE COVER FORCE (Rear Admiral Kuninori Marumo)

Light cruisers: *Tenryu, Tatsuta*
Seaplane tender: *Kamikawa Maru*
Three gunboats

CLOSE SUPPORT FORCE (Rear Admiral Aritomo Goto)

Light carrier: *Shoho*
Destroyer: *Sazanami*

SUPPORT FORCE, MAIN BODY (Rear Admiral Goto)

Heavy cruisers: *Aoba, Kako, Kinugasa, Furutaka*

Tulagi Invasion Force (Rear Admiral Kiyohide Shima)

Destroyers: *Kikuzuki, Yuzuki*
Minelayers: *Okinoshima, Koei Maru*
One transport
Auxiliary craft[13]

U. S. Navy Forces at the Battle of Coral Sea

(The nomenclature used by the U. S. Navy for its division of forces
was different from that used by the Japanese. The U. S. Navy used a
Task Force (TF) number for a large unit, a Task Group (TG)
number for a smaller unit within the Task Force, and a Task Unit
(TU) number for a still smaller force. When a Task Force divided
into groups, a decimal and another number were added; for example, Task Force 17, Task Group 17.2 and Task Group 17.3.)

Task Group 17.5 (Carrier Group)

Heavy carriers: *Yorktown, Lexington*
Destroyer screen: *Morris, Anderson, Hammann, Russell*

Task Group 17.2 (Attack Group)

Heavy cruisers: *Minneapolis, New Orleans, Astoria, Chester, Portland*
Destroyer screen: *Phelps, Dewey, Farragut, Aylwin, Monaghan*

Task Group 17.3 (from Australia)

Heavy cruisers: *Australia* (RAN), *Hobart* (RAN), *Chicago*
Destroyer screen: *Perkins, Walke*

Task Group 17.6 (Fleet Train)

Oilers: *Neosho, Tippecanoe*
Destroyer screen: *Sims, Worden*

Task Group 17.9

Seaplane tender: *Tangier*[14]

chapter 9

MIDWAY AND
THE ALEUTIANS
—PRELUDE

The Japanese victories had come so fast and with so few losses that they actually outpaced the planning of the Imperial General Headquarters and the staffs of the Army and Navy. Thus, the time from January to mid-April 1942 was spent in research and tentative planning for new operations, and was marked by disagreements within and between the Navy and Army. One naval staff group even suggested the invasion and occupation of Ceylon.[1]

When retreating Allied troops, planes, ships, and submarines backed up into Australia, and the Americans at once began building and fortifying a southern supply line for Australia, the Japanese knew that General MacArthur planned to use this continent as a base for his counterattack. Therefore, the Army wanted to capture Port Moresby, which was only 300 miles from Cape York, Australia. The Battle of the Coral Sea had stopped the first attempt at a direct onslaught, so the Army now proposed an overland attack on Port Moresby. This would be a prelude to a Japanese occupation of northern Australia, which would frustrate any offensive moves by General MacArthur.[2]

Admiral Yamamoto and the Navy also recognized the Australian threat to the newly-occupied southern regions, but they advocated a different way of neutralizing Australia: the interdiction of the American–Australian line of communications by the capture of New Caledonia, Samoa, and the Fijis (designated FS Operation). But Yamamoto believed that his most important task was to draw the U. S. Pacific Fleet into a decisive battle which, with a fleet inferior in numbers, it must lose. The key to his plan was an attack and occupation of Midway as soon as possible, at least by early June. Yamamoto felt that the Japanese could occupy the island before the U. S. Navy could muster an adequate defense. The capture of the island would draw out a counterattack by the U. S. Pacific Fleet, for which he would be waiting with a vastly superior force.

Midway, fittingly named, is very close to the geographical center of the Pacific Ocean. It is a circular atoll consisting of two islands: Eastern Island, with an area of 328 acres, and Sand Island, 850 acres. But despite its tininess, in June 1942 it became the fulcrum for any further extension of power by Japan.

At first the Japanese Army headquarters rejected the idea of occupying Midway. The Army feared that this would inevitably lead to an attack on Oahu, using troops it would rather use in the southern regions. The Navy, however, convinced them that this was not the purpose of the action and that the Army would not be called upon for a Hawaiian attack.[3] Yamamoto stubbornly held to his earlier unpopular view: Japan would lose a protracted war, and her only hope lay in a decisive battle, fought in the first six months, which would destroy the U. S. Navy in the Pacific and lead to a negotiated peace. An operation against Midway (designated MI Operation) was finally approved on 5 April; it included a raid on Dutch Harbor and the occupation of Kiska and Attu in the Aleutians (designated AL Operation), added as a distraction tactic.

It was up to Admiral Nimitz to counter this new threat. Although the Pacific Fleet was inferior in ships and planes, it possessed a valuable secret weapon: the Japanese naval code, JN-25, had been broken.[4] The U. S. Navy could thus anticipate Japanese moves and be prepared with what it had. It was this knowledge that had enabled Task Force 17 to thwart Operation MO. The Americans also knew that something was being planned for the Central Pacific and the Aleutians in late May or early June; thus they immediately sent the heavy carrier *Yorktown*, damaged at Coral Sea, back to Pearl Harbor for repairs. (The story of the repair of the *Yorktown* is incredible; when she arrived at Pearl Harbor on 27 May, it was estimated that it would take 90 days to repair her. But, with 1,400 men working night and day on her, she was able to sail from Pearl Harbor at 0900 on 30 May.)[5] The heavy carriers *Enterprise* and *Hornet* of Task Force 16 rushed back from the Southwest Pacific to Pearl Harbor. Command of Task Force 16 passed from Vice Admiral William F. Halsey, who was ill, to Rear Admiral Raymond A. Spruance. Everything possible was done to defend Midway; the Sixth Marine Defense Battalion was reinforced, leaving Midway with about 3,000 troops. A large submarine force and long-range search planes were sent out for reconnaissance, while the small island was crowded with whatever useful aircraft could be found.

It was vitally important to the Americans that the Japanese be unaware of what was taking place at Pearl Harbor. Because the *Yorktown* had disappeared after the Battle of the Coral Sea, the Japanese presumed her to be sunk, or at least out of action. They lacked hard information about other U.S. carriers, and it even seemed possible to them that none would be in the vicinity of Midway on the days of attack.

It was just as essential to Admiral Yamamoto that he have this knowledge. In March, K Operation had been instituted, a method of checking ships at Pearl Harbor. A long-range *I*-class submarine was sent to French Frigate Reef, where it refueled a large Kawanishi seaplane, which would then make a reconnaissance of Pearl Harbor. From 27 May to 30 May, however, the submarines could not approach their rendezvous point because the U. S. Navy, having discovered how the Japanese were using French Frigate Reef, had deployed a tanker and two destroyers there, thus depriving the Japanese of their seaplane reconnaissance during the crucial days of the *Yorktown*'s repair. K Operation was suspended on 30 May, and thus the Japanese Midway Force had no sure knowledge about American ships and their whereabouts.[6]

There was a further gap in Japanese naval intelligence. Thirteen *I*-class submarines were dispatched as a picket line between Pearl Harbor and Midway, for purposes of reconnaissance and attack. But they arrived after Task Forces 16 and 17 were already near Midway. Thus, as the mighty array of Japanese ships gathered for the Midway occupation and the "decisive battle," the Japanese admirals still did not know what U. S. Navy units were in the vicinity.

Nagumo's Carrier Strike Force was the first of the many Japanese naval forces to converge on Midway, having sortied from Hashirajima on 27 May, starting at 0400. Remaining behind for a later sortie were the Main Body of the Combined Fleet (with Admiral Yamamoto on board the *Yamato*), and Vice Admiral Kondo's Second Fleet, Strike and Support Force, Main Body.

While those who did not have command responsibility anticipated yet another easy victory, Vice Admiral Nagumo did not. He had driven his carriers hard since 7 December, and he knew that they needed extensive repair and maintenance. Yamamoto realized that he was once again throwing the dice; but this time he did not know the odds of the game, for he knew nothing about the location and number of the U.S. carriers he might encounter. Yet if the war were to be won, he believed, it must be won with this battle. He was ill with diarrhea and quite withdrawn at this time, but he did not alarm others with his doubts.

On the following day, the occupation transports, along with the *Jintsu* and her ten screening destroyers, left Saipan, while the Second Fleet's Occupation Support Force left Guam. On 29 May the rest of the fleet sailed. Seventy-one major warships of the Imperial Japanese Navy were headed towards 1,178 acres of land in the mid-Pacific. The following day, with the cancellation of K Operation, Yamamoto's fleet was now blind except for what its submarines and its scouting planes from land, carriers, and cruisers could spot. Admiral Nagumo's short-range radios had not received the message that K Operation had been called off, so he still assumed that the Kawanishi flying boats would report the number and location of any American carriers. He knew nothing about the American carriers at Pearl Harbor and near Midway. On 3 June the Aleutian diversionary force sailed (the date was west of the international date line).

On the morning of 4 June, first contact was made, when several ships of the Second Fleet Escort Force, still 670 miles from Midway, were seen by PBYs from Midway. Later that morning, B-17s attacked the Escort Force and its transports, without success. The convoy was also attacked that evening; the tanker *Akebono Maru* was torpedoed in her bow, but was still able to proceed, and the transport *Kiyozumi Maru* was strafed. Yamamoto now knew that the operation had been discovered.[7] But he had not expected the operation to be a surprise; the vital question was: what ships did the U. S. Navy have to respond with?

Admiral Yamamoto's basic plan was as follows: his carriers, guarded by two fast battleships, two heavy cruisers, one light cruiser, and twelve destroyers, would attack Midway at dawn on 4 June; however, if the observation planes, submarines, or K Operation discovered U.S. naval units, then the attack would be made on them instead. After the destruction of any U.S. ships in the area, the Midway attack would proceed. If a battle with a U.S. task force developed, or if resistance on Midway was stiffer than expected, Kondo's powerful Second Fleet forces, 200 miles to the west, would be used either to mop up the remnants of the shattered U.S. task force (preferably in a night battle) or to bombard Midway. If no task force were encountered, Admiral Yamamoto fully expected an

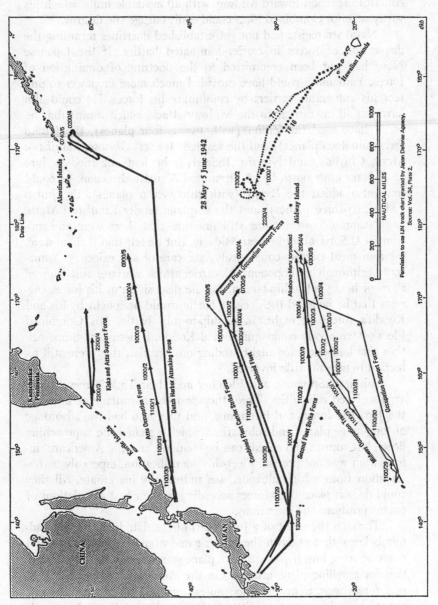

Approach Routes to Midway and the Aleutians, 28 May–5 June 1942

American reaction toward Midway with all available units, which his vastly superior Combined Fleet could easily engage and destroy.

Naval strategists had not yet established doctrines regarding the disposition of forces in carrier-dominated battles. If the Japanese Navy had not been committed to the doctrine of diminution of forces, Yamamoto could have provided much more firepower to protect his vulnerable carriers by combining his forces. He could also have put all his carriers in the Midway attack, which meant that he could have used the *Zuiho* (with twenty-four planes), the *Hosho* (with nineteen planes), and the seaplane tenders *Chitose, Kamikawa Maru, Chiyoda,* and *Nisshin.* Indeed, if he had not tried to lure U. S. Navy units north by his attempted Aleutian diversion, he could have also added the *Ryujo* (with thirty-seven planes), the *Junyo* (with fifty-three planes), and the seaplane tender *Kimikawa Maru.*

Nagumo, however, was still unaware that there were any substantial U.S. naval forces near Midway. But he felt that if there were, his four great carriers could easily take care of any exigency. Yamamoto, although a proponent of carrier-attack warfare, still showed signs of being battleship-bound, for the disposition of his forces suggests that he believed the decisive battle would be fought by his and Kondo's forces at night, in a ship-to-ship battle. His Combined Fleet's Main Body could quickly aid Kondo, if necessary. Since neither side had perfected night landing on a carrier, they were still reluctant to take the risks involved.

Admirals Spruance and Fletcher and their Task Forces 16 and 17 also faced difficulties. True, they had the advantage of knowing the Japanese forces and intentions, and they also had the advantage of long-range planes and submarines which watched the approaching fleets; but courses and speeds can be changed, and the Americans' information was not precise. Fleet-ship identification, especially by observation from a high altitude, was notoriously inaccurate. All they could do was place their forces according to their best calculations of enemy positions and intentions.

Through the night of 3 June (east of the date line) the U.S. admirals knew that at dawn the carrier game would begin: see first and don't be seen; but, if you are seen, place your ships in the best formation for repelling plane attacks. On the evening of 3 June the U.S. task forces were more than 300 miles northeast by east of Midway, about 400 miles east and a little to the north of Admiral Nagumo's planned launch point at dawn on 4 June (3 June for Nagumo, since he was west of the international date line).

During part of the night the two carrier forces closed on intersecting lines which would have crossed about 40 miles northwest of Midway. The two U.S. admirals were working from different premises. Admiral Spruance did not believe that the Midway-based planes which had attacked the convoy on 3 June, had found the main body of the Japanese force. Instead, his intelligence reports indicated that Nagumo's carriers would be somewhere northwest of Midway in time for an attack at dawn on 4 June; Spruance maneuvered accordingly. Admiral Fletcher of Task Force 17 was senior to Spruance and was in tactical command of both task forces; however, because Spruance had a competent carrier officer as his chief of staff, Captain Miles Browning, Fletcher allowed Spruance to command Task Force 16 on his own. As a result of this division of command, the three carriers could not fight as one unit, which diminished their effectiveness in the carrier battle. Admiral Nagumo, still unaware of any American ships in the vicinity, prepared to hit Midway early and hard, and at the same time sent out his cruisers' float planes in search patterns to the east and northeast.[8]

Table of Organization for Midway Attack, MI Operation; Combined Fleet (Admiral Yamamoto)

First Fleet, Main Body (Admiral Yamamoto)

Light carrier: *Hosho*
Battleships: *Yamato**, *Nagato, Mutsu*
Light cruiser: *Sendai*
Destroyers: *Fubuki, Shirayuki, Murakumo, Hatsuyuki, Isonami, Uranami, Shikinami, Ayanami, Yukaze*

First Mobile Force, Carrier Strike Force (Vice Admiral Nagumo)

Heavy carriers: *Akagi, Kaga, Soryu, Hiryu*
Battleships: *Haruna, Kirishima*
Heavy cruisers: *Tone, Chikuma*
Light cruiser: *Nagara*
Destroyers: *Akigumo, Makigumo, Yugumo, Isokaze, Hamakaze, Arashi, Kazagumo, Urakaze, Tanikaze, Nowaki, Hagikaze, Maikaze*
Fleet train: eight tankers

Second Fleet, Strike Force, Support Force, Main Body (Vice Admiral Nobutake Kondo)

Light carrier: *Zuiho*
Battleships: *Hiei, Kongo*
Heavy cruisers: *Atago, Chokai, Myoko, Haguro*
Light cruiser: *Yura*
Destroyers: *Murasame, Yudachi, Harusame, Samidare, Asagumo, Minegumo, Natsugumo, Mikazuki*
Four tankers

Second Fleet Escort Force (Rear Admiral Raizo Tanaka)

Light cruiser: *Jintsu*
Destroyers: *Kuroshio, Oyashio, Hatsukaze, Yukikaze, Amatsukaze, Tokitsukaze, Kasumi, Kagero, Arare, Shiranuhi*
Fifteen transports, with 5,000 troops
One tanker

Second Fleet, Occupation Support Force (Rear Admiral Takeo Kurita)

Seaplane tenders: *Chitose, Kamikawa Maru*
Heavy cruisers: *Kumano, Mogami, Mikuma, Suzuya*
Destroyer screen: *Arashio, Asashio, Hayashio*

Special Duty Force

Seaplane tenders: *Chiyoda, Nisshin*

First Supply Force

Destroyer: *Ariake*
Two freighters[9]

Japanese Carrier Strike Force Planes at Midway[10]

	Fighters	Dive Bombers	Attack Planes
Akagi	18	18	27
Kaga	18	18	27
Hiryu	18	18	18
Soryu	18	18	18
	72	72	90

Table of Organization for the Diversionary Aleutians Operation

Fifth Fleet, Main Body (Vice Admiral Boshiro Hosogawa)

Heavy cruiser: *Nachi*
Destroyer screen: *Inazuma, Ikazuchi*

Second Strike Force, Carrier Force (Rear Admiral Kakuji Kakuta)

Light carriers: *Ryujo, Junyo*
Heavy cruisers: *Maya, Takao*
Seaplane tender: *Kimikawa Maru*
Destroyer screen: *Akebono, Ushio, Sazanami, Shiokaze*

Attu Occupation Force (Rear Admiral Sentaro Omori)

Light cruiser: *Abukuma*
Destroyers: *Hatsuharu, Hatsushimo, Wakaba, Nenohi*
Two transports, with 1,000 troops

Kiska Occupation Force (Captain Takeji Ono)

Light cruiser: *Tama*
Destroyers: *Akatsuki, Hokaze*
Six transports with 550 troops[11]

U. S. Navy Forces at the Battle of Midway

Task Force 16 (Rear Admiral Raymond Spruance)

TASK GROUP 16.5

Heavy carriers: *Enterprise, Hornet*
Heavy cruisers: *New Orleans, Minneapolis, Vincennes, Northampton, Pensacola*
Light cruiser: *Atlanta*

TASK GROUP 16.4

Destroyers: *Balch, Conyngham, Benham, Ellet, Maury, Phelps, Worden, Monaghan, Aylwin, Dewey, Monssen*

Task Force 17 (Rear Admiral Frank Jack Fletcher)

TASK GROUP 17.5

Heavy carrier: *Yorktown*

TASK GROUP 17.2

Heavy cruisers: *Astoria, Portland*

TASK GROUP 17.4

Destroyers: *Hammann, Hughes, Morris, Anderson, Russell, Gwin*

Task Force 7

TASK GROUP 7.1 (Midway Patrol)

Twelve fleet submarines

TASK GROUP 7.3 (Oahu Patrol)

Four fleet submarines

FLEET TRAIN

Destroyers: *Blue, Ralph Talbot*
One tanker

FRENCH FRIGATE REEF

Destroyer: *Clark*
One tanker
Two tenders
Auxiliary craft

U. S. Navy Carrier Planes in Midway Operation[12]

	Fighters	Dive Bombers	Torpedo Planes
Yorktown	25	37	13
Enterprise	27	38	14
Hornet	27	37	15
	79	112	42

U. S. Navy Forces in the Aleutians

Task Force 8 (Rear Admiral Robert A. Theobald)

Heavy cruisers: *Indianapolis, Louisville*
Light cruisers: *Nashville*, St. Louis, Honolulu*
Destroyers: *Gridley, Gilmer, McCall, Humphreys*

TASK GROUP 8.2 (Surface Reconnaissance Force)

One gunboat

16. *The sinking of the British cruiser* Cornwall, *5 April 1942.*

17. *Japanese War Painting, "Naval Operation in the Indian Ocean," depicts the British cruisers* Dorsetshire *and* Cornwall *under attack by Japanese dive bombers, 5 April 1942.*

18. *Vice Admiral Shigeyoski Inouye,*
commander of MO Operation

19. *Rear Admiral Kiyohide Shima, com-*
mander of the Tulagi Invasion Force

20. *Rear Admiral Takeo Takagi, commander of MO Carrier Strike Force*

21. *Rear Admiral Aritomo Goto, commander of Support Force, MO Operation*

22. *The Japanese light carrier* Shoho *is sunk by American torpedo and dive bombers at the Battle of Coral Sea. She was the first Japanese carrier to be sunk in the Pacific war.*

23. *The U.S. carrier* Lexington *at the Battle of the Coral Sea, 7 May 1942. She erupts in a massive explosion as her fuel storage tanks are penetrated by flames. In the background, the carrier* Yorktown *steams away.*

One tanker
Fourteen patrol ships
Five Coast Guard cutters

TASK GROUP 8.4

Destroyers: *Case, Talbot, Sands, Dent, Brooks, Waters, Reid, King, Kane*

TASK GROUP 8.5

Submarines: six S-type submarines[13]

chapter 10

YAMAMOTO'S "DECISIVE BATTLE"

1942

4 June   Nagumo's carrier planes raid Midway and repel attacks from Midway's planes

4 June   Planes from the U.S. carriers *Hornet, Yorktown,* and *Enterprise* discover and attack Nagumo's four-carrier force, and sink the *Akagi, Kaga,* and *Soryu*

The air strike on Midway began to launch at 0430, and by 0445 it was assembled and on its way, at a speed of 125 knots.[1] At that time, the carriers were 210 miles from Midway; after launching, they closed on Midway, at a speed of 24 knots. The four carriers had launched a total of thirty-six attack planes, thirty-six fighters, and thirty-six attack planes carrying massive bombs weighing almost 1,800 pounds.[2] Knowing that U.S. planes on Midway would counterattack, the four ships provided a total of thirty-six fighters as combat air patrol. Nagumo was left with 126 planes, along with those that returned from Midway, for whatever else might arise.

As soon as Midway radar picked up the raiders, "General Quarters" was sounded, and by 0600 every plane capable of flying, about 120 in all, had taken off. The pilots' enthusiasm, however, outstripped the adequacy of their planes. As the Marine fighters tried to intercept the bombers, the Zero fighters in turn attacked them. The U.S. planes (old Buffaloes and Wildcats) were no match for the Zeroes, flown by pilots with a great deal of combat experience. It was now up to Midway's antiaircraft defense. At 0634, Japanese high-altitude and dive bombers began to attack. The raid was over in 20 minutes, and the Japanese planes rendezvoused from 0720 to 0730 for the return flight. The damage they had inflicted, however, was not enough to knock out Midway. Seventeen out of twenty-seven Marine fighters and pilots were lost; seven other planes were severely damaged.

At Midway, on Eastern Island, the Marine command post and mess hall were destroyed, and the powerhouse was severely damaged. On Sand Island, the Japanese, not wanting to repeat the error made in the Pearl Harbor raid, destroyed the oil tanks and seaplane facilities. Fires broke out in storehouses, gas dumps, and the hospital. Casualties were relatively light, though, and the airstrips were still operable.[3]

Japanese plane losses were extensive. Although no bombers were hit by American fighter interceptors, Midway's antiaircraft fire was intense and accurate. In all, 38 planes were lost and 29 were inoperable after the Midway strike—a total of 67 planes out of the 108 launched. That left 167 planes to meet the 230 that the U.S. carriers could muster. If Admiral Yamamoto had not kept the light carrier *Hosho* (with 11 fighter and 8 attack planes) back with his Combined Fleet, and the light carrier *Zuiho* (with 12 fighters and 12 bombers) with the Second Fleet, Strike and Support Force, the Japanese carrier force would still have had 210 planes; add the light carrier *Ryujo* (with 16 fighters and 21 attack planes) and the light carrier *Junyo* (with 22 fighters, 21 bombers, and 10 attack planes), both assigned to the Aleutians, and he would have had 300 planes. His assumption about the number of U.S. planes that might be encountered was indeed a serious miscalculation. Dividing his forces deprived him of valuable planes in an important air battle, and gave the U. S. Navy a sizable margin in carrier planes.

While the Midway attack was taking place, Admiral Nagumo ordered the heavy cruisers *Chikuma* and *Tone* to launch antisubmarine and search patrols, which they did between 0435 and 0500. Nagumo clearly did not expect to find an enemy task force, for his search patrols were merely pro forma exercises; although his two cruisers had a total of ten search planes, he committed only four to search missions and three to antisubmarine duty. In addition, his battleships each had three float planes, the light cruiser *Nagara* had a float plane, and the carriers had planes that could have been used on search missions.[4] All that can be said in Nagumo's defense is that he was told, when his force sortied from Hashirajima, that all the American carriers were in the South Pacific, and he had received no intelligence to the contrary. Nagumo also had more immediate problems, for he had started to be counterattacked from Midway before he had recovered his own planes, which were due back from their Midway strike at 0840.[5]

At 0553, when the U.S. forces on Midway received the first report of incoming Japanese planes, all planes that could fly were launched; some were to intercept Japanese planes, others to attack Japanese ships. A coordinated attack on Nagumo's carrier force had been planned. There were six Avengers (produced as a carrier-based torpedo plane but assigned in this instance to land-based duty), four B-26s (armed with torpedoes, to the amazement of their USAAF pilots), sixteen Marine Corps Dauntless dive bombers, and sixteen USAAF B-17s.

The attack on the carriers was anything but coordinated. The six Avengers, followed in line by the four B-26s, didn't wait to rendezvous with the others, but at 0715 made straight for the *Akagi*. The Japanese combat air patrol and antiaircraft guns shot down four of the Avengers; a fifth hit the deck of the *Akagi* and then rico-

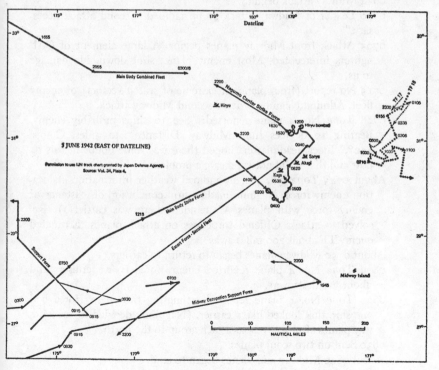

Battle of Midway, 5 June 1942

cheted into the sea. Only one, badly damaged, returned to Midway. The B-26s, hardly knowing the "drill", nevertheless attempted a torpedo attack. They didn't score either; two were shot down, and two returned to Midway, badly damaged. So far, the Japanese carriers had protected themselves.

From the Japanese side, the situation was recorded as follows:

0430 High-altitude attack units from Midway planes driven off by CAP and anti-submarine ships.

0500 Launched *Tone*'s No. 4 plane on search mission.

0520 Nagumo issued orders that, if conditions warranted it, a second Midway strike would be carried out. It was thought the planes (on the carriers) should begin changing (from torpedoes) to bombs.

0532 Enemy flying boats (PBYs) reconnoitering.

0555 *Tone*'s No. 1 plane message "See 15 enemy planes coming toward you." Admiral Nagumo decided they were coming from Midway.

0634 Midway attack begun.

0700 Leader of Midway attack group radioed "Second attack necessary."

0705 Attack from Midway planes begins. A large element of CAP fighters intercepted. Most enemy planes shot down. No damage to us.

0715 No report (from planes at extreme of search vectors) of enemy fleet. Admiral Nagumo ordered second Midway attack.

0728 *Tone* No. 4 plane reported: "See 10 ships probably enemy. Bearing 10 degrees from Midway. Distance 240 miles. Course 150°." Fleet headquarters hoped there was some doubt in this report and that it did not yet create a problem.

About 0745 *Tone* No. 4 plane radioed weather information at location enemy force. Nagumo made a firm conclusion of existence of enemy force with planes. Concluded there was carrier(s). Resolved to attack. Ordered torpedoes on attack planes. Estimated enemy TF about 200 miles away.

About 0750 Midway planes began to return to carriers.

0809 *Tone* No. 4 plane reported enemy force is five cruisers and about five destroyers.

0820 *Tone* No. 4 plane reported estimating the enemy force had one ship that looked like a carrier. (Nagumo) decided to use Midway planes after recovery as attack group to the north.

0830 Sent off two scout planes.

About 0840 Midway raid planes began to land.

0918 All landed.[6]

This was Admiral Nagumo's situation: his pilots had reported that a second strike on Midway was necessary. He had a second flight group ready on the flight decks of the *Akagi* and *Kaga*, armed with torpedoes and armor-piercing bombs for an attack on the U.S. naval force. But his air officer, Commander Minoru Genda, persuaded him that a second Midway attack was more urgent. Nagumo decided to lower his flight-deck planes to the hangar deck, and replace their torpedoes and armor-piercing bombs with fragmentation bombs, for use in a second Midway attack. At 0918 the surviving first-strike planes were to be rearmed with bombs and gun ammunition, and refueled for a second Midway strike. (The *Hiryu* and *Soryu* were not in this predicament, because their flight decks held properly armed dive bombers.) The *Akagi* and *Kaga* were highly vulnerable at this time; the presence of bombs, ammunition, and gasoline on their flight decks was an invitation to disaster. The hangar decks were also dangerous while the second attack force was being rearmed, for the crewmen, in their haste, were not taking the time to stow the torpedoes and bombs properly.

Then, when one of his observation planes sighted a U.S. naval force with at least one heavy carrier, Nagumo changed his mind and ordered that the hangar-deck planes, however they were armed, be raised to the flight deck, and that the flight-deck planes be put below. But since the carriers could not lower and raise planes at the same time, Nagumo needed time to make the switch. His ships were in proper formation and, in a few more minutes, his second strike force would be on its way to destroy the U.S. naval task force, whose exact location was now known. But the Americans did not give him those minutes. In this last hour, he had committed the most crucial miscalculation of the war.

During the night and early morning of 3–4 June, Task Forces 16 and 17 had been maneuvering into position for first discovery and battle, guided by their knowledge of the approximate position of the Japanese Carrier Strike Force. At 0430 the *Yorktown* launched ten dive bombers to search a 180-degree arc, northward to a distance of 100 miles. The Japanese Carrier Fleet, a little over 200 miles to the west, had just launched its raid on Midway. At 0534 the *Enterprise's* radio picked up a report that Japanese carriers had been sighted; then, at 0545, it picked up Midway's "enemy planes approaching" signal. At 0603 more information came in about the position of "two enemy carriers and battleships." Although the positions were not reported with great accuracy, the report gave both task forces a smaller area to search. Admiral Spruance, a cautious man, had thought that he should close to 100 miles before launching a strike, in order to diminish the risk of planes running out of fuel. But the planes actually had a range of about 200 miles, and after discussions with his senior officers, which overcame his concern about fuel, Spruance decided on a 200-mile flight. He had been listening to transmissions from Midway, and thought he might be able to catch Nagumo's carriers with their returning planes on them.

The U. S. Navy's ship formations in carrier battles were similar to those of the Japanese. The three American carriers did not fight as a group; even within Task Force 16, the two carriers separated, each with supporting ships in a ring screen defense. The Japanese also gave each of their carriers a separate ring screen defense; but in the first stage of the battle the four carriers were caught by surprise in a box formation.[7]

At 0702, Spruance ordered an all-out launch, and the full strike force was airborne by 0806. The force contained twenty Wildcat fighters, sixty-seven Dauntless dive bombers, and twenty-nine Devastator torpedo planes. (The Devastator was an exceptionally vulnerable plane; with a top speed of about 200 miles per hour, its run-in had to be low and straight, and to score a hit, it had to release its torpedoes very close to the target.) He also launched eighteen fighters as combat air patrol, and kept eighteen on deck to relieve them. Not

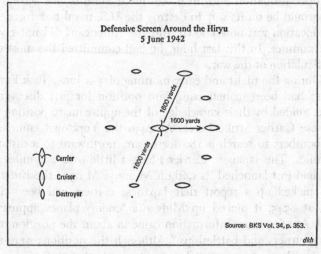

Line Drawing of the Defensive Screen Around the Hiryu

wanting to wait for all of Task Force 17's planes to be launched, Spruance abandoned his plans for a coordinated attack, and sent his dive bombers ahead at 0845.

In the meantime, the *Yorktown* launched seventeen Dauntless dive bombers, twelve Devastator torpedo planes, and six Wildcat fighters at 0838. Fletcher kept half his planes on the carrier as a precaution if reinforcements were needed. Fletcher delayed his launching and kept such a large reserve because he still could not be sure that there were only four carriers in the attacking force. He also sent up a combat air patrol of twelve Wildcats.

The *Hornet* had sent up thirty-five Dauntlesses and ten Wildcats, which were to keep contact with the fifteen torpedo planes. Because of poor visibility, however, the torpedo planes became separated from the others. Meanwhile, Nagumo, after recovering his planes, turned his force 90 degrees to the northeast. The *Hornet's* forty-five fighters and bombers could not find a Japanese carrier and were never in the battle. But her fifteen Devastator torpedo planes discovered the *Kaga*, and went ahead with their attack, without fighter support or dive-bomber diversion.

The Japanese combat air patrol fighters swarmed down on the Devastator column, flying single-file about fifty feet above the water, and at eight miles the Japanese antiaircraft guns began to find the mark. None of the planes succeeded in scoring a hit; all were shot down by the Japanese.[8] The BKS report was brief and understated: "0918 Enemy carrier planes begin torpedo attack. Defense fighter planes. Shot down a large portion of the torpedo planes."[9]

The *Enterprise's* torpedo squadron also became separated from its fighter escort, and in an attack on the *Kaga* about ten minutes after the *Hornet's* planes, they met the same fate. The Zeroes and antiaircraft fire were extremely effective; many attackers were shot down before they could release torpedoes, and no hits were scored by those who did. Ten of the fourteen planes were shot down.

The third group of torpedo planes, coming from the *Yorktown*, escorted by six fighters, made their attack at 1000 against the *Soryu*. Again they made no hits and only five planes got close enough to launch torpedoes. Their fighter protection was overwhelmed by Zeroes, and all but two of the attacking planes were shot down. Out of the forty-one Devastators that attacked, only six had survived; no hits were scored.

A curious entry is made in the BKS battle report for 1000: "The observation plane reported that the enemy in the vicinity (previously) reported by *Tone* No. 4 was not seen; this was not reported to the communications officer." This information would have been useful (particularly, as it turned out, to Captain Tomeo Kaku of the *Hiryu*), for in a carrier contest of hide-and-seek, locating and tracking the enemy is half the battle. The three U.S. carriers had gone south after launching.

In spite of their dismal failure, the torpedo-plane attacks set the stage for an effective follow-up strike. The Japanese carriers had maneuvered so extensively in defending against the torpedo-plane attacks that they had not been able to launch any of their own planes to augment their combat air patrol. Also, the attacks brought the Japanese combat air patrol down close to sea level, thus leaving the carriers unprotected against high-flying dive bombers. Antiaircraft gunners and observers were also unprepared for high-flying planes. During this half-hour, the carriers' box formation was disrupted, and the *Hiryu* became separated, to the north of the other three carriers.

The U.S. carrier-plane attack had so far been a complete failure. Formations that should have stayed together had become separated, while others could find neither a target to attack nor "friendlies" to protect. The Japanese carriers' position had been plotted, but their course was subsequently changed. Spruance had launched dive bombers from the *Enterprise* and *Hornet* at 0752, ahead of the torpedo planes, which were slower and more vulnerable, and for whom fighter protection was essential. The *Enterprise*'s bombers arrived at the estimated point of contact at 0930, but saw nothing. Moreover, they had become separated from their fighter escort, which had mistakenly identified the *Hornet*'s torpedo squadron as the *Enterprise*'s bombers. These fighters had spotted the Japanese carrier formation at 0910 but did not break radio silence. Tragically for the *Hornet*'s torpedo-plane pilots, the *Enterprise*'s fighters circled above the attack at 19,000 feet, awaiting an order from the *Enterprise* to enter the fray.

The *Enterprise*'s dive bombers searched to the southwest, then at 0935 turned to the north. At 0955, a chance event occurred which changed the course of the battle. The destroyer *Arashi* was spotted, steaming at flank speed to the northeast; the *Enterprise* bomber group immediately turned to follow her, correctly guessing that the lone destroyer was rejoining the Japanese carrier force.

Earlier that morning the U.S. submarine *Nautilus*, by following Midway planes' reports, had found herself in the middle of the Carrier Strike Force.[10] Undamaged by a Japanese depth-charge attack at

0900, she came to periscope depth at 0920. At 0925 she fired a torpedo at a battleship and missed, then dived and again survived a depth-charge attack. The destroyer *Arashi* was returning to the carrier force after depth-charging the *Nautilus* when the *Enterprise's* flyers saw her.[11]

Without this stroke of good fortune, the *Yorktown's* seventeen dive bombers would have had to attack the Carrier Strike Force without any help. The *Yorktown's* planes had launched at 0806, and Lieutenant Commander Maxwell F. Leslie, their group commander, correctly calculating where the enemy fleet would be, found it shortly after 1000. The battle plan called for the dive bombers to attack before the torpedo planes, but the *Yorktown's* torpedo planes had not waited to make a coordinated attack. Even as the *Yorktown's* torpedo planes were being slaughtered, her seventeen dive bombers struck, going after the *Soryu* from 14,500 feet. They faced almost no opposition, since the Japanese combat air patrol and the ships' guns in the carrier force were preoccupied with attacks by the low-flying torpedo planes.

The Soryu

The *Soryu*, like the other three carriers, was in a precarious situation. Unlaunched dive bombers were on the flight deck, and the rest of the carrier's planes (except for airborne fighters) were being refueled and rearmed on the hangar deck. Bombs and torpedoes had not been properly stowed, and gas lines were open. The carrier was especially vulnerable to a dive-bombing attack.

Although the ratio of hits against such little opposition was low —three 1,000-pound bombs out of thirteen—the bombs were well-placed. One bomb exploded just in front of the forward elevator, a second struck near the port side, forward of the center elevator, and the third hit near the port side of the after elevator. The first bomb penetrated to the hangar deck, and the resulting explosion flung the forward elevator back against the starboard island bridge. The second bomb hit the planes on deck, and the exploding gasoline, bombs, and torpedoes engulfed the flight deck in sheets of flame. The third bomb penetrated the flight deck and did similar damage aft. The attack lasted from 1025 to 1030, with no *Yorktown* planes destroyed. The *Soryu*, completely ablaze with ammunition exploding, lost rudder control and went dead in the water, shortly after 1040. The captain, seeing the fires were out of control, ordered his crew to abandon ship at 1045; nearby ships raced to the scene and began to pull the living from the sea. The heavy cruiser *Chikuma* sent a cutter at 1112 to aid in the rescue work. The rescued men were transferred to the destroyers *Hamakaze* and *Isokaze*.

Admiral Nagumo, who could not judge the situation on the *Soryu*, radioed an order at 1655 that the two rescue destroyers withdraw to the northwest to screen the carrier. The *Isokaze* replied: "*Soryu* cannot make way by herself," and questioning the special screening order, she added: "Cannot anticipate *Soryu* getting under way even if fires extinguished." The same reply was repeated by the *Isokaze* at 1802: "Do not estimate *Soryu* can get under way on own power. Surviving crew has abandoned ship." Soon after the bomb hits, the *Soryu*'s commanding officer Captain Yanagimoto suffered severe burns, and was forced to pass his command on to his subordinate officer. His staff repeatedly pleaded with him to seek safety by boarding another ship, but he adamantly refused. At about 1045, after ordering his men to abandon ship, he plunged back into the flames, seeking battle death (*senshi*).

About 1900 the *Soryu*'s fires became more violent. Admiral Nagumo, on board the light cruiser *Nagara*, organized a fire-fighting unit and began preparations to get it on the *Soryu*. But she began to sink at 1912, and went under three minutes later. She gave a final shudder, when, at 1920, a huge underwater explosion occurred in her grave. It was impossible to get exact casualty figures, for while the ship's complement was 1,103, there were many civilians, most of them newsmen, on board. An unofficial figure of 718 killed was calculated from those missing from the ship's roster.[12]

The Akagi

The thirty-seven bombers from the *Enterprise*, divided into two squadrons under the command of Lieutenant Commander Clarence McClusky, finally spotted three of the Japanese carriers shortly after 1000. The flight leader ordered one squadron to attack the *Akagi*, while his squadron attacked the *Kaga*. The *Akagi* had no more warning or protection than the *Soryu*. The Dauntlesses held their dives all the way down to about 1,600 feet before releasing, but only two of their bombs found the mark; one hit the edge of the midship elevator, while a second struck the port quarter. (It was recorded by surviving officers of the *Akagi* that "the enemy dive bombers attacked gallantly.")[13]

Instantly the *Akagi* was ripped by explosions and fire. The first bomb had penetrated the elevator shaft and detonated the improperly stowed torpedoes and bombs. This hit alone would have been fatal. The second bomb exploded among planes which were shifting their armaments from bombs to torpedoes. Again, flames from the exploding gasoline, bombs, and torpedoes swept across the flight deck. At 1029 Captain Taijiro Aoki ordered the flooding of torpedo and bomb magazines. The forward section was immediately flooded, but the magazines aft could not be flooded because the shafts that dogged the doors had been bent by the explosions. The fire in the after magazine, however, was put out, after the damage party spent two and one-half hours working their way through midship elevator debris on the deck. At 1032 Aoki ordered that the carbonic acid gas fire-extinguisher equipment be activated in the hangar deck, which he hoped was still sealed off; but this did not stop the fires. A minute later the *Akagi* had to turn to port to avoid a four-plane torpedo attack. Then at 1036, her after starboard engine went dead and her speed dropped to 12 knots. At 1040 a single U.S. torpedo plane was observed, and the *Akagi* turned, to meet it bow on. At that moment, her rudder jammed and all her engines stopped immediately. She was in a severe predicament, with her only operable armament being the No. 1 and No. 2 25-mm antiaircraft guns located on the very bow. The torpedo plane, however, did no damage; the main danger facing the *Akagi* was the rapidly spreading fire. The captain ordered full power on the water pumps, but because they had been damaged, they could not furnish an adequate stream.

At 1043 the fighter planes situated near the island bridge exploded, driving all personnel away from the bridge and communications room. Then the *Akagi*'s radio went silent. Admiral Nagumo, realizing the fires would not be extinguished and needing radio communication to direct the Carrier Strike Force, decided to shift his flag. He and his staff boarded the screening destroyer *Nowaki* at 1046, and eventually ended up in the light cruiser *Nagara*.

By 1100, Aoki had heard nothing from his engine room for an hour. He sent another "do-or-die" squad to try to repair the ship's rudder, but their repairs held up for only a short time. At 1120 the fire on the foredeck suddenly blazed up with tremendous force. Therefore, at 1130 the captain ordered that all survivors who were not actually in the damage-control crews be transferred to the destroyers *Nowaki* and *Arashi*. Five minutes later more torpedoes and bombs on the hangar deck began exploding, increasing the intensity of the fires, and driving the captain and his staff from the flight deck to the anchor deck, where they continued to exercise command.

No sooner were they on the anchor deck than the ship's engineer reported the complete destruction of both the operations room and engine room, along with the hangar deck and communications room. Aoki signalled "Trying to extinguish fires completely outside the flight deck." Apparently he still hoped to seal the hangar deck and use carbonic acid gas to put out the fire. But by 1300, Aoki had run out of ways to save his ship. At 1338 he ordered the Emperor's picture transferred; twelve minutes later, the *Akagi* went dead in the water and started drifting. About 1500 the fires on the deck again erupted violently, and the deck of the forward communications room was hit by explosions. By 1600 the crew and wounded had been evacuated to the destroyers.

Captain Aoki fought stubbornly to keep his ship alive. At 1820 he sent out a party to look at conditions in the engine room, but intense heat drove the group back. By 1915 the chief engineer was certain the ship could not move herself. The captain had already concluded the fire was out of control and, because the ship was dead in the water, at 1920 he signalled to Admiral Nagumo that he had transferred his crew. It was then decided to sink the *Akagi*, by destroyers' torpedoes. At 1925 the captain ordered all hands to abandon ship, and at 2000, the destroyers *Arashi* and *Nowaki* began taking the last survivors on board.

On the *Akagi's* anchor deck, a furious argument was taking place. Captain Aoki's staff was pleading with him to abandon ship; he answered that the *Akagi's* fate was also his own, because of their close bond. Reluctantly, the staff tied him to part of the anchor deck and left, with him smiling. But the carrier was slow in sinking. Flight officer Masuda and other staff members, disobeying orders, returned to the *Akagi* at 0030 and forcibly transferred Aoki to the *Arashi*.

On 5 June at 0450 the order came from Admiral Yamamoto: "From a distance between 1,000 meters to 1,500 meters fire from the four destroyers Mark 93 torpedoes (charge: 500 kilograms)." The *Akagi* sank at 0500. The official casualty total was 221 men killed, a remarkably small number, given all the fire and explosions on board her. (Her normal complement at this time was 1,630 men; of these, 63 were Nagumo's staff members.) The survivors were transferred to the battleship *Mutsu*.[14]

The Kaga

The attack on and sinking of the *Kaga* was quite similar to that of the *Akagi*. The *Kaga*, too, was evading what the First Air Fleet War Diary called a "scissors" torpedo-plane attack at 1022. Suddenly, nine dive bombers were observed coming out of the clouds. Because the *Kaga*, like the *Akagi*, had been concentrating her defenses against the torpedo planes, the lookouts were slow to spot the *Enterprise's* dive bombers. The *Kaga* turned sharply to starboard and sent up a strong barrage of antiaircraft fire, but she was hit by four bombs, the first striking the starboard quarter, the second and third bombs hitting in the vicinity of the forward elevator, and the last exploding in the center of the flight deck. The force of the second bomb blew out all the windows on the bridge. The forward part of the ship was enveloped in smoke from exploding munitions and the resulting fires. As the first bombs began to hit, the captain ordered emergency steering. It would be his last order. The third bomb hit directly in front of the island bridge, shattering the planes on the flight deck, destroying the flight deck itself, and killing most of those on the bridge, including the captain. The last bomb penetrated to the hangar deck and exploded in a fiery blast.

On the flight deck there were fighter planes which had completed rearming but had not yet been launched. Flight Officer Takahisa Amagai, who had been on the bridge, was not seriously wounded and at once took over command of the ship. Every effort was made to fight the fires, but they were too intense to extinguish, even with carbonic acid gas. Moreover, the fire-fighting water pumps had been destroyed. When Amagai decided that the fires could not be controlled, he ordered, at about 1325, the transfer of the Emperor's picture to the destroyer *Hagikaze*. He also decided to evacuate the ship and, accordingly, he sent an orderly to inform crew members in the engine room, since all phone contact had been lost. But the fires were so intense that the orderly could not deliver the message.

"Abandon Ship" was ordered at about 1700, and the destroyers *Hagikaze* and *Maikaze* began to take survivors on board.[15] At 1800 Yamamoto ordered Destroyer Division 4 (the destroyers *Arashi*, *Hagikaze*, *Nowaki*, and *Maikaze*): "Await orders and guard *Kaga*." Later it was told: "Your duty is to be the strike force for *Kaga* and *Soryu* in your charge." Finally, at 1925, the forward gasoline storage tank caught fire, two tremendous explosions occurred, and the *Kaga* sank. Her normal complement was 1,708 but it was, as usual, impossible to know precisely how many were on board. There were about 800 men killed, many of them from the engine-room gang.[16]

chapter 11

DEFEAT AT MIDWAY;
THE ALEUTIANS
MISADVENTURE

1942

3 June	Japanese carriers raid Dutch Harbor
4 June	The *Hiryu*'s planes severely damage the *Yorktown*, and in turn the *Hiryu* is mortally damaged
4 June	Admiral Yamamoto orders Admiral Kondo to bombard Midway
5 June	Japanese carriers raid Dutch Harbor
5 June	Japanese occupy Attu Island (AQ Operation)
5 June	The *Hiryu* sinks
5 June	Admiral Yamamoto orders general withdrawal
5 June	The heavy cruisers *Mikuma* and *Mogami* collide
5 June	U.S. carrier planes sink the *Mikuma*
7 June	Japanese occupy Kiska (AOB Operation)
7 June	Japanese submarine *I-168* sinks the crippled *Yorktown*

The Hiryu

In the confusion of the various land- and carrier-based air attacks on the Carrier Strike Force, the *Hiryu* and her defense ring of ships ended up some distance to the north of the three stricken carriers. Having escaped notice, the *Hiryu* was thus able to launch two attacks against the *Yorktown*, herself separated from Task Force 16. Both waves of the *Hiryu*'s planes had hit the *Yorktown* hard, but at the same time, many planes were lost; all that remained were five dive bombers, four torpedo planes, and six Zero fighters which were used as combat air patrol. The *Hiryu*'s Captain Kaku knew that more U.S. carriers were nearby, although he did not know how many. A third attack against them was planned, first for 1630, then postponed until 1800 while the crew ate their evening meal. That postponement proved to be fatal.

While the *Hiryu*'s pilots were in the midst of their meal, thirteen dive bombers, which had come in hidden by the sun, attacked the carrier, while eleven others attacked her escorting battleships and cruisers. The attack came as a complete surprise. The watch called out the warning and the *Hiryu* began to take evasive action. The first three bombs missed, but then the carrier was hit four times in rapid succession. The first hit blew the forward elevator up against the island bridge. All four bombs were closely spaced (two were amidships and two forward of the port island), completely ripping apart the flight deck. Fires from bomb hits broke out in several places, and bombs and torpedoes in the hangar deck began to explode, inflicting serious damage. Despite her damage the carrier was still able to maintain 30 knots.

All hands except for the gunners were trying to fight the fires, but their means were limited, because the fire-fighting equipment had been destroyed; men began rigging up buckets on lines to get water from the sea. The *Hiryu* was in the center of a formation ten miles in circumference, with four destroyers close beside her, pouring streams of water from their hoses onto her fires. She was still maintaining 28 knots, although the brave engine-room gang faced almost certain death.

Eventually the fires spread to the lower deck, and the engines went dead. No longer able to function in the heat and flames, the engineers made desperate attempts to escape—but their compartment's steel plates had become red-hot, and only a few made it out. The ship began flooding and soon developed a 15-degree list to port. At about 0158 another explosion ripped her, increasing the fires' intensity. It was then clear that the ship simply could not be saved. Captain Kaku, after receiving approval from Admiral Tamon Yamaguchi (commanding officer of Carrier Division 2, with his flag in the *Hiryu*), at 0230 ordered the crew to prepare to abandon ship. At 0250 the crew was assembled, and Kaku and Yamaguchi descended from the bridge. The Emperor's picture was given to a junior-grade lieutenant, charged with the duty of transferring it.

An intensely emotional scene followed on the deck. Kaku and Yamaguchi gave inspirational speeches to the crew, telling them that victory would come, and assuring them that they were not responsible for the loss of the ship. The two officers exchanged ceremonial cups of water; then the ensign was lowered and the men sang their national anthem, "Kimigayo." Finally, at 0315 the captain ordered the men to abandon ship. The first man off was the officer carrying the Emperor's picture; then the rest of the crew began transferring to the two rescuing destroyers, the *Kazagumo* and *Makigumo*. Captain Kaku and Admiral Yamaguchi remained on board and refused to allow their staff officers to stay with them. Tranquil in the face of disaster, they admired the beauty of the moon for a few moments—and then went to their cabins and committed *seppuku*.

As his last command, Admiral Yamaguchi ordered the *Makigumo* to torpedo the *Hiryu*. Two torpedoes were launched from the destroyer, but only one hit the mark. Nevertheless, it was judged that the torpedo damage would cause the carrier to sink, so the destroyers headed back to rejoin the light cruiser *Nagara* and Admiral Nagumo. But early the next morning, an observation plane from the light carrier *Hosho* reported that it had spotted the *Hiryu* still afloat with people on board, waving their caps at the plane. When Admiral Nagumo received this report, he sent the *Tanikaze* to the carrier's reported position to rescue survivors. However, the *Tanikaze* was attacked en route by enemy planes from Midway and was therefore late in arriving on the scene; meanwhile, the *Hiryu* had finally sunk during the forenoon watch. There were seventy men that the destroyers had left aboard the *Hiryu*; thirty-five of them survived by launching a cutter, and were later rescued by a U.S. destroyer on 19 June. Also, surviving Japanese airmen who had been aloft with no carriers to receive them had been forced to land in the ocean; twenty-seven of them were rescued by American ships and planes. In all, 416 men from the *Hiryu* were killed, most of them engine-room personnel.[1]

The Yorktown

At 1030 on 4 June, three of the four big Japanese carriers in the Carrier Strike Force were out of the battle; but to the north, the *Hiryu* as yet remained untouched. The Japanese observation planes had spotted the U.S. carriers, but were confused about their locations. Because Admiral Fletcher in the *Yorktown* was separated from the *Hornet* and *Enterprise*, the Japanese spotters reported anywhere from one to four enemy carriers (the "four" being a duplicated sighting of the same two carriers). Although the early loss of the three carriers had been a stunning blow, Japanese staff officers believed that enemy losses from the attacks on the Japanese carriers had also seriously depleted U.S. air strength. Admiral Nagumo felt the battle might still work out to a draw, if not a Japanese victory. Powerful help was on the way; Admiral Nobutake Kondo's Second Fleet was speeding toward the battle at 28 knots, and about 200 miles behind him came Admiral Yamamoto's Combined Fleet. Each force had one light carrier; also the light carriers *Ryujo* and *Junyo* had been recalled from the Aleutians. Admiral Yamamoto had not given up on an eventual occupation of Midway or on a decisive battle with what remained of the American forces. But his plans all depended on the *Hiryu*.

Admiral Hiroaki Abe, commander-in-chief of the Second Fleet, which guarded the Carrier Strike Force, was put in tactical command by Admiral Nagumo when Nagumo left the *Akagi*. At 1050, Abe signalled the *Yorktown*'s location to the *Hiryu* and ordered her to attack the *Yorktown* immediately with full force. Because of the number of enemy torpedo planes that had attacked, it was deduced that there must be two enemy carriers.

The *Hiryu* had used attack planes carrying bombs against Midway, so that her dive bombers were the only planes properly armed for a carrier strike. The remaining attack planes were being rearmed with torpedoes. At 1058, the *Hiryu* sent her ready planes in on the first strike, consisting of eighteen dive bombers, accompanied by six Zeroes. The strike group was given the *Yorktown*'s location by the heavy cruiser *Chikuma*'s No. 5 float plane and led to it by further radio reports. At the same time, the *Hiryu* was landing planes from the three stricken carriers, including Zeroes from the *Akagi*'s combat air patrol. Then at about noon, the *Hiryu* launched nine fighters as her cover, and prepared to launch her torpedo-armed second wave. Meanwhile, Nagumo brought his protecting warships back into formation to give the *Hiryu* maximum antiaircraft protection.

The *Yorktown* was also preparing herself for the expected counterattack. Radar picked up the *Hiryu*'s first wave, overestimated as thirty or forty planes, at a range of 40 miles. The *Yorktown* had twelve fighters aloft as combat air patrol. On deck, refueling, were twelve more fighters which had just been relieved, plus three fighters that had been involved in the strike on the Japanese carriers. Overhead waiting to land were the surviving *Yorktown* dive bombers that had sunk the *Soryu*. When the Japanese approached, the bombers were waved off, gas pumps were shut down, carbonic acid gas was readied, and a reinforced fighter patrol prepared to intercept, while the *Yorktown's* defensive screen of two cruisers and six destroyers also prepared for action. Shortly before noon the Japanese dive bombers began their attack. Three of their bombs hit the *Yorktown*: the first exploded on the flight deck, starting fires which spread to the decks below. The second bomb struck near the smoke funnel, and destroyed three of the boiler ventilators. Without operable uptakes, five out of the six boilers in the engine room lost their fire and the engines stopped. The *Yorktown's* speed dropped to six knots, and by 1220 she was dead in the water. A third bomb exploded deep in the ship, on the fourth deck, but prompt flooding and use of carbonic acid gas prevented the nearby gasoline and ammunition from exploding. But, because the second bomb had knocked out the island bridge's communication systems, radar, and plotting room, at 1315 Admiral Fletcher shifted his flag to the nearby heavy cruiser *Astoria*, and ordered the heavy cruiser *Portland* to take the *Yorktown* in tow. The *Yorktown's* boilers remained intact, ventilation was restored, and by 1340 four of her engines were functioning and she was moving at a speed of 20 knots. The deck crew began fueling more fighter planes, and it looked as if the *Yorktown* was back in business.

Meanwhile at 1331 the *Hiryu* launched her second wave: ten torpedo planes and six fighters. The small number of planes was largely because of losses suffered in the Midway attack. As before, the *Chikuma's* No. 5 plane led the *Hiryu's* planes to the *Yorktown*, and despite heavy antiaircraft and fighter resistance, they pressed home their attack. The defensive screens' radar had again picked up the oncoming raiders, and the *Yorktown* had twelve fighters ready to intercept the incoming enemy planes. Nevertheless, the determined Japanese pilots broke through, despite the loss of five of their ten attack planes and three of their six fighters. Two torpedoes hit the *Yorktown* on her port side at 1430, causing explosions and fires; the *Yorktown's* port-side fuel tanks were destroyed, her rudder jammed, her power connections were lost, and she began to list to port. Her predicament was especially critical because the emergency repair job performed on her at Pearl Harbor had not fully restored her watertight integrity. Fearing that she would soon capsize, Captain Elliott Buckmaster ordered the *Yorktown* abandoned at about 1500; 2,270 of her men survived and were picked up by destroyers.

Admiral Fletcher decided to abandon the *Yorktown* and join Admiral Spruance. Wanting to be in position for a battle on the next day and to avoid attack if an undiscovered fifth Japanese carrier appeared, Task Forces 16 and 17 retired eastward until midnight, and then reversed course to be in position to protect Midway from the northeast. The destroyer *Hughes*, detached to stand by the *Yorktown* during the night of 4–5 June, reported that the *Yorktown* probably could be saved, so the minesweeper *Vireo* was sent from French Frigate Reef to attempt a tow. Later the destroyer *Gwin* joined the *Vireo*. The *Yorktown*, although listing 25 degrees to port and down a bit by the head, was still afloat, so Fletcher and Buckmaster decided to try to salvage her. The destroyers *Hammann*, *Balch*, and *Benham* were sent with a salvage party to try to bring her to port. The *Hammann*, on the *Yorktown*'s starboard beam, put a salvage party on board, while a four-destroyer antisubmarine defense ring guarded her from a distance of 2,000 yards.

All this protection was to be in vain, however. A Japanese search plane had spotted the *Yorktown* at 0700 and reported her location and condition. Admiral Yamamoto sent submarine *I-168*, which had shelled Midway on 5 June, to the *Yorktown*'s location. The submarine evaded the destroyer screen and at 1330 fired four torpedoes: one missed, two went under the *Hammann* and hit the *Yorktown*, and the last hit the *Hammann* square amidships. The destroyer sank in three minutes, while the stubborn *Yorktown* finally sank on 7 June at 0600.[2]

End of the Battle of Midway

It is difficult to imagine the scene on board Yamamoto's flagship, the battleship *Yamato*. In only a few hours, four giant carriers that had ranged across the seas from Hawaii to the Indian Ocean without a battle scar were suddenly gone. Admiral Yamamoto appeared stunned when the loss of the *Akagi*, *Kaga*, and *Soryu* was reported to him. His hope was temporarily restored when he was told that the *Yorktown* had been sunk and that the *Hiryu* was still afloat and unharmed, fighting back. He had at first been surprised to find any U.S. carriers; then he had been led to believe there were only two, so that the *Hiryu* would face even odds. Moreover, his powerful Second Fleet and Main Body would soon be on the scene. Thus, in his view, all had not yet been lost.

At 1220 on 4 June he ordered the Aleutian Second Mobile Force and Kondo's Second Fleet to meet his Main Body, northwest of Midway, on 5 June at 1200, and ordered the group carrying the Midway occupation troops to retire temporarily to the northwest. As the day progressed, however, his information became more accurate and his perception of the situation more grim. He now knew there had originally been three large U.S. carriers, and shortly after 1700 he also knew that his large carriers were no longer operative. Nevertheless, he gave up slowly. At 1915 he signalled to his officers that the enemy was fleeing to the east and that he should be pursued and destroyed; all the Midway units, together with the Combined Fleet, would execute a surprise attack on Midway and occupy it, after which all ships would rendezvous at 0300 on 5 June.[3] Admiral Nagumo, reporting back at 2130 that he had transferred to the *Nagara*, was guarding the defenseless *Hiryu* against nearby enemy ships which he believed to include at least two carriers. He added that if the U.S. carriers made a new attack his force could not oppose it, and that he would be unable to cooperate with the Main Body in a night battle. He then continued on a northwesterly course while protecting the *Hiryu*. Upon receiving this signal, Admiral Yamamoto, considering Admiral Nagumo too conservative, replaced him with Admiral Kondo at 0055.[4] Kondo was still under orders to bombard Midway that night.

Kondo had already started a dash for Midway before he received orders to bombard the island. He used his eight heavy cruisers, one light cruiser, and ten destroyers in a battle line with four miles between ships, on a northeasterly course, to attack Midway and to seek out the American force. The light cruiser *Jintsu* and ten destroyers were not far behind Kondo's force, and Nagumo's two battleships, two heavy cruisers, and twelve destroyers were only 125 miles away from Kondo.[5] Behind these forces came two fast battleships, the *Hiei* and *Kongo*. Kondo detached Cruiser Division 7 (the *Suzuya*, *Kumano*, *Mogami*, and *Mikuma*) under Admiral Takeo Kurita, to shell Midway at 0200. But Admiral Yamamoto's forces were too far behind the Carrier Strike Force, and Kondo signalled that he could not start the bombardment until 0300. Then, after only an hour, his force would be open to daylight air attack by the American carriers that Admiral Yamamoto had every reason to believe were in the vicinity. Kondo's own Main Body, rushing to back up his advanced Cruiser Division 7, would also be exposed to air attack. With only two light carriers, carrying thirty-one planes, the Japanese would not have their decisive battle, fought at night, but instead would face a daylight encounter, chiefly between American carrier planes and Japanese surface ships. Reluctantly, Yamamoto ordered a general withdrawal at 0255 on 5 June. The various units were to rendezvous at a point northwest of Midway. Kondo's force, except for Cruiser Division 7, joined the Main Body at 0815, and Nagumo's forces at 1300.[6] MI Operation had been cancelled, and would never be resurrected.

On the American side, Admiral Spruance had played it cautiously during the night. His plane supply was depleted, and he had no desire to engage Task Forces 16 and 17, with their vastly inferior surface-ship protection, against a Japanese armada, even if the Japanese had lost their four carriers. His carriers would be useless in a night battle, for his pilots had not yet perfected night carrier landings. Furthermore, he still was not certain that there were no more Japanese carriers in the area. So he withdrew to the east early in the night, in order to avoid being trapped by Yamamoto's considerable force. At midnight he reversed course, to be in position to protect Midway from the northeast if a battle should erupt the next day.

At the time of Yamamoto's general withdrawal order, the Japanese Cruiser Division 7, with the destroyers Asashio and Arashio, was only 80 miles from Midway.[7] But trouble lay ahead, for there were three U.S. submarines still on station west of Midway. The U.S. submarine Tambor had seen Kurita's force headed toward Midway. When Kurita turned back, a U.S. submarine was sighted at 0118 and a signal "red-red" ("emergency 45-degree port turn") was flashed. At that time the cruisers were in single column—the Kumano, the Suzuya, the Mikuma, and the Mogami. The Mogami's navigator, thinking she was too far from the Mikuma, shifted her several degrees to starboard to close the gap. But it was not the Mikuma he had seen—it was the Suzuya. Consequently, he rammed the Mikuma on her port quarter. At first it looked as if the Mogami had suffered the most damage, for her bow, back to turret No. 1, was bent almost at right angles to port, and fires were breaking out all over her, while the Mikuma had only suffered ruptured oil tanks on her port side, amidships. Admiral Kurita left the two destoyers and the Mikuma behind to guard the crippled Mogami and continued at full speed to the ordered rendezvous. The Mogami's speed was reduced to 12 knots; but, more seriously, the Mikuma was leaving a tell-tale trail of oil.[8]

Back at Midway, at dawn all available PBYs were sent on a search mission, out to a distance of 250 miles, followed by twelve USAAF B-17s. Midway had been shelled by the submarine I-168 for several hours, and the U.S. submarine Tambor had, at 0300, reported Japanese heavy cruisers sailing east toward Midway; thus, Midway was preparing itself for any eventuality. At 0630 a PBY signalled that two battleships leaking oil were proceeding east, 125 miles from Midway. The B-17s were ordered to attack them at once, but they could not find their intended victims. Second Marine Air Wing Command at Midway at once sent off the remaining Marine planes: six Dauntlesses and six Vindicators. At 0745 they spotted the oil slick, which led them directly to the damaged Japanese ships. The attack began at 0805, with the Dauntlesses dive-bombing and the Vindicators glide-bombing. Defensive antiaircraft fire was heavy and accurate. The planes managed only six near-misses, but one Vindicator, already badly damaged, crashed into the after turret of the *Mikuma*. Fire spread over the deck and was sucked into the starboard engine-room ventilator, killing the engine-room crew. Now the *Mikuma* had to slow to the *Mogami*'s speed. No casualties were reported from the *Mogami* or the *Arashio* and *Asashio*. At 0828 eight of the B-17s found the group, but did not hit any of them.

Admiral Spruance was still guided by caution, for earlier reports that Admiral Kurita's cruiser force was steaming east, 90 miles from Midway, indicated that the battle might be resumed. Incomplete PBY reports regarding the burning *Hiryu* made him believe that the Japanese might still have two heavy carriers, albeit damaged ones, in the area. At the time of the American pilots' last look at the *Hiryu* on 4 June, the U.S. planes had been attacked by Zeroes. These were in fact the *Hiryu*'s homeless combat air patrol, but Admiral Spruance could not be sure that they were not from another carrier. At 0600 on 5 June he had placed his force 130 miles to the northeast of Midway; then three hours later he changed course to the west and began to ponder his possible targets. If any Japanese carriers were still afloat, they were his first priority. He launched twenty-six dive bombers from the *Hornet* and thirty-two from the *Enterprise* at 1543; they searched on a 30-mile arc to the northwest, but found nothing. On the return flight, however, they spotted the destroyer *Tanikaze*, which had been sent to see if the *Hiryu* was still afloat; she was then returning to the Carrier Strike Force. The *Tanikaze* was having a tough day—she had already undergone two separate B-17 attacks, and now she was being assaulted by fifty-six dive bombers. Nevertheless, by skillful evasion tactics, she again avoided injury and even succeeded in downing a dive bomber by antiaircraft fire.[9]

Admiral Spruance finally gave up hope of finding and attacking Yamamoto's main forces, but the two crippled cruisers could be his almost for the asking. At 2040 he took a westerly course, to be in position to attack them on the morning of 6 June. At 0800, twenty-six dive bombers and eight fighters took to the air from the *Hornet*. At 1045, thirty-one dive bombers, three torpedo planes, and twelve fighters followed from the *Enterprise*. Then at 1330 the *Hornet* launched a third attack of twenty-four bombers and eight fighters.

The *Mogami* was hit twice in the first attack at 0945; one hit on the No. 5 turret killed all the men manning it. In the second attack at 1230 she was hit twice more and burst into flames. The third attack at 1445 killed all ninety crewmen in one engine room. Nevertheless, despite all this damage, she made it to Truk on 14 June, although she remained in a Japanese shipyard until 10 July 1943.[10]

Although she was of the same class, the *Mikuma* did not survive the successive attacks. She was mauled so badly by the first two attacks that the captain ordered the crew to abandon ship. The *Arashio* could not come too close to her because of the heat, so her crewmen jumped into the water to be picked up by the destroyer. The third attack at 1445 set off the *Mikuma*'s torpedoes.[11] Immediately thereafter the two destroyers abandoned the *Mikuma* and she sank during the night. The following day the *Arashio* was ordered back to see if the *Mikuma* was still afloat, but large patches of oil and debris were all that was there, although one more man was rescued. The *Mikuma*'s complement was 888, of whom about 240 were saved.[12] The *Mogami*'s casualty list is not known precisely, but there were at least 300 crewmen killed.

Even though almost every Japanese ship outside the Main Body underwent air attack at one time or another from 4 June to 7 June, no other serious hits or casualties were inflicted. The battleship *Haruna* was dive-bombed on 6 June at 1700, but suffered no casualties.[13]

The Battle of Midway was over. Colonel Ikki's Special Naval Landing Force troops, which were to occupy Midway, were sent back to Saipan while two heavy cruisers (the *Haguro*, and the *Myoko*), three destroyers (the *Asagumo*, *Minegumo*, and *Natsugumo*), and the seaplane tender *Chitose* were sent to Wake to make decoying radio traffic. The plan was to entice Spruance and his carriers to come to Wake, where they could be attacked by the *Chitose*'s planes and by Wake's land-based planes.[14] In the meantime, the Combined Fleet returned to Empire waters. The Japanese public was not told about the loss of the four carriers; crewmen were denied shore leave, and newsmen were kept on board for some time, in order to keep secret the extent of the catastrophe. Only gradually did the Japanese public become aware of the loss of this decisive battle. The Japanese losses were great: about 2,200 crewmen lost their lives, as did most of the crack pilots of the 234 planes lost (and Japan was producing few well-trained replacements), and four heavy carriers and a heavy cruiser were sunk.

Midway *was* indeed the "decisive" battle of the war in the Pacific. If it had been won by the Japanese, it is unlikely that it alone would have brought about the defeat of America, but it surely would have prolonged the war. However, Japan's loss of the decisive battle doomed the Japanese Navy and insured the ultimate defeat of Japan, for she could never match the industrial capability of the United States in the production of weapons and hardware. Even with the resources of the South Seas, her supply lines would later become vulnerable to air and submarine interdiction.

Why did Admiral Yamamoto lose at Midway? A commander and his staff should make their estimate of a situation using all available information, and if that information is inadequate or its accuracy is questionable, they should assume the worst. Yamamoto, however, assumed a favorable situation and made his battle plans accordingly. His basic mistake was an unfounded assumption that there were no U.S. carriers in the vicinity of Midway, because his pilots in the Battle of the Coral Sea had reported that both the *Lexington* and *Yorktown* had been sunk. A commander cannot act on such information—he must have proof, and there was no hard proof that the *Yorktown* had been sunk. Yamamoto also assumed that the *Hornet* and *Enterprise* were still in the Southwest Pacific. It does not excuse him that he did not know his JN-25 code had been broken, which was why the U.S. carriers raced back to Pearl Harbor. He should have assumed, for whatever reason, that the carriers were back in Pearl Harbor and could be sent to the Midway area before 4 June. It is true that he tried to discover what was happening at Pearl Harbor before invading Midway, but K Operation failed and was finally called off on 30 May, leaving him without any reliable information about the ships at Pearl Harbor. His failure to dispatch his *I*-class submarines sooner to form a picket line was inexcusable, but their failure to report any task forces in the Midway area only confirmed his basic belief that there would not or could not be such a force. Therefore his estimate of the situation presumed the best possible conditions and was not verified by factual data.

From his assumptions came the fatal disposition of his numerous forces. Nagumo's forces would destroy Midway's defenses, and then take care of any U.S. ships in the vicinity. If more help was needed to invade Midway, Kondo's powerful group could bombard the island and cover an invasion by Colonel Ikki's 5,000 crack SNLF troops. Yamamoto was certain that eventually (and probably quickly) the U. S. Pacific Fleet would attempt a counterattack. His Combined Fleet would now have spanned the 500 miles between Nagumo's Carrier Strike Force and Kondo's strong Strike Force. The entire Japanese naval force would be concentrated, and, hopefully in a night ship-to-ship battle, it could easily destroy what the U. S. Navy could send.

Admiral Nagumo fought in strict accordance with Yamamoto's estimate of the situation. It can be inferred from the battle data that he simply did not expect any enemy carriers to be as nearby as Pearl Harbor. One curious point here is that the Japanese documents state that Nagumo could not be informed that K Operation had been cancelled on 30 May because of the weakness of his radio receivers—yet during the battle he was in radio communication with Yamamoto. Perhaps no one thought it necessary to inform Nagumo that there was no longer a K Operation. At any rate, Nagumo's assumption that K Operation was still going on reinforced his belief there would be no U.S. carriers in the vicinity.

Nagumo's air reconnaissance was grossly inadequate; he had sent out only four cruiser catapult planes on search patterns. Before making his aerial attack on Midway he could have waited to make a thorough search and then have attacked Midway, if nothing was found. As it was, Midway's planes did no damage to his Carrier Strike Force. The confusion involved in changing the armament of his planes after the *Tone*'s No. 4 plane sighted an enemy carrier was also the fault of his inefficient communications system.

The failure to concentrate all of the Japanese carriers, including the light carriers *Ryujo* and *Junyo*, was a mistake. Yamamoto could have concentrated his heavy carriers in one place, his light carriers in another; or he could have scattered his light carriers, leaving them to do the air reconnaissance. Midway was such a close battle that the presence of four, or even of only two light carriers could have reversed the battle. One can't help but wonder why Yamamoto felt that he needed the light carrier *Hosho* with his Combined Fleet, when it was out of range of any American aircraft (except possibly B-17s which were not greatly feared). Likewise, given the 200-mile distance between Nagumo and Kondo, why did Kondo need the light carrier *Zuiho*?

Ironically enough, Yamamoto, the originator of carrier raids, still showed signs of being overly battleship-conscious. He seemed to believe that, regardless of what Nagumo did, Midway would be occupied and an eventual night battle would bring victory to the Japanese.

But there are things to be said for Yamamoto. He showed courage and command responsibility by abandoning the operation when he did, for if he had persisted, he would have met two U.S. carriers in the daylight, with inadequate carrier protection for his ships. The result could have been an even greater catastrophe. One suspects that, when the news of the loss of the *Hiryu* became certain, Yamamoto knew that the war was lost. Yet as a faithful servant of the Emperor, he set himself the task of doing the best he could with what remained. Thus, the Combined Fleet went home, and was reorganized between 10 and 14 July to make new plans and to meet new exigencies. Perhaps the brilliant Japanese political scientist Masao Maruyama is correct when he explains, in his investigation of the Japanese subconscious sense of history, "Ikioi," that the expression "Ko narimashita"—"It happened this way"—is acceptable to the Japanese while "Ko shimashita"—"I (or some man or men) made it happen this way"—is not, for it offends the Japanese sense of logic. Thus, history had destined what had occurred, and Admiral Yamamoto would still be commander-in-chief of the Combined Fleet with all its responsibilities.[15]

Aleutians Misadventure (AL Operation)

The AL Operation was primarily a diversionary action which, even if it did not succeed in drawing any major units of the U. S. Navy northward, would still cause an element of uncertainty and consternation. The operation was commanded by Vice Admiral Boshiro Hosogaya, who kept his heavy cruiser the *Nachi* and two destroyers as a support force, near Paramushiro on the northernmost island of the Kurile chain. Rear Admiral Kakuji Kakuta was commander-in-chief of the Fifth Fleet, Northern Force, Second Strike Force, consisting of the two light carriers *Ryujo* and *Junyo*, two heavy cruisers and three destroyers. Kakuta sailed from Ominato, at the northern tip of the main island of Honshu, during the afternoon watch of 28 May, planning a 3 June air strike on Dutch Harbor in the Aleutians. Also in motion were the invasion forces for the occupation of Attu (AQ Operation) and Kiska (AOB Operation).

The Dutch Harbor raiders began their run in without detection on 2 June.[16] Dutch Harbor was in the early stages of naval and mili-

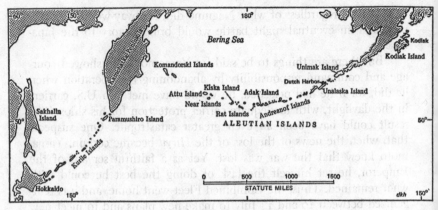

The North Pacific

tary development—it had a USAAF airfield, an oil-tank farm, holding about 25,000 barrels, and a radio station. There was also Fort Mears—an army barracks, and a beached barracks ship (the *Northwestern*), a hospital, and a PBY base, with the seaplane tender *Gillis*. On 3 June, the harbor held the destroyer *Talbot*, the submarine S-27, a Coast Guard cutter, and two army transports. At sea guarding the Aleutian chain was Admiral Theobald's Task Force 8, with his flag in the heavy cruiser *Nashville*. He had two heavy cruisers, three light cruisers, and four destroyers; on 5 June, they were 500 miles south-southeast of the Japanese Northern Area Force.

At 0300 on 3 June, Admiral Kakuta's force was about 180 miles southwest of Dutch Harbor, making its way in the usual dense fog and nasty weather. From that point the *Ryujo* launched fourteen attack planes covered by three fighters, and the *Junyo* fifteen bombers with thirteen fighters. Because of poor visibility, the *Junyo*'s planes could not find the target, so they returned to the carrier. Of the *Ryujo*'s planes, nine attack planes with her three fighter planes suddenly saw the Dutch Harbor installations below them at 0808. The seaplane tender *Gillis* had detected their approach by radar, and "General Quarters" had been sounded, but none of the ships had been able to clear the harbor by the time of the attack. Antiaircraft fire was powerful, and the raiders also met a few P-40 fighters. They reported back to Admiral Kakuta that they had seen two submarines and five destroyers at Makushin Bay. By 0830 the raid was over, leaving the tank farm ablaze, the hospital and Fort Mears bombed, and several PBYs destroyed in the harbor. One Japanese bomber was brought down by antiaircraft fire.

Admiral Kakuta immediately launched a strike against the five destoyers at Makushin Bay. This strike, at 0945, consisted of fourteen attack planes, fifteen bombers, and twelve fighters, with four observation planes added. The ever-changeable Aleutian weather hid Makushin Bay from the raid, so that the planes returned to the carriers at 1050, having seen nothing. They did, however, run into some more P-40s, and one Zero was shot down. After recovering the planes at 1200, the Japanese naval force turned to the southwest.

Yamamoto then ordered Kakuta to make a preinvasion bombardment of Adak, but the weather was so foul that Admiral Kakuta elected to make a second strike on Dutch Harbor. (The Adak invasion was later cancelled.) Again he was able to launch in the fog, escaping detection. At 1604 on 5 June he sent off nine attack planes, eleven bombers, and eleven fighters. Once more fair weather exposed Dutch Harbor to attack. The destruction of the oil farm was completed, the hospital was again hit, and the beached *Northwestern* suffered severe damage. The two raids on Dutch Harbor killed thirty-two Americans. While the raid was going on, Kakuta's carrier force was spotted and underwent attack by B-17s and B-26s, which managed only a few near-misses which did no damage, and lost two planes in the process. The raiding Japanese planes then returned to the two carriers, having lost one fighter.

Just as his planes were landing, Kakuta received a signal from Yamamoto, who was then in trouble at Midway, that AL Operation was "temporarily postponed." The force stood by, 600 miles southsouthwest of Kiska, until returning to Empire waters on 24 June. Attu and Kiska were occupied, without resistance, on 5 June and 7 June, respectively. Admiral Theobald and Task Force 8 never succeeded in coming into contact with the Japanese during the AL Operation. For both sides the Aleutians campaign was an exercise in futility. It did not distract Admiral Nimitz from Midway, and the occupation of Attu and Kiska gained Japan nothing and eventually caused the loss of valuable ships and men.

section 4

OVEREXTENSION OF THE DEFENSE PERIMETER

chapter 12

PAPUAN PENINSULA AND GUADALCANAL

1942

Mid-June	Japanese begin construction of airfield on Guadalcanal
4 July	Allied plane discovers construction of Guadalcanal airfield
21 July	Japanese occupy Buna
29 July	Japanese capture Kokoda
7 August	First U. S. Marine Division invades Guadalcanal and Tulagi
9 August	U. S. Marines eliminate Japanese troops at Tulagi
24 August	Unsuccessful Japanese invasion of Rabi Island in the Louisiades, Milne Bay (RE Operation)
6 September	RE Operation cancelled
18 September	Japanese Army shifts focus from Papuan Peninsula to Guadalcanal
12 December	Last Japanese convoy to Buna

1943

3 January	Elimination of Japanese Army forces at Buna, Gona

The shocking Japanese defeat at Midway and the loss of four precious first-line carriers stunned the naval section of Imperial Headquarters. For a few weeks there was even apprehension in the naval command that there might be an immediate American counterattack in home waters. Thus, during July the Imperial Japanese Navy concerned itself with defense. The Japanese "Victory Fever" had broken—into the sweat of sudden despair. Defeated in its "decisive battle," the Japanese Navy had to make readjustments; it was not yet prepared to say that the war was lost. The fleets were rearranged to support ongoing operations, and new plans for a successful "decisive battle" began to be researched.

Wars have a momentum of their own, however. Attu and Kiska had to be kept in supplies and guarded, even at the cost of increasing the number of Japanese ships to do so. Cleanup operations in the Philippines had to be continued. Lae and Salamaua had to be supplied. Both the Army and the Navy recognized the threat that the growing forces of General MacArthur in Australia posed, but they disagreed on the methods of thwarting him. The Navy wanted to interdict his line of supply by capturing Samoa and the Fijis (FS Operation). To do that, they planned first to occupy Nauru and Ocean islands. (They were finally taken on 25–26 August 1942, but never served as a springboard for FS Operation.)

There was latent hostility between the Navy and Army, and the Army, the more powerful section at Imperial General Headquarters, continued to plan its campaigns as if the prewar Navy was still intact, taking it for granted that there would be ships to provide sufficient transport escort, supply, and invasion cover. In fact, even after Midway the Army continued planning as if the losses at Midway were of little consequence, an attitude that hastened the Navy's final defeats. The Army's strategy to counter General MacArthur was to extend the Japanese defense perimeter to include even north Australia. Thus, Port Moresby was still an urgent objective, and to establish protection from the east for MO Operation, the Army mounted, as one operation, the invasion of the Papuan Peninsula and Guadalcanal.

It had been standard Japanese military doctrine to make advances only under air cover. But they would have to go beyond the range of air cover to make a direct assault on Port Moresby. Therefore, they would first occupy islands in Milne Bay, on the Papuan Peninsula at the southern end of New Guinea, which would furnish airfields from which planes could cover the Port Moresby operation. In like fashion, Tulagi and nearby Guadalcanal could furnish airfields on the eastern flank. In planning this extension of the defense perimeter, Imperial General Headquarters made a fatal and illogical error. Both the Milne Bay and the Guadalcanal operations were beyond the range of adequate air cover, and the naval forces used to support these campaigns were extremely vulnerable, since Midway had decimated Japanese carrier-based air power.

Even before the Army had precipitated the battle of Guadalcanal by beginning the construction of an airfield there, it began plans and preparations that by the last of August would become a major interlocking operation in both Guadalcanal and the Papuan Peninsula. Lae and Salamaua could not furnish the necessary means of moving against Port Moresby. The Army, therefore, came up with a new operation (code-named "RI"), to occupy Buna (and nearby Gona), at the east trailhead of the Kokoda path, which would lead them directly into Port Moresby, over the 7,000-foot-high Owen Stanley Mountains. To that end, on 21 July, 2,000 troops were landed west of Buna, and by 29 July, they had captured Kokoda. The convoy to Buna had consisted of two high-speed transports, the light cruiser *Tatsuta*, the minelayer *Tsugaru* and the destroyers *Asanagi*, *Yuzuki*, and *Uzuki*. By 21 August the Army had landed 13,500 troops for the overland assault on Port Moresby.

The Army found its task a bit more than it had anticipated. Because of the bad weather Lae and Salamaua airfields could not provide adequate air cover; meanwhile, the Japanese soldiers and their line of supply were subjected to frequent air raids from Australia, Milne Bay, and Port Moresby. Moreover, the operation was being attempted under the worst possible conditions. Heat, humidity, torren-

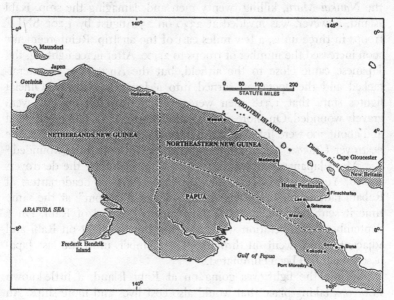

New Guinea

tial rains, mud, dysentery, and tropical disease combined to decimate the ranks of the invaders, while those still alive were weakened by malnutrition and illness. General MacArthur had responded to the danger in the Papuan region at once, and by mid-September Port Moresby had been heavily reinforced by two brigades, while Australian troops were contesting every mile of the Kokoda trail. In mid-August an Australian brigade was sent to Milne Bay to protect the airfields there.[1]

The Japanese Navy, in support of the Army, was forced to overextend its forces. While the battle of the Eastern Solomons was fought on 24 and 25 August, in an effort to land reinforcements on Guadalcanal, an invasion force (code-named RE Operation) was being put ashore at Rabi Island in the Louisiades in Milne Bay, at the very southern end of New Guinea. (Samarai Island was also earmarked for later invasion.) The Army desperately wanted air cover for RI Operation and for bombing Port Moresby and the north Australian airfields. Japanese ships assigned originally to the Milne Bay attack were the light cruisers *Tenryu* and *Tatsuta*, and the destroyers *Yuzuki, Oite, Urakaze, Hamakaze,* and *Tanikaze*.

RE Operation was a disaster.[2] On the approach, about 50 miles northeast of Rabi Island, ten bombers from Port Moresby attacked the *Nankai Maru*, killing twenty men and damaging the ship. Rabi Island, however, was invaded at 2330 on 25 August by 1,202 SNLF troops in three units, a few miles east of the airstrip. Reinforcements soon increased the number of troops to 2,400. After fierce fighting, the Japanese came close to the airfield, but the Australians counterattacked and the operation turned into a Japanese debacle. Official figures state that 1,318 men were evacuated, of whom 312 were gravely wounded. On shore, it was estimated that 311 had been killed and about 700 were listed as missing. In support of the operation, the destroyer *Urakaze* suffered one crewman killed and three wounded.[3]

More Japanese ships were sent to help, including the destroyers *Arashi, Yayoi,* and *Isokaze*. The Outer South Seas headquarters at Rabaul radioed on 5 September, "Try to get them out"; at the same time it sent reinforcements to Guadalcanal instead of Rabi. On 6 September RE Operation was called off, but the fight on Rabi and adjacent islands went on throughout September, until the last Japanese soldier had been eliminated.

While the fight was going on at Rabi Island, a little-known story was taking place that would also cost lives and more ships. An SNLF unit of 353 men (the Tsukioka Unit) was ordered to explore the islands at the southern tip of Papua, looking for good locations for communications and meteorological stations. It had left Rabi Island in seven small ships on 24 August, and had landed in the Goodenough Island group at Taupota Island on 25 August. After the battle for Rabi Island was lost, there was no necessity for the Tsukioka Unit to remain where it was. Besides, it was running into its own difficulties, for it had been spotted by an Australian plane after leaving Taupota, and on 25 August it was attacked at Goodenough Island by ten fighter planes from Port Moresby, and lost its outside communication.

Finally on 10 September the destroyers *Isokaze* and *Yayoi* were sent out from Rabaul on a search-and-rescue mission. On the next day at 1300, east of Normanby Island, the destroyers were attacked by a group of USAAF B-17s and B-25s. This unit, based in Australia, was General MacArthur's air force, under Major General G. C. Kenney. The *Yayoi* was hit aft and her steering machinery was destroyed. She underwent continuous air attack thereafter, and finally sank at 1715 on 11 September. The *Isokaze*, too, had been attacked and jarred by near-misses. On hearing the *Yayoi*'s message that she was sinking, the *Isokaze* went at full speed to the radioed location, but all that could be seen there was oil and debris—no survivors in the water. But not all hands had gone down on the *Yayoi*; some had made it to Normanby Island. The *Yayoi*'s survivors were later discovered by enemy aerial observation. Finally, after several unsuccessful attempts at rescue, on 25 September the destroyers *Isokaze* and *Mochizuki* left Rabaul, made a landing on the north coast of Normanby Island, and took off eighty-three of the *Yayoi*'s crew.

The Tsukioka Unit had an even more difficult time. After 2 September it sent parties by two canoes to try to reach Buna, in order to give the unit's location on the east side of Goodenough Island. One canoe arrived, and thereafter the unit was supplied by air drop; then, however, the Australians landed 800 troops to clean it out, and fierce fighting erupted. On 1 October, the submarine *I-1* left Rabaul and on 3 October rescued seventy-one of the men in the unit and brought home the ashes of thirteen who had been killed in battle. She was then sent out again, but after she was subjected to bombing, it was realized that submarine rescue was impractical, so the light cruiser *Tenryu* was pulled off Guadalcanal duty to make the next try. She left Rabaul on 22 October, arriving at what was understood to be the rendezvous point, only to be met by the small-arms fire of 200 Australians ashore. Not being able to locate the

Tsukioka Unit, the *Tenryu* returned to Rabaul. When the Tsukioka Unit's new location became known, the *Tenryu* made a final effort on 26 October. Traveling at top speed, she arrived at Uere Island and took off the last of the men. In all, 261 of the 353 men in the unit were saved.[4]

On the Kokoda trail, the Japanese Army could only advance to within 32 miles of Port Moresby. On 28 September the 25th Australian Brigade attacked what it thought were the Japanese Army's front-line positions, but found them to be deserted—the Army had retreated and set up defensive positions at Buna and Gona, guarded by a final defense line at the Kumusi River.

The dwindling garrison there was doomed when the Army decided, on 18 September, to give priority to the Guadalcanal campaign. This did not mean that Buna and Gona were immediately and totally abandoned; but the convoys to bring in new troops met with such furious air attack, causing damage to destroyers and transports, and further loss of men and materiel, that the Eighteenth Army finally was forced to abandon Buna's and Gona's defense to the men already there.

A later attempt was made on 17 November to send in two convoy groups. The first group, carrying 1,000 troops, was escorted by the destroyers *Kazagumo*, *Makigumo*, *Yugumo*, *Oyashio*, and *Kagero*. It arrived at Buna without incident and unloaded its cargo of men and materiel. The second convoy, carrying 500 men and escorted by the destroyers *Oyashio*, *Umikaze*, and *Kawakaze*, left Rabaul the next day at 0200 and arrived at Buna at 1700. Unloading was completed by 1945. It was a bright moonlit night, however, and the ships came under heavy air attack, with the *Umikaze* and *Kawakaze* both suffering damage.[5]

As the Japanese Army retreated down the Kokoda trail onto its bases at Buna and Gona, the Kumusi River became the vital last line of defense. As the Kumusi River battle at Buna increased in intensity, more Japanese troops and guns were brought in, as well as artillerymen and airfield construction men. It was decided to land the main body of the 21st Brigade at Buna. Troops were loaded in the destroyer *Shiratsuyu*, while the destroyers *Makigumo*, *Yugumo*, and *Kazagumo* served as escort. The convoy left Rabaul on 28 November, and on the next day it received the inevitable air attacks. The *Shiratsuyu* suffered a direct hit on her bow, and although she had few casualties, her speed was reduced to 10 knots. The *Makigumo* caught fire from several near-misses. The two crippled destroyers retired to Rabaul, leaving only the *Kazagumo* and *Yugumo* to make it to Buna, carrying a minimum of supplies.[6]

One more major attempt was to be made to supply Buna with some 642 men of the Oda Unit. On 12 December five destroyers, the *Arashio*, *Kazagumo*, *Yugumo*, *Inazuma*, and *Isonami*, took on the troops, left Rabaul, and arrived at a disembarkation point some 30 miles northwest of the Kumusi River battle. Air attacks again began, and the *Isonami* received minor damage. The convoy was then recalled; 591 men had disembarked and reached their units, while another 51 had disembarked but were lost. From then on, Buna and Gona received only trickles of men and supplies, usually brought in by barges, but the Navy made no more attempts at organized convoys. The Japanese Army had abandoned the Buna–Gona troops to take care of themselves, which eventually meant their total annihilation.

Buna and Gona had been written off, because the life-and-death struggle then going on at Guadalcanal demanded so much attention that the lower Papuan Peninsula could not be saved. The last of the Japanese troops there were eliminated—they did not surrender—on 3 January 1943. The casualty list included about 12,000 Japanese troops, along with those in the Navy that were killed and wounded. The Australians lost 5,700 men, and Americans, 2,800.[7] The Japanese Imperial Headquarters had violated the very principle that had brought it success up to this time when it landed troops beyond land-based air cover. In doing so, it turned the Japanese back on the road that would lead them to final defeat. From then on, the Allies would be operating under land-based air cover. Moreover, at the Papuan Peninsula and at Guadalcanal, the Japanese Navy, forced to operate under enemy air assaults without carrier-based air cover, began to experience a rate of attrition that it could not sustain. Japanese destroyers were being sacrificed in operations for which they were neither fitted nor intended.

Guadalcanal

In July and August of 1942, the Japanese Navy was under a strain even to provide warships to protect their shipping in the Greater East Asia sphere, or to protect troop convoys to areas such as Burma, the Philippines, Lae, Salamaua, and Buna. The Japanese military leaders expected that MacArthur would eventually counterattack up through New Guinea toward the Philippines, as part of his opera-

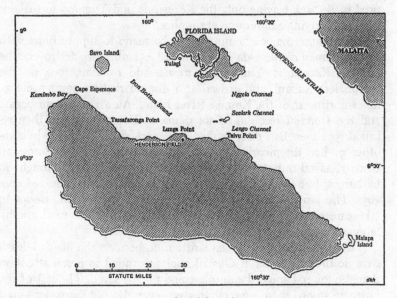

Guadalcanal

tions to reach Tokyo. They also saw the threat of counterattack through the central Pacific as part of Nimitz' offensive. They did not, however, foresee that the occupation of Tulagi on 2 May would lead to the opening of a third road to Japan: up through the Solomon chain to Rabaul. The extension of the defense perimeter to Tulagi, to be developed as a seaplane base, and the later occupation of Guadalcanal in order to build an airfield was a routine operation, one more piece to be fitted into a larger strategy. The American reaction at first also was a routine measure to protect the life line to Australia. Neither side had any idea of the immensity of the struggle that was to take place there. Just as Midway was the turning point in the war at sea, Guadalcanal would be the turning point in the war on land.

Guadalcanal is a mountainous island at the bottom of the Solomon chain, 2,500 square miles in area. Its climate is abominable; the heat, humidity, and torrential rains are never-ending, and malaria-bearing mosquitoes and a host of tropical diseases thrive in its lush jungles. An English-owned plantation engaged in raising copra was the only reason that any Europeans lived there. Yet the waters around this island for six months were to be the scene of an almost constant struggle between the Japanese and the Allied fleets. Those waters became the scene of more than half-a-dozen major battles, most of them fought at night, ship-to-ship. At first by accident, later because of pride, and then finally in desperation, Guadalcanal became the place the Japanese wanted at all costs to hold. But by trying to keep it and dislodge the U. S. Marines on it, Japan critically diminished her fleet, losing battleships, carriers, cruisers, and especially destroyers, in a war of attrition she could not possibly win. When she finally decided to withdraw what remained of her Guadalcanal forces, in KE Operation, Japan's naval strength had become so eroded that the American march north could not be stopped. It is true that the Japanese Navy fought efficiently and well in the battles around Guadalcanal, and then in the numerous battles during her retreat toward Rabaul; indeed, Japan was clearly the victor in many of these encounters. But she could not afford to pay the price in ships that the United States could, and did. Even when the Japanese did not lose a destroyer, they had to delay her overhaul, making her less efficient.

The battles around Guadalcanal and in the Solomons wasted the Japanese Navy, denying it the opportunity for that one decisive battle that would destroy the U. S. Pacific Fleet. U. S. Navy ships were increasing in number and introducing new devices: radar was being improved, eventually leading to the development of radar-controlled guns. Even so, Japanese ships, especially destroyers, could counter these advantages for a while, because Japanese lookouts had very good vision and excellent optics, and Japanese torpedoes were vastly superior to those of the Allies. The Japanese had evolved excellent fighting tactics from their battle experience: use torpedoes first if possible, don't reveal a ship's position by gunfire unless necessary, and use searchlights sparingly, depending instead on flares dropped from float planes.

Tulagi was quickly developed into a seaplane base by the Japanese. They paid little attention to Guadalcanal until mid-June, when they began sending in convoys carrying labor troops to build an airfield. Tulagi contained the main garrison, while Guadalcanal had 2,000 troops, most of them engineer and labor corps units. Work on the airstrip went slowly, since no Allied counterattack seemed imminent.

The United States was somewhat alarmed by the occupation of Tulagi and the development of a seaplane base there; but it was the discovery on 4 July that the Japanese were constructing an airfield on Guadalcanal that spurred the United States into action aimed at de-

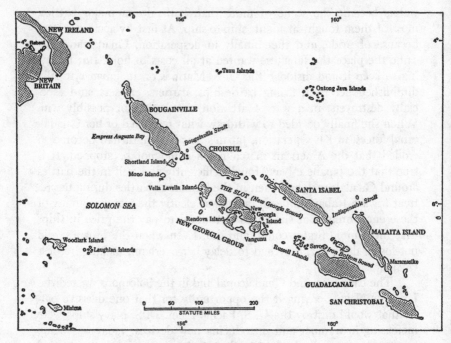

The Solomon Islands

nying Japan such an advantage. Early in the war, the United States had considered occupying one of the islands in the southern portion of the Solomon chain. MacArthur now saw Rabaul as an obstacle to his plan to go up the coast of New Guinea and through the Bismarck Sea on his way back to the Philippines. Moreover, the United States had men specially trained for swift amphibious campaigns: the U. S. Marine Corps. While MacArthur was pleading for Army regulars and was getting only green draftees, two of the Marine Corps' divisions lay idle.

Therefore, on 2 July 1942, the Joint Chiefs of Staff decided to use the Marine First Division, already on its way to Nouméa, to recover Guadalcanal and Tulagi in Operation Watchtower. The directive was much broader, however, than just the occupation of Guadalcanal and Tulagi; it was also to seize and occupy New Britain, New Ireland, and New Guinea, ending with the capture of Rabaul. The first step was to be the capture of the Santa Cruz Islands, Tulagi, and neighboring areas; Guadalcanal was not even mentioned by name.[8] The forces to undertake the operation were put together swiftly, and, as might be expected in such a quickly organized effort, they lacked proper balance, sufficient logistical planning, and an adequate fleet of warships to escort the invading Marines.

The American naval force in the invasion of Guadalcanal and Tulagi had an Air Support Force made up of three heavy carriers, (the *Saratoga*, *Enterprise*, and *Wasp*), the battleship *North Carolina*, five heavy cruisers, one light cruiser, sixteen destroyers, and three tankers. The Marine First Division was carried in fifteen transports, with close cover of eight cruisers and a screen of destroyers.

About 10,000 Marines assaulted Guadalcanal on 7 August 1942, and by evening they had overrun the Japanese camp, occupied the unfinished airfield, and forced the 2,500 Japanese labor troops and a guard unit of 150 troops into scattered flight.[9] The rest of the division (6,000 men) was put ashore at Tulagi, where most of the regular Japanese troops were; it was only after a vicious battle, in which the Japanese fought to the last man, that Tulagi was secured, at 0000 on 9 August.

There was jubilation among Americans in the rear echelons in the Southwest Pacific, and among the American public, for with these landings the Americans had wrested territory from the Japanese for the first time in the war. But there was nervousness among those in the immediate expedition, for although the men had been put ashore, their supplies had not been unloaded yet. American naval officers were uneasy, too, because they well knew that Japanese air power could devastate surface ships. This feeling even extended to the carrier cover group which was some 120 miles from the Guadalcanal area. Admiral Fletcher, in charge of the Air Support Force, had promised to stay in the vicinity for 48 hours to provide air cover defense against the Japanese air attacks that would inevitably come; however, he gave cover for only 36 hours and, at 1807 on 8 August, withdrew to the southeast. Admiral Richmond Turner, commander-in-chief of the amphibious forces at Guadalcanal, had estimated that he needed four days to unload the necessary supplies for the Marines ashore. Now, rather than 96 hours of air cover, or even 48, he would be given only 36 hours.

Vice Admiral Gunichi Mikawa, commander-in-chief of the Eighth Fleet, Outer South Seas Force, had the responsibility of dislodging the intruding U. S. Marines. The units available at Rabaul were well-equipped and ready, having been posted for the Rabi Island operation. Mikawa responded decisively, using everything that he had—519 soldiers were loaded in two transports, which set sail at

2200 on 7 August. However, at 1255 on 8 August, because of the strength of the Marine units that had captured the Guadalcanal airfield, the convoy was ordered to return to Rabaul. In doing so, while just off Cape St. George, the *Meiyo Maru* (5,627 tons) was torpedoed by the submarine S-38 at 2125; she sank in five minutes, with 373 of her men lost.[10]

As soon as he had been informed of the situation on 7 August, Mikawa was ordered by Yamamoto to attack the ships at Guadalcanal and Tulagi with all available land-based bombers.[11] Although intercepted by the American Air Support Force planes, the Japanese airmen set fire to one transport, the *George F. Elliott* (which eventually sank), and caused the later sinking of the destroyer *Jarvis*.[12] The air attacks were continued on 8 August, and by 9 August they were unopposed by American planes.

Meanwhile, Mikawa was gathering his warships to take on the American transports and the escorting warships. At Rabaul he had the heavy cruiser *Chokai* (his flagship), the light cruisers *Tenryu* and *Yubari*, and the destroyer *Yunagi*. The heavy cruisers *Aoba*, *Kako*, *Kinugasa*, and *Furutaka* had just sortied from Kavieng on the morning of 7 August, and he ordered them to rendezvous with his four ships, east of Bougainville.[13] The rest of Mikawa's ships were on a Buna convoy. The rendezvous was made at 1400 on 7 August, and Admiral Mikawa's force headed south, planning to engage the Allied warships and destroy the invader's transports in a night battle. The fact that Admiral Mikawa could muster only one destroyer clearly shows the burden that was placed upon the Navy in guarding Japan's vast defense perimeter.

The American ships covering the Guadalcanal occupation knew that the Japanese would respond quickly by air, by submarine, and probably with a task force; so during 8 August, several groups carried out air reconnaissance. Mikawa's force was first spotted at 1026 by an Australian pilot, but it was incorrectly identified as including three cruisers, three destroyers, and two seaplane tenders. The force was again spotted, heading south through Bougainville Strait (and again incorrectly identified) at 1101. Because of poorly worded reports and inaccurate descriptions, Admiral Turner could not deduce that both reports referred to the same force. Various search planes were to keep the Japanese ships in sight: the Navy's PBYs and B-17s, the Hudsons and B-17s of General MacArthur, and, before the departure of Admiral Fletcher's carrier force, his scout planes. One area was poorly covered; it was the very area most likely to be used by a counterattacking fleet, called the "Slot"—the U. S. Navy's name for the area between Choiseul, New Georgia, and Santa Isabel.

For some reason, Turner was not told that the Slot had not been searched by the Air Support Force planes. All he knew was that a Japanese fleet containing seaplane tenders was somewhere to the north. Quite correctly, Turner assumed that such a force would not make a night attack. He simply had not been supplied the correct information (which had been inexcusably delayed) from Australia or from the Air Support Force; he was thus not properly alerted to Mikawa's approach. It was not Turner's indifference or lack of precaution that led him to believe that there would be no night battle on 8–9 August. The accusation often made that Turner's division of ships was faulty is unfair; given the information that Turner had, the three formations were proper (if not properly alert) for the operations anticipated that night.

With transports to guard just east of Guadalcanal's Lunga Point and at Tulagi, the Support Force was divided into three parts, each with assigned sectors to patrol. The Southern Force consisted of the heavy cruisers *Australia* (RAN), *Chicago*, and *Canberra* (RAN), and the destroyers *Patterson* and *Bagley*. Its patrol area stretched from the transports at Lunga Point, to Savo Island, to a distance about halfway to Tulagi. This force was placed so that it could block any entrance made between Cape Esperance and Savo Island. The Northern Force which contained the heavy cruisers *Vincennes*, *Astoria*, and *Quincy*, and the destroyers *Helm* and *Wilson*, made a box-shaped patrol. Its eastern boundary was a line running north from the transports to the west of Tulagi, and northwest from that line to Savo Island. The Northern Force was to block off the western approaches of the bay formed by Guadalcanal and Florida Island. The Eastern Force, which covered the area east of the line between Lunga Point and Tulagi, was composed of the antiaircraft light cruiser *San Juan*, the light cruiser *Hobart* (RAN), and the destroyers *Monssen* and *Buchanan*. It was to cover any enemy approach from the east. The destroyers *Blue* and *Ralph Talbot* were posted as a picket line to the northwest of Guadalcanal and Tulagi. Their line, at its outer limit, placed them 20 miles apart. The officer in tactical command of the Support Force was Admiral V. A. C. Crutchley (RN).

It was planned that the unloading of the transports would continue through the night. Admiral Turner, on board the transport *McCawley* at Lunga Roads, was alarmed by the premature departure of the carriers, and summoned Admiral Crutchley from his flagship the *Australia* at 2032. Crutchley had earlier requested such a conference to clarify the confused situation. Rather than travel the 20 miles by small boat, Crutchley went to the conference in the *Australia*, thus weakening the Southern Force, and placed Captain Howard D. Bode in the *Chicago* in tactical command. Expecting the British admiral back by midnight, Captain Bode simply turned in, leaving the Support Force with no tactical commander. Moreover, all hands, from admiral to the lowest rating, were exhausted by the activity, excitement, and heat of the past two days, so the Support Force was placed in Condition Two, with half the watch on duty. Thus, as Mikawa approached, the officer in tactical command was asleep, the Support Force was widely dispersed, and the ships were in no condition to enter a fight on a minute's notice. From the 1026 report of the presence of seaplane tenders, the force was expecting a plane attack at dawn.[14]

24. The great Japanese battleship Yamato, flagship of Admiral Yamamoto. She and her sister ship the Musashi were the largest battleships ever built.

25. *The Hiryu in flames after the first attack by U.S. dive bombers at the Battle Midway, 5 June 1942. Her flight deck and forward elevator have been hit, but she shows no signs of a list and is not making way.*

26. *Bombs fall in Makushin Bay, during the first Japanese attack on Dutch Harbor, 3 June 1942.*

27. *Vice Admiral Gunichi Mikawa, commander of the Eighth Fleet, Outer South Seas Force.*

28. *Photograph taken from a Japanese cruiser during the First Battle of the Solomon Sea, 9 August 1942, shows the U.S. cruiser* Quincy *being illuminated by searchlights from the heavy cruiser* Aoba.

chapter 13

FIRST BATTLE
OF THE SOLOMON SEA

(USN Title: Battle of Savo Island)

1942

9 August   First Battle of the Solomon Sea

17 August Japanese begin reinforcement efforts for Guadalcanal and bombardment of Henderson Field

As his force steamed south through intermittent squalls on the dark night of 8 August, Admiral Mikawa had his own worries too, for he did not know of the departure of Fletcher's carriers, and he needed up-to-the-minute information on what he could expect at Tulagi and Lunga Point. Therefore, his cruisers continued to launch search planes all day long, from early morning until twilight. At 0043 on 9 August, his force was in a single two-mile column headed southeast by south, led by the flagship *Chokai*, followed by the *Aoba*, *Kako*, *Kinugasa*, *Furutaka*, the light cruisers *Tenryu* and *Yubari*, and the destroyer *Yunagi*. A minute later, the U.S. destroyer *Blue* was sighted about five and one-half miles due south.

The Japanese column, with all its guns bearing on the picket-line destroyer *Blue*, veered to port three degrees. When the *Blue*, however, showed no evidence of having observed the column, Mikawa swung back to his original course. Earlier, at 2300, the *Chokai* had catapulted a plane to provide illumination; the *Kako* did the same three minutes later, and at 2308 the *Furutaka* launched one of her planes to illuminate and act as a shell-spotter during the battle. Mikawa then at 0108 issued the order to enter the bay from the south side of Savo Island. At 0125 he ordered "independent command" and then at 0131 he further ordered, "Every ship attack." For the next seven minutes the seven ships followed the *Chokai*, at a speed of 26 knots. They saw the destroyer *Ralph Talbot* on her picket run, about eight miles off their port bow; however, the Japanese column was still not discovered. It was reported to Mikawa that a third destroyer had been observed. The *Chokai*, immediately after issuing the attack order, spotted the silhouettes of the heavy cruisers *Canberra* (RAN) and *Chicago*, and at 0138 she launched four torpedoes at them at a range of 5,000 yards and ordered all ships to open fire. Immediately after launching, other silhouettes of Allied ships were seen, and Mikawa ordered that the area be illuminated. All Mikawa's ships were now firing torpedoes, a weapon the Japanese heavy cruisers had that the U.S. cruisers lacked.

Directly ahead of the *Chokai's* column lay the *Canberra* and *Chicago* and the destroyers *Bagley* and *Patterson* of the Southern Force. It was not until 0143 that the *Patterson* discovered a number of Japanese ships closing on them. The alarm was then sounded, but it was much too late. Directly on the Japanese column's port beam at about 5,000 yards the ships of the Northern Force were doing their box patrol (actually crossing Mikawa's "T", had they known an enemy force was there). The Southern Force, now fully exposed by the illuminating flares dropped from the float planes, received fire from the *Chokai, Aoba,* and *Furutaka*. At 0143, just as the *Patterson* sounded her alarm, two torpedoes ripped into the *Canberra* on her starboard side, followed immediately by devastating gunfire salvos. The *Canberra* barely had time to fire two torpedoes and a few shells before she went dead in the water and began listing. Fires broke out and her crew began to struggle to keep her afloat. She was out of the battle, almost before being aware that there was one.

The remaining cruiser in the Southern Force was the *Chicago*. The battle had been under way for several minutes before the *Chicago's* sleeping Captain Bode, the officer in tactical command, could be aroused and bring his ship into action; but he also was too late. At 0147 a torpedo hit the ship's bow, severing part of it. As Bode struggled blindly to get into the battle, a shell knocked off his cruiser's foremast. The *Chicago* could not find the Japanese warships, which by now had turned hard to port in pursuit of the Northern Force. Bode completely miscalculated the location of Mikawa's force and steered his ship away from the battle, without using his radio to alert the Northern Force. The *Bagley* never managed to get in the fight; thus, the entire Southern Force had been eliminated from the battle in six minutes.

At 0144, in the darkness of a night battle, the *Furutaka* had become separated from the other Japanese ships. To avoid a collision, the *Chokai* turned northward at full speed, followed by the rest of her column. After nine minutes, new formations had been established, with the *Furutaka* and the *Tenryu* in column and the *Yubari* close on their port side. In the starboard column were the *Chokai, Aoba, Kako,* and *Kinugasa,* about 1,000 yards from the *Furutaka's* group, but opening eventually to 7,500 yards. Admiral Mikawa was worried about the three Allied destroyers he had earlier observed, so at 0138 he detached the *Yunagi* to retrace his original course in order to protect his rear. The *Yunagi* and the two picket destroyers never saw each other, but at 0210 the *Yunagi* fired torpedoes and shells at the *Jarvis*, without effect.[1] She had already been

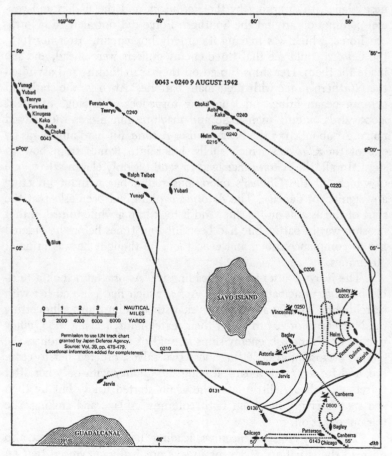

First Battle of the Solomon Sea

hit, however, in the air raids of 8 August, and eventually sank, en route to Australia.

Both columns were now headed directly toward the Northern Force, which was still carrying out its box patrol. Straight lines projected along the paths of the two columns would have completely enclosed the Northern Force. When the *Patterson* saw the Japanese column make a 90-degree turn to port, she paralleled it, and a one-sided fire fight ensued. The *Patterson* was hit on her Y turret and set afire; meanwhile Mikawa's ships were moving out of her range. The *Bagley* was not prepared for battle, and by the time she had her torpedoes ready for launch, the Japanese ships were too far away.

Difficult as it may be to believe, the dropping of flares by Japanese planes, the warning by the *Patterson*, and the flashes and general commotion around the Southern Force did not alert the Northern Force, which was making its orderly box circuit. After her turn, the *Chokai* could see that three enemy cruisers were ahead, and she made for them. Her ships turned on their searchlights, and assaulted the Northern Force with their main batteries. At 0147, the starboard column began firing and launching torpedoes at a range of about 4,000 yards, adding high-angle and machine-gun fire as they closed range. At about 0157 the heavy cruiser *Astoria*, hit hard amidships by one of the *Chokai*'s 8-inch shells, burst into flames from bow to stern. In all, the *Astoria* managed to send off only eleven salvos, one of which hit the *Chokai*'s operations room, but without inflicting any significant damage. The *Astoria*'s captain had been asleep at the start of the assault on his ship, and it took him a while to realize that his ship was in battle. She had been hit four times before he ordered her to commence firing, and even then, he thought he was firing at "friendlies."

The heavy cruiser *Quincy*, leading the *Astoria*, also took a terrible beating, principally from the *Aoba*, which had exposed her with searchlights. The Japanese, however, with burning ships silhouetting the Northern Force, turned off their searchlights, leaving the *Quincy* unable to distinguish enemy ships. Afraid of firing on friendlies, the *Quincy*'s captain, after letting loose two salvos, ordered her to cease fire, and turned to starboard, leaving the *Quincy* with only her after turrets available. A little later she again started firing, but by then she was receiving fire from both columns. Ablaze and sinking, she was out of action.

The heavy cruiser *Vincennes*, leading the cruiser formation, also misread the situation. Her captain was not really convinced that an enemy force was at hand until she was illuminated at 0150 by the *Kako*—which promptly hit the *Vincennes* squarely amidships, setting her planes afire. The *Vincennes* chose to close the Mikawa port column, but did little damage, and, after repeated hits by shells and torpedoes, she finally sank at 0250.

The screening destroyer of the Northern Force, the *Wilson*, added what firepower a destroyer's guns could, but did little damage and was ignored by the Japanese cruisers. She ended her fight when, after chasing an "enemy ship" at 0200, the ship identified herself as the *Bagley*. The destroyer *Helm* never saw any enemy ships, and held to her previous course until 0200. The Eastern Force never got into the battle; Rear Admiral Norman Scott, in tactical command, was puzzlied by what little he could see or hear on that dark night, with its constant rain squalls. Eventually he sent out four destroyers, but to a position far away from the actual battle. The transports ceased unloading during the battle, but ashore there was also very little precise knowledge of what was happening.

Admiral Mikawa now had an important decision to make. Should he go for the transports, which were then totally exposed? But such a tactic would leave him in enemy waters, susceptible to plane attacks at daylight. He did not know that Admiral Fletcher had retired with his three carriers; indeed, he did not even know how many more enemy ships there were in the vicinity.[2] Thus, he decided to order a retirement shortly after 0200. Turning north and then northwest at 0214, Mikawa's ships became scattered, with the *Aoba* by herself on the extreme starboard side of the force. In such bad weather, it would have been most difficult for Mikawa to reassemble his force. Again the question arises: What if he had decided to destroy the transports, leaving the Marines ashore without supplies? Would the U.S. forces still have been able to hold the island?

As Mikawa was trying to reform his column and head northwest, the *Ralph Talbot*, one of the picket-line destroyers, stumbled into the battle. She had heard the *Patterson*'s warning, and indeed had watched the battle from a distance, not really knowing what was happening. At 0215 she was discovered by the *Tenryu*, which illuminated her with searchlights. Immediately the *Furutaka* and *Yubari* joined the *Tenryu* in firing on the *Ralph Talbot* from ranges of 3,000 to 4,000 yards, and hit her on her torpedo-tube mounts. Lieutenant Commander Joseph W. Callahan of the *Ralph Talbot*, thoroughly puzzled by what had been going on, turned on his recognition lights, thinking that he was being shelled by Allied ships. This tactic must have puzzled the three Japanese ships, for they ceased fire for a moment; but soon the *Yubari* again trained a searchlight on the *Ralph Talbot* and recommenced firing. The U.S. destroyer was hit four times, burst into flames, and began to list; meanwhile, she had been able to launch only four torpedoes, which had no effect. But fortunately for her another rain squall hid her, and the Japanese ceased firing at 0223. If the *Ralph Talbot* contributed anything to the battle, it was only by way of confirming Admiral Mikawa's earlier decision to retire, for he still did not know how many other Allied ships there might be in the vicinity.

The battle was over. The *Canberra*, dead in the water and beyond help, was deliberately sunk by a "friendly" torpedo at 0800, after her surviving crew had been removed. The *Astoria* went down at 1215, after efforts to save her had failed. The *Quincy* sank at 0205, the *Vincennes* at 0250, and the *Ralph Talbot* had been badly damaged. It was the worst defeat the United States Navy had ever suffered: 1,023 men were killed, and 709 were wounded.[3]

On the Japanese side, the damage was recorded as follows:

The *Chokai:* 34 killed, 32 wounded; hull and armament hit in a number of places.

The *Aoba:* Direct hit on No. 2 torpedo mount, making torpedo tubes Nos. 1 and 2 inoperable. One torpedo damaged. Fire in torpedo room. Motor boat heavily damaged.

The *Kinugasa:* Very slight damage. One motor boat heavily damaged. 4 killed, 1 wounded.

The *Yubari:* One 4.5-inch shell penetrated hull but did not explode.

The *Furutaka, Kako, Tenryu,* and *Yunagi:* No damage.[4]

The Action Report of the heavy cruiser *Chokai* follows: (To get World Time Zone time, add two hours.)

Date: Aug. 8–9. Location: Off Tulagi

Name of Action: Night action off Tulagi

Action Details: On 8 Aug. while carrying out air searches from early in the morning, operated during the morning so as to conceal our plans. 1130. Sortied for Tulagi anchorage 2100. Launched plane # 1 to illuminate anchorage.

2240: "Prepare for attack!"

2246: "Action" ordered safely evaded enemy DD [*sic*] patrol line.

2331: "All forces to the attack" ordered. Subsequently, up to 0023 9 Aug. when the entire force began to withdraw, 5 large US British or Australian cruisers were sunk by gunnery or torpedo action.

0540: Arrived Rabaul, Tulagi Strait night action movement. (Author's note: add one hour to IJN time at Rabaul here for World Time Zone time.)

Ammunition Expended

Main battery: 302 rounds. Main battery AA shells: 6. 12 cm guns: 120 rounds. 24 mm guns ([sic]—undoubtedly 25 mm is meant): 500 rounds. Type-93 torpedoes: 8. Parachute flares: 15. Launching float flares: 10. 7.7 mm guns: 96 rounds.

Battle Results

Sank 2 large British cruisers, 3 large U.S. cruisers

Damage

Killed: 34. Wounded: 32. Hull and armaments hit in several tens of places.[5]

The *Chokai* overestimated the damage inflicted on the Allies; this often happens, especially in night battles. Corrections are made by higher authorities, after reconciling all battle reports.[6]

While it was virtually untouched in the battle of 9 August 1942, Mikawa's force did not return to Rabaul without any losses. The heavy cruiser *Kako* left Mikawa's force to sail to Kavieng on 9 August. At 0810 on 10 August, 70 miles from Kavieng, the *Kako* received three torpedo hits on the starboard beam from the U.S. submarine *S-44*. She sank at 0815, with seventy-one killed (including one civilian), and fifteen wounded (including one civilian).[7] After she had fought in a glorious Japanese victory, the *Kako*'s loss at the hands of an old "S"-type submarine was supremely ironic.

Admiral Mikawa is often criticized for passing up the exposed U.S. transports, which were his for the taking. Hindsight, however, cannot recreate the situation that Mikawa faced at that moment. He was cautious because he did not know what other enemy ships were in the area, and he worried that his force might be exposed at daylight to heavy carrier-plane raids which could inflict tremendous damage. Admiral Yamamoto, rather than criticizing Mikawa, sent him an official message of praise for his splendid defeat of the enemy.

In spite of the gravity of the U.S. defeat, Admiral Turner kept his transports unloading until late afternoon the same day and then finally weighed anchor and withdrew with his remaining warships. Thus, the United States had 15,000 Marines ashore, most of them on

Guadalcanal, and all Japanese opposition had been wiped out on Tulagi. They had a one-month's supply of food, but they were now dependent on the U. S. Navy's ability to keep the line of supply open. Work was started on finishing Henderson airfield and on setting up a five-mile perimeter defense against the Japanese troops on the island.

The crucial battle for Guadalcanal was about to begin. Neither side was willing to give up Guadalcanal, but neither side would be able to drive the other off the island. The Allies well understood its strategic importance, as did the Japanese, who, after 18 September gave its recapture priority over all other South Pacific operations. This gruesome, stubbornly fought struggle was to last almost half a year, exacting a tremendous price from both sides in lives and materiel. Neither side could have foreseen what the campaign there would entail, for both were willing to spend whatever was necessary for victory. Two stubborn bulldogs had entered a do-or-die fight.

The Japanese felt that Guadalcanal had to be reinforced and held, which meant that they had to control the seas around it. The Americans would have to eliminate the Japanese Army units on the island, and provide reinforcement and supplies to the American garrison. But most important of all, with the construction and use of Henderson Field, along with satellite fields, the Americans would have the permanent air power to resist Japanese reinforcement efforts and to counter Japanese naval or aerial bombardment.

Recontact with the rear echelon was made on 15 August when four destroyer transports (APDs) brought in aviation gas and ammunition. Then on 20 August, three APDs brought in three and one-half days' supply of food and got away safely. Henderson Field landed its first plane on 12 August, and on 17 August it was pronounced fit for dry-weather use. Planes from several sources were subsequently flown into Guadalcanal, the first ones being nineteen Wildcat fighters and twelve Dauntless dive bombers from the decks of the escort carrier *Long Island*, followed on 22 August by a squadron of P-400s.[8] The *Enterprise* flew in her dive bombers two days later and remained south of the island, out of Japanese air range, to stage more planes onto Henderson Field. Thereafter, Henderson was steadily supplied, although the loss rate at first was very high. At times the problem would not be a lack of planes to fly, but a lack of gas to fly them. But by the end of August, Guadalcanal had become an unsinkable (albeit stationary) aircraft carrier that could be captured only from within the island. The Americans had made Henderson into an all-weather field by using crushed coral; possession of the field had given them control of the sky, and thus of the sea, around Guadalcanal in daylight hours. But in the darkness of night the Americans would "button up" and the Japanese would regain control of the sea. It was indeed a new and strange phenomenon in naval warfare.

The first Japanese reinforcements came when a detachment of 113 SNLF troops was put ashore at Tassafaronga on 17 August, without incident. These troops had been escorted by the destroyers *Oite, Mutsuki, Mochizuki,* and *Uzuki.* The next night about 900 troops, the advance group from the Ikki Unit, were put ashore at 2300.[9] They had been brought from Truk and were placed on three high-speed ships for the run-in and landing, escorted by the destroyers *Umikaze, Yamakaze, Kawakaze, Suzukaze, Urakaze, Tanikaze,* and *Hamakaze.* Two strike forces accompanied the convoy, and after the uncontested landing, the destroyers *Asashio, Hagikaze,* and *Kagero* bombarded the seaplane base at Tulagi, while the destroyer *Arashi* shelled Henderson Field.[10] But the bombardment group had tarried too long, and on 19 August the *Hagikaze* was attacked near the Shortlands by two B-17s from Espiritu Santo and she received three bombs on her fantail at 1215. Thirty-three men were killed, thirteen wounded, and the *Hagikaze* was escorted to Truk by the *Arashi.*[11] The Ikki Unit went into battle immediately, without awaiting further reinforcements, and was virtually wiped out in the battle of the Tenaru River during the night of 20–21 August, suffering 777 killed and 30 wounded. Colonel Ikki, wrapped in a rising-sun flag, was killed leading the charge.[12] (It was Colonel Ikki who had been originally scheduled to lead the invasion of Midway.)

The Japanese Army command at Rabaul was still determined to recapture Guadalcanal and Tulagi quickly, but, inexplicably, it did not seem to realize that there were 15,000 U. S. Marines holding Guadalcanal. Therefore, the next reinforcement was attempted with only 1,500 men of the Kawaguchi Unit, 38th Brigade. But if the number of Marines at Guadalcanal was being underestimated, the Allied naval forces that might attack the Kawaguchi Unit convoy were not. The Combined Fleet at Truk was taking over from the Eighth Fleet, and preparing to meet the Allied forces in a major battle which would not only protect the convoys, but also defeat and destroy Allied naval power so that future Japanese reinforcements would not be threatened. Thus another major naval battle was in the making. In the meantime, all available Japanese air power was being employed in frequent raids on Guadalcanal, as additional Japanese aircraft flew into Rabaul. Japanese destroyers were also making the run down the Slot at night, bringing in small detachments. These runs, which occurred almost every night, had the added value of furnishing information about Allied ships in the Guadalcanal area.[13] Generally, after the deliveries had been made, the destroyers would bombard Henderson Field and the Marine encampment. There was little that could be done about such bombings, for it was known that the Japanese Combined Fleet was planning something, and Allied forces had to be assembled and ready for whatever might happen.

Still, by one means or another, supplies had to be delivered to the Marines on Guadalcanal. Two supply ships, escorted by the destroyers *Blue*, *Henley*, and *Helm*, were en route to Guadalcanal on 21 August. The *Blue* and *Henley* went ahead in the hope of catching a Japanese landing, and in order to reconnoiter the area for the approach of the Allied convoy. They soon entered "Iron Bottom" Sound, between Guadalcanal and Tulagi. (The Americans later gave it this name because of the number of warships sunk there.) At 0330 on 22 August both started a patrol pattern, using their inferior SC-type radar. At 0355, the *Blue* made a radar and sonar contact; then suddenly, at 0357 a torpedo slammed into the *Blue*'s stern. The Japanese destroyer *Kawakaze* had just landed reinforcements and was returning to Rabaul when she sighted the *Blue*.[14] Evidently her lookout's sharp vision had prevailed over the American SC radar. Both destroyers paid a price, however; planes caught up with the *Kawakaze* in the vicinity of the Shortland Islands and attacked her between 0730 and 0740, causing minor damage. The *Blue*, however, could not be towed out of Tulagi before the oncoming battle, so she was ordered scuttled on 23 August.

It was becoming clear to the Japanese that a significant battle was shaping up. The complacency reflected by Admiral Yamamoto's official praise for Admiral Mikawa after the First Battle of the Solomon Sea had begun to give way to concern, for the Japanese Army had not yet driven the U. S. Marines out, and the Americans now had an all-weather airfield which would give them control of the sea during daylight. One grand effort had to be made, then, to smash the Marines' naval lifeline. The Combined Fleet at Truk began to put its fleets in motion to carry out the Japanese grand strategy for the region and end the American threat to the Papuan Peninsula campaign and Rabaul.

chapter 14

SECOND BATTLE OF THE SOLOMON SEA

(USN Title: Battle of Eastern Solomons)

1942

23 August   Japanese Combined Fleet sorties to protect large convoy, to recapture Guadalcanal, and to destroy U. S. Southwest Pacific Fleet

24 August   Carrier battle

25 August   Admiral Yamamoto withdraws to the north

25 August   U.S. planes attack and repel Japanese convoy

For the Second Battle of the Solomon Sea, the Japanese had assembled a mighty array of 58 ships, with 177 carrier-based planes. In turn, the U. S. Navy, although it had only thirty ships, had 259 planes. This plane advantage was reduced when the heavy carrier *Wasp* with 83 planes was sent south on 23 August to take on oil, and was therefore not involved in the battle; thus the Japanese had 177 planes, the U. S. Navy 176. It was a peculiar sort of battle, resembling a match between two overly cautious chess players: one player lost a knight and a pawn, but endangered the other's queen; then both players quit the game.

Yamamoto had two purposes in mind in preparing for this battle. The Japanese Army's situation on Guadalcanal was critical, and major reinforcements were desperately needed. These could not be brought in without serious risk as long as the U. S. Pacific Fleet in the Southwest Pacific existed. The U. S. Navy also supplied planes and fuel for Henderson Field, and supplies and reinforcements for the Marines. The first objective, then, was to destroy the U. S. Pacific Fleet in the area, which would be accomplished by sinking the U.S. carriers, using Nagumo's carrier planes. The Vanguard Force of Rear Admiral Hiroaki Abe could protect the *Shokaku* and

Zuikaku against any enemy carrier strikes. After that, the Japanese carrier planes, aided by the Vanguard Force and then by Admiral
Kondo's powerful Main Body, Support Force (and, if needed, by the
battleship *Yamato*'s devastating 18-inch guns) could mop up any of
the American naval force that remained. Then Guadalcanal's Henderson Field could be put out of action permanently by Nagumo's
planes and ships.

His second objective was to keep the Americans from attacking
the Japanese troop convoy, with 1,500 reinforcements en route to
Guadalcanal. To that end, Henderson Field and the American garrison would be subjected to an intensive night bombardment by the
Eighth Fleet's four heavy cruisers, while Rear Admiral Raizo Tanaka
brought the convoy in to Tassafaronga. To aid in the second objective the light carrier *Ryujo* with her supporting ships was to be
placed 100 miles west of Nagumo's heavy carriers and 190 miles
northeast of Guadalcanal. From there, her planes could attack Henderson Field. (Morison, Vol. V, p. 87, infers that the *Ryujo* was set
out as "bait" to be located and attacked by U.S. carrier planes, thus
disclosing their position; but there is no known evidence that this
was so. The *Ryujo* had the Japanese Navy's latest heavy cruiser and
two good destroyers for protection. The Japanese probably decided
to take a calculated risk that the *Ryujo* could take care of herself.)

By this strategy, Admiral Yamamoto was again employing the
very division of forces that had contributed so heavily to his defeat at
Midway. He seemed incapable of devising a simple battle plan in
which all his ships, superior in number, could be brought to bear
against the U. S. Pacific Fleet. Admiral Nimitz at Pearl Harbor, and
the headquarters of the commander-in-chief, South Pacific (COM-
SOPAC), at Nouméa, were fully aware that Admiral Yamamoto was
coming out with most of the ships he could throw into battle. The
U. S. Navy also began gathering all of its available ships, knowing
that this battle was going to be a big one.

On the morning of 23 August, the Japanese naval forces were
headed southeast by south, on a line well to the east of the Solomon
Islands. The U. S. Navy fleet on the same morning was on a north-
northeasterly course about 150 miles east of Malaita Island, on a
course parallel to the Japanese forces. Both sides were cautious, as in
all carrier battles.

The first sighting was made by the Americans, when a reconnaissance plane based at the Santa Cruz Islands reported seeing a
troop convoy at 0950. Admiral Fletcher ordered the *Saratoga*'s planes

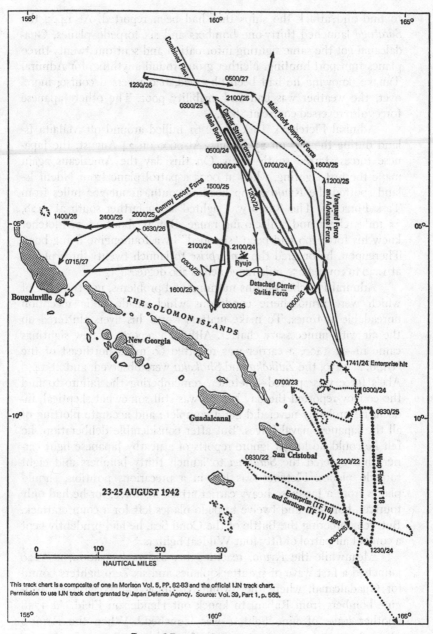

Second Battle of the Solomon Sea

to find and attack the ships that had been reported. At 1445, the *Saratoga* launched thirty-one bombers and six torpedo planes. Guadalcanal got the same sighting information and sent out twenty-three planes transport-hunting. Neither group found anything, for Admiral Tanaka, knowing he had been observed, had reversed course; moreover, the weather was bad and visibility poor. The other Japanese forces also reversed course at 1800.

Admiral Fletcher's Task Force 61 milled around off Malaita Island during the day on 23 August. At 0600 on 24 August, the Japanese forces started south again. On this day the Americans again made the first sighting, when at 0905 a patrol plane from Ndeni Island spotted the *Ryujo* group heading south, about 260 miles from Task Force 61. The *Ryujo* was sighted again farther south at 1128, 35 miles closer and still closing range. But at about 1100, Fletcher knew his force too had been "snooped" by a four-engine flying boat. Thereupon, he ordered the *Enterprise* to launch twenty-three planes at 1230 to cover a 250-mile range across 200 degrees.

Admiral Fletcher on this morning had problems, not the least of which were atmospheric conditions which made radio reception unreadable at times. To make matters worse, his flyers cluttered up the air with unnecessary chatter. Although reports of new sightings came in—at 1400, a carrier was reported 60 miles northeast of the *Ryujo*, at 1430, the *Zuikaku* and *Shokaku* were observed, and at 1440 Abe's force was spotted—Fletcher, remembering the failure to find the convoy reported the day before, was still somewhat skeptical; indeed, he probably never did get a complete and accurate plotting of all the Japanese naval forces. But after considerable deliberation, he felt he could no longer ignore reports of a nearby Japanese light carrier, and ordered the *Saratoga* to launch thirty bombers and eight torpedo planes. Fletcher was left in a precarious position, should planes from a Japanese heavy carrier attack his force, for he had only fourteen bombers and twelve torpedo planes left for a counterattack. But, remembering the Battle of the Coral Sea, he had prudently kept a combat air patrol of fifty-four Wildcat fighters.

Meanwhile the *Ryujo*, reaching her assigned position, at 1220 launched a first wave of six attack planes and six Zero fighters bound for Guadalcanal, where they would combine efforts with twin-engine bombers from Rabaul to knock out Henderson Field. At 1248 another wave of nine fighters was launched.[1] When the *Ryujo*'s planes began to appear on the Task Force ships' radar screen, the information was picked up by the *Enterprise* search force, which made for the raiding *Ryujo* planes 100 miles ahead of it, rather than go for the carrier from which they must have come. Shortly thereafter, Admiral Fletcher began to receive more information from PBYs and the *Enterprise's* planes—the *Ryujo* was located 200 miles away, a large carrier was located 60 miles north of the *Ryujo*, then at 1430 the *Zuikaku* and *Shokaku* were pinpointed 200 miles away. Ten minutes later, the Vanguard Force was located. But the bulk of his planes had already been sent out, and Admiral Fletcher simply did not have enough left for a strong strike. He tried unsuccessfully to divert the *Saratoga* group from the *Ryujo* to the *Zuikaku* and *Shokaku*; communications had become so difficult that he could not direct and control what was aloft.

The behavior of Tadao Kato, captain of the *Ryujo*, during this period was puzzling. After launching his planes, he turned north for an hour, and then at 1330 turned west. Soon thereafter he again reversed course, in order to be at the rendezvous point to recover his planes. During this entire period the *Ryujo* had kept her nine remaining fighters on board, although at 1341 her lookouts had reported a search plane. Then at 1351 a B-17 had emerged from the clouds and attempted to bomb the carrier. The *Ryujo* finally reacted to this by launching six fighters which chased the B-17 for a few minutes and then returned to cover the carrier. She was again attacked unsuccessfully by B-17s at 1455. Tameichi Hara, who commanded the destroyer *Amatsukaze* in the *Ryujo's* screen, claims that the *Ryujo* had seven fighters that could have been used as combat air patrol, but against the B-17s she only launched two, which then returned to their carrier. These seven fighters were not in the air when the *Ryujo* was attacked by carrier planes.[2] At 1400 her raiding planes signalled to the *Ryujo* that Guadalcanal had been successfully bombed and the raiding force had lost two fighters and three bombers. Another plane which was unable to return to the *Ryujo* was ordered to land at Ndemi Island, where the pilot was picked up by the destroyer *Mochizuki*.[3]

But the *Ryujo* would not be afloat to recover her planes, for the *Enterprise* group had found her, and the *Ryujo* did not have enough planes for an effective combat air patrol. The initial attack was by thirty dive bombers from *Saratoga* at 1557. According to a report made by Captain Kato, who survived the attack, she was able to evade all the bombs except a near-miss, but suffered a torpedo hit aft on her port side.[4] The screening *Tone* was also attacked by dive bombers and torpedo planes, but was not damaged. The *Ryujo's* rud-

der became jammed, causing her to move in circles; she was aflame
along her full length, and was soon listing heavily. Her planes, still
aloft from the Guadalcanal raid, were ordered to land at Buka, but
they did not have enough gas to do so. The *Amatsukaze* was ordered
alongside as "Abandon Ship" was signalled. Three hundred survivors
came on board, the last man being Kato; her normal complement
was 924 men. The *Amatsukaze* was in grave danger, for if the *Ryujo*
sank while the destroyer was alongside, the carrier would take the
Amatsukaze down also, since she had grappling hooks fastened on
the carrier, and the personnel were coming on board the destroyer by
way of wooden planks. Finally, the *Ryujo* sank at 2000. Her fourteen
planes soon arrived and circled over the rest of the force until they
finally splashed in the sea; seven pilots were rescued.[5]

Now it was the turn of the Japanese to strike back. Task Force
61 had been under constant surveillance ever since the *Chikuma*'s
float plane had made the first contact. Under the *Shokaku*'s flight
leader, the *Shokaku* and the *Zuikaku* began sending off planes at
1455: eighteen bombers and four Zero fighters from the *Shokaku*,
nine bombers and six Zero fighters from the *Zuikaku*. The two U.S.
carriers separated into two defensive groups, ten miles apart: the *Enterprise*, in the middle of a two-mile defensive ring made up of one
battleship, two cruisers, and six destroyers; and the *Saratoga*, similarly placed and guarded by two cruisers and five destroyers. Aloft, at
a distance of 25 miles, were fifty-three Wildcats as combat air patrol.
At 1638 the *Enterprise* was attacked simultaneously by dive bombers
and attack planes. The protective Japanese fighters prevented most
of the Wildcats from getting at the Japanese dive bombers. The Japanese planes met with severe antiaircraft fire, but the attack was
stubbornly pressed. The *Enterprise* took her first hit on the after
deck elevator, and the bomb tore through to the third deck before
exploding. A second bomb scored very close to the initial hit. Then
at 1645 a third bomb hit home aft of the carrier's island, but the explosion did little damage. Although the *Enterprise* was burning
furiously as the attack was ending, she had suffered no damage to her
hull; but she lost seventy-four men, with ninety-five wounded. Although carriers were evolving new techniques of protection, with
more antiaircraft guns, and more planes in the combat air patrol, the
Enterprise's protection had not been enough. The battleship *North
Carolina* also drew the attention of the attacking planes, but suffered
no damage. No attack planes carrying torpedoes were observed during this phase of the battle.

At 1600, the two Japanese carriers launched a second attack, which never discovered Task Force 61, however, due to the flight officer's plotting error—an error which probably saved the *Enterprise*. At first, the *Enterprise* worked up a speed of 24 knots and began recovering her planes. But because she was so seriously damaged, a domino effect began—one malfunction led to another, and finally the carrier's rudder jammed, which made towing impossible. If the second Japanese attack group had discovered her, she would have had no maneuverability. Eventually steering control was restored, whereupon Admiral Fletcher turned south, withdrawing from battle. Most of the *Enterprise*'s planes landed at Guadalcanal to bolster further the island's air defenses, and the *Wasp*, having refueled, was steaming northward to meet Fletcher. Thus, Guadalcanal, even without the *Enterprise* to feed planes into Henderson Field, still had air protection and a means of getting plane reinforcements.

When the first Japanese attack group retired to the north, there were still U.S. planes scattered in the air: thirteen bombers and twelve torpedo planes. From the *Saratoga* five torpedo bombers attacked the Main Body, Advance Force of Admiral Kondo, but without result. Two of the dive bombers were more fortunate; at 1740 they spotted the seaplane tender *Chitose*, which had almost no armor protection. Near-misses set her planes on fire and loosened her port plates, putting her port engine room out of action. Prompt action, however, saved her and she returned to Japan via Truk for repairs.[6] Admiral Kondo, still eager to continue the action, joined his Vanguard Force at 1630 and went searching to the south, hoping to find ships to engage in a night battle. At 2330, finding nothing, he retired to the north. One phase of the battle had ended.

But the cause of the battle still remained: the Japanese convoy with 1,500 troops, bound for Guadalcanal. Leaving the Shortlands, it was spotted at 0223 on 25 August by an American flying boat. The weather worked against the success of the mission, for the moon was bright, although there were scattered clouds. It had been a tough night on Guadalcanal, as most of them were. Planes catapulted from the cruisers covering Tanaka's convoy had bombed Henderson Field and the Marine encampment, using anti-personnel fragmentation bombs (nicknamed "daisy cutters" by the Marines).[7] As the troop convoy approached Taivu Point at 0740, the light cruiser *Jintsu* was in the process of joining the destroyers *Kagero*, *Isokaze*, *Kawakaze*, and *Yayoi*, which had also been bombarding Henderson Field. She came under fire from four planes which emerged from the scattered clouds, and took a bomb hit from a carrier plane between her A and B turrets. Her radio shack was ruined, so that her officers could not direct operations. At first, because it was thought that the planes were "friendlies," no ship returned fire. Crewmen on the *Jintsu* feared that the fire would spread to the forward powder magazine, so the captain ordered the magazine flooded. Soon the fires were brought under control.

While the *Jintsu* was solving her own problems, others were being created. At 0807 another group of enemy planes attacked, and the largest transport, the *Kinryu Maru*, in the center of the convoy, received one bomb hit and a severe strafing. At once she was enveloped in flames, which were fed by the ammunition she was carrying, and lost way. The *Jintsu's* commander, Rear Admiral Raizo Tanaka, at once ordered the *Yayoi, Mutsuki,* and patrol ships *No.* 1 and *No.* 2 to go to the transport's assistance. At the same time, he ordered the other two transports (the *Boston Maru* and *Taifuku Maru*) to retire, screened by destroyers *Kawakaze* and *Umikaze* and by patrol ships *No.* 34 and *No.* 35.

The *Mutsuki* was proceeding with the rescue of the *Kinryu Maru* personnel when at 1027 the group was attacked by three B-17s, and the *Mutsuki* was hit in the engine room. The *Kinryu Maru* and *Mutsuki* survivors, including the *Mutsuki's* captain, were picked up, mainly by the *Yayoi*, which rushed the badly wounded to the naval hospital at Rabaul. The *Mutsuki* was sunk then by a "friendly" torpedo at 1053 to prevent her falling into American hands.

The *Jintsu* and the destroyers *Kagero* and *Suzukaze* acted as direct guards to get the convoy out of the range of enemy air power. A little later, the *Jintsu* was instructed to return to Truk for repairs at once and to transfer the flag to the *Suzukaze*. Admiral Yamamoto, seeing the danger to the convoy, ordered the *Zuikaku*, accompanied by three destroyers, to provide air cover; at the same time, twenty-two land-based planes and thirteen Zero fighters attacked Guadalcanal. The convoy made it back to the Shortlands safely. Admiral Yamamoto ordered that the troops in the convoy be sent back to Guadalcanal at once, in smaller and swifter ships. Meanwhile, the Outer South Seas Force Headquarters ordered two destroyers to perform a nightly bombardment of Guadalcanal.

It is difficult to understand Yamamoto's thinking in this battle. He had brought out a large number of ships; he had lost the *Ryujo*, had seen the *Chitose* damaged, but his two heavy carriers had come through unscathed. Only the poor flight direction of the last wave of

Japanese plane attackers robbed the Japanese of a more heady victory. Yet, he cautiously withdrew his main forces to the north and did not return to the attack. If he was seeking a battle to destroy the U.S. fleet in the Southwest Pacific and had initially risked his two heavy carriers to do so, then why, after he knew that the *Enterprise* had been seriously damaged and his pilots reported only one large U.S. carrier left, did he retire?

His Vanguard Force, with Kondo's Main Body, did dash south for a night battle but then immediately returned. Surely a study of American tactics would have alerted the Japanese to the tendency of American carriers to disengage at night when enemy ships were likely to be looking for them. The U.S. fleet carriers could not use their planes at night and were vulnerable to ships' guns; moreover, their protective warship screen was outnumbered by the Japanese forces. Nevertheless, the Eighth Fleet's four cruisers did not bombard Guadalcanal, but sent in only their float planes, carrying light bombs. Tanaka's daylight convoy, being unprotected, suffered severe damage. Were thoughts of Midway inhibiting Admiral Yamamoto?

On the American side, there was timidity, too—but there was good reason for it. At least one carrier had to be afloat to serve as a steppingstone south of Guadalcanal to feed planes to Henderson Field. The worst marks for the U. S. Navy, as at Midway, were for lack of proper flight control and abominable radio discipline among pilots. Admiral Frank Jack Fletcher's staff never had a chance to direct the planes in the air. Task Force 61 was, indeed, fortunate to come out of the battle with as little damage as it did.

Table of Organization for the Second Battle of the Solomon Sea

Combined Fleet (Admiral Yamamoto)

SUPPORT FORCE, MAIN BODY

Battleship: *Yamato*
Escort carrier: *Taiyo*
Destroyers: *Akebono, Ushio*[8]

THIRD FLEET, CARRIER STRIKE FORCE,
MOBILE FORCE, MAIN BODY (Admiral Nagumo)

Heavy carriers: *Zuikaku, Shokaku*
Destroyers: *Kazagumo, Yugumo, Makigumo, Akigumo, Hatsukaze, Akizuki*

THIRD FLEET, DETACHED CARRIER STRIKE FORCE,
MOBILE FORCE, MAIN BODY (Rear Admiral Chuichi Hara)

Light carrier: *Ryujo*
Heavy cruiser: *Tone*
Destroyers: *Amatsukaze, Tokitsukaze*

Second Fleet, Support Forces (Vice Admiral Kondo)

VANGUARD FORCE, CLOSE SUPPORT (of Carrier Strike
   Force, Rear Admiral Abe)

Battleships: *Hiei, Kirishima*
Heavy cruisers: *Kumano, Suzuya, Chikuma*
Light cruiser: *Nagara*
Destroyers: *Nowaki, Tanikaze, Maikaze*

SUPPORT FORCE, MAIN BODY (Vice Admiral Kondo)

Seaplane tender: *Chitose*
Heavy cruisers: *Atago, Maya, Takao, Myoko, Haguro*
Light cruiser: *Yura*
Destroyers: *Kuroshio, Oyashio, Minegumo, Hayashio, Natsugumo,
   Asagumo*

STANDBY FORCE

Converted carrier: *Junyo*

SUPPORT FORCE FOR FLEET TRAIN

Battleship: *Mutsu*
Destroyers: *Harusame, Samidare, Murasame*

**Eighth Fleet, Outer South Seas Force,
Reinforcement Force (Vice Admiral Mikawa)**

CLOSE COVER FORCE (Vice Admiral Mikawa)

Heavy cruisers: *Chokai, Aoba, Kinugasa, Furutaka*

CONVOY ESCORT FORCE (Rear Admiral Tanaka)

Light cruiser: *Jintsu*
Destroyers: *Kagero, Mutsuki, Yayoi, Isokaze, Kawakaze, Suzukaze,
   Umikaze, Uzuki*

TRANSPORT FORCE

Three transports with 1,500 troops
Four patrol boats[9]

U. S. Navy Forces in the Second Battle of the Solomon Sea
Task Force 61 (Vice Admiral Fletcher)
TASK FORCE 11

Heavy carrier: *Saratoga*
Heavy cruisers: *Minneapolis, New Orleans*
Destroyers: *Phelps, Farragut, Dale, Worden, McDonough*

TASK FORCE 16

Heavy carrier: *Enterprise*
Battleship: *North Carolina*
Heavy cruiser: *Portland*
Light cruiser: *Atlanta*
Destroyers: *Balch, Benham, Maury, Ellet, Grayson, Monssen*

TASK FORCE 18

Heavy carrier: *Wasp*
Heavy cruisers: *San Francisco, Salt Lake City*
Light cruiser: *San Juan*
Destroyers: *Farenholt, Aaron Ward, Buchanan, Lang, Stack, Sterett, Selfridge*[10]

Japanese Carrier Planes Involved in the Second Solomon Sea Battle
Main Body
FIRST ATTACK

	Fighters	Carrier bombers
Planes used	10	27
Planes destroyed in the air	3	17
Planes crash-landed in sea and lost	3	1
Total lost	6	18
Returned to carrier	4	9

SECOND ATTACK

	Fighters	Carrier attack
Planes used	9	27
Planes destroyed in the air	0	4
Planes crash-landed in sea and lost	0	1
Total lost	0	5
Returned to carrier	9	22

CAP (Combat Air Patrol)

	Fighters
Planes used	35
Planes destroyed in the air	1
Planes crash-landed in sea and lost	1
Total lost	2

Support Force (the Ryujo)

GUADALCANAL ATTACK

	Fighters	Carrier attack
Planes used	15	6
Planes destroyed in the air	2	3
Planes crash-landed in sea and lost	1	1
Total lost	3	4

CAP (*Ryujo*)

	Fighters
Planes used	7
Planes destroyed in the air	0
Planes crash-landed in sea and lost	0
Total lost acting as CAP	0

Lost Planes, All Carriers

31 *fighters*
29 *carrier bombers*

Planes Fit for Action on 26 August

41 *fighters*
25 *carrier bombers*
34 *carrier attack*[11]

chapter 15

GUADALCANAL—
THE MISERY GROWS

1942

28 Aug.–2 Sept.	4,700 Japanese reinforcements land on Guadalcanal
12–16 September	Japanese attack, and fail to capture, Henderson Field
15 September	Submarine *I-19* sinks the heavy carrier *Wasp*
17 September	Imperial General Headquarters decides to reinforce Guadalcanal with Japanese Army's 17th Division
18 September	Japanese Army decides Guadalcanal campaign takes priority over Papuan campaign
18 September	7th Regiment U. S. Marine Corps reinforces Guadalcanal garrison
9–15 October	Japanese Army feeds in 17th Division by nightly convoys
11–12 October	Battle of Cape Esperance
13 October	United States reinforces Guadalcanal with 164th Regiment of Americal Division

Imperial General Headquarters still vastly underestimated the number of U. S. Marines on Guadalcanal; they guessed there were at most 4,000. The Japanese still faced the same problems: reinforcing the island, destroying the Marine units, and gaining control of the airfield. The disaster that befell the Japanese convoy on 25 August demonstrated that daylight convoys could not survive attacks by the Henderson Field planes; therefore a sufficient number of soldiers had to be brought in at night.

The Americans, with at least one heavy carrier always stationed to the south, had to supply the growing number of Marines on

Guadalcanal and Tulagi, reinforce them when necessary, prevent new Japanese troop landings, and drive off the Japanese troops that were already on the island. For the next month or so, then, the air was under American control in the daytime, for a distance of 250 miles (the range of the SBDs on Guadalcanal), and supplies, gas, and planes were flown in or brought by ship. Small numbers of reinforcements with supplies would also make the run in, often with considerable losses. It was true that Japanese planes were bombing Guadalcanal almost daily, sometimes in massive raids; but, although American planes and supplies could be destroyed and a few men killed in bombing raids, it would take more than that to regain Guadalcanal. Moreover, the Japanese were suffering significant losses in ships, planes, and pilots.[1]

The U. S. Marines held on precariously, into the last days of August. In this stalemate the Japanese had two options: the island would either have to be taken from within, by feeding in enough men and equipment by night, or another major sea battle would have to be fought to drive the U. S. Navy away, thus thwarting its "supply and protect" role at Guadalcanal. They finally decided to attempt first to bring in adequate reinforcement at night. A reinforcement unit of 350 men with supplies, escorted by three destroyers (the *Umikaze, Kawakaze,* and *Isokaze*), was landed without incident, east of Taivu Point on 26 August at 2300. A second unit of 128 men was successfully landed the next night, northwest of Taivu Point.

In Rabaul a more extensive reinforcement program was being put together. A first landing on 28 August would reinforce the Japanese Army with 1,250 troops; then the destroyers would escort a second landing, set for 29 August, which would bring in 750 troops on three fast destroyer transports. A third landing, on 30 August, would put 1,000 more Japanese soldiers on Guadalcanal. The next night a fourth landing of 650 troops, under Major General Kiyotake Kawaguchi, who was to be the new commander-in-chief at Guadalcanal, would be made; then in the fifth and last landing, 1,080 men would be put ashore. In all, the Japanese troops on Guadalcanal would be augmented by more than 4,700 men. All landings would be escorted by destroyers, and after the men had been debarked, the destroyers would proceed to bombard Henderson Field.

The first landing attempt in the large reinforcement effort showed that a convoy should not leave the Shortlands staging area too early; it sailed 28 August, and by 1700 on that same day, it had received its first plane attack. Between 1820 and 1847 the destroyers *Amagiri*, *Asagiri*, *Yugiri*, and *Shirakumo* were jumped by ten SBDs from Henderson Field. The *Asagiri* was mortally hit, and sank almost at once, with sixty-two men killed and her ammunition and supplies lost. The *Yugiri* took a bomb on her smoke funnel, and her after deck was strafed, but she suffered only moderate damage, as did the *Shirakumo*. But both destroyers had to be assisted back to the Shortlands, the *Shirakumo* being towed by the *Amagiri*.

Despite reports at 1300 from the float plane of the heavy cruiser *Aoba* that two U.S. transports, one cruiser, and two destroyers were in Tulagi Harbor (and, an hour later, at Lunga Point), the second convoy group, after some hesitation at Eighth Fleet headquarters, was allowed to sail and arrived off Taivu Point at 2330, escorted by five destroyers (the *Fubuki*, *Shirayuki*, *Hatsuyuki*, *Kawakaze*, and *Umikaze*), and disembarked the reinforcements.

This was the situation as the next inevitable battle began to take shape: every day, usually at noon, Japanese planes raided Henderson Field and the Marine encampment, Tulagi, and anything afloat in the area. On 30 August, in a raid meant as a diversionary maneuver for the landing that night by the Kawaguchi detachment, the Japanese planes managed to catch a converted destroyer, the *Colhoun*, and sink her. The flow of supplies to the Americans, even though U.S. planes controlled the sky during most daylight hours, was barely adequate, and there was often not enough aviation fuel.

At night, Japanese transports and destroyers made the dash from the Shortlands to Taivu Point, disembarking men, artillery, anti-tank guns, ammunition, and rations, bombarding Henderson Field, and then making a fast run back to their Shortlands base. Both sides were undermanned and undersupplied; the Marines had difficulty in establishing a defense perimeter around Henderson Field, but the Japanese lacked the manpower to wrest the field away, and their reinforcements were never enough to alter the balance. Moreover, the Japanese Army forces, which had moved inland to escape daylight bombing, found their strength being sapped by jungle diseases and malnutrition. On 31 August the Japanese Army designated Guadalcanal as its major objective, and placed the operation in Papua on a secondary basis. Finally, on 18 September, it was decided to concentrate on Guadalcanal alone.[2] The battle for Guadalcanal had grown into a monster that Imperial General Headquarters had never foreseen.

Beyond the range of Japanese land-based planes there were three

U.S. carriers, guarding against a conventional landing backed by a Japanese fleet, and feeding planes into Henderson Field. But there was no safety here either; on 31 August, at about 0746, the Japanese submarine *I-26* launched six torpedoes at the *Saratoga*, one of them hitting her on her starboard side, amidships. The damage was not excessive, for a bulge built into the ship absorbed the shock at the point of explosion; but the carrier had to retire to be repaired.

At first, the strain on the Japanese destroyers was not severe. One by one, they were being taken out of service and returned to Truk or Japan for modernization, which involved removing their X turrets (two 5-inch guns) and replacing them with two triple 25-mm. mounts. Eventually, between thirteen and twenty-one such guns were added, along with additional 13-mm. guns. Each destroyer was also equipped with four depth-charge throwers and thirty-six depth charges. (Before, depth charges had been rolled off the fantail on two depth-charge racks.) In addition, their minelaying and minesweeping equipment was removed.

Although these destroyers had been built for surface action (and indeed, in the next year they would see plenty of that), the increasing threat from the air and from under the sea forced them to use new weapons, even at the expense of older ones that were also needed. As the struggle over Guadalcanal and the Slot continued, the Japanese destroyers were being dangerously overworked. All of them needed full overhauls, but the exigencies of war made that impossible, and thus their speed and efficiency slowly began to deteriorate.

The next naval engagement came on the night of 4–5 September. The nightly troop delivery (which the Americans had nicknamed the "Tokyo Express") had embarked in swift destroyer transports, carrying more of General Kawaguchi's unit, escorted by the destroyers *Yudachi*, *Hatsuyuki*, and *Murakumo*. But they were not the only ships in the area; the U.S. destroyer transports *Little* and *Gregory* were on patrol and ferry service between Guadalcanal and Tulagi. At 0100 on 5 September the three Japanese destroyers opened fire on Guadalcanal. Believing that the destroyer bombardments were only a nuisance submarine bombardment, the *Little* and *Gregory* set off from their positions off Lunga Point to investigate, trusting that their radar would disclose any larger warships. Unfortunately for them, a PBY which had also seen the firing ejected flare parachutes which illuminated the American ships; then the *Yudachi* opened fire, and her superior armament sank both ships in short order. The Japanese destroyers, satisfied with their kill, started home at 0135.[3]

It was now becoming even more evident at Rabaul that Guadalcanal and its airfield would have to be captured from within before the Japanese Navy could have any freedom of movement. General Kawaguchi therefore continued to build up his forces with nightly high-speed runs by destroyers, small craft, and barges brought slowly from island to island. Most of the 35th Brigade was landed in this manner between 29 August and 7 September, reinforcing what was left of the Ikki unit. General Kawaguchi, with about 3,500 troops, made a fruitless effort to attack and defeat the Marines and capture Henderson Field on 12 September; but this attack had failed by 16 September, and caused more than 1,100 Japanese casualties.[4] So once again the "Tokyo Express" would have to run overtime to bring in replacements. With the heavy defeat of both the Ikki and Kawaguchi units, it was decided on 17 September that the Seventeenth Army would commit a full division to Guadalcanal. Still Imperial General Headquarters and the headquarters at Rabaul had vastly underestimated Marine strength at 7,500—there were actually 11,000.[5]

But the Marines still lacked the strength to mount an annihilating offensive to clear the island, because of losses from casualties and disease, and because of the troops needed to maintain the five-mile defense perimeter around Henderson Field. These factors spread the available forces very thin. It was finally decided to bring in the 7th Marine Regiment, which left Espiritu Santo on 14 September in six transports, escorted by cruisers and destroyers. To protect the convoy, the heavy carriers *Hornet* and *Wasp* gave distant cover, 100 miles to the south. The *Wasp* was to protect both the convoy and her own contingent (made up of the battleship *North Carolina*, three cruisers, and seven destroyers) from air and submarine attack.

By the afternoon of 14 September, the convoy had been "snooped" by a Japanese flying boat. Then, at about 1430 on 15 September, the *I-19* fired four torpedoes at the *Wasp*. Three of them struck her—two on the starboard side, forward, and another almost amidships. Immediately fires swept across her deck; she had been mortally wounded. Then at 1452, the *I-15* torpedoed the battleship *North Carolina* on her port side, forward; moments later, a torpedo smacked into the destroyer *O'Brien*, ripping off her bow. The *Wasp* erupted in a huge explosion at 1500, and "Abandon Ship" was ordered 20 minutes later. Because of the hopelessness of her condition, she was torpedoed by the destroyer *Lansdowne*, and sank at 2100; twenty-four of her planes were saved, however, by being landed on the heavy carrier *Hornet*. Since there was no fire on the *North Carolina*, she made it back to Pearl Harbor; but the *O'Brien*, after receiving temporary repairs at Espiritu Santo and Nouméa, sank on 19 October, on her way back to the United States, 2,800 miles from the place where she had been torpedoed.

Although the 7th Marine Regiment convoy had retreated during the night of 15 September after the disasters suffered by the cover force, Admiral Richmond Kelly Turner, deciding that the situation at Guadalcanal was serious enough to risk a bold action, brought the convoy in anyway. Between the bad weather and heavy raids on Rabaul by MacArthur's planes, the Japanese planes had been grounded, allowing the convoy to reach Lunga Point safely. At 0550 on 18 September, the Marines began going ashore, covered by a bombardment from the destroyers *Monssen* and *McDonough*. The transports were not attacked while returning to their base.[6]

The situation of the U. S. Navy forces guarding Guadalcanal to the south was becoming desperate: they had only one fleet carrier and one battleship, while the Japanese had two heavy carriers, several more light carriers, and a host of battleships, cruisers, and destroyers. Yet, strangely enough, even though the Japanese clearly had superior strength, they lurked just beyond the horizon as the convoy of U. S. Marines was brought in.

Yamamoto's thoughts at this point have not been officially recorded, and are difficult to infer. He knew that the U.S. naval forces in the Southwest Pacific were inferior to his; but he also knew that back in American shipyards there were two dozen nearly completed heavy carriers, along with battleships, cruisers, destroyers, and submarines, all being built at a pace that Japanese industry could never equal. One can only speculate, then, that he wanted to save his main fleet for the "decisive battle"; such a decision, however, threw an even heavier burden on his already overworked destroyers.

With the land battle on Guadalcanal stalemated during September and the first part of October, the Japanese Navy, though unwilling to send the Combined Fleet down from Truk for another major battle, stepped up its bombardment of Henderson Field and the Marine positions, while the Army continued to bring in new troops, arms, munitions, and food. Gradually, the Japanese, desperate to knock out Henderson Field, added more and larger ships to the nightly bombardment groups. The situation, with Japan pouring in reinforcements for a decisive battle and the Americans also anxious to prepare for the next inevitable Japanese assault, could be expected to produce another major naval battle—and it did, on 11-12 October.[7]

Battle of Cape Esperance

Japan hoped to eliminate American troops not only from Guadalcanal, but also from Tulagi, Rennell, and San Cristobal. To this end, Japanese troops were brought in from China, the Dutch Indies, and the Philippines, and sent, by way of Truk, to Rabaul and the Shortlands, for the nightly run of the "Tokyo Express." Lieutenant General Harukichi Hyakutake, commander-in-chief of the Eighteenth Army, took over command, replacing Major General Kawaguchi.

The Navy cooperated by bringing in the new troops, by damaging Henderson Field and destroying as many of its planes as possible with nightly bombardments and stepped-up air raids, and by preventing American reinforcement. With the American air menace eliminated, Admiral Yamamoto would then be free to "apprehend and annihilate" U. S. Navy forces in the Solomon Seas region. In reality, the decisive factor was Henderson Field—as long as the field functioned, Japanese forces within a 250-mile limit were subject to daylight air attack, which made a sustained naval bombardment of Guadalcanal impossible.

The Americans could read their enemy's intentions, as Japanese Army reinforcements poured in, as the intensity of the nightly bombardment increased, and as the introduction of new Japanese air units escalated the air war. Obviously, new American troops would also have to be brought in. Early in October the U. S. Joint Chiefs of Staff decided to commit the Americal Regiment with 2,800 men to Guadalcanal's defense.

The Americans knew that the Japanese would contest the convoy, with ships and aircraft. To bring in the regiment, U. S. Navy forces were divided into four groups. The distant cover force of the heavy carrier *Hornet* was positioned 180 miles southwest of Guadalcanal, while the battleship *Washington* was 50 miles east of Malaita. Rear Admiral Norman Scott's Task Force 64, composed of the heavy cruisers *San Francisco* (flagship) and *Salt Lake City*, the light cruisers *Boise* and *Helena*, and the destroyers *Farenholt*, *Buchanan*, *Laffey*, *Duncan*, *McCalla*, was near Rennell Island, providing close support for the fourth group, made up of two transports and eight

converted destroyers, under Rear Admiral Turner. The reinforcement operation, which faced a potentially overwhelming Japanese Combined Fleet, would be similar to the "Tokyo Express"—
they would make a dash for Guadalcanal and disembark at midnight, in order to expose the force to the fewest possible hours of air
attack. The transports sortied from Nouméa on 9 October.

On 9 October, the Japanese light cruiser *Tatsuta* and nine destroyers started bringing in General Hyakutake's troops, along with
the general himself. The flow continued, and in a week's time,
22,200 men, with adequate arms and supplies, had been landed on
Guadalcanal.[8] Eleven destroyers had been used in the massive reinforcement. "X Day," the beginning of the grand offensive to drive
the Americans from Guadalcanal, was set for 14 October.

The Japanese convoys were resisted with everything that Henderson Field had. On 10 October, returning to the Shortlands, the
gathering Japanese ships were attacked by forty-two enemy planes
with bombs and torpedoes. While no serious damage was suffered,
the attack strengthened Vice Admiral Gunichi Mikawa's determination to neutralize or eliminate Henderson Field. Accordingly, on
11 October he sent a task force under the command of Rear Admiral
Aritomo Goto to bombard the airfield and provide cover for that
night's convoy. The task force consisted of the heavy cruisers *Aoba*,
Kinugasa, and *Furutaka*, and the destroyers *Hatsuyuki* and *Fubuki*.
These ships would cover a large convoy carrying a considerable part
of the Second Division of the Japanese Army.[9]

The Japanese were unaware of Admiral Scott's Task Force 64
and the reinforcements it was bringing in. Long-range reconnaissance
had given Admiral Scott accurate intelligence of the position and
time of arrival of the two Japanese forces; the advantage, therefore,
was Scott's, and the situation was the reverse of that in the battle of
Savo Island. Scott set his trap carefully. At 2228 Task Force 64 was
14 miles north-northeast of Cape Esperance, heading for Savo Island. Scott intended to launch from each of his four cruisers
Kingfisher planes, which would find and, at the proper time, illuminate the Japanese ships; he succeeded in launching only two, however. At 2235 he formed the force into a single column, with three
destroyers in the van, then four cruisers followed by two destroyers.
Admiral Goto's three heavy cruisers were in a single column, with a
destroyer on each beam of the lead cruiser, steaming south-southeast.
Scott's ships had old and new types of radar, but nearby land rendered both undependable. Goto, however, had excellent lookouts,

one of whom spotted the glare of a burning Kingfisher that had mal-
functioned and caught fire. But Goto, not expecting Task Force 64
to be there, disregarded potentially revealing clues, right up to the
opening of the battle.

At 2250 a Kingfisher spotted three ships in the reinforcement
convoy, six miles from Savo Island. As usual before a night battle,
confusion prevailed. At 2308 the light cruiser *Helena*'s late-model SG
radar picked up Goto's force, but she did not report the force's location and bearing until 2323. The Kingfishers were of little help, for
engine malfunction forced one down at 2330, and the remaining
plane again reported spotting only the reinforcement group. Admiral
Scott continued to cruise between Savo Island and Cape Esperance,
ready to intercept any Japanese bombardment group. The inability
of the flagship *Salt Lake City* to decipher various ill-worded messages
received from 2342 to 2352, informing her of the course and distance
of Goto's force, was a classic foul-up; Scott knew the Japanese force
was nearby, but it could have been anywhere in an arc of 135 degrees. Moreover, because he had just executed a difficult reverse col-

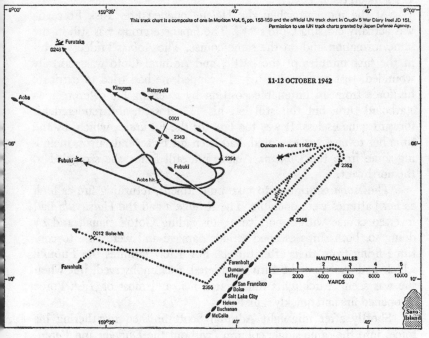

Battle of Cape Esperance, 11–12 October 1942

umn movement at 2332, his destroyers were scattered. The destroyer *Duncan*'s skipper knew, by his fire-control radar, exactly where Goto's force was, and, assuming that all the other U.S. ships also knew, he began a destroyer charge at 30 knots—but no one followed him. Finally, the *Helena*, which had been tracking by radar, informed Admiral Scott that enemy ships could be seen at 5,000 yards. At 2346 the *Helena*'s captain turned on her searchlights and opened fire on the ships of the still unsuspecting Admiral Goto, with 5- and 6-inch guns.

At 2346 the U.S. forces were steaming on a northeasterly course in a single column, consisting of the destroyers *Farenholt* and *Laffey* and the four cruisers, followed by the destroyers *Buchanan* and *McCalla*. The destroyer *Duncan* was about four miles northeast of Scott's force, within 500 yards of the heavy cruiser *Kinugasa*. As firing opened, the *Duncan* pumped several salvos into the heavy cruiser *Furutaka* and then took on the destroyer *Hatsuyuki*. However, within minutes the *Duncan* had been hit in her engine room, and after numerous other hits, she was out of the battle, and eventually sank on the next day.

At the moment when the *Helena* opened fire, Task Force 64 was actually crossing Goto's "T". The Japanese group was still in the same formation and on the same course. The *Aoba*'s bridge was hit in the first minutes of the battle, and Admiral Goto was mortally wounded. Just after seeing his "T" capped, he had tried to extricate his force from an untenable position by reversing his column, in a starboard turn; but this still left his "T" crossed, and rendered his forward guns useless. It was too late for the *Furutaka*, which, by the time her reverse was executed, had been hit by several salvos, including some from the *Duncan*. Ablaze but still firing, she struggled to the northwest.

The *Aoba* continued to take punishment, returning fire as long as her batteries were operable. The *Kinugasa* and the *Hatsuyuki* had reversed course with a port turn, misreading Goto's signal, and by doing so, both ships escaped serious damage and were able to continue firing from their after turrets. For a few minutes the *Fubuki*, which had executed the turn as ordered, was unobserved; but when she was seen, searchlights illuminated her, and most of Task Force 64 opened fire and quickly sank her.

Shortly after midnight Admiral Scott finished regathering his forces into the same single column (without the *Duncan* and *Farenholt*), now pursuing the Japanese. But the *Kinugasa* was still full of fight (and probably was helped for a few minutes by the *Aoba*, *Furutaka*, and *Hatsuyuki*). At 2400, she fired on the heavy cruiser *Salt Lake City* at a range of 8,000 yards, her shells falling just astern the U.S. ship. A Japanese torpedo attack narrowly missed the light cruiser *Boise*, which was rejoining the column; then at 0012 the *Boise* was hit by a gun salvo, her hull penetrated in four places. The *Kinugasa* also fired at her for four minutes. Finally the *Salt Lake City* broke column and interposed herself between the *Boise* and her attackers. The fire fight continued until 0016, with the *Salt Lake City* hit twice. The *Boise* was also further damaged when an 8-inch shell pierced her No. 1 turret and a 6-inch shell penetrated her forward powder magazine below the waterline, causing a tremendous explosion which killed all the men in her forward turrets, powder-handling rooms, and magazines.

The *Furutaka* took quite a beating before she finally sank. Her Action Report states that at 0149 her No. 3 turret was hit, at 0151 the No. 2 torpedo tube was hit, at 0154 a salvo penetrated her forward starboard engine room, and a minute later her after port engine room was hit. At 0205 her main batteries were no longer operative and her forward port engine room had been hit and flooded. "Abandon Ship" was ordered at 0220, and she sank at 0248, 22 miles from Savo Island. No casualty figures were given, but her normal complement was 604. Although the destroyers *Murakumo* and *Shirayuki* rescued 400 men from the water, some of these were killed when the *Murakumo* was severely damaged by air attack, when she was on her way to the Shortlands. The *Aoba's* Action Report records that she received direct hits on her No. 2 and No. 3 turrets, with the No. 3 turret exploding and starting fires. But Japanese heavy cruisers were made of sturdy stuff; although she received some forty hits from 6- and 8-inch shells, she was still able to retire at 30 knots. The only damage to the *Kinugasa* was to two motor boats; she was back in action shelling Tulagi on 14 October. The *Hatsuyuki* also received minor damage to her hull from two hits. On the American side, one light cruiser was heavily damaged, one heavy cruiser moderately damaged, one destroyer sunk, and one destroyer, the *Farenholt*, moderately damaged (from both enemy and "friendly" hits).

Admiral Scott broke off the chase at 0200. Meanwhile at Tassafaronga Point the Japanese convoy disembarked its troops and cargo without interference from Task Force 64. But on its return trip to the Shortlands on the morning of 12 October, the convoy was attacked by seventy planes, and the *Natsugumo* was sunk, while the *Murakumo* was badly damaged, and eventually scuttled.[10]

The Japanese losses were caused primarily by Admiral Goto's blind conviction that there was no U.S. task force in the area. The battle itself was one of the very few night conflicts in which the Japanese Navy did not show a clear superiority.

The battle could be called an American victory, if tonnage of ships sunk or disabled were totalled. However, confused communications, failure to pass on vital information at once, and the single-column formation of the U. S. Navy forces prevented it from becoming a disastrous defeat for the Japanese—and, as at the battle of Savo Island, the invading convoy was able to carry out its task and return. But Admiral Turner, in turn, was able to land the 164th Regiment of the Americal Division on 13 October. Thus, the Guadalcanal deadlock tightened, and another major naval battle became inevitable—for success in the land battle depended on naval bombardments, naval battles, and air supremacy, while escalation merely prolonged and intensified the struggle.[11]

Table of Organization, Battle of Cape Esperance

Eighth Fleet (Rear Admiral Aritomo Goto)

OUTER SOUTH SEA FORCE, BOMBARDMENT FORCE

Heavy cruisers: *Aoba, Furutaka, Kinugasa*
Destroyers: *Hatsuyuki, Fubuki*

CONVOY ESCORT FORCE (Rear Admiral Takaji Joshima)

Seaplane tenders: *Chitose, Nisshin*
Destroyers: *Akizuki, Asagumo, Natsugumo, Yamagumo, Murakumo, Shirayuki*[12]

U. S. Navy Table of Organization

Task Force 64 (Rear Admiral Norman Scott)

Heavy cruisers: *San Francisco, Salt Lake City*
Light cruisers: *Boise, Helena*
Destroyers: *Farenholt, Buchanan, Laffey, Duncan, McCalla*[13]

chapter 16

GUADALCANAL— THE BATTLE EXPANDS

1942

13–15 October	Japanese begin daily heavy raids, and nightly bombardments by Japanese battleships and heavy cruisers. Allied situation becomes critical
15 October	Daylight Japanese convoy attempts landings, and suffers heavy damage in ships, troops, and supplies
23 October	Japanese renew land battle
25–27 October	In support of land battle, Japanese Combined Fleet seeks battle with U. S. Navy forces. Carrier battle of Santa Cruz Islands
26 October	Japanese call for more reinforcements

Once the main strength of General Hyakutake's army had been delivered into Guadalcanal during the Battle of Cape Esperance, the Japanese were determined to end the Guadalcanal and southern Solomons campaign. The overall plan called for a massive coordinated land attack to wrest Henderson Field from the Americans. Preparations would include the construction of a new airstrip at Buin at the southern tip of Bougainville, so that greater fighter protection could be given to the Japanese bombers. Bombing runs would make Henderson Field inoperable by day so that convoys could bring in troops, heavy artillery, and all other military supplies necessary to insure success in the upcoming land battle. Meanwhile, the Navy would intensify its night bombardments of Henderson Field, using new thin-skinned anti-personnel high-explosive (APHE) shells, designed for shelling the airfield and Marine positions from a battleship's 14-inch guns. In preparation for the final victory which would annihilate both land and naval forces in the area, Admiral Yamamoto's Combined Fleet sortied from Truk on 11 October, and hovered to the north awaiting word that the field had been taken.

On 13 October Henderson Field was not in bad shape; it had ninety planes, divided equally between dive bombers and fighters.[1] Then at noon, all hell broke loose, when twenty-four high-flying Japanese bombers made extremely accurate runs over the field, leaving it a mass of craters. Two hours later, fifteen more bombers further devastated the field. Working furiously, the Seabees succeeded in getting the holes filled by nightfall. But no sooner was this done than two 8-inch howitzers, brought in by the Japanese during the battle of Cape Esperance, began putting new holes in the field (although they were silenced for a while by counterfire from three U.S. destroyers).[2] But the worst was yet to come. After midnight the battleships *Kongo* and *Haruna*, lying out of range of shore batteries, bombarded Henderson Field and the Marine positions for an hour and a half with the newly developed APHE shells. The two battleships were joined by the light cruiser *Isuzu* and destroyers *Oyashio*, *Kuroshio*, *Hayashio*, *Umikaze*, *Kawakaze*, and *Suzukaze*. The *Haruna* fired 483 rounds from her main batteries and 21 from secondary batteries, while the *Kongo* fired 430 rounds from her main batteries and 33 from secondary batteries.[3] When it was over, Henderson Field was ablaze with burning gasoline and planes; by daylight, only seven dive bombers and thirty-five fighters were operational, with scarcely any fuel left to power them.

Admiral Takeo Kurita was determined to give the Americans no respite. At 1200 Henderson took an aerial bombing, followed an hour later by a repeat. With the sky and the sea seemingly secure in Japanese hands, a large convoy, carrying the last elements of the Army's Second Division, came down the Slot at 14 knots during the night of 14–15 October, bound for Tassafaronga. There were six transports carrying the troops, escorted by the destroyers *Shiratsuyu*, *Ariake*, *Yudachi*, *Shigure*, *Akizuki*, *Harusame*, *Samidare*, and *Murasame*. By 0645, they had reached their disembarkation point.[4]

That night, Admiral Mikawa's flagship, the heavy cruiser *Chokai*, along with the *Kinugasa* and the destroyers *Amagiri* and *Mochizuki*, lay offshore and from 0149 to 0216 pumped 5-, 6-, and 8-inch shells onto the airfield.[5] At dawn on 15 October the defenders of Henderson Field saw the anchored Japanese troop convoy, only ten miles away. At that moment Henderson Field had only four dive bombers and ten P-40 fighters, and no aviation fuel. A frantic search turned up enough gasoline hidden away in the jungle to enable the remaining planes to make one round trip to the convoy, which would be covered by destroyers' antiaircraft fire and by Japanese fighter planes.

The Americans' situation on 15 October was indeed desperate, but they made use of everything they had, and shortly after noon, transport planes came in from Espiritu Santo with gasoline, and additional B-17s were flown in. But the heavy Japanese air raids continued. At 1545, thirty Japanese planes raided the field, and at 1845 thirty more made a second raid; but Henderson Field's antiaircraft fire was accurate and vicious, and seventeen Japanese planes were shot down. As the day wore on, the Japanese began to discover that, even with the meticulous planning and tremendous effort they had put forth, and even though the skies over Guadalcanal were almost completely under their control, the sea was still too dangerous for daylight convoys.

First a B-17 bombed the ships at Tassafaronga at 0700. Then the convoy was attacked by twenty-five carrier-based bombers from 0930 to 1045; one transport was hit and set afire. At 1220, another B-17 made a bombing run. More attacks by carrier planes were made from 1140 to 1230, and another transport was damaged. Although they had unloaded swiftly, the Japanese sustained heavy losses in troops, munitions, and supplies. Under the threat of more attacks, two transports weighed anchor and began retiring to the north. A final wave of twenty planes arrived at 1315; shortly thereafter, the *Kyushu Maru*'s munitions exploded, and she was beached. Still not completely unloaded, the three undamaged transports were ordered to retire at 2300. General Hyakutake now had all his forces ashore for X Day, but they were without many necessary supplies.

Meanwhile, Henderson Field's travail continued. Starting at 0027 on 16 October the heavy cruiser *Myoko* sent in 465 main battery rounds, while the heavy cruiser *Maya*'s main batteries delivered 450 rounds. The destroyers *Umikaze*, *Kawakaze*, and *Suzukaze* acted as supply ships, and destroyers *Naganami*, *Makinami*, and *Takanami* screened, and added their fire. At 0120, the force retired to the north.[6]

Although the Southwest Pacific had always been given a lower priority in men, ships, planes, and supplies than Europe, President Roosevelt and the U. S. Joint Chiefs of Staff, recognizing the gravity of the situation on Guadalcanal, began to consider what could be done.[7] First there was a change in leadership; Vice Admiral William F. Halsey relieved Vice Admiral Robert L. Ghormley as commander-in-chief, South Pacific on 18 October. More ships, including the new battleship *Indiana*, then in the Atlantic, were ordered to the Southwest Pacific. The U. S. Army's 25th Division, on Oahu, was ordered south. Four dozen fighter planes in the Central Pacific were ordered into the imperiled area, two dozen fleet submarines were sent south, more B-17s were given to Admiral Aubrey Fitch at Espiritu Santo, and the repaired *Enterprise* was sent at full speed to meet the *Hornet*. Finally, President Roosevelt ordered the Joint Chiefs of Staff to hold Guadalcanal, adding, "My anxiety about the Southwest Pacific is to make sure that every possible weapon gets into that area to hold Guadalcanal."[8]

No matter what high decisions were being made in Washington, the American troops on Guadalcanal were fighting every day for their very existence. The Japanese Army's general offensive opened on 22 October as a double-envelopment movement on Henderson Field, with X Day set for the next day. While outnumbering the field's defenders, the Japanese had the worst tactical position, for they were operating in a jungle without trails, in torrential rains, against fixed American defenses. The western Japanese flank failed in its attack on 23 October, but on 24 and 25 October the eastern flank came within yards of overrunning the last American defensive position of the airfield. This offensive was one of the most vicious land battles in the Pacific, fought with zeal and bravery on both sides, under almost unbearable conditions, by weakened and disease-ridden soldiers.[9]

On the morning of 26 October the Japanese finally halted their general offensive, and the call went out for more reinforcements; they would make another try sometime in November. The 38th Division was called for; meanwhile, Tanaka's "Tokyo Express" would continue to run. Nothing on Guadalcanal had really changed; both armies were determined, but even more exhausted, sick, and undermanned.

During the battle both navies lost ships which had been bringing in supplies or operating in the waters around Guadalcanal. The U.S. lost the destroyer *Meredith* and the fleet tug *Vireo*, while the destroyer seaplane tender *McFarland*, carrying munitions, was damaged and had to be towed into Tulagi. On 20 October the heavy cruiser *Chester* was torpedoed by the *I-76* and severely damaged.

During the land battle the nightly run of the "Tokyo Express" had continued. The Japanese Army had promised to capture Henderson Field by 25 October; and in order to provide the final push to sink American shipping at Tulagi and assist the Army forces, the Navy made a daylight raid with a First Attack Unit made up of the destroyers *Akatsuki, Ikazuchi,* and *Shiratsuyu.* (The *Shikinami* was also attached to this group, but acted as guard for a convoy.) As a follow-up, meant to trap the American defenders between the Japanese land forces on one side and a naval bombardment on the other, a Second Attack Unit, made up of the light cruiser *Yura,* and the destroyers *Akizuki, Murasame, Harusame,* and *Yudachi,* was dispatched to the Slot.[10]

The First Attack Unit entered Tulagi Harbor just after 1000, had an inconclusive fire fight with two U.S. minesweepers, sank a fleet tug and a patrol craft, and then taking up a position off Lunga Point, began to fire on the American positions. Once again the Japanese ships were outgunned by coastal batteries; both the *Akatsuki* and the *Ikazuchi* were hit, and the three Japanese destroyers had to retire behind a smoke screen. The presumption that Henderson Field would soon be in Japanese hands had undoubtedly prompted Vice Admiral Mikawa, the Outer South Seas Force commander at Rabaul, to order the attack.

The *Yura's* group never reached its destination. While in Indispensable Strait, the ships came under air attack from six B-17s, and the *Yura* and *Akizuki* were hit. After transferring her crew to the *Murasame,* the destroyers *Harusame* and *Yudachi* sank the *Yura* at 1820; the force then retired to the north.[11]

Why did the Japanese risk having these two units approach Guadalcanal in the daylight? The record leaves little doubt that the Navy fully believed Army reports that Henderson Field would be held by the Japanese by dawn on 25 October. The first assault mission, not expecting counterfire, was to bombard pockets of resistance after clearing the area of U.S. ships. The second assault group would assist the Army with gunfire support and would also land reinforcements. Yamamoto, waiting to the north, must have been chagrined when he heard of the Army's failure to deliver Henderson as promised—and justifiably so, for the Army had never even signalled to the naval forces that it had failed to take the airfield.

Battle of the Santa Cruz Islands

With the Army's failure to recapture Guadalcanal and "annihilate the enemy," Yamamoto could wait no longer to execute the naval part of the Imperial General Headquarters' orders. He sent his powerful Combined Fleet south again, to destroy the U.S. naval forces supporting Guadalcanal. On the American side, the newly appointed COMSOPAC, Vice Admiral Halsey, was equally determined to hold his position, and ordered: "Attack—Repeat—Attack." Neither bulldog would let go.

The disposition of Yamamoto's ships shows that he still believed in a division of his forces; but this time he placed his Carrier Strike Force in the rear with battle fleets in the van, hoping that the U.S. carrier planes would go for the battle fleets instead of the carriers. As usual, Yamamoto remained at Truk in the battleship *Yamato*.

The American plan of battle was as before, with two Task Forces under the over-all command of Vice Admiral William F. Halsey, South Pacific Force, at Nouméa. Task Force 16, under Rear Admiral Thomas C. Kinkaid, consisted of one fleet carrier, the *Enterprise*, with a support force of the battleship *South Dakota*, the heavy cruiser *Portland*, and an antiaircraft cruiser, the *San Juan*. It was screened by eight destroyers. Task Force 17, under Rear Admiral George D. Murray, had the fleet carrier *Hornet*, the heavy cruisers *Northampton* and *Pensacola*, and two antiaircraft cruisers, the *San Diego* and *Juneau*. It had a screen of six destroyers.

Serving as a battle line, Task Force 64 under Rear Admiral Willis A. Lee had the battleship *Washington*, the heavy cruiser *San Francisco*, two antiaircraft cruisers, the *Helena* and *Atlanta*, and six destroyers.

When Yamamoto sent his forces south on 25 October, their disposition was thus: Admiral Abe's Force was 60 miles south of Nagumo's Mobile Force, Main Body, on a course that would pass to the east of Malaita Island. The Advance Force guarded Nagumo's carriers to the west, and the *Junyo*'s air group was still farther west. Admiral Fitch's B-17s and PBYs had done good reconnaissance work and had spotted the Japanese groups coming south. Yamamoto knew this, and fearing a trap, he reversed his Strike Force to the north on 25 October, leaving his Vanguard Force, which did not reverse course, still farther south of the carriers. He knew from his own reconnaissance planes that an American task force lay east of Rennell Island and north of Ndeni Island of the Santa Cruz group, but he did not know how many carriers were in it—he did not yet know that the *Enterprise* had returned to the area.

At 1800 the Japanese Strike Force again turned south, but there was uneasiness about what the Americans had waiting. That anxiety was intensified when, at 0250, the *Zuikaku* was surprised by a bomb, landing about 1,000 feet off the starboard beam, dropped by a plane she had not detected. (The sky for the next two days was filled with cumulonimbus clouds—good cover for planes, and therefore dangerous for ships.) At 0400 all the Japanese forces again reversed course.

On the American side, Task Forces 16 and 17 set a northwesterly course during the night, which at dawn left them some 30 miles north-northeast of Ndeni Island and about 220 miles from Nagumo's carriers. Again the game of "hide and seek" began. Despite Admiral Kinkaid's knowledge of the *Zuikaku*'s location at 0512, the advantage this time lay with the Japanese. Kinkaid awaited further reports from his patrol planes.

A report at 0300 from a PBY which had spotted Nagumo's carriers was not delivered to Admiral Kinkaid until 0512. Lacking this information, at 0500 he launched sixteen SBDs from the *Enterprise*, carrying 500-pound bombs, on a search and attack mission covering a 200-mile arc to the north. Two planes of this group spotted the Vanguard Force at 0617, reported its position, sent another location report at 0630, and continued north—failing, however, to find the carriers. But at 0650 two more of the group did sight the Japanese carrier force and reported its location to Kinkaid; they were attacked by the carrier group's combat air patrol, but escaped into the towering cumulonimbus clouds. Two more pilots from the *Enterprise* picked up the location coordinates, and at 0740 dive-bombed the unsuspecting light carrier *Zuiho*. One bomb smashed her flight deck, aft, leaving a 50-foot crater; since the *Zuiho* could no longer recover planes, she was ordered back to Truk after launching her aircraft. Thus what began only as a search mission resulted in the elimination of a Japanese light carrier at the outset of the battle. One more group of two planes also attacked the heavy cruiser *Tone* at 0626, but without effect.

At 0650 a Japanese cruiser launch plane spotted the U.S. carriers; Nagumo immediately readied his planes. The first attack unit of sixty-two planes was launched from the *Zuikaku, Shokaku,* and *Zuiho* at 0755, along with a combat air patrol. A second attack unit of twenty-four planes was launched from the *Shokaku* at 0810, along with twenty from the *Zuikaku* at 0845; this group was then joined by twenty-nine planes from the *Junyo*.

The *Hornet* didn't get her first strike of twenty-nine planes airborne until 0730, to be followed by the *Enterprise*'s nineteen planes at 0800; then at 0815 the *Hornet* sent off twenty-five more planes.

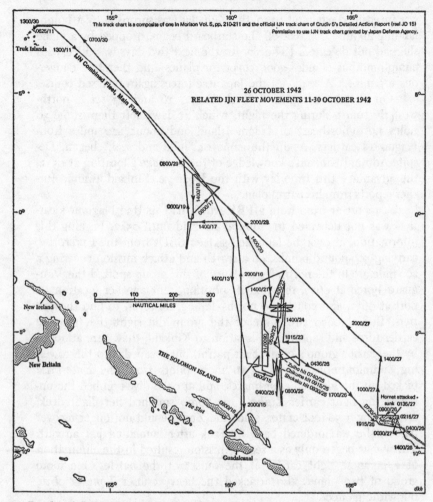

Battle of Santa Cruz Islands, 26 October 1942, and Related IJN Fleet Movements 11–30 October 1942.

Admiral Kinkaid kept thirty-eight fighters as cover for the two American carriers. Thus at the same time that the Japanese were attacking with 135 planes, the Americans were attacking with 73. The attacking air groups passed each other—sometimes peacefully, sometimes breaking into dogfights. The *Enterprise* lost eight planes in her strike group in tangling with Japanese fighters while less than halfway to the target.

At 0859, the American combat air patrol sighted Japanese dive bombers at 17,000 feet, but the U.S. fighters were too close and too low to render maximum protection. The ring of defending ships could not stop the Japanese planes that had broken through. The attackers concentrated on the *Hornet*. (The *Enterprise* was hidden in a rain storm, and Admiral Kondo believed that only one carrier was in the area.) First, at 0910 the *Hornet* was hit on her flight deck, on the starboard quarter. Then a Japanese pilot rode his plane into her, hitting the funnel and going through the flight deck, where his two bombs exploded. Attack planes torpedoed her twice in her engine room. The *Hornet* went dead in the water, and was then smashed by three more bombs—one hitting the flight deck, and two exploding four decks below. Another plane rammed the *Hornet*'s bow, ruining the forward elevator shaft. The attack had lasted only ten minutes. By 1000 the *Hornet* had her fires out and was taken in tow.

At that time, the *Enterprise*, which was now visible, was also attacked by dive bombers, but because of newly installed antiaircraft guns on the carrier and her escort ships, the Japanese managed only two hits and one near-miss. The first bomb hit well forward and exploded deep in the ship; the second landed abaft the forward elevator shaft, exploding in the hangar deck and the deck below, while the near-miss loosened plates in the starboard quarter. Fourteen attack planes with torpedoes made a run at the *Enterprise* at about 1030, but none scored a hit; however, the destroyer *Smith* was struck on her bow by a torpedo plane, and the destroyer *Porter* was torpedoed at 1002 by a Japanese submarine. The destroyer *Shaw*, after taking off the *Porter*'s men, sank her with gunfire.

The *Junyo*'s strike arrived at 1121 but scored only a near-miss on the *Enterprise*; however, the *South Dakota* and *San Juan* were hit and damaged. The Japanese attacks were finally over, and the *Enterprise*, which was having difficulty landing planes, sent her bombers to Espiritu Santo and retired south at 1400.

Attempts to tow the *Hornet* were ineffective, and all but essential men were ordered to abandon ship at 1440. Planes from the *Junyo* and the *Shokaku* torpedoed her again at 1520, flooding her damaged engine room. At 1540 she underwent still another dive-bombing, followed at 1550 by another in which she received a bomb on her flight deck, on the starboard quarter. At 1720 the *Junyo*'s bombers got a last hit into the now-empty hangar deck. By dark the *Hornet* had been abandoned. The destroyers *Mustin* and *Anderson* fired four torpedoes apiece into her, but she refused to go down, so the remaining U.S. forces then left her ablaze, retiring south. (She was finally sunk the next day by the destroyers *Makigumo* and *Akigumo*, from the Vanguard Force.)

The *Hornet*'s initial strike of fifty-two planes was scattered and poorly placed, and by the time the *Shokaku* and the blazing *Zuiho* were discovered at 0918, the *Hornet*'s group was down to fifteen SBDs; those not shot down in the previous dogfights had become separated. Nevertheless, by using cloud cover and diving through Japanese fighters, the dive bombers succeeded in hitting the *Shokaku*'s flight deck with four 1,000-pound bombs, putting her out of the battle. This three-carrier group continued on a northwesterly course, with only the *Zuikaku* still operational. Sixty miles to the west, however, the *Junyo*, which had been closing Nagumo's carriers, was still in the fight.

The surviving U.S. planes were disorganized; the *Hornet*'s torpedo planes could not find the *Shokaku*, and at 0931 when they did find and attack the heavy cruiser *Suzuya* of the Vanguard Force, they made no hits. The *Hornet*'s second strike group also found the Vanguard Force instead of the carriers. The heavy cruiser *Chikuma* was jumped at 0902 by six torpedo planes, but she avoided their torpedoes. At 0915, however, she was attacked by twenty-one enemy aircraft, including nine dive bombers, which scored direct hits on both the port and starboard sides of the bridge, killing most of the bridge personnel. At 0939 she was damaged by three near-misses which sprayed metal over her deck. Before the attack was over, she had taken two more direct hits, one of them penetrating to the engine room. Crippled, she retired toward Truk, having lost 190 men, with 154 wounded. The Action Report of the heavy cruiser *Tone*, also in the Vanguard Force, mentions attacks by about fifty-one enemy planes from 0857 to 1000, including an attack by ten torpedo planes from 0951 to 0955. The Action Reports of other ships in the Vanguard Force show that they also were under attack, and the destroyer *Teruzuki* suffered minor hull damage and moderate casualties.

The Mobile Force carriers steamed northwest from 0600 to midafternoon. Nagumo transferred his flag to the destroyer *Arashi* at 0930, and at 1230 the *Zuikaku*, with a screen, detached herself from the two damaged carriers, once again turning to the southeast. (Nagumo finally boarded the *Zuikaku* at 1530 on 27 October.) This course was followed until sundown; then the carrier broke off the battle and retired through Indispensable Strait. At 0055 one of her escort destroyers, the *Teruzuki*, was narrowly missed during a PBY bombing run, suffering seven men killed.

The *Junyo* had turned southeast at 1100, but at 2000 she reversed course and, heading north, joined the *Zuikaku* during the night. At about 1100 the Vanguard Force also turned southeast and continued on that course until 1830. Admiral Abe, after a box search course, retired to the north; it was his two destroyers that sank the *Hornet*. The Advance Force of Admiral Kondo paralleled the Vanguard Force, following a box search route farther south, about 60 miles south of the *Hornet*.[12]

The battle was over. The U. S. Navy had lost a heavy carrier and a destroyer, and had suffered damage to a battleship, a heavy carrier, a heavy cruiser, and an antiaircraft light cruiser. But the *Enterprise's* losses had not been heavy, and because the *Hornet's* planes had landed on her, she was restored to nearly full air strength when she retired. Nevertheless, the U.S. carriers had taken a beating. The *Enterprise* was withdrawn because she was now the only U.S. carrier which could serve as a staging base for planes sent to Guadalcanal; planes from rear land bases could reach Guadalcanal by refueling on the *Enterprise*.

The Japanese also suffered extensive losses: one light carrier moderately damaged, one heavy carrier severely damaged, one heavy carrier slightly damaged, two destroyers damaged, and one heavy cruiser badly damaged. Yamamoto decided to withdraw to the north because he had lost more than 100 planes to the U. S. Task Force's increased antiaircraft firepower. His pilots were as brave as before, but not as skillful, for a great many of his best pilots had been killed. Yet at this time he was very close to real success. If he had only pressed the attack, he might have eliminated the *Enterprise*, the only remaining carrier in the Pacific which could feed planes into Henderson Field. But his two undamaged carriers simply did not have enough planes left to continue the fight. Moreover, he feared not only the *Enterprise*, whose whereabouts were still unknown, but also the planes at Espiritu Santo, which had performed well in both search and attack. A determining factor in this battle was the additional antiaircraft firepower on newly arrived U.S. ships; not only was the number of antiaircraft guns increased, but the U. S. Navy began using an American adaptation of the Swedish Bofors—40-mm. guns in twin and quadruple mounts. Once again, it had been proven that a combat air patrol could not stop determined Japanese bombers and their fighter escorts; nor was the ring defense around the carriers effective. But most U. S. Navy ships would soon be bristling with these new antiaircraft batteries and the amount of fighter cover provided would be increased. Thus, the number of Japanese planes shot down would be vastly increased in future battles.

While search operations were well executed by both sides, poor communications again handicapped the U. S. Task Force commanders, for the Americans had all the information they needed to make a successful first strike; that information had not, however, been communicated to the right people. Japanese communications and battle intelligence were good, even though their cruiser and battleship launch planes did not have the range of the PBYs and B-17s from Espiritu Santo.

At the moment, the situation at sea and on Guadalcanal was still stalemated. The Americans did not have enough land forces to go on the offensive, and at sea they had only one damaged carrier available, although carrier and battleship reinforcements were on the way. Japanese naval forces had once again failed to isolate Guadalcanal. On land and at sea, a final showdown lay ahead.

Table of Organization, Battle of the Santa Cruz Islands; Combined Fleet (Admiral Yamamoto in the <u>Yamato</u>)

Third Fleet, Carrier Strike Force, Mobile Force, Main Body (Vice Admiral Chuichi Nagumo)

Heavy carriers: *Shokaku, Zuikaku*[13]
Light carrier: *Zuiho*
Heavy cruiser: *Kumano*
Destroyers: *Amatsukaze, Hatsukaze, Tokitsukaze, Yukikaze, Arashi, Maikaze, Teruzuki, Yamakaze*

Second Fleet, Advance Force (Vice Admiral Nobutake Kondo)

Heavy cruisers: *Atago, Takao, Maya, Myoko*
Light cruiser: *Isuzu*
Destroyers: *Kawakaze, Makinami, Suzukaze, Takanami, Umikaze, Naganami*

Second Fleet, Close Support Force (Vice Admiral Takeo Kurita)

Battleships: *Kongo, Haruna*
Destroyers: *Harusame, Kagero, Murasame, Samidare, Oyashio, Yudachi*

Second Fleet, Vanguard Force, Main Body
(Rear Admiral H. Abe)

Battleships: *Hiei, Kirishima*
Heavy cruisers: *Suzuya, Tone, Chikuma*
Light cruiser: *Nagara*
Destroyers: *Akigumo, Isokaze, Kazagumo, Yugumo, Makigumo,*
    Tanikaze, Urakaze, Teruzuki

Second Fleet, Air Group Force (Rear Admiral Kakuji Kakuta)

Light carrier: *Junyo*
Destroyers: *Hayashio, Kuroshio*
12 submarines

Fleet Train

Destroyer: *Nowaki*
4 oil tankers

Eighth Fleet, Outer South Seas Force, Guadalcanal Attack Force
(Vice Admiral G. Mikawa in heavy cruiser Chokai at
Shortland Islands)

ASSAULT FORCE

Destroyers: *Akatsuki, Ikazuchi, Shiratsuya*

BOMBARDMENT FORCE (Rear Admiral Tamotsu Takama)

Light cruiser: *Yura*
Destroyers: *Akizuki, Harusame, Samidare, Murasame, Yudachi*[14]

U. S. Navy Table of Organization

South Pacific Force (Vice Admiral William Halsey,
at Nouméa)

TASK FORCE 16 (Rear Admiral Thomas Kinkaid)

Heavy carrier: *Enterprise*
Battleship: *South Dakota*
Heavy cruiser: *Portland*
Light cruiser: *San Juan*
Destroyers: *Porter, Mahan, Cushing, Conyngham, Preston, Smith,*
    Maury, Shaw

TASK FORCE 17 (Rear Admiral George D. Murray)

Heavy carrier: *Hornet*
Heavy cruisers: *Northampton, Pensacola*
Light cruisers: *San Diego, Juneau*
Destroyers: *Anderson, Borton, Hughes, Morris, Russell, Mustin*[15]

chapter 17

THIRD BATTLE
OF THE
SOLOMON SEA

(USN Title: Battle of Guadalcanal)

1942

13 November	First phase: wild melee between Japanese force, with two battleships, cruisers, and destroyers, and U. S. Task Group 67.4. Heavy losses on both sides; the battleship *Hiei* sinks. U. S. Task Group prevents bombardment of Guadalcanal
14 November	Second phase: Japanese force of three cruisers and two destroyers bombards Henderson Field
15 November	Third phase: battleships duel. Japanese scuttle the damaged *Kirishima*
15 November	Admiral Tanaka brings in rest of Army 38th Division in eleven high-speed transports, but incurs heavy losses in ships, troops, and supplies

The situation on Guadalcanal was becoming unendurable for both sides. The U. S. Navy, with severely depleted forces and a badly damaged carrier, was still determined to bring in the foot soldiers needed to break the land stalemate. To prevent the Japanese from playing the same role, Halsey began collecting units to block Japanese reinforcements. There were enough planes and pilots at Henderson Field, although they also needed constant reinforcement because of losses from frequent large-scale Japanese air raids and the ensuing air battles. Halsey still kept the *Enterprise* on station south of Guadalcanal, carrying civilian workers who were repairing her damages.

Bringing in the 38th Division was the next task facing the indefatigable Admiral Tanaka and his "Tokyo Express." But at the same time, the Japanese Navy was just as determined as the Americans to isolate Guadalcanal. With both sides having such similar objectives, it was inevitable that a new and bigger naval battle would occur.

Both the Americans and the Japanese proceeded to carry out a massive troop buildup, during the three months from 7 August to 12 November.

Troops on Guadalcanal, 7 August to 12 November

	Japanese	American
7 August	2,200	10,000
20 August	3,600	10,000
12 September	6,000	11,000
23 October	22,000	23,000
12 November	30,000	29,000[1]

For two weeks after the Battle of the Santa Cruz Islands, the same tense situation persisted, and the unbending determination of both sides stiffened. American ships brought in troops and supplies by day, sometimes bombarding the Japanese land positions; then the Japanese ships would deliver troops by night, and bombard Henderson. Between 2 and 10 November, sixty-five destroyers and two cruisers, all loaded with troops, brought in the Japanese Army's 38th Division. During that time, there were occasional confrontations. An American transport was torpedoed by the submarine *I-20* and beached on 7 November, and on 12 November, the destroyer *Buchanan* was damaged by friendly antiaircraft fire, while the heavy cruiser *San Francisco* was damaged by a Japanese plane which crashed into her after section. On 7 November the destroyers *Naganami* and *Takanami* were damaged in an air raid; the next night the destroyer *Mochizuki* suffered a torpedo hit from a PT boat.[2]

The initiative for the upcoming battle was taken by the Japanese. It would be another massive and prolonged effort; Yamamoto planned to bring men and supplies down to Tassafaronga Point on the night of 14–15 November, using eleven well-escorted high-speed *Maru* transports, backed by Admiral Kondo's Attack Group. This movement would be preceded by two heavy bombardments of Henderson by battleships, cruisers, and destroyers on 12–13 and 13–14 November. Halsey knew that these naval units were gathering, and he used every available ship to meet them. At the same time, he had to provide adequate protection for the *Enterprise* and get as many troops onto Guadalcanal as he could manage.

Admiral Turner had made it successfully to Guadalcanal and had unloaded most of his troops and supplies on 12 November; knowing that a Japanese force was headed south, he cleared his transports. The Support Group stayed on to prevent a night bombardment, although Rear Admiral Daniel J. Callaghan knew that his Task Group 67.4 was inferior to the Japanese in firepower, for the two battleships guarding the *Enterprise* were too distant to give aid, and Admiral Halsey still would not risk sending the *Enterprise* north.

The disposition of Admiral Abe's Bombardment Force and the arrangement of the shells in his big ships' magazines strongly suggest that his primary objective was a devastating bombardment of Henderson Field and the U. S. Marine positions. He was, however, aware that Turner's transports, guarded by warships, well might be in the region; thus, he took a calculated risk by choosing to make the bombardment first.[3]

As Abe's force came south at 1530, it entered an intense tropical storm, and the force was still in bad weather as it neared Savo Island at 2400 on 12 November. He ordered his ships to reverse course, for the storm had seriously impaired visibility. The reversal disrupted his planned disposition of forces.

Once the weather cleared at 0040, another reversal was ordered. By the time the Bombardment Force was approaching Guadalcanal after rounding Savo Island, the light cruiser *Nagara* and the battleships *Hiei* and *Kirishima* had formed a central column. Directly on the column's starboard beam were the destroyers *Ikazuchi*, *Inazuma*, and *Akatsuki*, while the destroyers *Yudachi* and *Harusame* were directly ahead. On the column's port beam were the destroyers *Amatsukaze*, *Teruzuki*, and *Yukikaze*, followed by the destroyers *Asagumo*, *Murasame*, and *Samidare*. The two reversals had disrupted and scattered Abe's destroyers, and most of the Japanese ships did not know where the others were.

The gun turrets still contained anti-personnel high-explosive (APHE) shells, and the 14-inch armor-piercing (AP) shells were at the back of the ammunition magazines, stored behind the APHE shells. Clearly, Admiral Abe was planning to bombard Henderson Field.

Suddenly at 0142 the *Yudachi* sighted enemy ships. At once, the APHE shells had to be sent down to the magazine, while other

APHE shells were removed and stacked in order to get at the AP shells, which then had to be sent up to the turrets. For eight minutes the situation was critical, much like Admiral Nagumo's situation when he was changing his planes' armament from bombs to torpedoes at Midway; if an enemy shell had hit a gun turret, causing a flash back to the magazine, the ship would have been utterly destroyed. But the Americans gave Abe those eight minutes, as the two forces closed at 40 knots.

The U.S. ships' formation was also faulty, for they were in a single column, which gave them no destroyer screening and no opportunity for massed destroyer-torpedo attacks; thus the same mistakes made in previous night battles were being repeated. At 0130 the column was halfway through a turn from northwest to north. The destroyers *Cushing, Laffey, Sterett, O'Bannon,* the light cruiser *Atlanta,* and the heavy cruiser *San Francisco* had already executed a change of course. The heavy cruiser *Portland* was turning, but the light cruisers *Helena* and *Juneau,* and the destroyers *Aaron Ward, Barton, Monssen,* and *Fletcher* were still on a northwesterly course. At 0150 began what was probably the most confused, close-ranged, and horrendous surface engagement of the war.[4]

As early as 0124 the *Helena,* which had an improved search radar system but was placed toward the rear of the column, had detected enemy ships. Admiral Callaghan ordered a slight change of course to starboard for a head-to-head battle, and thus put his formation in a position for its "T" to be crossed. Enemy contact reports continued to be sent to Callaghan, but poor communications made them only partially intelligible to him. The talk between ships (TBS) was overloaded because it was carrying both tactical control messages and information requests.

Admiral Abe may have been given enough time to change ammunition, but his force was still in disarray, with each ship unaware of the location of most of her sister ships. Finally, the battle opened at 0150 when the destroyer *Akatsuki* and the battleship *Hiei* illuminated the *Atlanta* and opened fire, while the *Akatsuki* also launched torpedoes. The U.S. column was just beginning a charge which took them into the middle of Abe's force. The *Atlanta* returned fire from her port and starboard turrets, hitting the *Akatsuki*'s searchlight. The *Hiei,* having turned to port, opened fire with all eight of her 14-inch guns, at what was point-blank range for a battleship—4,500 yards. The first salvo tore the *Atlanta*'s superstructure to shreds, killing Admiral Scott and almost everyone else on the bridge. Then the

Akatsuki's torpedoes slammed into the *Atlanta*, which lost way. The *Atlanta* managed only one salvo, which fell 2,000 yards short of the *Hiei*.

But the *Hiei* and the *Akatsuki* paid a price for using their searchlights. The *Hiei* at once drew fire from the four lead American destroyers, at ranges of 300 to 2,000 yards. The small destroyer guns and machine guns riddled the *Hiei*'s topside, and fires broke out across her deck. Admiral Abe, blinded by his own fires and confused about the whereabouts of his units, gave little direction during the rest of the battle. The *Hiei*'s fires drew salvos from almost every battery within range, including the 8-inch guns of the *San Francisco*. Abe then ordered his battleships to retire to the north; the *Kirishima* turned first, with the *Hiei* following. The onslaught of metal soon thereafter knocked out the *Hiei*'s communications systems.

The *Akatsuki*, caught in a crossfire between the *San Francisco* and a U.S. destroyer (probably the *O'Bannon*), sank at once, taking down almost all of her crew. In the meantime, the *San Francisco* began firing at an unidentified ship, probably the friendly *Atlanta*. Realizing she was probably firing on one of her own, Admiral Callaghan ordered her at 0155 to cease firing. Seconds later, the *Kirishima*, on the *San Francisco*'s port bow, fired her 14-inch batteries, scoring repeated hits; then, on her starboard beam, the destroyers *Inazuma* and *Ikazuchi* joined in. The combined salvos leveled the flagship's bridge, killing nearly all hands, including Admiral Callaghan.

By now, matters were simply out of hand; with Abe silent while the *Hiei* fought for her life, and both American admirals dead, the battle developed into a Pier 6 brawl. The U.S. column continued northwest, passing the *Hiei* close on the port side and the *Kirishima* to starboard. With Abe's formation scattered and the American column continuing on course, each Japanese ship had to duel independently with the American ships; identification of individual ships became almost impossible.

At about 0150, the second van destroyer, the *Yudachi*, turned south, running along the U.S. column at flank speed. Turning west, she cut through the line, almost colliding with the *Aaron Ward*, and then paralleled the U.S. ships to the northwest. During her run she launched eight torpedoes at the *Portland*, one or more of which hit the American cruiser, bending the plates in her stern so that she could only flounder around in circles. The *Yudachi* was finally hit at

0220 and, heavily damaged, she went dead in the water; her survivors were rescued by the *Samidare*.

The *Amatsukaze* and *Yukikaze* also turned south, first seeking out the flagship *Nagara*, then passing her, heading for the enemy column. (The *Yukikaze*, however, again reversed course to close the *Nagara*.) The *Amatsukaze* was joined by the *Akatsuki* (which was sunk immediately thereafter), *Inazuma*, and *Ikazuchi*. The *Nagara* fired star shells to outline targets for the three destroyers. The *Amatsukaze*, spotting five or six U.S. ships still in column, launched eight torpedoes at about 3,000 yards, scoring hits on the *Barton*, which exploded and sank at 0159. The *Amatsukaze* next spotted the *Juneau*, which was dueling with the *Yudachi*. Although outgunned, the *Amatsukaze* got in a hit that set the U.S. light cruiser afire. The *Amatsukaze* then turned northwest toward the *Hiei*, and at 0213 came suddenly upon the *San Francisco*, which was silent because the *Kirishima* had knocked out every one of the heavy cruiser's 8-inch turrets. The *Amatsukaze* raked her with gunfire, and launched four torpedoes; they were launched too close, however, which prevented the torpedoes from arming before they thudded into the *San Francisco*. (Torpedoes must run about 500 yards before arming themselves.) The *San Francisco* was by now a badly mauled ship, ablaze from bow to stern. The *Amatsukaze* then took on the *Helena*, only to receive one hit on her fire director station, and another which tore into her radio room, directly beneath the bridge. The hydraulic system was destroyed, which in turn knocked out the turrets and rudder. The *Amatsukaze* began to go in circles, afire and damaged by near-misses, with forty-three of her crew dead. The *Helena* suddenly ceased fire, and the *Amatsukaze*, using manual rudder and bringing her fires under control, withdrew at 20 knots.

But the *Helena* immediately had more troubles when the destroyers *Asagumo*, *Murasame*, and *Samidare*, originally in the van, but at the rear of Abe's group by 0150, finally entered the battle. The *Helena* was badly damaged in the bitter duel that followed.

The battle was over by 0200. The *Kirishima*, hit once by an 8-inch shell, had withdrawn early, along with the *Nagara*, which led the withdrawal of most of the surviving destroyers. The *Hiei*, battered by more than thirty hits, looped around Savo Island to the west, ablaze and barely able to make way, accompanied by the destroyers *Shigure*, *Shiratsuyu*, *Yugure*, and *Teruzuki*, and later joined by the *Yukikaze*.[5] The *Yudachi*, dead in the water, was abandoned in Iron Bottom Sound and later sunk by the *Portland*. The *Ikazuchi* had been hit well forward, with nineteen of her crew killed. The *Murasame* was hit in her forward boiler room, while the *Akatsuki* was sunk, with all hands lost (her normal complement was 200). Admiral Abe's intended bombardment of Henderson Field had been thwarted.

But the Americans had suffered extensive losses. The destroyers *Barton* and *Laffey* were sunk, and the *Atlanta*, left a shambles by 14-inch shells and torpedo hits, was finally scuttled in the early night hours of 13 November. The disabled *Portland* and the *Aaron Ward* were towed to Tulagi, while the *Cushing* and *Monssen*, abandoned and afire, finally sank during the afternoon of the 13th.

The *Hiei* was just north of Savo Island; although she was without a working rudder, the Japanese had not given up on her. But she was pounded the next day by U.S. dive bombers, torpedo planes, and B-17s from Henderson Field and the *Enterprise*, and by 1430, she could no longer make way. Her crew was taken off her at 1800, and she sank soon thereafter—the first battleship the Imperial Japanese Navy had lost in the war. The surviving U. S. Navy ships retired through Indispensable Strait: the *Helena, San Francisco, Juneau, O'Bannon, Sterett,* and *Fletcher.* At 1101, a torpedo from the submarine *I-26* surprised the *Juneau*, which immediately sank.

Despite Abe's failure to bombard Henderson, and the loss of a battleship, Yamamoto remained determined to bring in the 38th Division to Guadalcanal. He ordered Kondo's Strike Force, Main Body, then at Ontong Java Atoll, about 500 miles east of Rabaul, to save the *Hiei* and be available for bombardment on 14–15 November. Although the *Hiei* sank, Kondo continued on his southerly course, escorting the troop convoy (scheduled to arrive at sunset on the 14th), and on the way assimilating six ships from Abe's force. The Outer South Seas Force of Vice Admiral Mikawa would also participate in the second night bombardment of Henderson; it started south from the Shortlands, on a course east of the Slot.

Task Force 16 with the *Enterprise* remained south of Guadalcanal, looking unsuccessfully for Japanese carriers. (The converted carrier *Junyo* was too far north to be detected or to enter the battle.) The *Enterprise* could have reinforced Henderson, but Rear Admiral Thomas Kinkaid, even in this crisis, still refused to move the carrier farther north. Task Force 64, under Rear Admiral Willis August ("Ching") Lee, with two battleships and four destroyers, was too far away to block Mikawa's force. Thus, Guadalcanal was wide open to a night bombardment. Mikawa arrived just north of Savo Island at

0030; from 0128 to 0205, his heavy cruisers *Chokai*, *Maya*, and *Suzuya* (each with ten 8-inch guns, using APHE shells) poured 1,370 rounds onto the field, with help from the destroyers *Mochizuki* and *Amagiri*. In the meantime, the rest of Mikawa's force acted as a screen to the west.

The two forces reunited at 0800, and within minutes they were jumped by dive bombers from Henderson Field. At 0836 the *Kinugasa* sustained a direct hit on a forward gun mount and several near-misses; fires broke out and she began to take on water. An hour later, after she had corrected her list and extinguished her fires, she was attacked once more by three dive bombers. Near-misses stopped her engines and, drifting without power, she was abandoned and finally sank at 1122, 15 miles west of Rendova Island, with fifty-one of her crew lost. The *Chokai* was also damaged by strafing and near-misses, while a plane crashing into the *Maya* damaged a high-angle gun, two searchlights, and a torpedo tube, and killed thirty-seven men. The *Isuzu*, made unnavigable by near-misses, began to take on water, and was towed to the Shortlands and then to Truk. The *Michishio* also suffered damage and casualties.[6]

The shelling of Henderson Field had not been effective, but Guadalcanal still had to be reinforced, and the eleven troop transports were scheduled to make their delivery that night. Yamamoto decided to protect the vital convoy with one more onslaught on Henderson Field, this time using the big punch of Admiral Kondo's Strike Force, Main Body, reinforced by Abe's surviving ships.

The U. S. Navy was equally determined to stop both the troop convoy and any further bombardment of Henderson. Because of accurate air reconnaissance, there was no doubt in Halsey's mind about the size, location, and objectives of the Japanese forces. He split his forces, keeping Task Force 16's carrier, the *Enterprise*, to the south, while sending Task Force 64 under Admiral Lee to stop both Kondo and the transports. By 2100, Lee's two new battleships (with 16-inch guns), and four destroyers were nine miles west of Guadalcanal, waiting for Kondo and the transports.[7]

Admiral Kondo knew he would be opposed. As he approached Savo Island he had sent forward the light cruiser *Sendai* and her three destroyers as a distant screen. At 2210 they were ten miles northeast of Savo Island, heading almost due south, when the *Sendai* spotted Lee's Task Force 64 about five miles off her port bow, on a southeasterly course. Admiral Shintaro Hashimoto, commanding the Sweeping Force, detached the destroyers *Ayanami* and *Uranami* to loop around Savo's western side to search and perhaps attack, while the Volunteer Bombardment Force was several miles behind the *Sendai*. On receiving the *Sendai*'s report, Kondo detached the *Nagara* and four destroyers, and sent them almost directly south, so that they passed west of Savo Island. His own force of one battleship, two heavy cruisers, and two destroyers held to its southeasterly course for a few minutes and then also turned south.

Lee's line of battle was composed of the destroyers *Walke*, *Benham*, *Preston*, and *Gwin*, and the battleships *Washington* and *South Dakota*. They were being stalked by the *Sendai* and the *Shikinami*, while the *Uranami* and *Ayanami* maneuvered to set an ambush. Lee ordered a change of course to starboard (due west) in column, at 2252. At 2300, the *Washington*'s superior radar system detected the *Sendai* at 16,000 yards, and tracked her until she was seen at 2312. At 2317, the *Washington* fired a salvo of nine 16-inch shells at 11,000 yards; the *Sendai* made smoke and, with the *Shikinami*, withdrew to the north.

The *Ayanami* and *Uranami* were just coming around Savo Island when they were spotted by the *Walke*, *Benham*, and *Preston*, which fired the opening salvos at 2322, at a range of 10,000 yards. The *Nagara* and her four destroyers, paralleling the *Ayanami* and *Uranami* 1,600 yards to the north, were fired on by the *Gwin* at 2335. The five Japanese ships quickly responded with gunfire and torpedoes, and the *Gwin* had soon received hits in her engine room and on her stern. She was able to continue on course, however, protected by the *Washington*, which had veered a few degrees to interpose herself between the *Gwin* and her attackers.

In the meantime, the *Uranami*, *Ayanami*, and Kondo's close screen all launched torpedoes. The *Walke*, hit repeatedly by gunfire, began to lose way to port; then, at 2338, a torpedo ripped into her, and she sank four minutes later. The *Nagara* battled the *Preston* for a few minutes, but the latter was no match for the Japanese light cruiser. Shells from the *Nagara* penetrated the *Preston*'s engine rooms, blew off her rear stack, leveled her deck from bridge to stern, and set her afire; she sank at 2346. The *Benham* was also severely mauled, with her bow blown off by a torpedo, and she retired to the west. None of the American destroyers had managed to launch any torpedoes. By 2340 Admiral Kimura's Screening Force reversed course to the east, passing within a few hundred yards of Savo Island. The only Japanese ship damaged up to this point had been the

Ayanami, which was scuttled at around midnight. Her crew was removed by the *Uranami,* which then retired to the north.

During this phase of the battle, the two U.S. battleships were seeking bigger game. The *Washington* trained her secondary batteries on the *Nagara,* but with no effect. Then Task Force 64 suffered another misfortune. At 2333 the *South Dakota's* circuit breakers tripped, leaving the ship without electric power to operate lights, radar, or turrets for three minutes. By the time her power had been restored, she had lost the *Washington* by turning to port while her sister ship had turned to starboard; both ships had to change course in order to clear the damaged American destroyers. Thus, the *Nagara* had one more chance, and she launched eight torpedoes at the *South Dakota*—but none hit.

It was Kondo's intention, of course, to bombard Henderson. The force assigned to do it had been sailing in a box formation northwest of Savo Island, from 2316 to 2340. Suddenly, the *Nagara's* destroyers turned their searchlights on the *South Dakota,* giving the Bombardment Force a target for its shells and torpedoes. The *South Dakota* immediately received hits from the *Kirishima's* 14-inch guns and fire from nearby ships; however this attention given to the *South Dakota* caused the Japanese ships to overlook the *Washington,* which had set a parallel course at about 8,000 yards. She overwhelmed the *Kirishima* with a deadly salvo from her 16-inch guns at 0005. The *South Dakota* added more of the same, and by 0012 the *Kirishima* was doomed: afire, rudderless, and rapidly taking on water. The *Takao* and *Atago* were also damaged in the barrage, and withdrew to Kure. The light cruiser *Nagara* was also damaged and sent back to Japan for repairs, taken out of action for more than two months. In all, the Japanese ships suffered 249 men killed, 84 wounded.[8]

Kondo cancelled the bombardment and, making smoke, set a course to the northeast at 0030, while the destroyers *Asagumo, Teruzuki,* and *Samidare* took in the *Kirishima's* survivors. No attempt was made to save her; her sea cocks were opened, and she sank at 0323, seven miles northwest of Savo Island.

With the remainder of his convoy needing as much protection as it could get, Admiral Tanaka dispatched the destroyers *Kagero* and *Oyashio* to attack any enemy warships near Tassafaronga. The two destroyers fired torpedoes at the *Washington* at 0039, but none hit. In any event, what was left of Task Force 64 was retiring to the south, for the damage on the *South Dakota* had been so extensive that she had to be sent stateside for repairs. She had taken more than forty hits from the *Kirishima*, the *Atago*, and the *Takao*.

Thus ended one of the biggest, most bitterly fought battles in naval history. Again the Japanese had been thwarted in their attempts to neutralize Henderson Field for the protection of Admiral Tanaka's convoy. But Yamamoto and Tanaka were still determined to bring in the 38th Division, and the convoy, which had been marking time near the Shortlands, started south again on 14 November.

Every air group within range knew that Tanaka was coming: the Marine pilots on Guadalcanal, the *Enterprise*'s pilots, who used Henderson Field as a stopover, and Admiral Fitch's B-17 pilots at Espiritu Santo. At 1250 eight B-17s, seventeen Dauntlesses, eight Avengers, and eight fighters attacked the convoy, sinking two transports and damaging a third which limped back to the Shortlands. Destroyers removed the soldiers and supplies from the transports. Then at 1430 a second wave of twenty-four Dauntlesses and eight B-17s set another transport afire; again the soldiers were transferred to destroyers. The third wave came in at 1530: five Dauntlesses and eight B-17s, which sank two transports. The last wave of seventeen Dauntlesses and four B-17s hit at 1715, setting afire one transport. In the end, the Japanese had only four transports left, and 400 men had been killed.

For a while Tanaka wavered in indecision. At 1730 he began to retire to the northeast, but at 2000 returned to a south-southeasterly course and by 0215 he was at Tassafaronga. It was a bright night and he immediately started unloading men and supplies. His convoy at once came under artillery fire from Lunga Point and was attacked from the air. All four transports were hit, set afire, and beached; miraculously, however, none of the destroyers received serious damage. They left at daybreak, and the artillery and air attacks, joined by gunfire from the destroyer *Meade*, began to concentrate on the men and supplies that Tanaka had landed on the beach. The failure of the convoy caused a deep feeling of depression in the Japanese Army headquarters at Rabaul, for it was felt that these transports carried the aspirations of the whole Seventeenth Army. All that had been delivered of the 38th Division and subsidiary units were remnants of two infantry regiments, one battalion, an engineers regiment, and the commissariat—a total of 2,000 men out of about 10,000 that had embarked. Also landed were 1,500 bags of rice (a four-day supply) and 260 rounds for mountain howitzers. (The ammunition dump was bombed and destroyed that same day.)[9]

The cost to the Japanese had been prohibitive: two battleships, one heavy cruiser, three destroyers, and eleven transports totalling 77,606 tons had been sunk. Adding to the cost were several damaged warships, the many planes that had been downed trying to provide aerial support, and the loss of almost 5,000 of the 7,000 men of the 38th Division.

The Imperial General Headquarters did not budge an inch in their objective of controlling Guadalcanal, but obviously the use of the major elements of the Combined Fleet could neither sink the "land carrier" Henderson Field, nor destroy the naval forces that Halsey could muster. The last major sea battle for Guadalcanal had been lost, and the Japanese Army was on its own. Nevertheless, the Imperial General Headquarters still hoped to save Guadalcanal. Although no more big convoys were assembled, trickles of men and supplies were sent down the Slot almost every night.

Yamamoto simply did not wish to risk his carriers and other major warships by using the Combined Fleet in an assault on the island and on the *Enterprise*. Such an assault might well have succeeded; but, ever since August 1942, battles involving elements of the Combined Fleet had always resulted in serious losses for the Japanese Navy, particularly among its destroyers. The bold Admiral Yamamoto of 7 December 1941 had become a more cautious leader. Nevertheless, he was still hoping for a decisive naval battle, and that battle could have been fought around Guadalcanal; then if the naval battle had been won, the land battle could also have been won. But Yamamoto apparently never saw Guadalcanal as the place for the kind of decisive battle that he envisioned; moreover, as a naval man, although he cooperated with Imperial General Headquarters in trying to bring the troops in to the island, he probably never understood Guadalcanal's true significance. But subsequent events proved how important these battles were; from the Third Battle of the Solomons on, the retreat of the Japanese armed forces would not end until Japan surrendered.

**Table of Organization,
Third Battle of the Solomon Sea (divided into three days)**

12-13 November 1942

**Third Fleet, Advance Force, Raiding
(Bombardment Force, Volunteer Attack Force, Admiral Abe)**

(Note: This was one of the first times that the title "Volunteer Attack" was used by the Japanese Navy. Literally, the compound word "teishin" means "bravely (offer) body" or "volunteer". It may well signify a changed psychological attitude toward the war. Before, victory was always assumed, but now sailors were being asked to seek death, presaging the "kamikaze" concept.)[10]

Battleships: *Hiei, Kirishima*
Light cruiser: *Nagara*
Destroyers: *Akatsuki, Inazuma, Ikazuchi, Amatsukaze, Yukikaze, Teruzuki, Asagumo, Harusame, Murasame, Samidare, Yudachi, Shigure, Shiratsuyu, Yugure*

13-14 November 1942

Outer South Seas Force, Bombardment Force (Admiral Nishimura)

Heavy cruisers: *Maya, Suzuya*
Light cruiser: *Tenryu*
Destroyers: *Kazagumo, Michishio, Makigumo, Yugumo, Mochizuki, Amagiri*

Outer South Seas Force, Support Force, Main Body

Heavy cruisers: *Chokai, Kinugasa*
Destroyers: *Arashio, Asashio*

14-15 November 1942

Attack Force, Main Body (Henderson Field Bombardment) (Admiral N. Kondo)

Battleships: *Kirishima, Hiei*
Heavy cruisers: *Atago, Takao*
Light cruiser: *Nagara*
Destroyers: *Teruzuki, Inazuma, Asagumo, Oyashio, Shirayuki, Hatsuyuki, Samidare, Kagero*

SWEEPING FORCE (Admiral Shintaro Hashimoto)

Light cruiser: *Sendai*
Destroyers: *Uranami, Shikinami, Ayanami*

CONVOY FORCE

11 high-speed transports

DESTROYER ESCORT FORCE (Admiral R. Tanaka)

Destroyers: *Hayashio, Oyashio, Kagero, Mochizuki, Amagiri, Umikaze, Kawakaze, Haganami, Suzukaze, Takanami, Makinami*

Mobile Force, Advance Force

Converted carrier: *Junyo*[11]

SUPPORT FORCE, MAIN BODY

Battleships: *Kongo, Haruna*
Heavy cruiser: *Tone*
Destroyers: *Hatsuyuki, Shirayuki*[12]

U. S. Navy Table of Organization

Task Force 67

TASK GROUP 67.1 (TRANSPORT GROUP)

Transports: *McCawley, Crescent City, President Adams, President Jackson*

TASK GROUP 67.4 (SUPPORT GROUP)

Heavy cruisers: *San Francisco, Portland, Pensacola*
Light cruisers: *Juneau, Helena*
Destroyers: *Barton, Monssen, Cushing, Laffey, Sterett, O'Bannon, Buchanan*

TASK GROUP 62.4

Light cruiser: *Atlanta*
Destroyers: *Aaron Ward, Fletcher, Lardner, McCalla*
3 attack cargo ships

TASK GROUP 64

Battleships: *Washington, South Dakota*
Destroyers: *Walke, Benham, Gwin, Preston*[13]

第五編

section 5

DEFEAT OF THE IMPERIAL JAPANESE NAVY

chapter 18

DEFEAT AT
GUADALCANAL
AND THE ALEUTIANS

1942

30 November	Battle of Lunga Point (USN Title: Battle of Tassafaronga) Admiral Tanaka's "Tokyo Express" defeats Task Force 67. Japanese successfully land supplies and troops
31 December	Imperial General Headquarters decides to evacuate Guadalcanal (KE Operation)

1943

2–3 February	Japanese evacuate first echelon of troops
4–5 February	Japanese evacuate second echelon of troops
7–8 February	Japanese evacuate rear guard from Guadalcanal
26 March	Battle off Attu Island (USN Title: Battle of Komandorski Islands)
11 May	United States successfully invades Attu
28 July	Japanese successfully evacuate troops from Kiska (also called KE Operation)

Because of the heavy losses in men and ships, on 12 December the Japanese Navy proposed evacuation. This would not mean immediate abandonment; Tanaka would continue to bring in supplies and small troop units. But the Japanese Army leaders opposed this proposal. General Imamura, now in charge of the Seventeenth Army with 50,000 fresh troops, arrived in Rabaul to prepare a reinforcement effort for 1 February. However, on 31 December the Imperial General Headquarters agreed to the evacuation. It decided to rely upon a new line of defense in New Georgia.[1]

In the meantime, Tanaka brought in supplies in rubberized metal containers lashed to his destroyers' sterns. Making a fast run in to Tassafaronga Point, he would cut the lines, and the supplies would drift ashore or be brought ashore by swimming soldiers (or be destroyed by American planes, PT boats, or artillery fire). Meanwhile, the Japanese Army's situation on Guadalcanal worsened drastically each day as disease and lack of food and ammunition took a greater toll. Yet an American offensive on 19–22 November was stopped, and the lines of both sides remained much the same until February, when the survivors of the Japanese Army were taken off the island by the Navy.

The situation was also changing for the Americans. Gradually in December the original Marine detachments, after four months' duty, were relieved by new Marine and Army regiments. By 9 December the Americans had 40,000 troops on Guadalcanal, while the Japanese had only 25,000. Henderson Field was enlarged, satellite airfields were added, and Tulagi was made a PT-boat base, with fifteen PT boats and their tender.

Halsey could not assume, however, that the Japanese would not make another major effort. After 24 November he received intelligence that there was a build-up of Japanese shipping (including scores of motor-driven barges) at the Shortlands base, and at Buin, at the southern tip of Bougainville. Suspecting that this might presage another reinforcement attempt, he put together a new Task Force 67, composed of newly arrived cruisers and destroyers. Actually, no Japanese effort was being planned, but Tanaka was leaving supplies and a few men in small boats off Tassafaronga, every fourth day. When it was reported that eight destroyers and four transports had been sighted and they would be off Guadalcanal by 30 November, Halsey ordered Task Force 67 to intercept and destroy the Japanese ships.

For the last naval battle of Guadalcanal, the Americans had a heavy ship advantage. The Japanese Supply Force consisted of a Strike Force of the destroyers *Naganami* (flagship) and *Takanami*, and a Transport Force of the destroyers *Makinami, Kagero, Kuroshio, Oyashio, Kawakaze,* and *Suzukaze*.[2] Task Force 67, commanded by Rear Admiral Carleton H. Wright, was divided into Task Group 67.2, with the heavy cruisers *Minneapolis, New Orleans, Pensacola,* and *Northampton,* and the light cruiser *Honolulu;* and Task Group 67.4, with the destroyers *Fletcher, Drayton, Maury,* and

Perkins. Two destroyers, the *Lamson* and *Lardner*, were attached late and were used as rear guard.

Wright was determined not to repeat the errors of previous disastrous battles. He placed a ship with improved radar in each cruiser group. He made certain, moreover, that the talk between ships would not use ambiguous code words and the circuits would be used only for command orders. He drew up a new battle formation, abandoning the old single column; instead, the group on the engaged side would use radar and, on spotting the Japanese ships, would launch a massive torpedo attack and then peel off to unmask cruiser guns. The cruisers would then open up before the enemy came within 12,000 yards. Searchlights would not be used; instead, cruiser float planes flying from Tulagi would illuminate the Japanese column. Unfortunately for Wright, new to the command and the ships in it, the battle did not go according to plan.

Battle of Lunga Point
(USN Title: Battle of Tassafaronga)

At 2230 on 30 November, Tanaka's eight destroyers were on a southerly course, nearing Tassafaronga Point. Suddenly the *Naganami* reported enemy ships. At that time, the destroyers had been nearing the location where their cargo drums and troop-carrying cutters would be put overboard. Tanaka, ever alert, at once ordered his ships to prepare for battle. A few minutes later the *Takanami* veered off to screen the port side.[3]

At 2238 the U.S. formation executed a simultaneous turn to the west. Task Group 67.4's four destroyers were in the port van, only 3,500 yards from the flagship *Minneapolis*, instead of acting as an advanced picket line, as planned. Two miles to the rear were the two belatedly attached destroyers. At 2306, Admiral Wright's radar picked up Tanaka's screen, at a range of 13 miles. On approaching Iron Bottom Sound, Wright had ordered his Tulagi-based float planes aloft.[4]

At 2316, the *Fletcher* requested permission to launch a torpedo attack on Japanese ships on her port bow. Despite Wright's earlier instruction that such an attack should be made at first sighting, he inexplicably waited four minutes before answering "Affirmative." By that time the Japanese destroyers, now in at least four groups, had to be fired on from astern, so that torpedoes would have a longer following run. The *Fletcher* and the *Perkins* launched a salvo of tor-

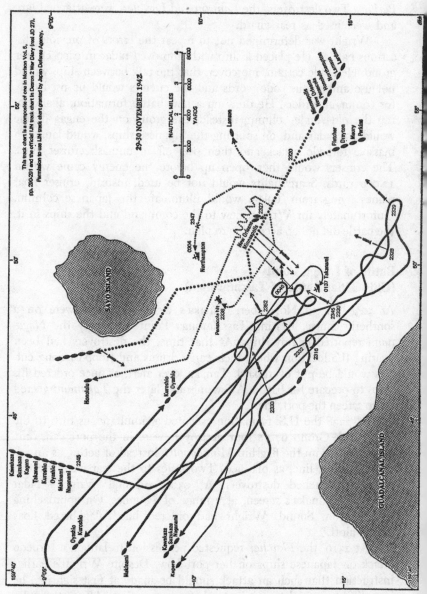

This track chart is a composite of one in Morison Vol. 5,
pp. 290-291 and the official IJN track chart in Desron 2 War Diary (reel JD 27).
Permission to use IJN track chart granted by Japan Defense Agency.

29-30 NOVEMBER 1942

NAUTICAL MILES

YARDS

SAVO ISLAND

GUADALCANAL ISLAND

Battle of Lunga Point (USN Title: Battle of Tassafaronga), 29–30 November 1942 pedoes at 2321; but the *Maury* could not find a target, and the *Drayton*, which had the same difficulties, launched two. Then the destroyers did not peel off, but set a course to join the main column.

At 2320 gun flashes from the opening salvos of the *Minneapolis* and the *New Orleans* were seen by Tanaka's ships, thus giving them targets. Tanaka had not stumbled into an ambush, and his destroyers reacted with the skill that long training and experience had instilled in them. The *Takanami*, as screen, was closest to the targets, immediately fired a torpedo salvo and began to receive 8-inch shell fire in return; she then reversed course starboard. Being alone and closest, her "blip" on the U.S. ships' radar screens was largest, and she took fire from the entire line of U.S. ships. When she returned fire, she was further pinpointed. Unable to take the beating, she sank shortly after reversing course. Before going down, she launched a cutter full of soldiers that landed safely on Guadalcanal; nevertheless, 211 of her men were lost.

The *Kagero*, *Makinami*, *Kuroshio*, and *Oyashio*, at that time the ships farthest to the southeast, released their cargo and reversed course, paralleling the U.S. ships. The *Kuroshio* launched four torpedoes on her turning course at 2329 and four more two minutes later; meanwhile, the *Oyashio* fired a spread of eight at 2330, claiming two hits. The *Kagero*, on her run south, had exchanged gunfire at 2320, and after reversing course launched four more torpedoes. The *Makinami* followed suit and then the pair withdrew to the northeast. The *Kawakaze* and the *Suzukaze*, after their unloading operations, also joined the battle. Beginning at 2330, headed southeast, the *Kawakaze* launched a total of nine torpedoes, while the *Suzukaze* fired eleven rounds from her main battery. The *Naganami*, on a retiring course, at 2333 launched a full salvo of torpedoes, and in turn, received a shell fragment on her funnel with minor casualties.

At 2327 the first two of the nearly fifty Japanese torpedoes in the water hit the *Minneapolis*—one in the bow, forward of turret No. 1, and one in the No. 2 engine room. With sixty feet of her bow bent down, she lost way, and after firing three more salvos, she lost power in her forward turrets. She was out of the battle and was eventually towed into Tulagi.

The *New Orleans* was next in line; swerving to avoid ramming the *Minneapolis*, she steered into a torpedo, which tore into her powder magazine and split the ship into two parts. The bow forward of turret No. 2 floated past the rest of the ship, while the main section was afire and losing speed. Nevertheless, damage control kept her afloat, and under her own power she made Tulagi.

The number three ship, the *Pensacola*, turned to port to avoid collision with the two cripples ahead of her—but she was not spared either. At 2338 a torpedo slammed into her port side, amidships, causing flooding of her after fire room, rendering three turrets powerless and raising havoc topside from the huge fires erupting on deck. She, too, limped into Tulagi.

The *Honolulu*, next in line, kept the damaged ships between herself and the Japanese torpedoes, and thus escaped a hit. Last came the *Northampton*. She was hit by two torpedoes at 2347, which caused massive damage; fires broke out, the ship was abandoned at 0150, and finally sank at 0304.

None of the van destroyers were damaged, but they were so busy doing rescue work and screening the *Honolulu* that they were out of the battle. The two rear-guard destroyers had not been issued Task Force 64's recognition lights code, and, upon flashing on the wrong ones, they took friendly fire. They then steamed east until Tanaka's departure, and finally were ordered to return to assist in rescue work.

Tanaka had again done the impossible. Not only had his six destroyers delivered their cargo (200 drums apiece) and landed troops, but they and their screen had also engaged a superior force, sinking one heavy cruiser and mauling three more, while losing only one destroyer. Use of their superior 24-inch torpedoes instead of their guns made Tanaka's ships seem as elusive as ghosts to the Americans. The Americans' tragedy was caused by a combination of circumstances, which were effectively exploited by Tanaka's tactics. In November 1942 U.S. naval units were still not well-trained in night battle. Furthermore, the Americans were forced by conditions half a world away to use ships that had not worked together; they were using poor destroyer tactics and inferior torpedoes. Nor was the use of radar helpful, because it caused the U.S. ships to train all their heavy guns on the closest Japanese ship, the *Takanami*, while the others were left untouched.

Although the decision to evacuate the Japanese troops from Guadalcanal had been made and the evacuation was being organized, the troops that were already on the island were in desperate need of food, medicine, and munitions, and could not be ignored. Therefore Admiral Tanaka still had to make his deliveries, however difficult and costly they might be. For the 3 December run of ten destroyers he had air cover for part of the time, and the run was made without incident. On 7 December he used eleven destroyers for the night convoy; on meeting an initial air attack, the *Nowaki* received minor damage. But off Cape Esperance, the group came under PT-boat attack and at 0100 the *Teruzuki* received two torpedo hits, which damaged her so badly that she was scuttled at 0400. The destroyers *Arashi* and *Naganami* landed their contingent of 155 men and rescued 138 of the *Teruzuki*'s crew. (Her normal complement was 290.) On 7 December, the Japanese also began using submarines to get men and supplies into Guadalcanal.

The Eighth Fleet dispatched these convoys only when there was no full moon. They had developed a new route for Tanaka—by way of the Shortlands and Munda—to give him more air cover. Still, troops on Guadalcanal had to wait three weeks for Tanaka's next try. (The Japanese resorted to air drops on 20–26 December, but because of poor radio communications only half of them were successful.)[5]

In the meantime, the Japanese continued to lose ships. The light cruiser *Tenryu*, escort for the invasion of Madang (north of Finschhafen in New Guinea), was torpedoed by the U.S. submarine *Albacore*, at 2015 on 18 December, ten miles from Madang. The venerable old cruiser went down at 2300 with twenty-three of her crewmen lost. On 25 December the destroyer *Uzuki* collided with the torpedoed *Nankai Maru* and suffered flooding. In the Slot on 26 December, the destroyer *Ariake* came under air attack, and a near-miss set the ship ablaze, killing twenty-eight and wounding forty. The ships at Rabaul for the evacuation of Guadalcanal (KE Operation) attracted MacArthur's B-17s during the last part of December; the destroyer *Tachikaze* was bombed, and lost her bow, while three other destroyers suffered damage. The light carrier *Ryuho*, after leaving Yokosuka on 11 December, was torpedoed the next day and had to return to drydock; then on 10 January 1943, the U.S. submarine *Trigger* torpedoed the destroyer *Okikaze*, sinking her near Yokohama.[6]

On 2 January 1943, when Tanaka resumed his run, with ten destroyers carrying provisions and ammunition, his ships came under attack from nine B-17s. The *Suzukaze* was damaged by a near-miss, and was shepherded back to the Shortlands by a destroyer; meanwhile Tanaka, now with eight ships, continued south. On his arrival, he was met by eleven PT boats, which launched eighteen torpedoes at his ships, but by adroit seamanship, he evaded the torpedoes—but the drums cast overboard were then destroyed by the PT boats. On 5

January, subchasers landed 1,200 Japanese Army troops and 1,200 11-pound bags of rice at Kamimbo Bay. On 10 January, eight of Tanaka's destroyers delivered 250 drums and repulsed a PT-boat attack, sinking two of them, while the *Hatsukaze* suffered only minor damage.

On 14 January, KE Operation began. With an escort force of nine destroyers, Tanaka was bringing in the Matsuda Unit of 600 men, which was to act as rear guard for the evacuation. On the run back, the *Arashi*, *Tanikaze*, *Urakaze*, and *Hamakaze* suffered minor damage from Henderson Field's Dauntlesses, for Tanaka had stayed longer than usual at Guadalcanal.

The evacuation took place on three different nights. On 2–3 February one light cruiser and twenty destroyers evacuated the first group of 4,935 men, at Cape Esperance and Kamimbo Bay. While the evacuation was under way the convoy was attacked by PT boats, but with no damage sustained. But the destroyer *Makigumo* hit a mine off Savo Island; the *Yugumo* tried to take her in tow, but the destroyer went under, the only ship lost. The second evacuation force, with a light cruiser and twenty destroyers, picked up, at the same locations, another 3,921 men on the night of 4–5 February. This force also came under aerial attack from about thirty planes, with the destroyer *Maikaze* suffering some damage; she was towed to the Shortlands by the destroyer *Nagatsuki*. The final evacuation convoy on 7–8 February took off troops from Guadalcanal and Russell Island—a total of 1,796 men. The convoy consisted of eighteen destroyers for Guadalcanal and two for Russell Island. On the way south it was attacked by thirty-five planes. The destroyer *Isokaze* received moderate damage, with ten men killed, but the operation was over—the total number of men saved by KE Operation was 10,652.[7]

The operation was truly an amazing feat, almost impossible to explain. The known presence of so many Japanese warships drew resistance only from planes and PT boats. One destroyer was sunk (but that by a mine), and two suffered moderate damage. If the Japanese could not get their men on the island without suffering unacceptable losses, how could they accomplish a total evacuation so easily? In fact, the American land forces on the island were unaware, until 1625 on 9 February, that there were no longer any Japanese troops on the island.

The Japanese Navy had been prepared for major resistance; stationed to the north was a Strike Force made up of six heavy cruisers, two light cruisers, a minelayer, eleven destroyers, and the heavy car-

29. Rear Admiral Raizo Tanaka, leader of the "Tokyo Express," which brought Japanese troops in to Guadalcanal in nightly runs.

30. Four Japanese torpedo bombers come in low, in a raid on the Lunga Roads anchorage at Guadalcanal. The planes on the far left and far right are about 15 feet above the water.

31 Japanese track chart of the Battle of Cape Esperance taken from microfilmed

32. A Japanese plane attempts to torpedo the U.S. battleship South Dakota *at the* Battle of the Santa Cruz Islands

33. *Japanese torpedo and dive bombers attack the carrier* Hornet *at the Battle of the Santa Cruz Islands, 26 October 1942.*

34. *The battleship* Hiei. *She was sunk at the Third Battle of the Solomon Sea,
13 November 1942, by U.S. bombers and torpedo planes. She was the first battleship
to be lost by the Japanese during the Pacific war.*

rier *Zuikaku*, whose fighters protected against convoy-raiding planes. The light carrier *Zuiho* and the converted carrier *Junyo* were also on station.[8]

Thus, the travail of the emaciated and exhausted Japanese troops had finally ended. According to Japanese records, 31,358 men of all services landed on Guadalcanal, and 10,652 were evacuated. The rest were killed in battle or by disease, or listed as missing. On 21 January 1943 the fighting ended at Buna, Gona, New Guinea; but there was no evacuation attempt—the Japanese troops, over 14,000 of them, fought to the last man.[9]

Guadalcanal could not have been held as long as it was, or evacuated so successfully, without the genius of Admiral Raizo Tanaka, who ran the "Tokyo Express" and the evacuation effort. Unfortunately his extraordinary feats were not rewarded—he finished the war with a desk job, first at Singapore and then in Burma.

The Japanese defense perimeter could not be maintained at the extent originally planned. The inevitable American advance against new targets, all the way to Okinawa, would make use of the very tactics that had brought the Japanese such spectacular success in the war's early stages. American advances and naval maneuvers now would be covered by land- and carrier-based aircraft. Other vicious naval battles had yet to be fought and lost; but the Japanese defense perimeter had been broken, and would be constantly pushed back or eroded by MacArthur's drive north through New Guinea and the Solomons, and Nimitz's offensive through the Central Pacific. Guadalcanal and New Guinea were the turning point, for there would be no more Japanese advances. Japan had overreached herself, with disastrous results.

The Aleutians

The Japanese occupation of Attu and Kiska in the Aleutians had opened a new theater of operations—but it was one that gave Japan no advantage. For the Japanese, it was not a new road leading to the invasion of Alaska, and was never meant to be. But the occupation of American territory, however insignificant, wounded American pride and caused an overreaction by the United States. Both sides wasted ships, men, and supplies that could have been better used elsewhere, on this near-arctic wasteland. But such is the psychology of war that both sides feel that any known enemy position must be fought and captured. Nevertheless, Attu and Kiska posed such a slight danger to the United States that they could have been ignored, except for routine surveillance.

Both Kiska and Attu are situated in one of the world's worst weather zones; one must deal with perpetual cold, fog, squalls (williwaws), and a terrain almost as completely unsuited for construction of airstrips as the climate is for flying. Yet Imperial General Headquarters had to provide for the men stationed on these two desolate islands. The garrison on Attu numbered fewer than 3,000, while that on Kiska numbered about 5,000; but the men had to be fed, supplied with munitions, supplied with construction crews and tools to build airfields, and protected against invasion. The islands were also within range of both U. S. Navy and Army Air Force bombers, whose raids made life miserable for the Japanese garrisons.[10]

Japanese ship losses were usually caused by submarines. The destroyer *Nenohi*, escorting the seaplane carrier *Kamikawa Maru* off Agattu on 4 July, was smacked by a torpedo on her starboard side amidships, launched by the *Triton*, and sank with only 36 of her crew saved, out of her normal complement of 228. The following day, off Kiska, the U.S. submarine *Growler*, launching four torpedoes, managed to sink the destroyer *Arare* and severely damage the destroyers *Shiranuhi* and *Kasumi*. In a USAAF raid on Kiska on 16 October, a bomb hit squarely on the destroyer *Oboro*, which exploded and sank, with no survivors, while the destroyer *Hatsuharu* was severely damaged.

Both sides worked hard to improve their positions for their next round. The Japanese labored, in vain, to build an airfield and strengthen the defenses on Kiska and Attu. The Americans made the first move, occupying Adak on 30 August 1942, and by 14 September they had airstrip and seaplane bases in operation there which could provide fighter cover for USAAF raids on Kiska. Then on 12 January 1943 the Americans occupied Amchitka, only 60 miles from Kiska, with a good harbor and terrain suitable for airstrips.

Battle off Attu Island
(USN Title: Battle of Komandorski Islands)

The Japanese believed Kiska would be the first American invasion point, so their convoys braved the winter weather to bring in men and supplies. In turn, the Americans, determined to interdict the convoys, sent a Task Group into the area between the Kamchatka Peninsula and Attu, south of the Komandorski Islands. At that same time, headed for the same area, Vice Admiral Boshiro Hosogaya was bringing in three large *Marus*, escorted by every ship the Fifth Fleet, Northern Force could muster. What followed was an old-fashioned long-range ship-to-ship duel that lasted almost four hours.

At 0500 on 26 March 1943, a Japanese column of eight warships and two transports steamed northward; in the van were the heavy cruisers *Nachi* and *Maya*, followed by the light cruisers *Tama* and *Abukuma*, the destroyers *Wakaba*, *Hatsushimo*, and *Ikazuchi*, two of the *Marus*, and the destroyer *Inazuma*, which brought up the rear. On a parallel course, about 20 miles southeast of the Japanese column, came Task Group 16.6 in two columns: the destroyer *Coughlan*, the light cruiser *Richmond*, and the destroyers *Bailey* and *Dale*, five miles on the port side of the column of the heavy cruiser *Salt Lake City*, and the destroyer *Monaghan*. At 0500, radar on two ships picked up at least five ships, seven to twelve miles to the north. At once the American group began forming a single column: the *Bailey*, *Coughlan*, *Richmond*, *Salt Lake City*, *Dale*, and *Monaghan*.

The Japanese force had been nervously alert in the hours before dawn, and the *Inazuma*, the rear guard destroyer, reported seeing ship silhouettes at 0400. At first Hosogaya believed that the ships sighted were the destroyer *Usugumo* and a third *Maru*, which were due to meet with the convoy. But after a *Nachi* lookout's report at 0508, other spottings followed rapidly, and at 0515 the *Abukuma* relayed specific information about nearby enemy ships. The Japanese commanders now knew that they were in for a battle, and the transports slipped away to the northwest, screened by the *Inazuma*. At 0530, the *Abukuma* and her destroyers turned in column to starboard, acting as a screen. At 0542 the *Nachi*, *Maya*, and *Tama* also turned to starboard, paralleling the *Abukuma*'s column. At the same time, Task Group 16.6, now with the two cruisers in column, screened on both sides by two destroyers, began turning in column to the west, in pursuit of the transports.

At 0542 both sides opened fire simultaneously at about 20,000 yards; two minutes later the *Nachi* launched two salvos of four torpedoes each. Shortly thereafter, the Japanese cruisers split into three groups: first the *Abukuma* turned to the southwest, paralleling the American ships on their port quarter. Then at 0547 the *Tama* took up the same course, close by the *Abukuma*'s port side. The *Maya* and *Nachi* held their course with 24,000 yards separating the two forces, thus blocking the Americans from returning to their base.

Fought at long range, it was a duel of heavy cruisers. The *Nachi*

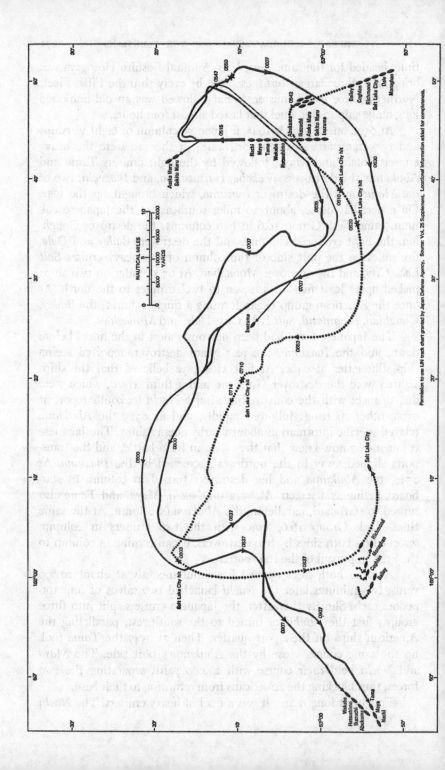

and the *Maya*, after an initial salvo at the outranged *Richmond*, concentrated on the *Salt Lake City*; meanwhile, any aggressive U.S. cruiser actions could be countered by Hosogaya's lighter forces. The American officer in tactical command, Rear Admiral C. H. McMorris, faced a dilemma, for he was clearly outnumbered in ships and weight of guns. Undaunted, at 0542, he turned his column to port on a southwesterly course. At that moment the *Salt Lake City* and the *Maya* and *Nachi* opened fire, at a range of about 20,000 yards. The two Japanese cruisers continued in a long looping turn to starboard, trying to cut the American force off from its base; this maneuver placed the *Maya* and *Nachi* in the undesirable position of making their chase astern the American ships. At 0550 the *Salt Lake City* scored a hit on the bridge of the *Nachi*, and two minutes later hit her torpedo tubes. It was inevitable, though, that the *Salt Lake City* would have to pay the price for the one-sided duel. The *Maya* hit her midships catapult planes with an 8-inch shell at 0610. She was hit again at 0620 on her quarterdeck, probably by the *Nachi*.

The *Tama* had tried to close the American column, but her Action Report mentions no torpedoes or shells fired. She withdrew to the northwest, placing herself between the U.S. force and the *Marus*. The *Abukuma* also closed the U.S. ships' starboard side, but then chose to veer in arcing turns to the northwest. She was fired on at 0653 and 0707 but was not hit. Hosogaya elected to play a cautious game, wanting to protect his convoy and yet maneuver to destroy the U.S. force. To do so, he continued to turn his two heavy cruisers and four destroyers to starboard until, by 0657, they were steaming on a northwesterly course. Although the *Maya* and the *Nachi* were newer and faster, their stern chase forced them to zigzag, both to unmask their stern turrets and to avoid plowing into a torpedo attack. Thus they could not close range on the American group. At 0707 the *Maya* and *Nachi*, 21,800 yards east of the *Salt Lake City*, blocked Admiral McMorris from getting at the transports. But McMorris' concern rapidly shifted to saving the *Salt Lake City*; at 0702 she had begun to lose steering control, thus losing her ability to chase splashes. She was hit a third time at 0710, by a shell from the *Maya* which went straight through the main deck to the hull, below the waterline.

The *Salt Lake City* was in trouble and requested a smoke screen, which was effectively provided by her destroyers beginning at

CAPTION: *Battle off Attu (USN Title: Battle of the Komandorski Islands),* 26 March 1943

0718. At 0803 the *Abukuma* scored one last hit on her, ruining her after gyro equipment and flooding the after engine room. Eventually her speed fell off, as water flooded her fire rooms, and at 0855 her engines stopped. By this time she had turned back on a southeasterly course. Although by then the *Salt Lake City* was hardly visible, the *Abukuma*, almost directly astern her, was still trying to score from long range. Also the *Hatsushimo* had fired five torpedoes at the *Salt Lake City* at 0857, while the *Wakaba* launched five at her screen, which was now steaming east on her starboard quarter. None of the torpedoes hit, however. The *Salt Lake City* finally got underway again at 1000, but by then, the battle was over; Hosogaya's force was headed southwest escorting the transports back to Paramushiro.[11]

Because the battle was fought at long range for nearly four hours, it is not surprising that the naval track charts of the two forces do not match. The Japanese track chart does not show the loss of way of the *Salt Lake City* when she was most vulnerable, nor does it record a torpedo attack by the destroyers *Bailey*, *Coughlan*, and *Monaghan*. U.S. records show that at 0900 and 0903 the *Bailey* was hit twice starboard, one shell penetrating to the electric generators; then at 0903 she launched five torpedoes and turned east, ordering the other two destroyers to follow her.

According to the *Maya's* Action Report, she was unhit, but her own gun blasts set fire to her No. 1 float plane. The *Abukuma* and the *Tama* received no damage. The *Nachi*, however, took the brunt of the fire, mainly from the *Salt Lake City*; her Action Report records two hits at 0555 and 0848. The *Hatsushimo*, the *Inazuma* and the *Wakaba* were not hit.[12]

Admiral Hosogaya, although justifiably concerned for his transports, had been overcautious; even with a decidedly superior force, he received nearly as much damage as the Americans. He never closed range to take on the crippled *Salt Lake City* and her protecting lighter ships. His light cruisers did not make an all-out attack, and his destroyers did not make a typical Japanese torpedo attack. The battle might easily have been a Japanese victory. Hosogaya was retired from naval service a month later.

Admiral McMorris probably displayed more courage than judgment in his actions. Although he did not get at the Japanese transports, he saved a heavy cruiser from a perilous situation and prevented the reinforcement of Kiska.

The Aleutian phase of the war was concluded when, leapfrogging Kiska, the U. S. Army landed 11,000 troops at Attu on 11 May

1943, opposed by some 2,500 Japanese troops. The fighting was bitter, ending on 29 May with the Japanese forces wiped out, except for twenty-eight prisoners. With Attu lost, the Imperial General Headquarters decided to attempt another KE Operation, for Kiska.[13] It started on 26 May with the use of thirteen *I*-class submarines, but was abandoned after seven of them were lost. Having no stomach for another "Tokyo Express," the Japanese decided to evacuate the island by ship; through good meteorological work and skillful execution, the troops were brought off the island without the Americans realizing that it had been done. A Japanese task force, advised that fog would cover its approach, left Paramushiro on 21 July; slipping into Kiska Harbor (a dangerous mission in the fog) at 1740 on 28 July, two cruisers and six destroyers took on the garrison of 5,183 in 55 minutes and were on their way back to Paramushiro.[14]

Not knowing about the evacuation, an American invasion force of about 35,000 landed at Kiska on 15 August—to find, after two days' sweep and search, only four abandoned dogs. Still, the Americans had learned something important from this turn of events, a lesson also being learned in New Guinea and the Solomons: by leapfrogging the Japanese positions, certain islands could be taken merely by being systematically isolated.

chapter 19

RETREAT IN NEW GUINEA AND THE SOLOMONS

1943

3–4 March	Battle of the Bismarck Sea. Fifth Army Air Force planes, using new tactic of skip-bombing, decimate Japanese convoy en route to Lae
7–16 April	Yamamoto's I Operation, to eliminate Southwest Pacific enemy airfields by air attack, fails
18 April	USAAF P-38 interception kills Admiral Yamamoto at Kahili. Admiral Koga succeeds as commander-in-chief
21 June	Allies inaugurate Munda, New Georgia invasion operation
6 July	Battle of Kula Gulf, Solomons
13 July	Battle of Kolombangara, Solomons
6–7 August	Battle of Vella Gulf, Solomons

With the loss of Buna, Gona, Guadalcanal, and Attu and Kiska, Japanese strategy had to become more defensive. Garrisons in the Solomons and New Guinea had to be strengthened and supplied, convoys had to be organized to take raw materials to Japan and bring back troops and materiel for the Army's defense bastions and Navy's bases. Only in Burma were faltering offensive operations still under way. Yamamoto still wanted the "decisive battle," but in 1943 he had no hard plans to bring it about. Victory fever had subsided, but the samurai spirit had not; now a determination to yield no more territory without making the enemy pay a tremendous price came to pervade Japanese strategic thinking. A "Hundred Years' War" became the national slogan.

On the American side, too, it was a time for regrouping and replanning the drive on Tokyo. MacArthur would attempt to return to the Philippines, via New Guinea and the Bismarck Archipelago. Nimitz, with Marines and Army troops at hand, would come up through the Solomons and drive Japan from Rabaul and Truk. He would also follow the old "Rainbow Five" strategy of recapturing the islands lost earlier in the Central Pacific, and then driving through the Marshalls to the Marianas and Carolines. In the United States, scores of new carriers and other warships and submarines were becoming available, and rather than hanging on by a fingernail, American forces could soon begin the process of smothering the Japanese Army and Navy on land, sea, and in the air. More and better planes and well-trained pilots, and scores of excellent submarines with improved torpedoes were arriving in the Pacific.

The Japanese planes would soon be equalled if not outmatched by American planes. Although Japanese plane production would always be adequate, the planes would not be appreciably improved; moreover, there was no effective program to train replacement pilots, so that the ability of Japanese pilots deteriorated swiftly. The truly skillful corps of aviators had been almost wiped out; the loss rate had been too high at the battles of Coral Sea, Midway, Guadalcanal, and New Guinea. The Japanese knew from their experiences running the Slot that the greatest danger that a convoy faced was from aircraft, and that if outlying garrisons had to be supplied, the convoy destroyer escorts needed more protection from planes. Also in 1943 Japanese destroyers had lost their edge on the U.S. submarines, which would soon begin their deadly attacks on the lifeline from the South Seas to Japan as well as on convoys to garrisons. As Admiral Yamamoto had always known, Japan could not cope with American industrial might. The Japanese would still fight with zeal and skill, but at a cost that, in the long run, could not be borne.

Battle of the Bismarck Sea

The Japanese Army was determined to hold Lae and Salamaua in New Guinea, as a western anchor protecting Rabaul and eventually the Philippines. When the Australians built a naval base at Milne Bay and began building an airfield at Wau, forty miles southwest of Lae, the Japanese Army reacted characteristically by reinforcing Lae with another regiment. To further protect New Guinea, it landed nearly 10,000 men at Wewak on 19 January 1943. Three months later, it reinforced Hollandia and began constructing a road from Madang to Finschhafen. To transport troops and supplies, it also brought in large barges that could hug the coast, travelling by night, and thus avoid air attacks.

General Imamura, commander-in-chief of the Eighteenth Army, could not allow the Australian base at Wau to remain, because its air power would make Lae and Salamaua untenable. Yet at the latter places he had only 3,500 troops, most of them ill and insufficiently supplied to drive out the Australians. It was decided that 6,900 more men had to be brought in, which meant a large transport force had to travel 260 exposed miles. Taught by their experience with the Tokyo Express, the Japanese planned carefully for the convoy. Planes would make massive raids on Allied airfields within range of the transports, and the convoy would be covered most of the way by fighter planes. It would await a weather front so that it could make the trip at least partially covered by clouds. Finally, the ships were carefully loaded with supplies and the units separated, so that the sinking of a ship would not mean the loss of all of some vital materiel or personnel. The convoy consisted of eight transports, totalling more than 28,000 tons, escorted by eight warships, all veterans

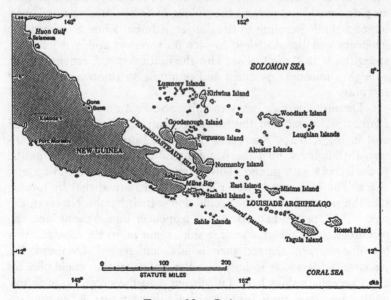

Eastern New Guinea

of the runs to Guadalcanal: the destroyers *Tokitsukaze, Yukikaze, Arashio, Asashio, Shirayuki, Uranami, Shikinami,* and *Asagumo.*

However well conceived, the plan fell apart for Rear Admiral Masanori Kimura, in command of the convoy. The convoy sortied from Rabaul on 28 February and skirted the northern coast of New Britain under a weather front the next day. Despite the front, however, the convoy was spotted by a B-24 at 1600. The air cover could not continuously protect the sixteen ships; moreover, the weather front would hide Australian fields, making the planned massive raids ineffective. Worst of all, the Fifth Army Air Force (VAAF) of Lieutenant General George Kenney had been heavily reinforced, especially by newly equipped B-25s, for which new tactics had been devised. Eight 50-caliber machine guns, installed in the vacated cone that had housed the bombardier, would strafe the target ship (on whose decks were the Japanese troops), while a 500-pound bomb with a five-second delayed fuse would be skipped into the ship, preferably amidships. The delayed fuse would give the B-25 time to get out of blast range, and the bomb, exploding near the hull of the ship, would rupture her below the waterline.

The convoy was well tracked, and just as it was turning into Dampier Strait, it was attacked on 3 March at 1015 by thirty-four heavy bombers flying at 5,000 feet. The convoy's inadequate combat air patrol could not prevent the sinking of two transports and damaging of a third. Reacting to the danger, Admiral Kimura ordered the *Yukikaze* and the *Asagumo* to pick up survivors and make a flank-speed run with them to Lae. This the destroyers did, arriving in Lae at night, unloading 950 men and returning to the convoy the next morning.

Despite Kimura's heavy casualties he kept on course; and on 4 March the massacre of the convoy continued. General Kenney had sent in B-17s, B-25s, A-20s, and Australian Beauforts, covered by sixteen P-38 fighters. First the Beauforts came in deck-high, raking the packed decks with gunfire, bow to stern. Next came the B-25s and A-20s. The Japanese destroyer captains had learned that by turning into the aircrafts' course they could dodge their bombs. However, the new VAAF tactics had taken this maneuver into account, and the medium-sized bombers, two to a ship, again raked the topsides with machine-gun fire, skipped their bombs, and retired. Overhead, the Japanese fighters were so busy with the P-38s that they could offer no aid. Everywhere ships burst into flames, and the orderly convoy formation had soon turned into a chaotic disaster area of burning, exploding, and sinking ships. At 5,000 feet, the B-17s made leisurely runs over ships dead in the water. The attack lasted for an hour and three-quarters, and by noon, all six transports and four destroyers (the *Arashio, Asashio, Shirayuki*, and *Tokitsukaze*) were sinking or had been sunk. The remaining four destroyers took on as many survivors as they could and retired to the north.[1] After this battle, Japanese destroyers no longer felt relatively safe from bombing by large aircraft; until then, it had been the dive bombers that they had feared most. The Battle of the Bismarck Sea was the last time the Japanese sent transports into areas covered by enemy air power. If Lae and Salamaua were to be supplied, it would have to be by large barges coming from Cape Gloucester, New Britain. The attack on Wau was of course cancelled, and defenses on Lae and Salamaua began to wither away, for lack of reinforcements, food, medicine, and munitions. The death toll of the Battle of the Bismarck Sea was prohibitive for the Japanese; the ships had carried 5,954 troops in addition to ships' crews, but only 2,734 men survived.

Battle for New Georgia

Even after the failure of the Japanese to reinforce Lae, the struggle to hold the defense perimeter placed the responsibility of garrisoning and defending all the Japanese South Sea positions in the hands of the Japanese Navy's overburdened destroyers and air force. Rabaul held four airfields, and there was one each at Buka (just off the northern tip of Bougainville), Kahili (on the southern tip of Bougainville), Ballale (off the southern tip of Bougainville), Vila on Kolombangara, Munda (on the northwest tip of New Georgia), and the last at Rekata Bay on Santa Isabel. To reduce Rabaul, the United States would have to neutralize these strongholds. It was also agreed that Admiral Halsey would coordinate his offensive against Munda with MacArthur's campaign to push the Japanese Army out of the Huon Peninsula, New Guinea. May 1943 was tentatively set as the date for the beginning of both campaigns. In preparation for the main offensive, Japanese airfields were bombed by air attacks, interspersed with U.S. cruiser and destroyer bombardments of Munda; but these had just about as little effect as the Japanese Navy's former bombardments of Guadalcanal. In return, the Japanese planes mounted as many raids on American airfields as possible.

It was the task of the Japanese Navy, mainly using its destroyers, to bring in supplies to the expanding air bases; but it became increas-

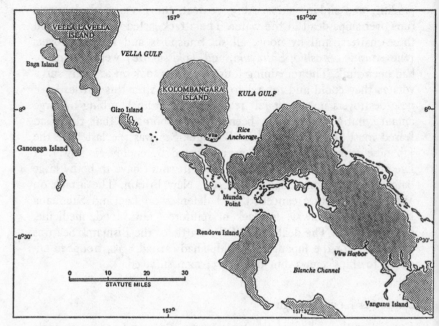

New Georgia

ingly likely that one of these missions would run into a U.S. bombardment force. The advantage lay with the U. S. Navy, because it had long-range plane reconnaissance and coast watchers who could report the movement southward of any Japanese naval force; at the same time, a U.S. naval force from Nouméa would probably be unobserved. Moreover, supply runs by the Japanese would be by small forces, while U.S. bombardment missions would include more and heavier warships. At this point, Yamamoto was becoming stingy in assigning ships to duty in the Solomons, for there still were other fronts to be considered, and he was saving his ships for the ever-elusive "decisive battle."

The first disaster for the Japanese came when the destroyers *Minegumo* and *Murasame* left the Shortlands at 1910 on 5 March, on a routine provisions run to Vila. (Their departure was spotted and they were reported as two light cruisers.) They went through Vila Gulf and Blackett Strait, and by 2330 they had unloaded and were headed back home. What they didn't know was that, coming up on a northeasterly course between Kolombangara and New Georgia, there was a U.S. bombardment force, consisting of the light cruisers *Montpelier, Cleveland,* and *Denver,* and the destroyers *Conway, Waller,* and *Cony.* The *Minegumo* and *Murasame* had just cleared Blackett Strait and settled in on a northwesterly course. At 0101, the *Murasame's* lookout spotted flashes of light; it was enemy fire at about 10,000 yards off the starboard bow. The first salvo straddled the *Murasame* with 6-inch shells. Within a minute she had been solidly hit; then she was smacked by a torpedo from the *Waller.* She exploded and sank at 0115, with no survivors; her normal complement was 200.

The *Minegumo,* now trapped, zigzagged northward. The U.S. ships began firing on her at 0106; she returned fire, but the newly developed radar-controlled guns of the U. S. Navy made the fight no contest. The *Minegumo* was hit repeatedly and sank at 0130. The ship was abandoned, but 174 men out of her normal complement of 180 managed to swim to Kolombangara.[2] No damage was sustained by the American ships and they proceeded to bombard Munda.

To prevent, or at least stall, the obvious Allied buildup for an offensive, Admiral Yamamoto ordered "I" Operation, which called for massive air raids on Guadalcanal and on MacArthur's bases at Port Moresby, Oro Bay, and Milne Bay. VAAF's air activity in New Guinea had been particularly bothersome; on 2 April it had caught a Kavieng convoy and severely damaged the heavy cruiser *Aoba* with a hit on her stern, putting her out of service, killing thirty-six, and wounding seventy-five. The destroyer *Fumizuki* also had to return to Yokosuka for repairs.

"I" Operation called for a reinforcement by land-based planes, flown from the four carriers of the Third Fleet at Truk. Several hundred planes made mass attacks on Guadalcanal on 7 April, Oro Bay on 11 April, Port Moresby on the next day, and Milne Bay on 14 April. But the great effort produced very little result; only one destroyer and four auxiliary ships were sunk. The operation was ended on 16 April and the decimated carrier planes that were left flew back to their ships.[3]

This operation proved to be Admiral Yamamoto's last command. The Americans had been monitoring a simple Japanese code and had a precise schedule of a series of visits Yamamoto planned to make to outlying bases, to improve troop morale. An ambush was set for him. On 18 April he left Rabaul for Kahili, and as usual was strictly on time. Sixteen P-38s, straining to the very limit of their gas supply, were sent to intercept his plane, and at 0935 one of them hit Yamamoto's plane and sent it plummeting into the jungle. The very

symbol of the Imperial Japanese Navy was dead.[4] Command passed
to Admiral Mineichi Koga. Allied officials may have felt that they
had exacted revenge for Pearl Harbor and destroyed an enemy genius, but Admiral Koga's strategy continued in the same pattern as
Yamamoto's. Even so, ever since the failure at Midway, Yamamoto
had seemed less decisive and aggressive; indeed, he seemed to know
that the war could no longer be won.

With the U. S. Navy preparing for the May (postponed to
June) offensive, U.S. ships were not sent up the Slot on interdiction
operations except for airfield bombardment missions. The Americans, however, began to mine Kahili Bay and the waters around
Bougainville by aerial drops, and Blackett Strait by ship. The mining
produced the following Japanese casualties:

> The destroyer *Kazagumo*—Kahili Bay. Slight damage, 3 April.
> The destroyer *Oyashio*—Blackett Strait. Dead in water, afire 8 May.
> Sunk next day by aircraft. Thirty-five men killed. 225 swam to
> Kolombangara.
> The destroyer *Kagero*—Blackett Strait. Dead in water, afire 8 May.
> Sunk next day by aircraft. Eighteen killed, thirty-six wounded.
> The destroyer *Kuroshio*—Blackett Strait. Sunk 8 May.

The remaining ship of the group in Blackett Strait on 8 May
was the destroyer *Michishio*. She struggled to save the two destroyers
and rescue their crews, but she herself came under air attack and
limped back to home port, seriously damaged. Three-quarters of Destroyer Squadron 2, Destroyer Division 15 had been wiped out on
8-9 May.[5]

Adding to the difficulty in finding ships to bolster the Solomons
bases, the ever-growing number of U.S. submarines based at Pearl
Harbor and in Australia were taking their toll, from Empire waters
to the Bismarck barrier. From January to April four destroyers—the
Hakaze, *Okikaze*, *Oshio*, and *Isonami*—were sunk by U.S. submarines.[6]

Japan could not afford such losses; her navy had started the war
with 110 destroyers, but by 1 July 1943 she had added only 14 more
and had lost 35, with others in shipyards for repair.

New Georgia

The first major Allied offensive in the Solomons began on 21 June
1943, and was directed toward the capture of Munda airfield. If

Munda fell, then the Japanese would be backed up to Bougainville, and everything south of there would be under constant air attack. The airfields at Munda and Vila had already been subjected to frequent air raids for some time, and by 21 June they could offer little or no opposition. The first step in the Munda invasion was to secure beachheads on nearby islands, and finally at Rice Anchorage, New Georgia for an overland assault on Munda. Thus, a major burden now fell on the Navy to reinforce Munda by landing troops at Vila on the southern tip of Kolombangara.

Vice Admiral R. Kusaka, commander-in-chief of Air Flotilla 11, did not have enough planes to stop the capture of beachheads near and on New Georgia; thus, his resistance was relatively weak and ineffectual. But Munda had to be reinforced quickly, and so some 4,000 Japanese troops were to be landed at Vila. The first echelon was carried on 5 July by the destroyers *Niizuki* (equipped with radar), *Yunagi*, and *Nagatsuki*.[7] Nearing Kolombangara at the same time that a strong U.S. naval bombardment force had just concluded shelling Vila and Bairoku Harbor, the three destroyers (using the *Niizuki*'s radar) launched a torpedo attack at 0015, at the range of 11 miles. The destroyer *Ralph Talbot*'s radar detected ships to the northwest at 0040, but before the American ships could react, one torpedo had hit the destroyer *Strong*, which sank an hour later. The source and nature of the explosion that ripped the *Strong* apart mystified the American command: they could not believe that a torpedo fired from the distance their radar indicated could be responsible. The blips on the U.S. ships' radar screens disappeared as the three Japanese destroyers, rather than tangle further with light cruisers and destroyers, went back to Buin with their troops still on board.

Battle of Kula Gulf

Rear Admiral W. L. Ainsworth's Task Group 36.1, retiring after bombarding Vila, received word on 5 July that a Japanese destroyer group was leaving Buin. Task Group 36.1, consisting of the light cruisers *Honolulu*, *Helena*, and *St. Louis*, and the screening destroyers *Nicholas*, *O'Bannon*, *Radford*, and *Jenkins*, reversed course and came north through Indispensable Strait, seeking a fight. The Japanese Reinforcement Force was divided into a Support Group (the destroyers *Niizuki*, *Suzukaze*, and *Tanikaze*), First Transport Group (the destroyers *Mochizuki*, *Mikazuki*, and *Hamakaze*), and

Second Transport Group (destroyers *Amagiri, Hatsuyuki, Nagatsuki,* and *Satsuki*). While the Americans had the advantage of weight and guns, and the Japanese destroyers would have to fight with troops on board, the Japanese also had their usual advantages—experience in this sort of battle, and their devastating 24-inch torpedoes.

As the Japanese destroyers went north, hugging Kolombangara on their port side, Rear Admiral Teruo Akiyama detached the destroyers *Mochizuki, Mikazuki,* and *Hamakaze* to land troops at Vila. Then at 0143 he sent the Second Transport Group arcing back southward, also for disembarkation, while the destroyers *Niizuki, Suzukaze,* and *Tanikaze* continued north, in column. The U.S. ships steamed on a northwesterly course, with the Japanese column 23,000 yards southwest of them. Contact was established at 0136 on 6 July. Admiral Ainsworth had thought the element of surprise was his, but the *Niizuki*'s radar had already picked up the U.S. ships at 0106. Akiyama's mission was to land troops, which is why the 0143 order for the Second Transport Group's reversal was given; but when he saw the size of his opposition, Akiyama knew he needed help, and at 0200 he ordered the transport ships to reverse again and enter the fight, even though troops were still aboard the transport destroyers.

At 0142 Ainsworth ordered a simultaneous change of course to port, shortening the range. Both groups still held their fire and eight minutes later Task Group 36.1 was back in column again, on a northwesterly course. The Americans' earlier mistakes were being repeated; the range was now down to below 11,000 yards, and no guns had been fired or torpedoes launched. As usual, the Japanese destroyers were trying for surprise torpedo attacks and avoiding the use of their guns, which would expose their location.

The battle was finally joined when at 0157 Japanese torpedoes hit the water and the 6-inch U.S. guns opened fire. With radar gun control (or perhaps because of it), the fire of all U.S. ships was concentrated on the leading *Niizuki*; she was hit hard and often, and sank within a few minutes. In a minute after the battle opened the *Suzukaze* and *Tanikaze* had each fired an eight-torpedo salvo, made a 90-degree turn west to avoid the *Niizuki*, and then, making smoke, continued to the northwest, sustaining only minimal damage. The *Suzukaze* took hits on a searchlight and a torpedo mount and suffered moderate damage to her hull, the *Tanikaze* was hit once with a dud and suffered very slight damage, while the *Amagiri*, storming up from the south, took four hits, which disabled her electric power plant and radio compartment, and killed ten of her men.

At 0203 Admiral Ainsworth ordered a shift to a south-southwesterly course, but a minute later the first of the Japanese torpedoes hit the *Helena*, severing her bow back to her No. 2 turret. In the next two minutes two more torpedoes hit her, leaving her buckled in the middle.

The *Honolulu* and the *St. Louis* reopened fire at 0221, capping the "T" of the Second Transport Group. The *Amagiri*, suffering only slight damage, made smoke and, turning hard to starboard, launched torpedoes. The *Hatsuyuki*, behind the *Amagiri*, was hit by three duds which did heavy damage topside and in her engine room. Her hull was holed twice, and six men were killed. In turn she got off 20 rounds from her 5-inch guns. She retired, to rendezvous with the First Transport Group. The *Nagatsuki* took one direct hit, but was able to follow the *Satsuki* south; she ran aground, however, five miles short of Vila. The *Satsuki* tried to pull her off but gave it up as hopeless at 0400 and returned to Buin, leaving the *Nagatsuki's* crew on board their ship.

By 0235 the two forces were badly scattered; the *Helena* had been sunk but her bow section was still afloat. Admiral Ainsworth, thinking the battle was over, ordered a general retirement to Tulagi, which his flagship, the *Honolulu*, and the *St. Louis*, *O'Bannon*, and *Jenkins* began to execute. But the battle was not yet over. The destroyers *Radford* and *Nicholas* were rescuing the *Helena's* survivors after having made an hour's run to the northwest; meanwhile, 14,000 yards distant, the *Amagiri* was doing the same for the *Niizuki's* men in the water. The *Suzukaze* and *Tanikaze*, returning after a long run to the northwest, saw nothing and retired to Buin. The *Amagiri* and *Nicholas* saw each other, and abandoning rescue operations, they exchanged torpedo salvos. At 0534 they then resorted to their guns; the *Amagiri* was hit, made smoke, and retired, leaving the *Niizuki* behind. Casualties for the *Niizuki* were approximately 300 men killed. The *Mochizuki* of the First Transport Group chose to go to Buin via Kula Gulf, and again the *Nicholas* and *Radford* ceased rescue work and came out firing. No damage to either side resulted, however, from this skirmish.

The advantage now lay with the Americans; the *Helena's* survivors could be rescued, but the *Niizuki's* could not, and the *Nagatsuki* was stranded on the shore. Her crew finally left her, and by 1010 she was under attack by American planes. Succumbing to fire and explosions on the evening of 6 July, she sank. Meanwhile, the injured *Hatsuyuki* made it to Buin.

The Japanese had intended to land troops at Vila, but official records state that only about 850 out of 2,600 reinforcements were successfully disembarked; the rest were taken back to Kolombangara. The battle damage on either side was almost even—one light cruiser for two destroyers. The superior firepower of the U.S. force should have easily carried the day; however indecision and hesitation to open fire caused confusion and loss of initiative. Moreover, the U.S. ships still relied on guns with flash powder, rather than torpedoes, which the Japanese destroyers had used so effectively.

The superiority of Japanese night-fighting techniques was again demonstrated a week later on 13 July in the Battle of Kolombangara, when Admiral Ainsworth, with three light cruisers and ten destroyers, tangled with Rear Admiral S. Izaki's ships, in the same waters. The Japanese force, escorting four destroyer transports, was led by the light cruiser *Jintsu* and the destroyers *Mikazuki, Yukikaze, Hamakaze, Kiyonami,* and *Yugure*. Again the Japanese had better detection (they now could detect American ships' radar), better torpedoes, and better night-fighting tactics. The venerable *Jintsu*, veteran of the Tokyo Express, was lost with all her crew, but Japanese torpedoes sank the destroyer *Gwin* and scored damaging hits on Admiral Ainsworth's light cruisers *Leander* (HMNZS), *St. Louis,* and *Honolulu*. Thus it was clear that the Japanese could still fight night battles quite well, even when engaged in reinforcement tasks; nevertheless, they could not afford to keep losing ships, while the Americans continued to build more and more. These battles were two in a whole series of Pyrrhic victories for the Japanese.

The Japanese campaign to hold New Georgia was a replay, in smaller dimensions, of Guadalcanal. Both sides reinforced the original troops but in doing so the Japanese, having lost the air and facing growing U.S. naval forces, suffered further intolerable losses, and in the process, failed to provide enough troops and materiel to hold the island. After a desperate struggle fought in jungle terrain, Munda fell on 5 August. All Japanese troops on the island had been killed, evacuated, or taken prisoner by 20 September.[8]

Further Intrusion up the Slot

The naval battles continued with deadly regularity. At the same time heavier and heavier raids on Rabaul by MacArthur's planes, and on the other Solomons airfields by Halsey's carrier planes, cut down on air protection for the Japanese Navy. A raid by more than

200 planes hit Kahili on 17 July, and, while the damage done was not extensive, the crippled *Hatsuyuki* was sunk, with eighty-two of her crew killed. To illustrate the dilemma faced by the Japanese Navy: Rear Admiral Kusaka decided to send a large unit south on 19–20 July to drop off three destroyers carrying troops, while the rest of his force awaited a possible U.S. cruiser or destroyer run up the Slot. The Japanese force, including the heavy cruisers *Kumano, Suzuya,* and *Chokai,* the light cruiser *Sendai,* and nine destroyers, was spotted by two radar-equipped PBYs at 2148 on 19 July. The Japanese ships reversed course to assess the situation but were attacked by torpedo planes and bombers. The *Kumano* sustained a torpedo hit on her starboard quarter at 0246, and a dud bomb hit her on the starboard beam. She lost rudder control, but was able to limp home with a slight list. However, the same attack caught and sank the destroyers *Yugure* and *Kiyonami;* a total of 468 men from the two ships were lost.

Many Japanese ships were sunk while attempting to prepare for the expected next American invasion after the fall of New Georgia. While bringing troops to the Shortlands, the seaplane tender *Nisshin* was sunk on 22 July in Bougainville Strait, losing almost all hands. In fact, the loss rate was becoming so high that the Japanese Navy began using its large self-propelled barges, which could sail during the night and hug the inlets during the day, to transport troops to bolster defenses in the upper Solomons. A mine laid by VAAF slightly damaged the stern of the light cruiser *Nagara* at Kavieng 15 July. (She was repaired at Truk and back in service on 1 August.) On 27 July the destroyers *Ariake* and *Mikazuki,* carrying troops to strengthen the Tuluvu, New Britain garrison, ran aground near Cape Gloucester, and were pounded to pieces by VAAF planes the next day. VAAF planes on 2 August also severely damaged the destroyer *Akikaze* at Rabaul, putting her out of action until November.[9]

Battle of Vella Gulf

The next major encounter occurred the night of 6–7 August. Four Japanese destroyers, the *Hagikaze, Arashi, Kawakaze,* and *Shigure,* the first three carrying troops and supplies, were steaming by their usual route toward Kolombangara. The convoy, spotted at 1630 near Buka, was expecting night action, which it would get from Task Group 31.2: the destroyers *Dunlap, Craven, Maury, Lang, Sterett,* and *Stack*. No U.S. cruisers were available, and for the first time this would be a destroyer-versus-destroyer action. The U.S. destroyers would not have to act as screens for cruisers and would have a six-to-four advantage.

The Japanese column entered Bougainville Strait at 2100 and by 2320 it was northeast of Vella Lavella, where its course was changed to south-southeast. Sailing orders had prescribed that the four ships follow one another by 545 yards, but the *Shigure*, her engines overworked, lagged by 1,500 yards. She was especially concerned because of the plane spotting, and had trained her torpedo tubes to port, since the shores of Vella Lavella on her starboard side were clear of ships. Visibility against the black background of Kolombangara was only 2,000 yards. At 2344 the *Shigure*'s lookout spotted several ships.

The U.S. group was divided into two columns: the *Dunlap*, *Craven*, and *Maury* to port, and the *Lang*, *Sterett*, and *Stack* to starboard, both columns steaming northeast by north. The *Dunlap*'s radar spotted ships at 2333, ten and one-half miles to the north. The advantage again was with the U.S. ships, for by continuing course, they would close distance for a port torpedo attack at a range of 6,000 yards. At 2341 the *Dunlap*, *Craven*, and *Maury* launched twenty-four torpedoes, three minutes before the *Shigure* made her sighting. Just as the *Shigure* launched a salvo of eight torpedoes, three torpedoes struck the *Arashi* in her engine room and she burst in flames; a few minutes later she was hit by gunfire and another torpedo. The *Kawakaze* took one hit from the same salvos, causing her magazine to explode and setting afire her entire forward section. The *Hagikaze* caught fire too, being hit twice, and lost power. The *Kawakaze* sank at 2352, and the *Arashi* at 0017, followed by the *Hagikaze* at 0018. Torpedoes barely missed the *Shigure*, which had had time to turn and comb their wakes. But in turn, the *Shigure*'s torpedoes also missed. She reversed course, made smoke, and retired to the north at 2345, after passing through the wreckage of the *Arashi* and the *Hagikaze*.

The port column of Task Group 31.2 turned to the east to avoid the Japanese torpedoes at 2344, and then almost south at 2352 to rake the ships still afloat. The starboard column turned to the west at 2352, also opening up on the Japanese ships. The two columns then reformed and retired to the south. Only sporadic gunfire had come from the crippled destroyers, and no damage to U.S. ships had been incurred. The Japanese lost 1,210 soldiers and sailors; only 310 men were rescued from Kolombangara.[10]

The defeat was a severe loss to the Japanese—of three more destroyers and over a thousand men—and it was a humiliation to Japanese destroyer men who had intense pride in their performance record, particularly in night torpedo battles. It also showed that U.S. destroyers, when they were not tied down as screens to larger ships, could also win night battles.

COLLAPSE OF
THE OUTER
DEFENSE PERIMETER

1943

30 June	Japanese lose Nassau Bay, isolating Lae and Salamaua
15 August	Japanese lose Barakoma Bay, south of Vella Lavella, isolating Japanese Army on Kolombangara
17 August	Japanese establish barge base at Horaniu, north Vella Lavella, for evacuation of Japanese troops on bypassed Kolombangara
18 August	Battle off Horaniu
14 September	Japanese lose Salamaua
15 September	Japanese lose Lae
2 October	Japanese lose Finschhaven
6 October	Battle of Vella Lavella
6–7 October	Japanese evacuate last troops from Vella Lavella
1 November	U. S. Marines invade Bougainville at Empress Augusta Bay
2 November	Battle of Gazelle Bay (USN Title: Battle of Empress Augusta Bay)
5 November	Rabaul suffers massive and destructive raid by planes from two U.S. carriers. Loss of Rabaul as effective naval base
11 November	Rabaul receives second air raid by planes from two U.S. carriers
26 November	Battle off Cape St. George, Solomons. Last ship-to-ship battle in the Solomons

With Munda lost, the nearest Japanese force was on Kolombangara. As at Attu, American strategy called for bypassing Japanese-held islands and letting them wither away. General MacArthur had instituted a variation of this strategy on 30 June by occupying Nassau Bay, 17 miles south of Salamaua, thus cutting it and Lae off from further help. In the Solomons, Barakoma Bay on the southern end of Vella Lavella was occupied by American forces on 15 August. Vella Lavella lay 40 miles northwest of Vila and 60 miles south of Ballale, which was just south of Bougainville. In a sense, island-bypassing was like a game of checkers, and Kolombangara had been jumped. The U.S. invasion force suffered air attacks, but superior American air power pounded Kahili, Ballale, and the seaplane base at the Shortlands and provided an effective combat air patrol for the amphibious invasion fleet sailing the 200 miles from Guadalcanal. This operation demonstrated again the principle that whoever controls the air also controls the sea and land.

The move again caught the Imperial General Headquarters by surprise. Not wanting to repeat previous mistakes by landing Japanese troops on the north sector of Vella Lavella, it decided instead to strengthen the Rabaul defense perimeter at Bougainville and get the Japanese troops out of Kolombangara. At Vella Lavella, a barge-staging base for the Kolombangara evacuation was to be established. To do this, Army and SNLF troops were to be brought in by twenty barges from Buin on 17 August. The movement was screened by four destroyers: the *Sazanami, Hamakaze, Shigure,* and *Isokaze.* In reaction, the U.S. destroyers *Nicholas, O'Bannon, Taylor,* and *Chevalier* sailed northward, intent on destroying Japanese barges and warships.

Battle off Horaniu

As the Japanese destroyers and barges came south on 17 August, they underwent a bombing attack at 2038 and another at 2400. There were no Japanese casualties; however, the guarding destroyers' formation was in some disarray as the battle began.

Headed toward Horaniu, on the northeast end of Vella Lavella, were the barges, still more than 15 miles away. Some three and one-half miles to the northeast were the destroyers *Sazanami* and *Hamakaze,* headed northwest. Beyond them were the destroyers *Isokaze* and *Shigure* sailing abreast, trying to reform their column.

At 0029, the U.S. unit's radar detected enemy ships to its northwest at a distance of more than 11 miles. At 0040 the U.S. destroyers turned sharply to the west, which put them on a collision course with the barges. The Japanese destroyers, now also headed west, had spotted the American group at 0029, and orders were given by Admiral Matsuji Ijuin in the *Sazanami* to prepare for a port-side torpedo launch. Since the admiral's main responsibility was the protection of the barges, he had to bring his force before the U.S. destroyers, in order to draw the attack to his ships. Accordingly, at 0050 the Japanese destroyers turned south-southeast. The *Shigure* and *Hamakaze* had already launched torpedoes at 0046, but at the long range of over 12,500 yards, they were ineffective.

The U.S. destroyers, contrary to Admiral Ijuin's expectation, were more interested in a fight than a barge massacre. So Captain T. J. Ryan, the U.S. commanding officer, had turned toward the Japanese destroyers, his ships now abreast one another, which rendered the Japanese torpedo attack ineffective. With the distance closing, the U.S. destroyers turned due west at 0056. In response, Ijuin turned south. Thus at 0100 the two groups were sailing on reverse parallel courses, at a distance of 9,500 yards.

The *Sazanami* launched torpedoes at 0055, followed a minute later by fire from the *Hamakaze* and *Sazanami*; the range was long, however, and the fire was ineffective. In turn, the U.S. group had returned fire at 0059 after the *Chevalier* launched four torpedoes. The *Shigure* and *Isokaze* had set a westerly course about nine and one-half miles away, but turned south at 0050, inside the *Sazanami* and *Hamakaze*. While preparing another torpedo attack, the *Shigure* and *Isokaze* began drawing uncomfortably close fire. The two made smoke and began zigzagging, and returned fire at 0100, along with another torpedo launch. Although ammunition was being expended and plenty of water being churned up by both sides, neither had yet drawn blood. Then the *Hamakaze*'s radarman suddenly thought he detected a powerful U.S. force coming up from the south. On this information, Ijuin ordered a retirement to the northwest at 0100. The U.S. destroyers, still continuing north, finally managed a near-miss on the *Isokaze* at 0112, which wounded several and started small fires. The *Isokaze* at 0111 fired a futile parting torpedo salvo. The *Hamakaze*, nicked by near-misses, had suffered only minor damage, and the *Shigure* and *Sazanami* were not touched. Thus, the battle was over, with neither side having scored or been impressive. It had been fought at extremely long range for destroyers, and Admiral Ijuin had done his job of drawing the attack from the barges. During the battle the barges had scattered, and the U.S. forces sank only two. By 19 August, 390 of the barges' passengers had started constructing a barge base at Vella Lavella.[1]

Horaniu was occupied by Allied forces on 14 September; 600 Japanese troops and laborers were left on the northwest tip, awaiting evacuation, which was finally accomplished during the sea battle of 6–7 October. Kolombangara was evacuated by barges to Bougainville, via Sumbi Point and Choiseul. Almost 10,000 men were rescued in this manner, with the U. S. Navy unable to devise means to prevent it. The Japanese posts at Rekata Bay, Santa Isabel, Gizo, and Ganongga were also evacuated. Thus, the next line of Japanese defense was at Bougainville, with a garrison also still at Choiseul.

The final Japanese evacuation of the force that had operated the barge base at Horaniu, Vella Lavella brought about another naval battle and another Japanese victory. Even in withdrawal, the Japanese destroyers still showed great skill in night battles.

Battle of Vella Lavella

The plight of the 600 troops stranded on Vella Lavella could not be ignored. To evacuate them, Admiral Ijuin put together a Support Force, made up of the destroyers *Akigumo, Isokaze, Kazagumo, Samidare, Shigure,* and *Yugumo,* a Transport Force with the destroyers *Fumizuki, Matsukaze,* and *Yunagi,* and a separate group of some twenty barges and smaller craft. The sailing from Rabaul (and the barges from Buin) were reported during the afternoon of 6 October. At the moment, the U. S. Navy had only six destroyers available, in two groups of three: the *Selfridge, Chevalier,* and *O'Bannon;* and the *Ralph Talbot, Taylor,* and *La Vallette.* Captain Frank R. Walker's first group was 20 miles ahead of Commander Harold B. Larson's southern group. At 2235 the barges were steaming southeast, some 20 miles from their destination. Protecting them to the southwest were the destroyers *Akigumo, Isokaze, Kazagumo,* and *Yugumo* headed on a northeasterly course in column. Over eight miles away to the west were the *Shigure* and *Samidare,* steaming south for a rendezvous with Admiral Ijuin's main column. By splitting his forces, Ijuin hoped to confuse the Americans about his strength.

In turn, Walker knew that his units had been seen and he expected to run into a large force of Japanese destroyers. Nevertheless, he chose not to wait for Larson, and pushed on, with his three destroyers in column: the *Selfridge, Chevalier,* and *O'Bannon.* At 2231 U.S. radar detected ships ten miles north-northeast. What the U.S. radar had picked up was the Transport Force, which, acting on the sighting report, was retiring from the scene. As the two forces groped for each other (the visibility was poor in spots), Admiral Ijuin's force had also been misinformed by a report of an approaching U.S. force composed of four cruisers and three destroyers.

At 2230 the *Isokaze* thought she saw three enemy ships; this report was confirmed at 2238 by the *Kazagumo* and *Akigumo*, but the distance was overestimated as 11,000 yards. At 2235, Ijuin had turned his four destroyers sharply to port, and by 2238 they were sailing south. If this course were kept, Walker's "T" would be crossed. Walker maintained his course, however, in order to close the enemy. Ijuin then went into a series of complicated maneuvers that lost him his initial advantage. At 2245 he ordered a 45-degree simultaneous port turn, and three minutes later, a 90-degree turn to port; he was thus retiring, northwest of the U.S. destroyers, with the *Yugumo* on the port flank of the battle line, masking the other three destroyers. The *Yugumo* suddenly broke formation, making for the U.S. column. Both sides opened up at 2256 with guns and torpedoes; the *Kazagumo*, having become unmasked, could now also open fire.

The *Yugumo*'s torpedoes drew first blood when the *Chevalier* was hit at 2301 on her port bow, penetrating a magazine and tearing her bow off up to the bridge. The *O'Bannon*, next in line, then collided with the *Chevalier*. The *O'Bannon* was able to back off but she was out of the battle. The *Chevalier*'s loss was almost immediately avenged when gunfire and torpedoes tore the *Yugumo* apart; she sank within minutes. When Ijuin saw the *Yugumo*'s plight he turned south, forming a column and making smoke.

The *Selfridge*, now alone, continued to close the Japanese Transport Force, looping finally to the north. This brought her into a fight with the *Shigure* and the *Samidare*. The *Selfridge*'s guns repeatedly closely straddled the two, but they had already launched sixteen torpedoes and were returning fire. At 2306 a torpedo hit the *Selfridge* on her port side, forward; no fires broke out, but Walker's force was put out of action. All of the Japanese destroyers now retired, still fearing a larger force coming north. When Commander Larson arrived he saw nothing but wreckage and men in the water. The *La Vallette* sank the *Chevalier* with a torpedo after taking off 250 of her 301-man crew. The *Selfridge* and *O'Bannon* made it safely back to Tulagi.[2]

Meanwhile, the barges, the real cause of the battle, reached Horaniu, rescued all the troops, and returned them safely north. Other than the *Yugumo*, no Japanese destroyers were damaged; once again, the Japanese destroyers had shown that they were still masters of night fighting. Moreover, Captain Walker should certainly have waited for Larson's destroyers—but he seemed to have a little bit of *banzai* in him, too.

New Guinea

General MacArthur was to break through the Bismarck Archipelago by way of New Guinea. To that end, Lae, Salamaua, and Finschhafen had to be captured. With only a small portion of the U. S. Navy forces (and no carriers) assigned to him, he had to rely on land-based planes to cover his invasions and neutralize Japanese air power by pounding Japanese airfields at Lae, Salamaua, Finschhafen, Wewak, and Madang (with occasional massive raids on Rabaul). In turn, the Japanese Navy escorted troops from Cape Gloucester to Finschhafen, to be transported south by barges.

Overwhelmed by combined overland and amphibious attacks, air attacks and naval bombardment, Salamaua was lost by Japan on 14 September, and Lae on the following day.[3] No evacuation was possible in either place. Finschhafen was similarly lost on 2 October, and after an ineffective attempt to recapture it, Imperial General Headquarters shifted priority to the defense of Bougainville.[4] This released the VAAF which, starting on 12 October with a massive raid by 349 planes, began pounding Rabaul's defenses. The air attacks never ceased until Rabaul finally ceased to function as a naval base, early in 1944.

Bougainville

The next Allied target was Bougainville, the largest of the Solomon Islands, with an area of 3,380 square miles. Covered with forests, it is a rugged, mountainous island, with the usual rainy and humid climate. Its population was small (about 43,000), and its native inhabitants were extremely primitive. If it could be captured, Rabaul, only 170 miles from its northern tip, would be indefensible against American air power, both land- and carrier-based. Allied control of Bougainville would destroy the effectiveness of the Japanese airfields at Kahili, Buin, Kahara, Kieta, Tenekau, Buka, and Bonis; in the Shortlands at Ballale and the seaplane base at Faisi; and on Treasury and Choiseul islands. An amphibious landing always has its risks, but Admiral Nimitz reasoned correctly that, with the beginning of

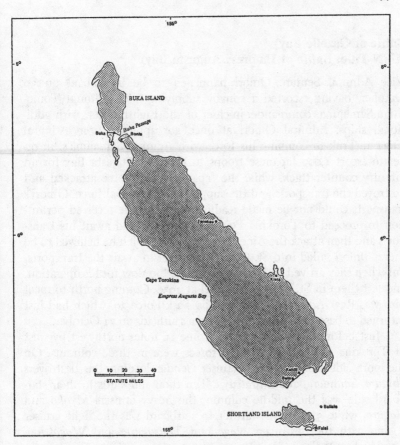

Bougainville Island

the Central Pacific offensive in mid-November, Admiral Koga would not send the Combined Fleet with its carriers against Halsey's operation in the Southwest Pacific.

To defend Bougainville, the Japanese had more than 50,000 men—but the chosen beachhead at Empress Augusta Bay was held by fewer than 3,000 men. The landings were made on 1 November by the 3rd Marine Division at Cape Torokina, which was defended by 270 men and one field gun. By dark, 14,000 Marines were ashore. The Americans expected immediate air and naval reaction, and so all transports, except for four which were partially unloaded, left the beachhead.

Battle of Gazelle Bay
(USN Title: Battle of Empress Augusta Bay)

Vice Admiral Sentaro Omori happened to be in Rabaul on 30 October, having escorted a convoy supplying Vice Admiral Tomoshige Samejima, commander-in-chief of the Eighth Fleet, with additional ships. Admiral Omori at once got approval from Admiral Koga at Truk to combine his force with Admiral Samejima's, in order to escort 1,000 Japanese troops to Empress Augusta Bay for an infantry counterattack, while the Japanese naval force attacked and destroyed the transports and the supporting U.S. naval force. Omori's transports could not be made ready in time, but he received permission to proceed to Torokina Point, where he would await his transports and then attack the American transports which he believed to be there. Omori sailed into St. George Channel to await the transports, but when they arrived he found them to be too slow for his operation, and left them in St. George Channel at 1930. Coming north to meet him was Rear Admiral A. S. Merrill's Task Force 39, which had just returned to base from bombarding Buka's airfields on 31 October.

Just before contact was made, some 19 miles northwest by west of Torokina Point, the Japanese forces were in three columns. On the port side was the light cruiser *Sendai* leading the destroyers *Shigure*, *Samidare*, and *Shiratsuyu*. Ten thousand yards to their starboard side was the middle column, the heavy cruisers *Myoko* and *Haguro*, while 5,000 yards farther to starboard was the light cruiser *Agano* with the destroyers *Naganami*, *Hatsukaze*, and *Wakatsuki*. They had set their course to the southeast.

On a northerly course came Task Force 39 with four light cruisers in column, screened at a distance of 1,000 yards on their starboard side by the van destroyers, and on their port side by the trailing destroyers. At the point of first contact, the Japanese force was almost 20,000 yards northwest of Task Force 39.

Admiral Omori did not conduct a good battle; the visibility was poor, he had no radar, his plane reports only confused him, and he tried maneuvers that were too complicated for a force that had been so hastily thrown together. Moreover, he had no idea what forces opposed him. First, his spotter plane reported three U.S. battleships and many cruisers and destroyers at Torokina Point. Then at 0126 the *Haguro* launched a catapult plane which at 0140 reported minelayers, one cruiser, and three destroyers, 20 miles south of Omori's ships. Omori then ordered a 180-degree simultaneous turn, a difficult maneuver for his closely spaced ships, operating in total darkness. He wanted both to confuse the enemy and to await further aerial reports. A short time later he ordered another 180-degree simultaneous turn. By this time his columns were in some disorder; the port screen was only about 300 yards away from the main column, and the *Samidare* was out of line. Shortly thereafter the *Shigure's* lookout sighted enemy ships, which completely surprised Omori.

Task Force 39 had been speeding north, and the *Montpelier's* radar had already detected the Japanese ships. At 0131 Admiral Merrill ordered his four van destroyers to veer off to port to attack the enemy. (What radar had so far spotted was the *Sendai's* screen.) Eight minutes later, Merrill's group executed a simultaneous turn which would free the rear-guard destroyers for a second torpedo attack. One minute after the *Shigure's* sighting, the *Ausburne, Dyson, Stanley,* and *Claxton* launched twenty-five torpedoes and then split into two units, the first two reversing course to starboard, the latter two doing the same, but then continuing their loop, so that they were closing the light cruisers.

The *Shigure* reported seeing two destroyers retiring and two paralleling the *Sendai's* column. The *Sendai* reacted with a hard turn to starboard, because it was likely that American torpedoes were headed for the column's broadside. But the earlier loss of formation now caused trouble, for the *Sendai's* turn was sharper than the *Shigure's* and they almost collided. The *Samidare,* in trying to avoid the *Sendai,* sideswiped the *Shiratsuyu,* crushing the latter's hull on her port side and buckling her deck. Both were out of the fight, although the *Samidare* still managed to launch eight torpedoes at 0152. The *Shigure* launched an eight-torpedo spread at 0148, and the *Sendai* a similar spread at 0150. But now the U.S. light cruisers had gone into action, opening fire at 0150, and, as usual, the American guns, guided by radar, were all trained on the biggest target. At 0151 the *Sendai* was hit squarely by the first three salvos from the four cruisers' 6-inch guns. She was almost literally smothered by flying metal, and erupted in flame.

Admiral Omori in the *Myoko* was startled to see the *Sendai* blaze up on his port beam; he thought she was ahead of him, in the port van. He tried to reform his ships by turning to port in a tight circle, coming out on a south-southwesterly course. In the meantime the *Agano* and her three destroyers closed the American ships.

When the order to reform came, the *Agano's* group turned in column hard to starboard, causing the *Myoko* and the *Haguro* to cut directly through it. The *Myoko* sliced off the bow of the *Hatsukaze* and smashed the destroyer's torpedo tubes. (The *Hatsukaze's* bow was still wrapped around the *Myoko's* bow when the *Myoko* returned to Rabaul.) The *Haguro* just barely missed a collision with the *Naganami* and the *Wakatsuki*.

In response, Admiral Merrill's light cruisers had been executing a complicated series of maneuvers including a figure eight, north and south; but as the *Myoko* and *Haguro* finally set their course straight south, the U.S. light cruisers headed southwest, four abreast, gradually edging into a westerly course, and then into a single column steaming due north. Finally a fire fight between the two Japanese heavy cruisers and four U.S. light cruisers broke out. The *Myoko* and the *Haguro* opened fire at 0215 and in turn were straddled by American fire. They launched twenty-four torpedoes at 0218, but neither side scored, and at 0229 Omori ordered a withdrawal.

The U.S. rear guard destroyers never made the torpedo charge expected of them; the *Foote* managed to blunder into a torpedo aimed at the cruiser column and had her stern blown off. She was towed, however, to safer waters.

The Japanese clearly lost this battle, even though they had the heavier guns. The *Sendai* soon sank; the *I-144* picked up Admiral Ijuin and 37 more of her crew, but the rest of the crew (her normal complement was 450) were lost. U.S. destroyers later sank the bowless *Hatsukaze* by gunfire; however, all but nine of her men had been rescued. The *Samidare* suffered two direct hits, but with collision damage and on manual steering, she made it back to Rabaul, as did the *Shiratsuyu*. The *Agano* suffered minor damage from a near-miss, and the *Haguro's* and *Myoko's* Action Reports indicate no casualties or damage. With the exception of the case of the *Sendai*, Omori's maneuvers and collisions hurt him more than did the torrent of 5- and 6-inch shells and the two dozen torpedoes thrown at his force. Because Omori was turned back, the Bougainville invasion could not be stopped.

Rabaul vs. Carrier Planes

After Omori's defeat, Admiral Koga decided to reinforce the Eighth Fleet in Simpson Harbor, Rabaul, since an American foothold on Bougainville could not be tolerated. He sent to Rabaul the Second Fleet's venerable ships: the heavy cruisers *Atago*, *Chokai*,

Maya, Takao, Mogami, Suzuya, and *Chikuma,* screened by the light cruiser *Noshiro* and four destroyers, under the command of Vice Admiral Takeo Kurita.

When the news of this reached Admiral Halsey, he had no heavy cruisers or battleships; they were in the Central Pacific preparing for the Tarawa–Makin landings. He did have Rear Admiral Frederick C. Sherman's Task Force 38, a fast carrier force built around the heavy carrier *Saratoga* and the light carrier *Princeton.* Halsey took the gamble of sending them to a launch point south of Torokina Point, 230 miles southeast of Rabaul, and launching all their planes at once, relying on surprise and a small Airsol (Aircraft Solomons Command) combat air patrol. The weather favored Task Force 38, for Sherman went north under clouds and in rainstorms, and although his ships were seen by aerial reconnaissance, they were not recognized as carriers. Instead, it was thought that the force was a reinforcing group sent to cover the Bougainville landing.

The Japanese task force arrived at Rabaul on 5 November at about 0700, and joined up with the light cruisers *Agano* and *Yubari,* and seven destroyers. The weather at Rabaul was bright and clear, ideal for a surprise raid. When the air-raid signal was sounded some time after 1000, most of the ships were in no condition to get under way and to leave the harbor for dispersal. The *Saratoga* and *Princeton* had launched at 0900, sending out fifty-two Hellcat fighters, twenty-three Avenger torpedo bombers, and twenty-two Dauntless dive bombers.

The planes were first seen at Rabaul at about 1020; the carrier pilots kept in a compact group until the moment of attack, so that they would have maximum protection against the Japanese fighters up to the very last moment. The raid lasted until about 1044, causing heavy damage to the Japanese ships. The *Atago* suffered three near-misses, her torpedo flasks were exploded, her hull, armament, and machinery were damaged, and twenty-two men were killed, with sixty-four wounded. The *Maya* had started to leave the harbor but was hit on her catapult plane flight deck; a chain of explosions and fires gutted all her engine rooms, making navigation impossible, and seventy men were killed, with sixty wounded. The *Chikuma* got off lightly, with some slight damage to her hull, armaments, and machinery, and she was able to leave for Truk at 2038, and sail for Eniwetok on 20 November. The *Mogami* cleared the harbor at 1037, but before that she had been hit and set afire, probably by a torpedo. The magazines for the No. 1 and 2 turrets were flooded. At 1045 she stopped all engines and concentrated on fire-fighting; that evening, because of the damage to her bow structure, she was escorted to Truk by the *Suzuya* and the destroyer *Tamanami*. The *Takao* received a bomb hit on the starboard side of her No. 2 turret, heavily damaging her hull and machinery. The *Suzuya*, which was just moving up to the *Naruto* for refueling when the attack started, took evasive action and escaped with light damage. The three light cruisers *Agano*, *Noshiro*, and *Yubari* received no damage. Of the destroyers, the *Fujinami* was hit by a dud torpedo, and the *Amagiri* and *Wakatsuki* suffered only light damage.[5]

The raiders returned to their carriers, which then sped south undetected. Rabaul's air defense had been able to down less than a dozen planes. No sooner had the Japanese fleet begun to sort out the disorder than an attack by the VAAF hit the fleet again, with twenty-seven B-24s and sixty-seven P-38s. The VAAF found no plane opposition, for Rabaul's fighters and bombers were out looking for Task Force 38; however, the raid inflicted no more damage on the fleet.

5 November 1943 was the beginning of the end for Rabaul as a Japanese naval base, although it would take many more raids to drive the Japanese out. For some reason, Japanese naval officers and men had loved Rabaul as a base; now, their most popular song about it had become tragically ironic: "Saraba, Rabauru-yo, mata kuru made wa" which meant, "Farewell Rabaul, until I see you again." The Second Fleet's heavy cruisers, withheld from battle during most of 1943, had suffered grievously at Rabaul.[6] Four ships were sent to Japan for repairs and they would be unavailable for months.

The VAAF kept up the pressure, with frequent raids. The loss of Japanese planes for the defense of the Rabaul base was serious, but the Japanese Navy still desperately needed to use the base. Therefore, Koga flew in 100 planes from his heavy carriers at Truk, further depleting his carriers' supply of planes and pilots. Task Force 38's attack had been so successful that it set the pattern for the U.S. carrier raids of the future; such raids were one of the three principal factors later said by Tojo to have caused Japan's defeat.

Admiral Halsey planned an immediate repeat attack. He had just secured the heavy carriers *Bunker Hill* and *Essex*, and the light carrier *Independence*, and by 8 November he had formed Task Group 50.3 under Rear Admiral Alfred E. Montgomery. One hundred eighty-three planes were put in the air on 11 November; but this time the Japanese were ready. Not only did they defend Simpson Harbor, but they prepared a return strike against the carriers. The U.S. carrier planes found fewer targets. In and outside Simpson Bay were the heavy cruiser *Maya*, the light cruisers *Agano*, *Noshiro*, and *Yubari*, and the destroyers *Kazagumo*, *Urakaze*, *Suzunami*, *Hayanami*, *Fumizuki*, *Umikaze*, *Naganami*, *Makinami*, *Fujinami*, and *Amagiri*. The Japanese carrier fighter planes were already aloft, and the U.S. strike was not flying with the same precision that it had shown before. Nevertheless, the *Noshiro* was attacked by torpedo planes outside the harbor at 0857, while a fierce rainstorm was in progress. She evaded the torpedoes but then got a strafing which put several holes in her bridge stack and severed three degaussing cables. At 0903 she underwent another torpedo attack, but again was not hit. The *Suzunami* was divebombed and sunk at 0820, while the *Yubari*, *Urakaze*, and *Umikaze* suffered only slight damage. The *Naganami* took a near-miss, then a bomb on her deck abaft the bridge, and had to be towed into port. The second U.S. carrier raid had lasted less than an hour.[7]

At 1200, the Japanese launched a strike of more than one hundred planes against Task Group 50.3. The U.S. ships' combat air patrol and screening destroyers, however, protected them against a hit, and the Japanese lost more than thirty-five planes; over Rabaul another twenty Japanese planes were downed. Only fifty-two of the planes sent from the Japanese carriers returned to Truk. Not only had Rabaul not been effectively defended, but the Combined Fleet carriers lost so many carrier pilots that Koga could not respond to the 20 November invasion of Tarawa. As in so many cases, Japanese reluctance to lose one part of the defense perimeter allowed another part to be overrun; now even the original defense perimeter was beginning to collapse because of inadequate naval support.

Battle off Cape St. George

When it appeared that the Allies would hold Bougainville, Japanese fear of landings on Buka began to grow. The Japanese Navy's position was that Bougainville was not a steppingstone but would be permanently held by the Allies; the Army, however, insisted that Buka was the real objective. The Army prevailed and consequently determined that the Navy should run in a convoy of some 900 soldiers to Buka, while evacuating 700 aviation personnel, for constant bombing of Buka's airfields had rendered them useless since 1 November. So once again the Navy had to put together a destroyer transport force to conform to the Army's strategy. The 25 November convoy was to be the last such "Tokyo Express."

The Buka Reinforcement Unit consisted of the troop-laden destroyers *Amagiri*, *Yugiri*, and *Uzuki*, screened by the destroyers *Onami* and *Makinami*. Air intelligence alerted Halsey, and he sent two destroyer divisions (from Destroyer Squadron 23) to intercept the Buka Unit: Destroyer Divisions 45 (the *Charles Ausburne*, *Claxton*, and *Dyson*) and 46 (the *Converse* and *Spence*).

The *Amagiri*, *Uzuki*, and *Yugiri* landed their troops at Buka, took on the aviation personnel, and headed home at 0045. But the two-destroyer screen was already running into trouble. The two U.S. destroyer divisions were guarding the western entrance to St. George Channel; if an interception were made, Destroyer Division (Desdiv) 45 could make a torpedo attack, covered by Desdiv 46; then the two could reverse roles. Radar contact was made at 0141, the Japanese screen being spotted. The *Onami* and *Makinami* were on the starboard side of the *Amagiri*, *Yugiri*, and *Uzuki*, headed west, well in advance of the destroyer transports. The destroyers *Charles Ausburne*, *Claxton*, and *Dyson* were the starboard column, headed north, with the destroyers *Converse* and *Spence* following, off Desdiv 45's port quarter. At 0145 Desdiv 45 turned directly east to close and attack the Japanese screen. At 0156 it launched torpedoes for a 4,500-yard run, turning south after the launch.

The *Onami* spotted the retiring destroyers at 0200, but thirty seconds later she took several torpedo hits, and sank immediately. The *Makinami* also took hits and almost buckled, but nevertheless stayed afloat. At that moment Desdiv 45's radar picked up the destroyer transports, 13,000 yards from their disintegrated screen. The destroyer transports turned north at flank speed, hotly pursued by Desdiv 45. The *Yugiri* launched torpedoes, but to no avail. Desdiv 45 opened fire at 0222 with the bow guns of all three ships, and the Japanese destroyer transports returned fire, both sides scoring near-misses. At 0225 the three destroyer transports separated, each veering off on a separate course 45 degrees apart, leaving Captain Arleigh Burke a choice of which to pursue. He chose the *Yugiri*, which was hit with gunfire at 0305. But the *Yugiri* did not give up easily; she circled to face her tormentors, and kept on firing her guns and launching torpedoes until she sank under the continued pounding at 0328. Meanwhile, Desdiv 46 had finished off the *Makinami*. Burke then tried to engage the *Amagiri* and the *Uzuki*, making a stern chase, but his efforts were in vain. The U.S. group retired at 0404, and the *Amagiri* and *Uzuki* lived to fight another day.[8]

Probably no one realized it at the time, but this was to be the last surface battle (the first of which had occurred at Savo Island on 9 August 1942) to be fought in the Solomons. There had been fifteen battles, twelve of which were night surface-ship contests. Because of the spectacular nature of carrier battles, many have regarded the Pacific war as a carrier war; but, on the contrary, most of the battles, especially those fought in the Solomons, were surface night fights. The Japanese either drew or won at least ten of these night struggles, but in doing so they reduced their destroyer strength (and, to some degree, their cruiser strength) to a point where they had to be more conservative, for the Japanese defense perimeter was being steadily diminished by invasions from New Guinea, the Admiralties, and the Central Pacific—and the Japanese Navy could do nothing about it. The Outer South Seas Force was renamed the Inner South Seas Force; but no naval engagement of any consequence took place from 25 November 1943 to 19 June 1944, after the loss of Saipan. In reality, the power of the Japanese Navy, especially in essential destroyer strength, had been broken, while the strength of the U. S. Navy was increasing at an incredible rate. The nature of the war at sea changed after 25 November; the Japanese Navy now surely faced ultimate defeat, short of a miraculous victory in a decisive battle—which never occurred.

At this point, Japanese strategic planning began to lose sight of reality and became obsessed with either fighting and winning an impossible "decisive victory," or seeking death in battle. Wars are usually fought long after one side's defeat is inevitable, and this was particularly true in the case of Japan, for the thinking of her military leaders came to be dominated by vestiges of Japanese mythology, rather than by reality. Japan had never been invaded, her people were thought to be descended from the gods, the land of Japan itself had been formed by the god Izanagi, and Japan was led by a semi-divine emperor. Therefore, Japan could not possibly be defeated; a "Divine Wind" would surely save her. And so the war had to be continued to the bitter end, which would mean the total destruction of the Imperial Japanese Navy.

Table of Organization for Battle of Gazelle Bay

Torokina Interception Force

Heavy cruisers: *Myoko, Haguro*

PORT SCREEN FORCE

Light cruiser: *Sendai*
Destroyers: *Samidare, Shigure, Shiratsuya*

STARBOARD SCREEN FORCE

Light cruiser: *Agano*
Destroyers: *Hatsukaze, Naganami, Wakatsuki*

U. S. Navy Forces at Gazelle Bay

Task Force 39 (Rear Admiral A. S. Merrill)

Light cruisers: *Montpelier, Cleveland, Columbia, Denver*

VAN SCREEN

Destroyers: *Charles Ausburne, Dyson, Stanley, Claxton*

AFTER SCREEN

Destroyers: *Spence, Thatcher, Converse, Foote*[9]

chapter 21

EBBING OF THE JAPANESE TIDE

1943

20 November	U. S. Marines invade Tarawa. Japanese lose Makin Island
24 November	Japanese lose Tarawa
26 December	MacArthur invades New Britain at Cape Gloucester

1944

2 January	Japanese bypassed at Sio, by occupation of Saidor
Jan.–Feb.	Japanese lose Sio, Madang, Green Island. U.S. forces occupy Emirau, Admiralties
1 February	Japanese lose Roi-Namur, Marshalls
5 February	Japanese lose Kwajalein, Marshalls
10 February	Japanese abandon Truk as main naval base
17–18 February	Massive carrier-plane and ship raid on Truk, destroying it as an operating naval base
21 February	Japanese lose Eniwetok
24 March	Japanese lose Los Negros, Admiralties
31 March	Admiral Koga disappears in flight to Palau. Admiral Soemu Toyoda becomes new commander-in-chief
3 April	Japanese lose Manus, Admiralties
22 April	Japanese lose Aitapi, New Guinea
26 April	Japanese lose Hollandia, New Guinea
21 May	Japanese lose Wakde and Sarmi
27 May	U. S. Army invades Biak
31 May–4 June	Japanese make first attempt to reinforce Biak

8–9 June   Battle off Biak

15 June   U.S. troops invade Saipan. Japanese Navy shifts attention to the Marianas

19–20 June   Battle of the Marianas (USN Title: Battle of the Philippine Sea). Loss of second "decisive battle" by Japanese Navy

1 September   Japanese lose Biak
              Saidor

Allied strategy changed toward the end of 1943. The large Japanese forces on Bougainville, Buka, Choiseul, New Britain, and New Ireland were not being challenged in battle; instead, on Bougainville the Allied forces established a safe defense perimeter and built air strips, thus cutting the Japanese Army off from food and munitions. Rabaul and Buka suffered constant air raids and became untenable; the latter was also subjected to naval bombardments. Bougainville's air power would prove to be invaluable to MacArthur in penetrating the Bismarck Archipelago.

In New Guinea, the 12,000 Japanese troops at Sio were eventually bypassed and stranded by a landing at Saidor on 2 January 1944, which had in turn been made possible by landings on New Britain at Cape Gloucester, on 26 December. The Japanese defenders retreated to Rabaul, were cut off and then left alone; however, Japan did not surrender Rabaul until the end of the war. MacArthur now controlled both sides of the Vitiaz Strait, which opened the road to northern New Guinea and the Admiralties (chiefly Manus Island). The Japanese survivors at Sio marched to Madang, which fell, forcing the Army to retreat further to Wewak. Green Island, 115 miles east of Rabaul, was lost in February 1944. Rather than assaulting strongly held Manus Island, MacArthur first took unoccupied Emirau, 70 miles northwest from Kavieng, then took Los Negros, easternmost of the Admiralties, on 24 March. Air strips were built at these places to cover further Allied invasions; then Manus Island and Wewak came under air attack. After a fierce battle, Manus was lost in April.

On 22 April MacArthur made a long leapfrog move into Aitape and then secured two invasion beaches 20 miles from Hollandia, New Guinea; then Hollandia itself was taken on 26 April. General Imamura's Eighteenth Army was practically wiped out in these campaigns, either in battle, or by disease and starvation after being driven into the jungle. Very few men surrendered.

MacArthur, wanting air bases for the invasion of Mindanao, landed on Wakde Island off the New Guinea coast on 19 May, and after a bloody two-day battle, Japan lost this outpost also. Next Biak Island was invaded on 27 May, but this action was met with renewed Japanese resistance. (Admiral Koga, unable to stop the Allies' rapid march north, was killed when his plane bound for Davao was lost in a storm on 31 March; Admiral Soemu Toyoda became the new commander-in-chief of the Combined Fleet, and he was determined not to lose Biak.)

The Central Pacific offensive against the Japanese began in late 1943. Makin and Tarawa were invaded on 20 November; Tarawa fell after a bloody three-day battle in which the SNLF troops fought to the last man, and Makin fell on 24 November.

The very heart of the Japanese strength in the Marshalls was the next objective. Heavy carrier strikes almost eliminated Japanese air power in the area, but did little to aid the land invasions. Roi–Namur fell on 1 February and, following very heavy air attacks

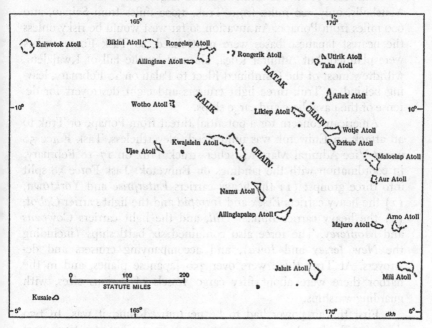

Marshall Islands

and battleship bombardment, a beachhead was secured on Kwajalein that same day. Again Japanese resistance was resolute, but the islands forming the atoll had been lost by 5 February.

The Combined Fleet could not respond to the westward threat because the U. S. Navy had increased the size of its Pacific fleet in all categories—Essex-class carriers, new battleships with 16-inch guns, cruisers, destroyers, and submarines. Thus the Combined Fleet was completely outclassed and outgunned. But at the same time, the Japanese Navy faced such a threat in the Central Pacific that it could not go to the aid of the beleaguered Japanese troops in New Guinea, the Admiralties, New Ireland, and New Britain. Admiral Toyoda truly faced a dilemma. Between 9 April 1943 and 14 February 1944 the Japanese Navy had lost thirty-three ships—twenty-five destroyers, five light cruisers, one escort carrier, one seaplane carrier, and one battleship. In addition to these outright losses, the shipyards in Japan were filled with damaged ships.[1] The only Japanese replacements were three carrier escorts, three light carriers, two light cruisers, nine destroyers, and two battleships converted to hybrid battleship-carriers—the Hyuga and the Ise.

Eniwetok Atoll was next. It is the largest island in the western Marshalls, only 700 miles from Truk, 1,000 miles from Saipan, and 600 miles from Ponape. An invasion so far west would be risky unless the nearest Japanese bases were neutralized, so Task Force strikes were planned; but Admiral Koga, alarmed by the fall of Kwajalein, withdrew most of the Combined Fleet to Palau on 10 February, leaving behind at Truk three light cruisers and eight destroyers for defense of the naval base and cargo ships.

American concern for a potential threat from Ponape or Truk to an attack on Eniwetok was unjustified. Nevertheless, Task Force 58 under Vice Admiral Marc Mitscher struck Truk on 17–18 February, in coordination with the landings on Eniwetok. Task Force 58 split into three groups: (1) the heavy carriers Enterprise and Yorktown; (2) the heavy carriers Essex and Intrepid and the light carrier Cabot; (3) the heavy carrier Bunker Hill, and the light carriers Cowpens and Monterey. The force also contained six battleships (including the New Jersey and Iowa), and accompanying cruisers and destroyers. At Truk there were over 350 Japanese planes, and in the harbor there were about fifty cargo vessels of various sizes, with guarding warships.

First the air power had to be neutralized—and it was. In two days of raids almost 300 Japanese planes were put out of action, most of them still on the ground. After the threat of Japanese air attack was eliminated, the planes and battleships made an almost complete slaughter of everything left afloat. Sunken Japanese ships included the light cruisers *Agano, Katori,* and *Naka,* the destroyers *Tachikaze, Fumizuki, Oite,* and *Maikaze,* thirty merchant ships, auxiliary craft, and two transports.[2]

As soon as the raid started, as many Japanese ships got under way as could. In one group were the light cruiser *Katori* and destroyers *Nowaki* and *Maikaze.* The *Maikaze* fought a brave but hopeless battle with the *New Jersey* and *Iowa,* and was finally sunk at 1343 by the heavy cruisers *Minneapolis* and *New Orleans,* her guns blazing away until the water closed over the turrets.[3] The only Japanese retaliation was a bomb hit on the heavy carrier *Intrepid,* which caused serious damage.

After the fall of Eniwetok on 21 February and elimination of Truk as a naval base, the Imperial General Headquarters had so many problems facing it that it could not solve any one adequately. The Allies simply bypassed the islands in the Marshalls that still had strong Japanese garrisons, like Woetje, Maloelap, Mili, Jaluit, making only occasional air raids. Majuro Lagoon became a staging area for the U. S. Navy. The new American strategy was based on the use of far-ranging carrier strikes, carried out by the Fifth Fleet under Admiral Raymond Spruance. Under Spruance was Vice Admiral Marc Mitscher's Task Force 58. As a new defensive tactic, a battle line under Vice Admiral Willis A. Lee, composed of seven new battleships, thirteen cruisers, and twenty-six destroyers, was placed well ahead of the carriers; their antiaircraft firepower was awesome.

Task Force 58 ranged far and wide with carrier strikes and ship bombardments, even aiding MacArthur's New Guinea campaign. The three routes to Tokyo had been consolidated into two when Rabaul was neutralized, and were soon to become one route when the U. S. Navy and Army would meet for the conquest of the Philippines. During this period, Admirals Spruance and Halsey alternated commands of the Fifth and Third fleets.

Task Force 58's raids were frequent and sometimes devastating. On 30–31 March, Palau, to which the Japanese had sent plane reinforcements, was raided. The destroyer *Wakatake* was sunk trying to clear the harbor, more than thirty Japanese planes were destroyed, and twenty-eight ships were sunk, a total of 129,807 tons.[4] Planes also mined the two passages into Palau. Similar U.S. raids hit Yap,

Woleai, Wakde, Sarmi, Sawar, Hollandia, and, for a second time, Truk.

The Japanese decided to hold an inner defense line through the Marianas, Palaus, West Dutch New Guinea, and the Dutch Indies; they code-named it KON Operation. Behind this line, troops were massed for deployment in danger zones, additional airfields were built, and the Combined Fleet was concentrated. As pressure from the U. S. Navy and MacArthur increased, the operation had to be constantly revised. The Japanese believed that the main thrust would be up from New Guinea to Mindanao, which was where they hoped to fight the "decisive naval battle." But MacArthur's surge northward could not be stopped. In May, Sarmi, then Wakde, New Guinea, 120 miles north of Hollandia, were invaded. MacArthur met fierce resistance and the Japanese were not eliminated until 1 September.

The Japanese tried desperately to hold Biak by reinforcements; it was hoped 22,300 Imperial Japanese Army troops could eventually be landed.[5] First the Japanese sent out a task force; but it was spotted early, and was recalled. It was decided a new tactic would have to be used. Troops were transferred to the heavy cruiser *Aoba*, the light cruiser *Kinu*, and the destroyers *Shikinami, Shigure, Uranami, Harusame, Shiratsuyu,* and *Samidare,* and taken to Sarong.

The Second Reinforcement Group sortied from Sarong at 0000 on 7 June, covered by Air Flotilla 23. The destroyers *Shikinami, Uranami, Shigure* carried 600 troops, while the destroyers *Harusame, Shiratsuyu, Samidare* towed troop-laden barges. The movement again was observed, and Admiral V. A. C. Crutchley (RN) went forth with a cruiser and destroyer force to intercept. At the same time, the Japanese group came under air attack on 8 June at about 1245; the *Harusame* was sunk, the *Shiratsuyu* was damaged, and the *Shikinami* and *Samidare* were slightly damaged. After the *Harusame*'s crew was rescued, the group again started toward Biak.

Contact was made with Admiral Crutchley's (RN) superior force at 2320. Vice Admiral Sakonju had no stomach for a fight, with his ships either loaded with troops or towing barges, so he cut the barges loose and headed north. A long-range stern chase duel ensued. First the Japanese destroyers missed their targets, then U.S. destroyers opened fire at 0018, at about 17,000 yards. (Crutchley had retired his cruisers, letting the destroyers fight it out.) The *Shigure* was hit five times, and the *Shikinami* also suffered some casualties. The battle ended at 0027 when the U.S. ships entered an area where the VAAF had permission to bomb any ship it saw.[6] Thus, Biak had

not been (and would not be) reinforced. Events shaping up elsewhere caused cancellation of KON Operation in favor of A-GO
Operation—the "decisive battle," to be fought in the vicinity of the
western Carolines. There the Japanese fleet could be helped by land-
based planes.

Battle of the Marianas
(USN Title: Battle of the Philippine Sea)

When Saipan was invaded by the United States on 15 June, the
Japanese Navy reacted in full force, with A-GO Operation now
shifted to the defense of Saipan, for the loss of Saipan and its adjacent islands would make Japan herself subject to the pounding of
long-range American bombers. The Navy, however, had wanted the
"decisive" battle to occur much farther to the southwest, for two
sound reasons: first, because U.S. submarine activity had created a
shortage of refined oil and when A-GO was activated, the Japanese
Navy did not have enough refined oil available to fight as far away as
the Marianas. Instead, it had to use unprocessed Borneo oil,
which was more volatile and thus a greater fire hazard, and contained
impurities that damaged ships' boilers. Second, the Japanese realized
that the disparity between the U.S. and Japanese fleets was so great,
in both number of ships and number of experienced carrier flyers,
that the Japanese Navy would have to be aided to a great extent by
land-based planes to fight its decisive battle. The original A-GO Operation had been planned with this need in mind.

But battles must be fought where the opportunity presents itself, and the opportunity was present in the Philippine Sea after 15
June. The Japanese Navy had been reorganized on 1 March 1944
into a First Mobile Fleet, similar to a U. S. Navy Task Force, with
separate units somewhat resembling the U. S. Navy Task Groups.
Vice Admiral Jisaburo Ozawa commanded this First Mobile Fleet,
and thus had the task of somehow creating the conditions that would
equalize the contending fleets enough to bring Japanese victory. His
plan, for which he held high hopes, was to subject the U.S. carrier
groups west of Saipan to attack from every land-based plane he could
get to Guam, Yap, and Rota. The U. S. Navy would have to depend
on carrier planes alone, and Ozawa's carrier planes had greater range
than the U.S. carrier planes, by 210 miles. He thus could stay out of
U.S. carrier-plane reach and launch his own strike craft; they would
hit the U.S. carriers (which would already have been damaged by land

planes), land at Guam to refuel and rearm, and give the American carriers a second strike on the way home.

But it didn't happen that way. The land-based planes failed to damage Task Force 58—although Vice Admiral Kakuji Kakuta, commander of the Base Air Force of the Marianas, located on Tinian, assured Ozawa that Task Force 58's attrition rate was bringing about plane and ship equality. But Spruance had ordered carrier raids on Iwo Jima and Chichi Jima, the staging areas for Japanese planes coming south, on 15 to 17 June; and Guam and Rota, the turnaround fields, would be wiped out by nearly continuous U.S. fighter attacks, beginning on 19 June. Thus the battle would be between carrier planes, without Ozawa's knowing so until after the battle was over. Admiral Spruance's primary worry was that Ozawa would try to slip around his own Task Force to get at the Saipan invasion transports, but he need not have worried; Ozawa, relying on the promised aid from land planes, was after a decisive battle against the U.S. carriers.

When the Japanese realized that Saipan was the point of invasion, Admiral Ozawa gathered part of his First Mobile Force at Tawitawi, the westernmost island of the Sulu archipelago. But Ozawa's forces were already being depleted even before he sailed from Tawitawi. On 14 May, the U.S. submarine *Bonefish* sank the destroyer *Inazuma* off Tawitawi; then on 5 June, the submarine *Harder* torpedoed and sank the destroyers *Minazuki* and *Hayanami* in the same area. On 8 June the *Harder* also sank the destroyer *Tanikaze*. Bad luck dogged Ozawa's progress; en route on 14 June the destroyer *Shiratsuyu*, dodging an imaginary torpedo, collided with the tanker *Seiyo Maru*. The destroyer's stern was neatly excised and her depth charges set off. She sank at 0347 on 15 June, with 104 of her men lost.

Ozawa chose a route up through the Philippines, and on leaving San Bernardino Strait, was spotted by the submarine *Flying Fish* on the evening of 15 June. Ozawa's force then bore to the southeast, where it met Admiral Matome Ugaki's force, which had been sighted coming up from the Halmaheras by the submarine *Seahorse*, on the evening of 15 June. At midday on 17 June, the fleet refueled and then took a northeasterly course. The second tanker train was observed by the submarine *Cavalla* early on the 17th. The *Cavalla*, at 2115 on the same day, by following the tankers, ran into Ozawa's Mobile Force. There was no doubt now in the minds of the Americans that the Japanese were looking for battle. While Spruance knew

from his submarines the general position of Ozawa's fleet, his search
planes on 18 June could find no ships, although they did spot Japanese float search planes. Ozawa, depending heavily on his land-based
planes both for accurate reconnaissance and massive attacks, received
no information whatever from them; but his own carrier planes managed to find most of Task Force 58. They had observed the northern
and southern edge—40 miles apart, giving Ozawa a good fix.

Ozawa's plan was to keep out of range while getting into a favorable position to strike. Spruance had different tactics; he used his
four groups, each with a ring defense, to block a direct lunge by
Ozawa at Saipan, but he was still concerned about the possibility
that Ozawa might slip around him to the north or south. Task
Group 58.2 was placed to the south; 12 miles to the north was Task
Group 58.3; another 12 miles to the north was Task Group 58.1; and
due east of the last group, again 12 miles away, was Task Group 58.4.
Fifteen miles west of Task Group 58.3 was Admiral Lee's Battle Line,
in a circle defense with a picket line of destroyers west of Lee's force.
If the Japanese carrier planes were to attack the U.S. carriers they
would have to pass through a wall of steel thrown up by the Battle
Line; then, outnumbered, they would have to fight off each carrier
group's combat air patrol and meet an antiaircraft barrage from the
escort ships. The Japanese land planes had done nothing, despite Kakuta's repeated (but totally false) reports, to diminish the U.S. carriers' strength or to secure Rota and Guam for a refueling and rearming stopover.

Meanwhile, Ozawa made his battle dispositions. At 0600 on 18
June, his main force of six carriers set a northeasterly course, reversing to south-southwest at 1540. At 2100 he detached his van force of
three light carriers under Vice Admiral Kurita on an easterly course,
while his group continued south until 0300, turned to the northeast
again, and was in launch position before 0900.

During the night of 18–19 June, the picture began to clear for
Spruance. His submarines did an excellent job of reporting Japanese
positions, and Ozawa had broken radio silence to order Guam-based
planes to attack at dawn, which gave Spruance HF/DF (high
frequency/direction finders) fixes. The two fleets were 300 miles apart
at 2023. Instead of closing distance, however, Spruance reversed
course, for he was still worried that if he went too far west Ozawa
would go around him. At 0630 Spruance began zigzagging, headed
roughly southwest by west. By this time Guam had only 50 (instead
of Ozawa's hoped-for 500) planes from Truk, Yap, and the Palaus.

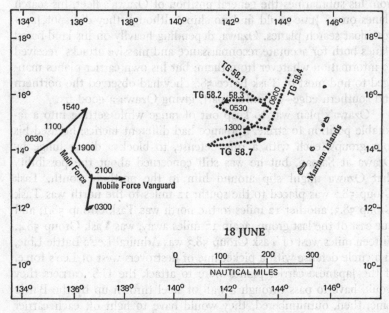

18 JUNE

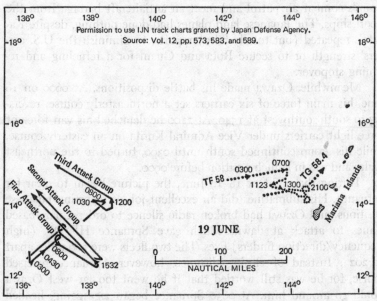

19 JUNE

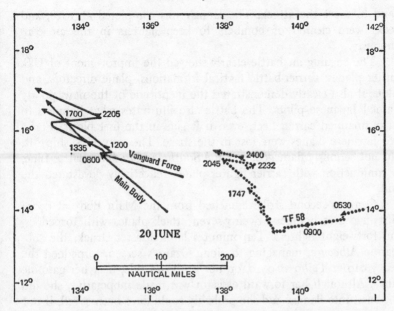

Battle of the Marianas (USN Title: Battle of the Philippine Sea), 18–20 June 1944

Kakuta simply would not leave these other fields unprotected against possible diversionary raids, although A-GO's success depended on there being 500 planes at Guam. He still reported to Ozawa that Guam was secure and well-stocked, and that its planes were inflicting heavy damage on Task Force 58. (There is no conceivable professional explanation for this misinformation, except Admiral Kakuta's desire to "save face.")

When U.S. radar showed Japanese planes approaching Guam on 19 June, Spruance launched planes to attack Guam first. The island came under attack at 0730, and when heavy fighter resistance was met, fighters from the *Belleau Wood*, *Cabot*, *Yorktown*, and *Hornet* were also launched as reinforcements. At 0807 more Japanese planes were detected by radar, also headed for Guam, but too few to cause any trouble.

The real battle was now beginning. Ozawa's Van Force launched sixteen fighters, forty-five fighters carrying bombs, and eight attack planes with torpedoes. Meanwhile, Spruance called back his planes from Guam. The first strike was detected by the Battle Line's radar at 1000, and at 1010 Admiral Spruance ordered every fighter on hand to meet the attack. The launch was completed at 1038, and decks were cleared of bombers to keep fighters in the air continuously.

The ensuing air battle clearly showed the improvement of U.S. carrier planes, carrier-battle tactical formations, plane directors, and pilots; it also clearly demonstrated the ineptitude of the new, poorly trained Japanese pilots. The battle also illustrates what happens to an outmanned carrier fleet, even if it gets in the first blows. Forty-two Japanese planes were lost in the strike. The only U.S. ship hit, but not seriously damaged, was the *South Dakota*. The Battle Line, in conjunction with carrier fighter planes, effectively devastated the raid.

Ozawa's second strike launched from the Main Body at 0900: thirty-five dive bombers, twenty-seven attack planes with torpedoes, and forty-eight fighters. Ten minutes later disaster struck; the submarine *Albacore*, managing to elude Ozawa's screen, torpedoed the heavy carrier *Taiho* at 0910, on her starboard side, near her gasoline tanks. Although her forward elevator was made inoperative, she did not burst into flames, and she probably could have been saved, if not for two other factors: her unrefined fuel oil gave off dangerous fumes, and her crew showed poor judgment by maintaining 26 knots and keeping all shafts open to ventilate the ship. At 1530 an explosion tore through the ship, and she literally erupted, her fires so hot that rescue ships could not get near her. She finally sank at 1728; out of a crew of 2,150, there were 1,650 lost.[7]

Most of the Japanese planes in the second strike were shot down by the Battle Line. The only U.S. damage was from a near-miss of the *Wasp*. Only 2 planes made it to Guam and Rota, and only 31 out of 110 planes survived. Still, Ozawa was persistent; this was the "decisive battle", and the only information he had on damages to Task Force 58 was taken from Kakuta's false reports. He launched strike three at 1000: fifteen fighters, twenty-five fighters with bombs, and seven attack planes with torpedoes. They evaded the Battle Line and came in from the north, because of an error in interpreting search-plane reports. Very few, however, found any targets, and thus only seven planes were lost. A strong fourth strike was launched at 1130: thirty fighters, nine dive bombers, thirty-three attack planes, and ten fighter bombers. They, too, were very badly misdirected. Ordered to land at Guam, forty-nine planes headed there; the rest found Task Group 58.2, inflicted no damage, and suffered heavily. The Guam-bound planes jettisoned their bombs and began landing, but only nineteen of them made the field, and these were chewed up by strafing carrier planes.

As far as Ozawa was concerned, he had given it his best shot, but had failed to seriously damage a single American ship. Further disaster hit him at once, when, at 1222, the submarine *Cavalla* got four torpedoes into the heavy carrier *Shokaku*. The carrier lost power and was engulfed in flame; despite valiant efforts to save her, the flames reached her magazines, and at 1510 she blew apart and sank. (Now the *Zuikaku* was the only carrier left from the Pearl Harbor raid.) Ozawa shifted his flag to the destroyer *Urakaze*, which, along with other destroyers, had been taking off the *Shokaku*'s crew.

Up to the end of strike four, Task Force 58 had been engaged only in defensive action, and because of the range, was launching no attacks of its own. Shortly after the sinking of the *Taiho*, the First Mobile Fleet steamed northwest in retirement, followed by the Van Force. But Ozawa was not retreating; his carriers had only 102 planes left, but reports from his fliers and Kakuta stated that a number of U.S. carriers had been sunk. Also, Kakuta had radioed him that a good number of his carrier planes were safely on Guam, and Ozawa still believed that Kakuta was calling in hundreds of additional planes to attack.

Ozawa then shifted his flag to the *Haguro* and eventually to the *Zuikaku*. Even with only 102 planes left, he still thought he was in the fight. Spruance had not undertaken a night search; his fleet was making 24 knots to the northwest, while Ozawa's force was limping along at 18 knots. A night sighting and a morning attack by Spruance might well have more seriously damaged the First Mobile Fleet, but as it was, Spruance did not know where Ozawa was and did not find out until 1540 on 20 June. Ozawa began to refuel in the afternoon, but at 1615 the *Atago* reported, by interpreting a radio call to Spruance, that Task Force 58 had spotted the Japanese forces.

Ozawa immediately halted refueling and, bringing his speed to 24 knots, headed northwest. Spruance now had a difficult decision. His pilots would have to travel a great distance and their flight back would be in the dark; he realized that many of his pilots might not make it back to the carriers. Nevertheless, he ordered an all-out strike at 1620; by 1636 eighty-five fighters, seventy-seven dive bombers, and fifty-four torpedo planes from the six heavy carriers and five light carriers were airborne.

The Japanese force was divided into three groups. The first group contained the *Zuikaku*, *Haguro* and *Myoko*, with a destroyer screen.

Some 19 miles southwest of this group was a second group: the converted carriers *Junyo* and *Hiyo*, the light carrier *Ryuho*, the battleship *Nagato*, and the heavy cruiser *Mogami*, along with another destroyer screen. Ten miles due south was the last group: the light carriers *Chitose*, *Chiyoda*, and *Zuiho*, with the battleships *Musashi*, *Yamato*, *Kongo*, and *Haruna*, the heavy cruisers *Takao*, *Maya*, *Atago*, *Kumano*, *Suzuya*, *Tone*, and *Chikuma*, and the rest of the destroyer screen. Tagging along were the six tankers, accompanied by more destroyers.

Ozawa could launch only about 80 planes before Task Force 58's 216 planes hit. In the raid, which lasted from 1840 to 1900, the *Hiyo* was hit twice by torpedoes and sank at 2032, two tankers were sunk, and the tanker *Genyo Maru* received three near-misses, became unnavigable, and was finally sunk by the *Uzuki*. Extensive damage was suffered by the carriers *Zuikaku* and *Junyo*, the *Chiyoda*, and the heavy cruiser *Maya*. The *Shigure* was hit by a small bomb, while the *Haruna* suffered one direct hit aft, two on her quarter deck which penetrated two lower decks, causing flooding and heavy topside damage, and two near-misses on her port bow which bent the hull and killed fifteen men.[8]

The "decisive battle" had again been lost; but Ozawa cannot be faulted for it. He was ordered into battle with a force half the size of the U.S. force. He fully expected, but did not get, the 500 planes from Kakuta which might have made the battle even. His biggest error was in taking on the heavily gunned Battle Line, a new U.S. tactical formation designed to draw planes away from the U.S. carriers; but that was the fault of the inexperienced Japanese pilots, not of Ozawa. He was misled in strikes three and four as to where Task Force 58 was, and was led to believe that Guam was a sanctuary —when it was a graveyard. It is difficult for an outmatched fleet and inexperienced flyers to do much better than Ozawa's did.

In retrospect, however, even if everything had gone right for Ozawa, it would have been a near-miracle if he could have prevailed against the great number of U.S. carriers, the number of vastly improved planes, and the new battle-line tactic, with its tremendous firepower capability. At best, some U.S. carriers might have been damaged or sunk, but many more were on the way. After a war of two and one-half years the Japanese were being crushed by the weight of U.S. ship construction, while Japan was having trouble getting raw materials from the South Seas to Japanese shipyards, in order to maintain the same number of ships she had before the war. Moreover, the precious oil that was a large factor in starting the war was not readily available in a form that could be used for ships' fuel. The plight of the Imperial Japanese Navy was now critical; but, as in a Greek tragedy, the drama had to be played to the last bitter scene by those who simply could not accept final defeat.

Table of Organization, Battle of the Marianas

First Mobile Fleet

MOBILE FORCE VANGUARD

Light carriers: *Zuiho, Chitose, Chiyoda*
Battleships: *Yamato, Musashi, Haruna, Kongo*
Heavy cruisers: *Atago, Takao, Maya, Chokai, Kumano, Chikuma, Tone*
Light cruiser: *Noshiro*
Destroyers: *Asashimo, Kishinami, Okinami, Tamanami, Hamakaze, Fujinami, Shimakaze*

"A" FORCE

Heavy carriers: *Taiho, Shokaku, Zuikaku*
Heavy cruisers: *Myoko, Haguro*
Light cruiser: *Yahagi*
Destroyers: *Asagumo, Urakaze, Isokaze, Wakatsuki, Hatsuyuki, Akizuki, Shimotsuki*

"B" FORCE

Converted light carriers: *Hiyo, Junyo*
Light carrier: *Ryuho*
Battleship: *Nagato*
Heavy cruiser: *Mogami*
Destroyers: *Michishio, Nowaki, Yamagumo, Shigure, Samidare, Hayashio, Hamakaze, Akishimo*
3 tankers, screened by the destroyers *Hatsushimo, Hibiki,* and *Tsuga*
2 tankers, screened by the destroyers *Yukikaze* and *Uzuki*
24 submarines

U. S. Navy Table of Organization

Fifth Fleet, Task Force 58

TASK GROUP 58.1

Heavy carriers: *Hornet, Yorktown*
Light carriers: *Belleau Wood, Bataan*

3 heavy cruisers
2 light cruisers
10 destroyers

TASK GROUP 58.2

Heavy carriers: *Bunker Hill, Wasp*
Light carriers: *Monterey, Cabot*
3 light cruisers
12 destroyers

TASK GROUP 58.3

Heavy carriers: *Enterprise, Lexington*
Light carriers: *San Jacinto, Princeton*
1 heavy cruiser
4 light cruisers
13 destroyers

TASK GROUP 58.4

Heavy carrier: *Essex*
Light carriers: *Langley, Cowpens*
4 light cruisers
14 destroyers

TASK GROUP 58.7—BATTLE LINE

Battleships: *Washington, North Carolina, Iowa, New Jersey,
     South Dakota, Alabama, Indiana*
4 heavy cruisers
13 destroyers

PICKET LINE of 25 SUBMARINES[9]

chapter 22

THE BITTER END

1944

23 October   U.S. submarines ambush Admiral Kurita's Strike Force A in Palawan Passage

24 October   Battle of Sibuyan Sea. Kurita loses the battleship *Musashi*

24–25 October   Battle of Surigao Strait. U. S. Navy defeats Admiral Nishimura's Strike Force C

25 October   Admiral Shima's Second Strike Force fails to support Admiral Nishimura. Admiral Shima retreats

24–25 October   Admiral Ozawa's carrier force without planes lures all of Admiral Halsey's Task Force 38 north, leaving San Bernardino Strait unguarded

25 October   Battle off Samar. Admiral Kurita's Strike Force A is defeated in air and ship battle

25 October   Battle off Cape Engaño. Admiral Ozawa's carrier fleet destroyed

26 October   Kurita's force comes under further destructive attack

26 October   Japanese Navy splits into two parts: one part at Inland Sea, one part near Singapore

26 December   Admiral Kimura's San Jose Intrusion Force is defeated

1945

7 April   The battleship *Yamato* is sacrificially lost

17 May   The last sea battle. The heavy cruiser *Haguro* is sunk by five Royal Navy destroyers off Penang, Malaya

The Battles of the Sibuyan Sea and Surigao Strait

After the fall of Saipan, Imperial General Headquarters knew that within a few months a massive new invasion would come, somewhere. But where the invasion would occur was the question; it could be at Mindanao, Taiwan, or even the Ryukyus. Therefore, Imperial General Headquarters prepared three separate plans for still another "decisive battle": SHO 1 Operation in the Philippines; SHO 2 at Taiwan; and SHO 3 in the Ryukyus.

Leyte Island in the mid-Philippines was invaded, between Tacloban and Dulag on the northwest side of the island, beginning on 17 October 1944. At once SHO 1 Operation was activated.[1] As before, Japanese war doctrine called for a complicated disposition of forces, and it was of the utmost importance that adequate air cover be provided to the various fleets by Philippine-based planes, for their carriers could no longer provide that cover.

But this concentration of Japanese air power, and its reinforcement from the north, had been anticipated by the planners of the invasion. The instrument used to prevent it was Halsey's Third Fleet, Task Force 38, commanded by Admiral Marc Mitscher. Its Fast Carrier Force had been expanded to nine heavy carriers and eight light carriers, carrying 1,178 planes and screened by a powerful Battle Line. Admiral Nimitz, knowing the Philippine invasion would be opposed by every plane Japan could provide, ordered Task Force 38 to go on a plane-destroying rampage starting on 20–21 September, when it bombed Luzon's airfields and shipping. The destroyer *Satsuki* was sunk in Manila Harbor when one bomb hit her forward and two amidships. Task Force 38 resumed its raids on 9 October, hitting Taiwan's thirty airfields, then on 12–13 bombing Luzon, and Luzon again on 17–18. As Japan kept feeding planes south, the U.S. carrier planes kept destroying them. By the time the Japanese fleets were in Philippine waters, Vice Admiral Shigeru Fukudome of the Sixth Base Air Force, in charge of land planes in the Philippines, could give the fleet admirals practically none of the air cover which Imperial General Headquarters had depended on to stop the invasion.

When SHO 1 was activated, most of the ships of the Japanese Navy were either at Lingga Roads off Singapore or in Japanese waters. The Table of Organization divided all available ships into five groups, and Admiral Soemu Toyoda, commander-in-chief, remained at naval headquarters in Japan.

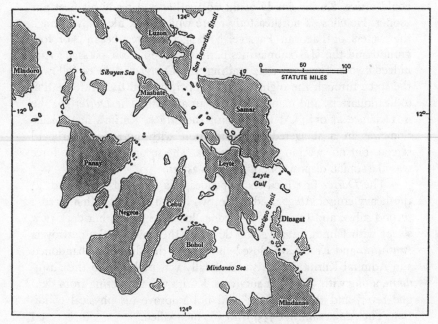

Map of Leyte Gulf

The Japanese plan of battle called for Admiral Ozawa's Mobile Force, whose carriers had almost no planes left, to "drag its cape" before Task Force 38; Japanese intelligence guessed that Admiral "Bull" Halsey would come charging after the carrier force, which would clear the carrier planes from Admiral Kurita's ships. Then Kurita's First Strike Force, Forces A and B, would form the north arm of a pincers movement coming through San Bernardino Strait against the invasion transports. Group C, under Admiral Nishimura, joined by the Second Strike Force of Admiral Shima, would form the southern arm, coming through Surigao Strait to join Kurita. The Transport Unit would land a small number of reinforcing troops on the west side of Leyte. 25 October was designated the day of battle. All depended upon Fukudome's providing the Leyte fleets with air cover, and on the absence of Task Force 38. The objective was to get at the transports, break up the invasion, and sink U.S. ships.

Kurita's First Strike Force sailed from Brunei Bay, Borneo, on 22 October at 0700. In reality the counterattack was coming too late and the Japanese naval forces had been too scattered, for the main body of transports would be gone by the time the Japanese ships could arrive. Kurita simply could not gather and ready his fleet any sooner. He chose a northeasterly route which took his ships through the waters of Palawan Passage, a dangerous area because of foul ground and the U.S. submarines patrolling the narrow passage.[2] And indeed two submarines were waiting; the *Darter* and *Dace* followed the force through the night of 23 October, flashed their information to headquarters, and maneuvered for an ambush. The *Darter* got the first chance at 0524. At the time of the attack, Kurita's first formation was in a staggered box formation with port and starboard screens but no sweeping van destroyers. The second unit of the force was in a similar disposition, 6,500 yards astern.

The *Darter* first fired six torpedoes at a range of 1,000 yards at the heavy cruiser *Atago*, and made two hits. The *Darter* then fired a second salvo, and two more torpedoes hit. The *Atago*, her deck now swept with flames, began going down by the bow. As the destroyers *Asashimo* and *Kishinami* closed the *Atago*, the ship was abandoned and Admiral Kurita, in the water, finally was pulled onto the *Kishinami*, along with 529 other survivors. Kurita was recovering from dengue fever, and this "dunking" did not improve his physical condition. The *Atago* sank at 0553, with 360 men killed.

No sooner had the *Darter* hit the *Atago* than she fired four stern torpedoes. Two of these found the heavy cruiser *Takao*, one smacking her starboard side under the bridge, and one hitting aft. She began to list, fires broke out, and with her boiler rooms flooded, she lost power; she was escorted part of the way back to Brunei Bay by the destroyer *Naganami*. It was now the *Dace*'s turn; launching four torpedoes, she blasted apart the heavy cruiser *Maya*, which sank at 0605, with 336 men lost (but, chiefly thanks to the destroyer *Akishimo*, 769 were saved).[3]

Admiral Kurita, now on board the battleship *Yamato*, still steaming on his planned course, entered the Sibuyan Sea heading north at 0630. By now the U. S. Navy knew that the Japanese had come out to fight, for both Nishimura's and Shima's forces had also been sighted. The next stage of the battle would be fought in the Sibuyan Sea, but, as Kurita knew, Admiral Fukudome's pilots would have to clear the sky for him; Kurita even catapulted his force's planes to strengthen Fukudome. But it was an impossible task, for Fukudome had less than 200 planes in the Philippines. He decided that he could best cover Kurita by attacking U.S. carriers rather than by acting as combat air patrol for Kurita. In three raids, mainly against Task Group 38.3 (Task Group 38.2, although closer to

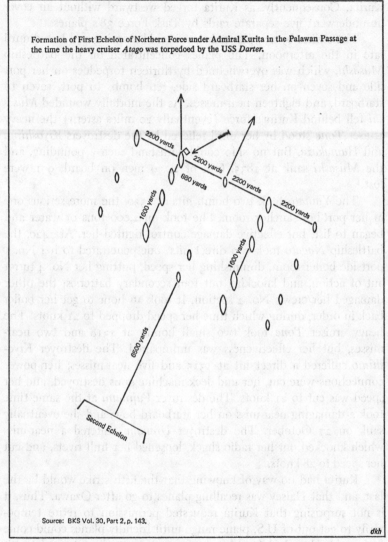

Formation of First Echelon of Northern Force under Admiral Kurita in the Palawan Passage at the time the heavy cruiser *Atago* was torpedoed by the USS *Darter.*

2200 yards

2200 yards

680 yards

1600 yards

2200 yards

2200 yards

1600 yards

6500 yards

Second Echelon

Source: BKS Vol. 30, Part 2, p. 143.

dkh

Formation of First Echelon of Northern Force under Admiral Kurita in the Palawan Passage, at the time the heavy cruiser Atago *was torpedoed by the* Darter.

Kurita, was, for the most part, overlooked), the Japanese slugged away, in furious air battles fought on the morning of 24 October. Although the light carrier *Princeton* was sunk, most of the Japanese planes were shot down, and there were scarcely any left to protect

Kurita. Consequently, as Kurita forged westward without air cover he underwent five separate raids by Task Force 38's planes.

The strikes by 259 planes began in mid-morning and lasted until late in the afternoon. The planes concentrated on the battleship *Musashi*, which was overwhelmed by thirteen torpedoes on her port side and seven on her starboard side, ten bombs to port, seven to starboard, and eighteen near-misses. As the mortally wounded *Musashi* fell behind Kurita's force (eventually 20 miles astern) the heavy cruiser *Tone* stood by her until relieved by the destroyers *Kiyoshimo* and *Hamakaze*. But no ship could withstand such a pounding, and the *Musashi* sank at 1835. Out of 2,279 men on board, 991 were lost.[4]

The *Yamato* took two bomb hits at 1330, the more serious one in her port-bow anchor room. She took on 2,000 tons of water and began to list, but effective damage control righted her. At 1420, the battleship *Nagato* took two direct hits: one penetrated to her No. 1 portside boiler room, diminishing her speed, putting her No. 4 turret out of action, and knocking out four secondary batteries; the other damaged her crew's No. 2 section. It took an hour to get her boiler back in order, during which time her speed dropped to 21 knots. The heavy cruiser *Tone* took two small bombs at 1318 and two near-misses, but her effectiveness was unimpaired. The destroyer *Kiyoshimo* suffered a direct hit at 1315 and five near-misses; her power connections were cut, her mid-deck machine guns destroyed, and her speed was cut to 21 knots. The destroyer *Fujinami* at the same time took a damaging near-miss on her starboard bow; and she eventually sank on 27 October. The destroyer *Uranami* suffered a near-miss which knocked out her radio shack, loosened her hull rivets, and cut her speed to 28 knots.

Kurita had no way of knowing that the fifth strike would be the last, and that Halsey was recalling planes to go after Ozawa. Thus, it is not surprising that Kurita requested permission to retire temporarily to get out of U.S. plane range until friendly planes could come to his aid. He asked for his own float planes to be returned to his ships, but Fukudome could not or did not comply with the request. On his own initiative Kurita reversed course and at 1500 sailed west until 1614; impossibly behind schedule for his rendezvous with Force C, he nevertheless turned east again to sail through San Bernardino Strait at night. He expected to run into Task Force 38 at dawn on 25 October.

Battle of Surigao Strait

Force C had sortied from Brunei Bay on 22 October at 1500. Nishimura's force, following a course between Mindanao and Negros, was bombed at 0918 on 24 October and the battleship *Fuso* had lost all her planes by fire; but Nishimura kept coming. In retrospect, one wonders if Nishimura really expected to get through and meet Kurita—and then what if Halsey returned? But to Nishimura an order was to be followed without time being wasted in discussion. He relished a night battle and apparently expected to win it with his two old battleships, the *Fuso* and *Yamashiro*, with their unique pagodas, along with the heavy cruiser *Mogami*, and four destroyers. He knew, because of the bombing, that he had been sighted and his course plotted, but he inexplicably made no attempt to get in touch with Admiral Shima or to wait for him.

But awaiting Force C was Admiral Kinkaid's Seventh Fleet's Battle Line, under Rear Admiral Jesse B. Oldendorf. Oldendorf set his trap carefully; he placed thirty-nine PT boats far down the strait, set up his first line of defense off Bohol Island on the north and Camiguin Island on the south, and then eleven more sections, strung to the east. Then Force C would be challenged by twenty-eight destroyers, divided north and south on a rough line with Dinagat Island. The next defense would come from the Battle Line, flanked right and left by light and heavy cruisers. Finally, in a position to cross Nishimura's "T", were the battleships *Mississippi, Maryland, West Virginia, Tennessee, California*, and *Pennsylvania*.

Nishimura had been informed by Kurita that Force A had been delayed and could not reach the Leyte rendezvous as scheduled; but this message did not deter Nishimura. His Force C tangled with the first group of PT boats at about 2200, and he signalled Kurita at 2400 that he was passing through Surigao Strait and would be at Leyte Gulf on schedule, and that he had seen enemy PTs but no other kinds of ships.[5] The Main Body entered the strait at 0015, with the destroyer *Michishio* 13,600 yards ahead of the column of the destroyer *Asagumo*, the battleships *Yamashiro* (flagship) and *Fuso*, and the heavy cruiser *Mogami*. Fifteen hundred yards off the *Yamashiro*'s starboard bow was the destroyer *Yamagumo*, and 1,000 yards off the port bow was the destroyer *Shigure*. Their speed was 20 knots.

Again torpedo boats picked up the Japanese ships, and both

sides fired star shells at 0102; but Nishimura ran this gauntlet of PT boats and was through them, without damage, at 0125. A new fight had begun to shape up ahead, with the first U.S. destroyer attack to occur at about 0200. Planning a scissors attack, two U.S. destroyers were on Nishimura's port bow and three were on the starboard bow. Force C now went into battle formation: a single column, steaming due north, with the four destroyers in the van, followed by the *Yamashiro, Fuso,* and *Mogami.* When the *Shigure* sighted the attackers, again Force C fired star shells, and at 0202 all ships opened fire. But already twenty-seven American torpedoes were bearing on Nishimura's ships, from a range of 8,000 to 9,000 yards. After launching, the five U.S. destroyers then began to retire. Instead of taking evasive action, Nishimura kept on course—and he paid for it. At 0207 the *Fuso* was hit by several torpedoes. She faltered, catching fire, and began to sink. Huge explosions ripped her into two parts, but both parts stayed afloat burning; finally, the after section sank an hour later. Both the Americans and Japanese were puzzled by what they thought were two burning ships. Apparently Nishimura did not know the *Fuso* had suffered this blow.[6] Perhaps no staff officer had dared to tell him.

Force C now had to run a gauntlet of more U.S. destroyers, which launched twenty more torpedoes at 0209–0211. Nishimura ordered evasive action, making two simultaneous starboard turns—but he had only put his destroyers directly in the path of the torpedoes. At 0220, the *Yamagumo* was hit and sunk; the *Michishio* sank at 0258; the *Asagumo* was hit and her bow was ripped off but she was able to retire; the *Yamashiro* was also hit. Nishimura sent his last battle report to Kurita at 0230: "Enemy destroyers and torpedo boats in north mouth of Surigao Strait. Two of our destroyers torpedoed and drifting. *Yamashiro* has one torpedo hit, not handicapped in ability to fight." And fight she had to, for another U.S. destroyer division jumped her at 0225.[7] A torpedo hit the *Yamashiro* and slowed her down to five knots, but she continued toward her enemy with her three main turrets knocked out. The *Asagumo* and the sinking *Michishio* also came under gunfire. Nishimura then issued an order for every ship to advance and attack enemy ships. But by this time the *Shigure* and the *Mogami* had turned from the *Yamashiro*'s bow and had begun retiring. A last U.S. destroyer division launched torpedoes at the *Yamashiro* but all missed; then after she turned to port at 0300, she took more torpedoes at 0311.

It had not been destroyers only that were attacking the *Yama-*

shiro. First the cruisers opened fire at 0251 at a range of over 15,000 yards. Then the Battle Line joined in at 0253, at a range of 22,800 yards. Finally, crossing Nishimura's "T", the six U.S. battleships began firing at 0310. No ship could take such a beating—blazing like

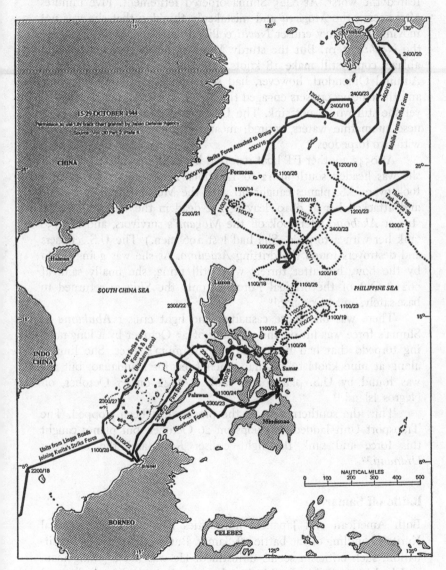

Battle off Leyte—Approach and Retirement, 15–29 October 1944

a furnace and dead in the water, the *Yamashiro* rolled over and sank at 0319.[8]

Admiral Shima's Second Strike Force was about 40 miles behind Force C. He had been listening to Nishimura's battle reports and feared the worst. At 0425 Shima ordered retirement. Five minutes after seeing the *Mogami* and mistakenly thinking that she was not moving, the heavy cruiser *Nachi* collided with her, badly damaging the *Nachi*'s stern. But the sturdy *Mogami*, although damaged and ablaze, could still make 18 knots, and she followed Shima's force. Admiral Oldendorf, however, had sent out a "clean-up" squadron, and three heavy cruisers engaged the *Mogami*, hitting her repeatedly; yet she still would not sink. The U.S. cruisers, on entering in Japanese submarine waters, retired; meanwhile, a PT boat missed her with two torpedoes.

At 0545 another PT boat reported her position and the fact that she was headed south at 12 to 14 knots. American air power now took over; U.S. planes caught up with the *Mogami*, trailing Shima, and attacked her at 0810, leaving her dead in the water. (The destroyer *Akebono* later took off the *Mogami*'s survivors, and at 1130 sank her with a torpedo. She had lost 196 men.) The U.S. cruisers and destroyers found the drifting *Asagumo*. As she was going down by the bow, her after turrets were still firing; she finally sank at 0621.[9] Out of the original Force C, only the *Shigure* returned to base safely, on 27 October.[10]

There was one more casualty. The light cruiser *Abukuma* in Shima's force was hit on the morning of 25 October by a long-ranging torpedo that had been fired at Nishimura's force. She limped along at nine knots to Dapitan, then tried for Mindanao, but she was found by U.S. planes and sunk at 1142 on 27 October, off Negros Island.[11]

Thus the southern arm of the pincers had been stopped. The Transport Unit landed its troops on 26 October, but planes caught this force and sank the light cruiser *Kinu* and the destroyer *Uranami*.[12]

Battle off Samar

Both American and Japanese authorities have criticized Admiral Kurita's handling of the battle off Samar. But if one considers his situation, such criticism seems unjustified. He was not a young man, and had been ill; his flagship had been sunk, he had been dumped

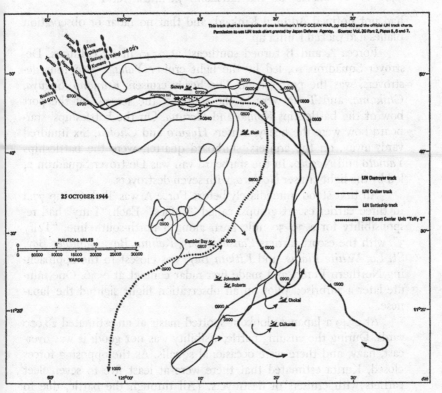

Battle off Samar, 25 October 1944

into the water, and transferred to a destroyer and then to the *Yamato*. He had lost the use of four of his heavy cruisers, the mighty battleship *Musashi* (sister ship of the *Yamato*), and a destroyer, with many other ships in his Force A suffering damage. He probably had not slept as he tangled all day with submarines and then, without cover, with U.S. planes. He had faced hard decisions, and now he had to leave the San Bernardino Strait with the expectation that all or part of Task Force 38 awaited him. He must have viewed the upcoming battle with feelings of weariness and trepidation, for he was human. Under the circumstances, perhaps only Hachiman, the god of war, could have done better.

As his fleet came out of the strait into the sea off Samar Island, he must have been amazed to find no ships waiting and no planes raiding. Surely there was a trap. It was incredible that Halsey, then chasing Ozawa's carrier force, had left the strait completely open, had not notified Admiral Kinkaid, and that no radar or observation planes had picked Kurita up.

Forces A and B turned southeast at 0540 in six columns. Destroyer Squadron 10, led by the light cruiser *Yahagi* with four destroyers, was the port screen. The heavy cruisers *Kumano*, *Suzuya*, *Chikuma*, and *Tone* were to the south of the screen, off the port bow of the battleships *Kongo* and *Haruna*. On the battleships' starboard bow were the heavy cruisers *Haguro* and *Chokai*. Six hundred yards away, on the cruisers' starboard quarter, were the battleships *Yamato* and *Nagato*. In the starboard van was Destroyer Squadron 2, led by the light cruiser *Noshiro*, with seven destroyers.

All that stood immediately before Force A was Task Group 77.4 in three carrier escort groups, called "Taffies." Each "Taffy" had responsibility for a 30–50 mile area, along a north-south line. "Taffy 3", with the escort carriers *Fanshaw Bay*, *Kalinin Bay*, *Gambier Bay*, *St. Lo*, *White Plains*, and *Kitkun Bay*, was closest to the approaching Northern Force, and made first radar contact at 0546. One minute later a surprised pilot on an observation flight sighted the Japanese.

At 0549 a Japanese lookout spotted masts at an estimated 28,000 yards. During the ensuing battle, visibility was not good; it was overcast, hazy, and there were occasional squalls. As the opposing forces closed, Kurita estimated that there were at least five to seven fleet carriers with cruisers or destroyers. (All through the battle, due to the poor visibility, he consistently overestimated the force he was fighting.) At 0552 he ordered an advance at 24 knots, and at 0553 turned his column to the east to strike at the head of the sighted ships. At 0558: "Open fire with front turrets." Then he ordered Destroyer Squadron 10 to also turn east, presumably to get in position for a torpedo attack. At 0603 he gave the order "Start attack." This order formed no battle lines and left each ship on her own commander's orders. Amazed sailors in Taffy 3 were startled when explosions from 18-inch shells began throwing colored water high in the air. (Warships used dyes of different colors so that a fire director on a ship could identify his ship's salvos.) When news of what was happening came into Kinkaid's headquarters, he was alarmed and angered by Halsey's having left the strait unguarded without notifying him. But he reacted immediately, and by 0612 every operative plane had been launched from all three Taffies.

The ensuing battle almost defies accurate description. Kurita, although surely believing he would come under air attack, did not form a ring defense. The battle has generally been described as one-sided—a mighty force charging down on almost defenseless escort carriers, each equipped with only one 5-inch gun and guarded by three destroyers and an equal number of smaller destroyer escorts. But that was not the truth of the matter, particularly from Kurita's vantage point. The Northern Force continued east, firing at indistinct targets until 0655, then began a slow loop south, enfolding Taffy 3 and driving it toward Leyte Gulf. As the Japanese ships maneuvered to close distance they came under increasing air attack from about 500 fighters, fighters with small bombs, and torpedo-armed planes from Task Group 77.4—the equivalent of the number of planes from five fleet carriers. Kurita tried with no air cover to get at the "jeep" carriers for almost four hours, while his force was under constant attack by swarms of planes. The Taffies' planes could land on Leyte's airstrips, refuel, rearm, and go back after Kurita's ships; thus the escort carriers did not have to land or launch planes after the initial takeoff. Kurita's ships were also forced to maneuver, breaking formation almost continuously to avoid the torpedo and bombing attacks. Poor visibility obscured some targets and made other targets appear larger than they were. Moreover, in order to comb the wakes of torpedoes, the *Yamato* had to reverse course for eight minutes, which resulted in Kurita's flagship's always being too far in the rear for him to analyze the situation correctly or control his ships well. Kurita could never get an accurate idea of what kind of air force he was fighting, or where they all came from. He did not know that he was facing no dive bombers, and, of course he was worried about the whereabouts of Halsey's Task Force 38. He also knew that the ships of the southern pincers had not made it. The battle became a melee, and when Japanese ships began to be hit, some starting to sink, an added burden was placed on the rest of his fleet; they had to destroy the U.S. ships ahead, fight off destroyers and constant air attacks, while trying to help stricken cruisers. No "textbook" attack could be made on Taffy 3.

The *White Plains* had three salvos straddle her from either the *Haruna* or the *Kongo*. Just as the Northern Force was getting in range, a rain squall hid Taffy 3 from 0607 to 0615, which allowed planes from the southern Taffies to have eight more minutes to come to the rescue, and allowed Taffy 3 to change course and open range. When the squall passed, Taffy 3's three destroyers made smoke, partially obscuring the escort carriers again. The U.S. destroyers then did what destroyers are built for and their officers trained to do—the

Hoel, Heermann, and *Johnston* charged the Northern Force. Five-inch shells did little damage to the *Kumano,* at the head of the heavy cruiser column; but the *Kumano, Suzuya, Chikuma,* and *Tone* also failed to register with their return fire. At 10,000 yards, the *Johnston* launched her ten torpedoes, made smoke, and plunged behind it. One torpedo hit the *Kumano* at 0627, almost severing her bow; her speed dropped to 14 knots and she veered out of column to port. At about the same time the *Suzuya* was bombed twice and severely damaged, causing her speed to drop to 23 knots, and making her veer off to port. The *Chikuma* and the *Tone* continued the attack, while the flag was shifted to the *Suzuya* and emergency repairs were undertaken on the *Kumano.* The *Johnston* received six hits, probably from the *Kongo,* but she nevertheless stayed afloat to fight once more, later that morning.

The *Haguro* opened fire at 0605, but she had to ward off a five-plane attack shortly thereafter, and then two more planes. Such time-wasting evasive action was typical of what the Northern Force was going through, still trying to get at the carriers. Kurita's ships were closed again by the *Hoel* and *Heermann.* A salvo from the *Hoel* missed the *Kongo* at 0653; the *Kongo* then took on the destroyer, hitting her repeatedly, leaving only the *Hoel's* A and B batteries operative. The *Hoel* launched torpedoes at the *Haguro;* all missed, but in evading the torpedoes the *Haguro* was hit at 0751 by a shell, starboard amidships, which caused her to fall out of line, going in circles. The *Heermann* also aimed at the *Haguro* while receiving near-misses in return. The *Heermann's* torpedoes missed the *Haguro* and the *Haguro's* shells missed the *Heermann.* The destroyer fired her remaining torpedoes at a battleship and then retired to the carriers. The *Hoel* took on the *Chikuma* briefly, and an air attack on the *Chikuma* drove her away; but her place was taken by the *Tone,* which seriously damaged the *Hoel.* The *Johnston* and the destroyer escort *Samuel B. Roberts* were sunk in this phase of the battle; still the destroyers had done their job, to the best of their ability.

For the Japanese, the purpose of the battle was to sink carriers and get to the transports at Leyte Gulf. While fending off planes, destroyers, and even destroyer escorts, the Northern Force sank one escort carrier. The *Gambier Bay* had been under the *Chikuma's* fire at 0730; then at 0741 she was hit repeatedly by fire from the *Haguro,* the *Chokai,* the *Noshiro* and a destroyer, finally sinking at 0807. The other carriers of Taffy 3 suffered moderate to severe damage. But Kurita was paying too high a price for mere "jeep" carriers (if he had even known they were escort carriers). The *Kumano* was limping back without a bow, the *Haguro* had been severely damaged, and the *Chokai* had been hit repeatedly, with holes in her bow, and her speed was dropping off. Allied planes then concentrated on the heavy cruisers *Chikuma* and *Chokai*. The *Chikuma* was hit once again by a torpedo. Both, with slowing speed, made excellent targets and were further damaged by bombs and torpedoes. The *Suzuya* was damaged by a near-miss at 0624; then at 0700, after another near-miss, the *Kumano* was ordered to retire through the San Bernardino Strait to Coron. The *Chokai* was so badly damaged, dead in the water, that the destroyer *Fujinami* took off her survivors and sank her with a torpedo. In turn, the destroyer *Nowaki* took off the *Chikuma*'s crew and scuttled her. At 0950, thirty planes attacked the *Suzuya*; at 1000 she took a torpedo in the bow, lost way, and began listing. After two more torpedoes, she sank at 1130.

At 0811 Kurita ordered: "Cease action, come north with me, 20 knots." He went due north until 0955, then looped a bit to the southwest at 1047, again heading toward Leyte. At 1115 he turned southwest, but had circled to a northerly course by 1136. He had made his decision to retire through San Bernardino Strait, basing his action on reports that Halsey's fleet was to his northeast—if so, it had to be fought. (After the war, Kurita refused to discuss his reasons for retirement.)

Although he had directed the battle poorly, Kurita's decision to retire was sound. He had sunk one escort carrier, two destroyers, and one destroyer escort. His own force, since leaving Burnei Bay, had lost one battleship, five heavy cruisers, and had suffered two heavy cruisers crippled. Practically all of the Northern Force had sustained some form of damage. He anticipated he would lose even more on 26 October before he got out of range of Allied air power. He knew that the southern arm of the Japanese pincers was undoubtedly destroyed. He did not know where Ozawa was and whether Ozawa had really pulled Halsey north, as planned.

The results of the battle proved conclusively that a very powerful surface fleet without air cover stood no chance—even against "jeep" carriers, screened by nothing larger than destroyers and destroyer escorts, but with enough planes and pilots to counterattack. If blame has to be assigned, it should rest not on the men who took the ships to sea on an impossible mission, but on Admiral Toyoda and the Imperial General Headquarters, for believing such a battle could be won against the massive sea and air power that they knew the U. S. Navy had available. It is true that Taffy 3 was defended with the utmost bravery and skill by her screen, but it was the air power of Taffies 1, 2, and 3 that made Kurita become so preoccupied with attacking planes that his battle formations became a secondary concern. Accurate gunfire control is difficult, if not impossible, for any ship constantly maneuvering against attacking planes.[13]

Battle off Cape Engaño

Admiral Ozawa well understood his role: to draw Halsey's Task Force 38 away from Kurita. His Mobile Force, Main Body (Northern Force) had one heavy carrier, three light carriers, two hybrid battleship/carriers, three light cruisers, and eight destroyers. What was more significant was that his two carrier divisions had a total of only 108 planes, and there were no planes on the hybrid battleship/carriers Ise and Hyuga.[14] Ozawa was sacrificial bait—and he knew it. When he heard on 24 October that Kurita was retiring, Ozawa also began to withdraw north. However, at about 2000 Toyoda issued an order to turn south and attack. Although Ozawa had received no news about Kurita during the night of 24–25 October, he proceeded to carry out his orders. But he now knew that Halsey was on his way north, and he knew what Halsey could do to his almost planeless carrier force.

By early morning 25 October, Ozawa had sent most of his planes to Philippine fields (Clark and Tuguegarao), leaving to only thirteen fighters the hopeless task of taking on all of Task Force 38's planes. By 0930 he had none left. The plan for the dispatched planes was to attack Task Force 38 and then proceed to the Philippines. Some found Task Force 38 and attacked, some did not; but very few from either group reached the Philippines, partially due to the lack of training of the pilots. Task Force 38 put a Battle Line ten miles in front of the carriers during the night, and dawn searches located Ozawa's fleet.

After seeing the approaching carrier planes at 0707, the Zuikaku and the light carrier Chitose launched eleven planes as combat air patrol. Ozawa had divided his Mobile Force into two groups. Group 5 had the Zuikaku and the light carrier Zuiho; they were screened by the light cruisers Oyodo and Tama, the destroyers Hatsuzuki, and Wakatsuki, the hybrid battleship/carrier Ise, the destroyers Kuwa and Akizuki. Directly astern was Group 6, with the light carriers Chitose and Chiyoda screened by the light cruiser Isuzu, the hybrid

35.   *The battleship* Kirishima, *which was sunk by gunfire from the U.S. battleships*
Washington *and* South Dakota, *15 November 1942.*

36. *Emperor Hirohito, at front center, with Japanese naval officers aboard the battleship Musashi at Yokosuka, in June 1943.*

37. *Japanese ships at Rabaul maneuver frantically to evade attacking U.S. planes, 5 November 1943. The photograph is taken from one of the Saratoga's planes.*

38. *The hybrid battleship-carrier* Ise. *After the extensive losses of carriers at the Battle of Midway, this ship and the* Hyuga *were converted into battleship-carrier by the addition of a flight deck aft.*

39. *Admiral Soemu Toyoda, the last commander-in-chief of the Combined Fleet.*

40. *Admiral Mineichi Koga, who succeeded Yamamoto as commander-in-chief of the Combined Fleet.*

41. *Vice Admiral Takeo Kurita,
leader of Fifth Fleet, First Strike
Force*

42. *Japanese Force "A" leaves Brunei on 22 October 1944, to take part in the Battle
of Leyte Gulf. The ships are, right to left, the battleships* Nagato, Musashi, *and*
Yamato, *and the heavy cruisers* Maya, Chokai, Takao, Atago, Haguro, *and* Myoko.

43. *Crewmen of the sinking carrier* Zuikaku *throw explosives over the side, during the Battle of Cape Engaño, 25 October 1944. The* Zuikaku *was then the only remaining carrier from the Pearl Harbor raid.*

44. *After a third devastating attack by torpedo and dive bombers, the* Zuikaku's *flag is lowered, as her crew salutes.*

45. The battleship Yamato, battered by bombs and torpedoes, is ripped by a final massive explosion as she sinks, 7 April 1945.

battleship/carrier *Hyuga*, and destroyers *Kiri*, *Shimotsuki*, *Sugi*, and *Maki*.

The American attackers split into two sections also. The first (80 planes) came in on the starboard bow of Group 5. The other section (50 planes) went down a center line between Groups 5 and 6 and then launched an attack on Group 6's starboard beam. Attacks proceeded then on both groups from all directions. The *Zuikaku* was hit by a torpedo early in the attack and developed a list to port, causing her speed to drop; she fell out of position, having also lost her radio communications. The *Ise* had two near-misses; the *Oyodo* took one direct hit and two near-misses but there was little damage. The *Akizuki* at 0750 took a hit, caught fire, and at 0756 exploded and sank. In Group 6, the *Chitose* was damaged, developed a distinct list to port, and her speed dropped. The first raid lasted from 0721 to 0759.

The *Zuikaku*, the last of the Pearl Harbor strike carriers, was the chief target of the raiders; she was attacked on all sides by torpedo planes and dive bombers. She answered ineffectively with rockets, to which were attached metal lines (in hope of snagging planes). As the attack progressed she was pelted with direct hits and penetrated by torpedoes; Ozawa decided to transfer his flag to the *Oyodo*.

The *Zuiho* underwent a heavy attack at 0731, was hit twice on the launching deck. She also suffered six near-misses aft, and a near-miss off her bow ruptured an oil tank. Fires broke out, she began to list, and by 0755 she started to lose speed.

Group 6 had not been neglected; 170 planes jumped it, and all ships replied with heavy fire, including the *Hyuga*'s main batteries. The light cruiser *Tama* was torpedoed at 0730 and began to lose way. The *Chitose* received a bomb on her port quarter which caused heavy damage, and her speed dropped drastically. The *Chiyoda* was pounced upon at 0724 from all sides, but due to the cooperation of the destroyer *Shimotsuki*, she was not hit. Because the *Chitose* was dead in the water, the *Shimotsuki* was sent to her aid. The light cruiser *Isuzu* was ordered to assist the light cruiser *Tama*. The *Chitose* sank at 0830 with 903 killed. Some of her crew was rescued by the *Shimotsuki*, but the destroyer was driven off by repeated air attacks.

Ozawa's force was now strung out over 35 miles. The northernmost force was the *Zuikaku*, the *Zuiho*, the *Ise*, and four destroyers. The *Tama*, trailing oil, was about halfway between this group and the *Chiyoda, Hyuga,* and the *Shimotsuki;* even farther back was the *Isuzu.*

The third attack, a big one, came in at 1205 and lasted for over an hour. A part concentrated on the *Zuikaku* and the *Zuiho;* the *Zuikaku* drew more than 100 bombers and torpedo planes. She received a torpedo on the port bow, immediately followed by seven more on both port and starboard sides. At the same time she took four direct bomb hits and various near-misses. The damage was too great; fires broke out and she lost way. When she began to list heavily, her captain, Rear Admiral Nakase, ordered the survivors to assemble on the fantail. The flag was lowered and the men began to abandon ship. She sank at 1314.[15]

It was the *Zuiho's* turn next. Starting about 1210, she took two torpedoes and four direct hits on the flight deck, and numerous near-misses. She slowed to 12 knots and soon lost steering power. At 1250 she suffered more near-misses and slowed to 6 knots. After a third wave attacked at 1332, and managed ten more near-misses, she had had it, sinking at 1426.[16]

At 1345, Halsey's planes concentrated on the *Ise,* but she survived the attack. They also jumped the sinking *Zuiho,* adding to the damage and confusion. The fourth attack, the largest—all available planes from five U.S. carriers—came in at about 1510.[17] It managed more than thirty near-misses on the *Ise*—but she still refused to go down. It was now time for the U.S. warships to go after the cripples and stragglers. Task Force 38's cruisers and destroyers sank the *Chiyoda* about 1547 by gunfire and torpedoes. (Most of her crew had already been taken off by the *Isuzu* and the *Maki.*) The *Hatsuzuki* was also sunk by this cruiser and destroyer group, at 1930, after putting up a gallant battle against impossible odds.

The *Tama* was sunk by the U.S. submarine *Jallao* later in the day, but the *Isuzu* and the *Oyodo* escaped. Among the destroyers, the *Akikaze, Wakatsuki, Shimotsuki, Maki, Kiri, Kuwa,* and *Sugi* also made it back to Japan. But the carrier arm of the Imperial Japanese Navy no longer existed.[18]

Kurita's Retirement from off Samar

Kurita's retirement was followed, and attacks were made by the escort carrier planes. The *Nagato* and the *Tone* were hit, but not enough damage was done to prevent their further withdrawal. Admiral Halsey, commanded by Admiral Nimitz to go after Kurita, at once split off Task Group 38.1 for that purpose. One hundred forty-seven sorties were flown by this group against Kurita's ships, but no further damage was done. The destroyer *Nowaki,* which had been standing by the *Chikuma,* was caught by Task Group 34.5 (a group newly formed at 1601 to chase Kurita) and sunk by shelling at 0000 on 26 October. The destroyers *Hayashimo* and *Shiranuhi* were caught by Task Force 38 and bombed south of Mindoro 27 October; the former was beached, the latter sunk.[19]

After these devastating battles, Japan no longer had a fleet. One part of the Combined Fleet that had survived the decisive SHO 1 went south to Brunei Bay and then to Lingga Roads off Singapore, where there was lots of fuel, but little ammunition. The other part went to Empire waters—where there was ammunition but no fuel. The story of Japanese naval engagements was almost over, except for the dreary account of sinkings of ships by submarine and by plane. Only three more "battles" remained—one off Mindoro, one off Penang, and the last suicidal dash of the *Yamato.*

SHO 1 never had a chance against the forces opposing it. It was formed too late, and even if it had reached the Leyte beachhead there was no large transport force there to sink. It could have done some damage to beachhead facilities and auxiliary ships, but the price would have been far too great; all or some of Halsey's carrier groups would be recalled, and then the remaining Japanese ships would have been trapped.

By October 1944 the Japanese Navy was simply overwhelmed by the number and kinds of American ships, submarines, and aircraft; no operation could have succeeded. But the training of Japanese military officers was such that it was unthinkable to face surrender. The kamikaze planes were being built and pilots being recruited to meet and to destroy the next advance. Suicide submarines (*kaiten*) were also being produced. Plans were already being formulated that if Japan herself was invaded, every Japanese man, woman, and child would be organized as *teishin butai* (Volunteer Corps) to meet the invaders, even though the Japanese might be armed only with sharpened bamboo spears.

The battles for Leyte were a kind of *banzai* charge, and in that charge most of what remained of the Japanese Navy was destroyed. The war, however, would still go on until officials with more wisdom could capture the government and begin to lay plans to bring about a negotiated peace. Even with a devastated fleet, with her armies isolated, and her people hungry, it would take the catalyst of the atomic bombs dropped at Hiroshima and Nagasaki to bring the "peace" party to enough strength to persuade an Emperor who had never made a political decision finally to make one, and end the war.

SHO 1 was an exercise in utter stupidity. The Japanese officers knew it, but given their initial programming as Japanese and as naval officers, their orders had to be obeyed. Many brave men died on both sides, many good ships went down as a result of SHO 1. The Japanese war slogan that "spirit (Japanese) could prevail over materialism" was a fantasy rapidly being dissolved.

San Jose Intrusion Force

Although Japan had no fleet left, its few remaining ships were scattered from Paramushiro to Penang, and its leaders were certain that the Philippines had been lost, one more effort was made, in a bizarre raid that served no purpose. Imperial General Headquarters ordered General Yamashita to make a counterlanding at Mindoro, while a hybrid bombardment force/hit-and-run raid on Mindoro's airfields by infantrymen, in cooperation with Japanese warships, was planned. Named "Intrusion Force," it was led by Admiral Masanori Kimura in the heavy cruiser *Ashigara*, with the light cruiser *Oyodo* and the destroyers *Kasumi*, *Kiyoshimo*, *Asashimo*, *Kaya*, *Sugi*, and *Kashi*. It sortied from Camranh Bay on 24 December 1944, and it was not discovered until 1500 on 26 December, when it was spotted by a PBY pilot, about 200 miles northwest of San Jose.

The San Jose beachhead was totally undefended against a naval attack. Planes and ships were hastily gathered as Kimura arrived off the beachhead, remaining far enough out to avoid a PT unit trap. On its approach run, the force was under constant air attack; at 2001 the *Oyodo* received two direct hits and one near-miss, but was only slightly damaged. Then the *Kiyoshimo* was hit twice and severely damaged; fires broke out aboard her, and she straggled out of formation. After a hit by a PT-boat torpedo, she sank about 2025. The *Ashigara* at 2024 suffered a near-miss and dropped behind the main force for a while.

The force went forward, despite reports of formidable U.S. ships in the area, and bombarded San Jose and its airstrip for half an hour. That done, Kimura returned to Camranh Bay, having lost a brand-new destroyer and with his other ships the worse for wear—all to no avail.[20]

Last Surface Battle

With their defeat in Burma and with their garrisons scattered throughout southwest Asia, the Japanese did not have enough ships to evacuate or even to provision the Army. The heavy cruiser *Haguro*, accompanied by the destroyer *Kamikaze*, was to remove the garrison at the Andaman Islands. The two ships were sighted on 11 May 1945, steaming on a northwesterly course, by planes flying from the escort carrier HMS *Shah*. The two Japanese ships knew they had been sighted, and reversed course; however, because the Andaman situation was desperate, the two ships again turned and resumed their mission. Anticipating an evacuation attempt, Admiral H. T. C. Walker of the British Eastern Fleet tried to intercept them. He took his main body south to prevent detection. The escort carrier *Shah* sighted the *Haguro* the morning of 15 May, after the *Haguro* had once again reversed course. Walker, however, had detached a five-destroyer force for such an eventuality, and the *Venus*, *Verulam*, *Virago*, *Vigilant*, and *Saumarez* made radar contact at 2300. Using an often-practiced (but seldom-used) "star" destroyer attack formation, they attacked the *Haguro*, fought a close-range battle, and sent the pink-painted cruiser down at 0150, 45 miles southwest of Penang. The *Saumarez* was moderately damaged, while the *Kamikaze* escaped.[21]

Last Sortie of the Imperial Japanese Navy

This book, as a battle history, does not treat the kamikaze aspect of the war as naval battles, since no Japanese ships were directly involved. Nor does it cover the carrier raids that ravaged Japanese ships and naval facilities, for these cannot truly be called naval battles; Japanese warships in Japanese naval bases hardly fought back, for many were half-sunken ships, and others had had their armament removed. But, ironically, in the last real sortie of the Imperial Japanese Navy the ships were used as diversionary bait. A dash was to be made by the mighty battleship *Yamato* and accompanying ships, designed to draw off as many American carrier planes as possible, thus leaving the Allied naval forces vulnerable to a large-scale kamikaze raid.

The composition of this last force (code-named TEN GO) was: the *Yamato*, the light cruiser *Yahagi*, and the destroyers *Isokaze*,

Hamakaze, Yukikaze, Asashimo, Kasumi, Hatsushimo, Fuyuzuki, and *Suzutsuki.* Okinawa had been invaded 1 April 1945, and Imperial General Headquarters in desperation decided to throw in every soldier, airman, and ship to dislodge the enemy; 6 April was designated TEN GO Day. The Japanese were so short of oil at home that the *Yamato* had only enough to make it to Okinawa. If she made it, the plan was to beach her and use her 18-inch guns in support of the ground fighting. Many of the ships' captains were against the operation, preferring to be let loose as sea raiders—but orders were orders. At 1600 on 6 April the ships weighed anchor at Tokuyama and started what would be the last voyage for most. Cadets and ill personnel were taken off the ships before departure.

At 0400 on 7 April, the ships emerged into the North Pacific, southeast of Kyushu. At 0900 the *Asashimo* reported engine trouble and dropped out of line. The force was in a ring formation as it turned southwest at 1115: the *Yamato,* bristling with guns (some of them radar-controlled, but without gunners trained in their use), was in the center. The light cruiser *Yahagi* was the southern lead ship, with the other seven destroyers completing the circle. Fifteen minutes later, the *Yamato*'s officers knew that they had been sighted, for an Allied seaplane was spotted. At that time all the last catapult planes of the fleet were sent back to Kyushu.

Soon thereafter the report came that 250 planes were headed for the TEN GO force. At 1220 the *Yamato* signalled the presence of many planes, 33,000 yards off her port bow. Just then a short rain squall interfered with visibility. When it blew over, the battle commenced at 1232 as ships opened fire with all guns, even the *Yamato*'s largest batteries. The fleet had been jumped only 175 miles south of Kyushu, and the massacre of the last vestiges of the Japanese Navy had begun. The *Yahagi* took a terrific initial pounding; hit repeatedly by torpedoes, bombed, and strafed, her engine rooms were littered with dead men. Then the *Hamakaze* went down. The waves of hundreds of U.S. planes were virtually continuous; the *Suzutsuki* was afire and in trouble, and the *Kasumi* had lost rudder control. The *Yahagi* could take no more and sank, as did the *Isokaze.* The *Yamato* was first hit by bombs at 1240, and then by torpedoes on her port side at 1250. She took eight more torpedoes on the port side and two starboard; by 1405 the listing ship could not be righted, and "Abandon Ship" was ordered. The last torpedo hit at 1417 and caused the *Yamato*'s list to go to 20 degrees; finally, the ship erupted, sending a majestic cloud of smoke billowing upward in a column, thousands of feet above her. Survivors were taken off the *Kasumi*, and then the *Fuyuzuki* finished her off. The *Asashimo*, limping in the rear, had also been sunk. Four battered survivors, the *Fuyuzuki*, *Suzutsuki*, *Yukikaze*, and *Hatsushimo*, finally made it back to Sasebo. A massacre it had been; from the *Yamato*, there had been 2,498 killed; from the *Yahagi*, 446; from the four destroyers, 721.[22] The massive kamikaze raid, for which 3,665 men had been sacrificed, had consisted of only 114 planes, which damaged one U.S. carrier, one pre-1941 battleship, and a destroyer. With the sinking of the great battleship *Yamato*, the once-formidable Imperial Japanese Navy had ceased to exist.

Table of Organization, SHO 1

Fifth Fleet, First Strike Force, Main Body (Vice Admiral Kurita)

FORCE "A" (NORTHERN FORCE)

Battleships: *Yamato, Musashi, Nagato*
Heavy cruisers: *Atago*, Takao, Chokai, Maya, Myoko, Haguro*
Light cruiser: *Noshiro*
Destroyers: *Kishinami, Okinami, Haginami, Asashimo, Akishimo, Hamanami, Fujinami, Shimakaze, Hayashimo*

FORCE "B" (NORTHERN FORCE)

Battleships: *Kongo, Haruna*
Heavy cruisers: *Kumano, Suzuya, Chikuma, Tone*
Light cruiser: *Yahagi*
Destroyers: *Nowaki, Kiyoshimo, Urakaze, Yukikaze, Hamakaze, Isokaze*

FORCE "C" (SOUTHERN FORCE) (Vice Admiral Nishimura)

Battleships: *Yamashiro*, Fuso*
Heavy cruiser: *Mogami*
Destroyer screen: *Shigure, Michishio, Yamagumo, Asagumo*

ATTACHED TO FORCE "C" (Vice Admiral Shima)

Heavy cruisers: *Nachi, Ashigara*
Light cruiser: *Abukuma**
Destroyers: *Akebono, Ushio, Kasumi, Shiranuhi, Wakabe, Hatsushimo, Hatsuharu*

SOUTHERN AREA GUARD FORCE, TRANSPORT FORCE
(Vice Admiral Sakonju)

Heavy cruiser: *Aoba*
Light cruiser: *Kinu*
Destroyer: *Uranami*
4 destroyer transports

MOBILE FORCE, STRIKE FORCE (Vice Admiral Ozawa)

Heavy carrier: *Zuikaku*
Light carriers: *Zuiho, Chitose, Chiyoda*
Battleship/carriers: *Ise, Hyuga*
Light cruisers: *Oyoda, Tama, Isuzu*
Destroyers: *Maki, Sugi, Kiri, Kuwa, Hatsuzuki, Akitsuki, Wakat-suki, Shimotsuki*

SUPPLY FORCE

Destroyer: *Akikaze*
2 tankers
6 escort vessels

U. S. Navy Table of Organization (units pertinent to SHO 1)

Third Fleet: Admiral Halsey
(in the battleship New Jersey), Task Force 38

TASK GROUP 38.1

2 heavy carriers
2 light carriers
3 heavy cruisers
14 destroyers

TASK GROUP 38.2

3 heavy carriers
2 light carriers
2 battleships
4 light cruisers
18 destroyers

TASK GROUP 38.3

2 heavy carriers
2 light carriers
4 battleships
4 light cruisers
14 destroyers

TASK GROUP 38.4

2 heavy carriers
2 light carriers
1 heavy cruiser
1 light cruiser
11 destroyers

BATTLE LINE (Drawn from Task Groups 38.2, 38.3, and 38.4)
6 battleships with heavy and light cruisers and screening destroyers

Seventh Fleet: Escort Carrier Group, Task Group 77.4 (Rear Admiral Thomas L. Sprague)

"TAFFY 1" (TASK UNIT 77.4.1)

6 carrier escorts
3 destroyers
5 destroyer escorts

"TAFFY 2" (TASK UNIT 77.4.2)

same composition

"TAFFY 3" (TASK UNIT 77.4.3)

same composition, minus one destroyer escort
(On the 18 escort carriers there were 304 fighter planes and 199 torpedo planes—a total of 503 planes, the equivalent of the number of planes on six *Essex*-class carriers.)

BATTLE LINE (to guard Surigao Strait to the south, Rear Admiral Oldendorf)

6 old battleships (5 recovered from Pearl Harbor)
3 heavy cruisers
5 light cruisers
29 destroyers
45 PT boats

IN RETROSPECT

As a famous American Indian warrior, Chief Joseph, once remarked, it is easy to take up the rifle, but it is almost impossible to lay it down. When Japan picked up the gun on 7 December 1941 the decision, although hotly debated, was in the end rather easy, given the emotions of the time. In the European theater, Japan's allies had isolated England, controlled most of Europe, were threatening Cairo, and had pushed the Russians all the way back to Stalingrad. Public opinion in the United States was almost equally divided between the isolationists, who wanted no involvement in World War II, and the interventionists, who did. Moreover, the American armed forces were small and relatively poorly trained; they lacked modern equipment, and what little they did have was being loaned to the Allies.

Relations between Japan and the United States had become increasingly strained, beginning at the turn of the century. Not only did the United States oppose the Japanese wars with China and her takeover of French Indochina, but the United States consistently adopted policies which denigrated the Japanese as people and as a nation. Moreover, the Americans had little regard for the Imperial Japanese Navy; it was commonly thought that, in case of war, the United States Pacific Fleet could be in Tokyo Bay within ten days.

The Japanese were a proud people; their tradition of the *samurai* made them believe that action was to be preferred to words, and convinced them that they were unique, that their land, people, and Emperor had come from the Plains of Heaven. The Shinto ideology had been skillfully blended with an intense nationalism; it was believed that an obligation was due to the country and the Emperor that even death in battle could not repay. Moreover, Japanese industry before World War II had produced weapons for use on land, air, and sea that were equal or superior to those of the Allies. Japan had soundly defeated a "modern" European nation, Russia, in 1904–1905, had with little effort taken Tsingtao, China, from the Germans in 1914, and had beaten the Chinese easily in 1931–1932.

It was true that Russia had decisively beaten the Japanese Army with the Russian Far Eastern Army in border battles at Chêngkufeng in 1938 and Nomonhan in 1939; however, in 1941, Russia seemed to be losing to Germany. Besides, if ever Japan and Russia were to clash in the future, Japan would need raw materials, especially oil, to keep her military force at full strength.

A storehouse of these materials lay available in the South Seas. With the Netherlands crushed in Europe, England besieged, and the United States at the moment preoccupied with Europe, militarily weak and politically divided, the temptation to create a Greater East Asia Co-Prosperity Sphere was too great. Japan coveted the resources of Malaya, Burma, and particularly the Netherlands East Indies, and if the United States Pacific Fleet could be destroyed in one devastating blow, the Philippine Islands would not block a Japanese push southward. Meanwhile a defense perimeter, always extended under Japanese air cover, could be created if the war lingered on. Intelligent military leaders knew that the war with the United States must be won quickly. The hotheads in the Japanese military forgot, or did not comprehend, the industrial might of the United States; only a few, such as Admiral Yamamoto, saw this reality and understood the war must be short or Japan would lose.

So the decision was made, primarily by the Army and civilian ultra-nationalists—but the loyal Japanese naval officers and men participated in the effort with all their strength, hoping to make it a short war.

The coveted territory and the defense perimeter were captured, and the resources began to be used, in half the time that had been estimated before the war. Admiral Nagumo's Carrier Strike Force was able to range from Pearl Harbor to Ceylon, relatively untouched by enemy opposition, for more than four months. Thus a "Victory Fever" developed, and because the Japanese began to feel invincible, the original defense perimeter was extended beyond the range of land-based air cover—a grave strategic error.

America may have been divided on 6 December 1941, but it was furiously united after the Pearl Harbor raid, and the mighty American production machine began to go all-out. Japan's first setback was her unsuccessful Port Moresby invasion operation in May; then, when Yamamoto got his "decisive battle" at Midway in June 1942, his carrier fleet, a major instrument in the swift early success, was emasculated. The Japanese had lost their skilled pilots and had inadequate shipbuilding and pilot-training programs. Guadalcanal, an obsession of the Japanese Army, further depleted the Navy, which could not replace ships as quickly as the United States could. When Japan evacuated Guadalcanal in February 1943, for all practical purposes the war was finally lost.

But it was difficult to put down the rifle, especially for the Japanese, given their unique ideology and national pride—so the war was fought to its bitter and bloody end. The Japanese armed forces, even in retreat, fought resolutely but hopelessly; Japanese troops generally defended their territory to the last man, for extremely few ever surrendered.

The war in the Pacific has generally been regarded as a carrier war, but there were only five true carrier-versus-carrier battles. The great majority of the naval battles were ship-to-ship fights, many of them fought at night. Still, the presence of carriers on both sides played a major role in isolating specific battlefields.

In this book, the term "naval battle" refers to engagements between surface ships; excluded are plane raids on ships in a relatively undefended harbor, or plane raids on undefended convoys. There are two battles difficult to classify: the Battle of the Sibuyan Sea, 24 October 1944, and the Battle off Cape Engaño, 25–26 October 1944.

The Battle of the Sibuyan Sea is regarded as a battle, because the only reason that Admiral Kurita's Strike Force had no air protection was that Admiral Fukudome, in charge of all Japanese planes in the Philippine Islands, had disobeyed orders and used all his available planes to attack the U.S. carriers; in doing so, Fukudome's planes sank the light carrier *Princeton*. The Battle off Engaño is included because, although Ozawa's carriers and defending ships were without planes, some of his ships were sunk by gunfire from Halsey's warships.

With these classifications, the U. S. Pacific Fleet won two carrier battles, and three were draws. But in the ship-to-ship battles fought from the time of Guadalcanal to Cape St. George, most of them being battles fought at night, the Japanese won ten, and the Americans three. In the Aleutians, a long-range ship-to-ship battle was a draw. But after the Battle of Vella Lavella, on 7 October 1943, the Japanese won no battles, while the U. S. Navy won eight.

The Japanese were superb night fighters, for a number of reasons: long and more intensive drill in such tactics before the war; their swift, long-range 24-inch torpedoes; better flashless powder; sharp observation by lookouts, sometimes more effective than radar; excellent optical equipment; and better tactics in most cases. Japan had an advantage in battle because she had retained torpedoes on her cruisers, while the U.S. cruisers had not, to their disadvantage. The Japanese also made good use of float observation planes.

But the necessity of supporting the Japanese Army in the Solomons took its toll. Daylight plane raids up to the Shortlands, losses in battle, overwork without overhaul, and the lack of time and equipment because of battle demands gradually diminished the Japanese ships' efficiency and postponed the installation of new armament to combat the ever-growing peril from submarines and planes. After November 1943 the Japanese Navy deteriorated steadily; as Yamamoto had foreseen, Japan began to be crushed by the weight of American production.

It is difficult to see how Yamamoto can be called a great admiral, for his only great contribution was in planning the raid on Pearl Harbor. Even though the Japanese won most of their battles up to 1943, most of these battles were not fought under the direct command of Admiral Yamamoto, and when he did bring his Combined Fleet out, and carrier battles ensued, his tactics led to disaster. At Midway his Combined Fleet was too far in the rear, even more so than had been the case at the Battle of the Coral Sea; but he repeated the same mistakes again, at the Second Battle of the Solomon Seas and the Battle of the Santa Cruz Islands. Perhaps it was because, ironically, he was still battleship-conscious. At any rate, in Combined Fleet battles he never committed his whole force for a unified blow at the outnumbered U. S. Pacific Fleet. Furthermore, he never used the whole of his Combined Fleet when the Americans' situation was so grave on Guadalcanal, and Henderson Field could receive plane reinforcements only from one crippled U.S. carrier. In small and large operations he burdened his fleet and lost valuable ships by never planning one combined smashing blow. Yet he, better than anyone, knew time was against him and that he could not afford the attrition he was allowing the Navy to suffer.

Japan had glaring weaknesses throughout the war. At home, although patriotism always ran high, internal quarrels among the Army, Navy, and *zaibatsu* (industrial combines) severely hampered planning and production. Until the introduction of the new *"Raiden"* fighter (when both pilots and gasoline were in short supply), the Japanese planes were the same as those used on 7 December 1941. Japan's submarine warfare, geared to fleet action, had a very poor record, and her antisubmarine tactics were poor. It was not until 1943 that destroyers began discarding minesweeping and minelaying gear for "Y" depth-charge throwers, bringing each destroyer's total number of depth charges up to thirty-six.

Japan should have laid down her rifle before the Leyte invasion. Instead she desperately began to rely on bizarre methods of war: the kamikaze pilots, the suicide submarines (*kaiten*), and the *baka* bomb. After President Roosevelt's "unconditional surrender" statement, desperate plans were drawn up to arm every man, woman, and child with sharpened bamboo sticks, should an invasion of Japan take place.

But finally, with millions of Japanese troops dispersed and isolated, the Navy incapable of battle, and oil and gasoline almost gone, wiser counsels prevailed—but not until the dropping of the atomic bombs that destroyed Hiroshima and Nagasaki. It has often puzzled the Western world that the Japanese were so willing to fight to the death in battle and to commit the homeland population to the same fate, and yet in the end, they surrendered without such a sacrifice. But it was their unique regard for their Emperor that explains the contradiction. When told to die for their Emperor, they obeyed; when told by their Emperor to surrender, they also obeyed—with so little protest that the Western world was astounded.

APPENDIX A

Name, Date of Completion, and Fate of Major Ships of the Imperial Japanese Navy

In Commission, 7 December 1941

BATTLESHIPS (BB)

Fuso 8 November 1915 Sunk in Battle of Surigao Strait, 25 October 1944

Haruna 19 April 1915 Inoperable: half-sunk in shallows off Kure by TF 38, 27 July 1945

Hiei 4 August 1914 Sunk in Battle of Guadalcanal, 13 November 1942

Hyuga 30 April 1918 Converted to hybrid battleship/carrier

Ise 15 December 1917 Converted to hybrid battleship/carrier

Kirishima 19 April 1915 Sunk in Battle of Guadalcanal, 15 November 1942

Kongo 16 August 1913 Sunk by *Sea Lion* off Taiwan, 21 November 1944

Mutsu 24 October 1921 Sunk, non-battle explosion; Hashirajima Bay, Japan, 8 June 1943

Nagato 25 November 1920 Surrendered on 2 September 1945

Yamashiro 31 March 1917 Sunk in Battle of Surigao Strait, 25 October 1944

CARRIERS—HEAVY (CV), LIGHT (CVL), ESCORT (CVE)

Akagi (CV) 25 March 1927 Sunk at Midway, 4 June 1942

Hiryu (CV) 5 July 1939 Sunk at Midway, 5 June 1942

Hosho (CVL) 27 December 1922 Surrendered on 2 September 1945

Kaga (CV) 31 March 1928 Sunk at Midway, 4 June 1942

Ryujo (CVL) 9 May 1933 Sunk at Battle of the Eastern Solomons, 24 August 1942

Shoho (CVL) 15 January 1939 Sunk at Battle of the Coral Sea, 7 May 1942

Shokaku (CV) 8 August 1941 Sunk by *Cavalla* at Battle of the Philippine Sea, 19 June 1944

Soryu (CV) 29 December 1937 Sunk at Midway, 4 June 1942

Taiyo (CVE) 5 May 1941 Sunk by *Rasher* in South China Sea, 18 August 1944

Zuiho (CVL)   27 December 1940   Sunk in Battle off Cape Engaño,
   25 October 1944
Zuikaku (CV)   25 September 1941   Sunk in Battle off Cape Engaño,
   25 October 1944

HEAVY CRUISERS (CA)

Aoba   20 September 1927   Sunk at Kure by TF 38, 28 July 1945
Ashigara   20 August 1929   Sunk by RN submarine *Trenchant* off Su-
   matra, 8 June 1945
Atago   30 March 1932   Sunk by *Darter* at Palawan Passage, 23 Octo-
   ber 1944
Chikuma   20 May 1939   Scuttled after damage, Battle off Samar, 25
   October 1944
Chokai   30 June 1932   Scuttled after damage, Battle off Samar, 25 Oc-
   tober 1944
Furutaka   31 March 1926   Sunk in Battle of Cape Esperance, 11 Octo-
   ber 1942
Haguro   25 April 1929   Sunk by RN destroyers off Penang, 16 May
   1945
Kako   20 July 1926   Sunk by S-44 near Kavieng, 10 August 1942
Kinugasa   30 September 1927   Sunk in Battle of Guadalcanal, 14 No-
   vember 1942
Kumano   31 October 1937   Sunk at Dasol Bay, Philippines, by TG
   38.3, 25 November 1944
Maya   30 June 1932   Sunk by *Dace* at Palawan Passage, 23 October
   1944
Mikuma   29 August 1935   Sunk after Battle of Midway, 6 June
   1942
Mogami   28 July 1935   Sunk by IJN destroyer after Battle of Surigao
   Strait, 25 October 1944
Myoko   31 July 1929   Surrendered on 2 September 1945
Nachi   26 November 1928   Sunk by planes of TF 38, Manila Bay, 5
   November 1944
Suzuya   31 October 1937   Scuttled in Battle off Samar, 25 October
   1944
Takao   31 May 1932   Surrendered on 2 September 1945
Tone   20 November 1938   Sunk by planes off Kure, 24 July 1945

LIGHT CRUISERS (CL)

Abukuma   26 May 1925   Bombed off Negros, 24 October 1944, sank
   26 October 1944
Isuzu   15 August 1923   Sunk by *Charr* and *Gabilan* in Flores Sea, 7
   April 1945
Jintsu   31 July 1925   Sunk in Battle of Kolombangara, 13 July 1943

Kashii 15 July 1941 Sunk by TF 38 off Cape Varela, 12 January 1945

Kashima 31 May 1940 Surrendered on 2 September 1945

Katori 20 April 1940 Sunk in Battle off Truk, 17 February 1944

Kinu 10 November 1922 Sunk after Battle for Leyte Gulf by TG 77.4, 26 October 1944

Kiso 4 May 1921 Sunk by TF 38 planes near Manila, 13 November 1944

Kitakami 15 April 1921 Surrendered on 2 September 1945

Kuma 31 August 1920 Sunk by RN submarine *Tally Ho* off Penang, 11 January 1944

Nagara 21 April 1922 Sunk by *Croaker* south of Nagasaki, 7 August 1944

Naka 30 November 1925 Sunk in Battle off Truk, 17 February 1944

Natori 15 September 1922 Sunk by *Hardhead* off Luzon, 18 August 1944

Oi 3 October 1921 Sunk by *Flasher*, South China Sea, 19 July 1944

Sendai 29 April 1924 Sunk in Battle of Empress Augusta Bay, 2 November 1943

Tama 29 January 1921 Sunk after Battle off Cape Engaño by *Jallao*, 25 October 1944

Tatsuta 31 March 1919 Sunk by *Sandlance* off Yokosuka, 13 March 1944

Tenryu 20 November 1919 Sunk by *Albacore* off Madang, 18 December 1942

Yubari 31 July 1923 Sunk by *Bluegill* off Palau, 27 April 1944

Yura 20 March 1923 Damaged and scuttled off Savo Island, 25 October 1942

DESTROYERS (DD)

Akatsuki 30 November 1932 Sunk in Battle off Guadalcanal, 13 November 1942

Akebono 31 July 1931 Sunk by TF 38, Manila Bay, 13 November 1944

Akigumo 27 September 1941 Sunk by *Redfin* off Zamboanga, 11 April 1944

Akikaze 1 April 1921 Sunk by *Pintado* off Cape Bolinao, 3 November 1944

Amagiri 10 November 1930 Sunk by mine, south of Borneo, 23 April 1944

Amatsukaze 26 October 1940 Sunk by USAAF off Amoy, 6 April 1945

Arare   15 April 1939   Sunk by *Growler* off Kiska, 5 July 1942

Arashi   27 January 1941   Sunk in Battle of Vella Gulf, 7 August 1943

Arashio   20 December 1937   Sunk in Battle of Bismarck Sea, 4 March 1943

Ariake   25 March 1935   Stranded and sunk, Cape Gloucester, 28 July 1943

Asagao   10 May 1923   Surrendered on 2 September 1945

Asagiri   30 June 1930   Sunk by USMC planes, Savo Island, 28 August 1942

Asagumo   31 March 1938   Sunk in Battle of Surigao Strait, 25 October 1944

Asakaze   16 June 1923   Sunk by *Haddo* off Cape Bolinao, 23 August 1944

Asanagi   29 December 1924   Sunk by *Pollack* off Bonins, 22 May 1944

Asashio   31 August 1937   Sunk in Battle of Bismarck Sea, 4 March 1943

Ayanami   30 April 1930   Sunk in Battle off Guadalcanal, 15 November 1942

Fubuki   10 August 1928   Sunk in Battle of Cape Esperance, 11 October 1942

Fumizuki   3 July 1926   Sunk at Truk, 17 February 1944

Fuyo   16 March 1923   Sunk by *Puffer* off Manila, 20 December 1943

Hagikaze   31 March 1941   Sunk in Battle of Vella Gulf, 7 August 1943

Hakaze   16 September 1920   Sunk by *Guardfish* near Kavieng, 23 January 1943

Hamakaze   30 June 1941   Sunk in the battleship *Yamato*'s last sortie, 7 April 1945

Harukaze   31 May 1923   Surrendered on 2 September 1945

Harusame   26 August 1937   Sunk by USAAF off Manokawan, 8 June 1944

Hasu   31 July 1922   Surrendered on 2 September 1945

Hatakaze   30 August 1924   Sunk by TF 38 off Taiwan, 15 January 1945

Hatsuharu   30 September 1933   Sunk by TF 38, Manila Bay, 13 November 1944

Hatsukaze   15 February 1940   Sunk in Battle of Empress Augusta Bay, 2 November 1943

Hatsushimo   27 September 1934   Sunk by mine off Maizuru, 30 July 1945

Hatsuyuki   30 March 1929   Sunk by planes off Bougainville, 17 July 1943

Hayashio 31 August 1940 Sunk by USAAF off Cape Huon, 24 November 1942

Hayate 21 December 1925 Sunk by coastal guns at Wake Island, 11 December 1941

Hibiki 30 March 1933 Surrendered on 2 September 1945

Hokaze 22 December 1921 Sunk by *Paddle*, Celebes Sea, 6 July 1944

Ikazuchi 15 August 1932 Sunk by *Harder* off Guam, 14 April 1944

Inazuma 15 November 1932 Sunk by *Bonefish* near Tawitawi, 14 May 1944

Isokaze 30 November 1940 Damaged by TF 58, and scuttled south of Nagasaki, 7 April 1945

Isonami 30 June 1928 Sunk by *Tautog* off Wangiwangi, 9 April 1943

Kagero 6 November 1939 Mined and sunk by planes off Rendova, 8 May 1943

Kamikaze 28 December 1922 Surrendered on 2 September 1945

Karukaya 20 August 1923 Sunk by planes off Luzon, 10 May 1944

Kasumi 28 April 1939 Damaged by TF 58, and scuttled off Nagasaki, 7 April 1945

Kawakaze 30 April 1937 Sunk in Battle of Vella Gulf, 6 August 1943

Kikuzuki 20 November 1926 Sunk by carrier planes at Tulagi, 4 May 1942

Kisaragi 21 December 1925 Sunk by USMC planes off Wake Island, 11 December 1941

Kuretake 21 December 1922 Sunk by *Razorback* off Taiwan, 30 December 1944

Kuri 30 April 1920 Surrendered on 2 September 1945

Kuroshio 27 January 1940 Mined off Rendova, and sunk by planes, 8 May 1943

Maikaze 15 July 1941 Sunk by ship gunfire at Truk, 17 February 1944

Matsukaze 5 April 1924 Sunk by *Swordfish* off Bonins, 9 June 1944

Michishio 31 October 1937 Sunk in Battle of Surigao Strait, 25 October 1944

Mikazuki 7 May 1927 Sunk off Cape Gloucester, 28 July 1943

Minazuki 22 March 1927 Sunk by *Harder* off Tawitawi, 6 June 1944

Minegumo 30 April 1938 Sunk at Kula Gulf, 6 March 1943

Minekaze 29 May 1920 Sunk by *Pogy* off Taiwan, 10 February 1944

Mochizuki 31 October 1927 Sunk by planes off Rabaul, 24 October 1943

Murakumo 10 May 1929 Bombed, scuttled off Savo Island, 12 October 1942

Murasame 7 January 1937 Sunk at Kula Gulf, 6 March 1943

Mutsuki 25 March 1926 Sunk by USAAF off San Isabel, 25 August 1942

Nagatsuki 30 April 1927 Sunk off Devil Island, 6 July 1943

Namikaze 11 November 1922 Surrendered on 2 September 1945

Natsugumo 10 February 1938 Sunk by USMC planes off Savo Island, 12 October 1942

Natsushio 31 August 1939 Sunk by S-37 off Makassar, 8 February 1942

Nenohi 30 September 1933 Sunk by *Triton* off Agattu, 4 July 1942

Nokaze 31 March 1922 Sunk by *Pargo* off Cape Varella, 20 February 1945

Nowaki 28 April 1941 Sunk by ship gunfire after Battle off Samar, 26 October 1944

Numakaze 24 July 1922 Sunk by *Grayback* off Okinawa, 19 December 1943

Oboro 31 October 1931 Sunk by USAAF off Kiska, 16 October 1942

Oite 30 October 1925 Sunk by TF 38 off Truk, 17 February 1944

Okikaze 17 August 1920 Sunk by *Trigger* off Yokosuka, 10 January 1943

Oshio 31 October 1937 Sunk by *Albacore* off Manus Island, 20 February 1943

Oyashio 20 August 1940 Mined, and sunk by planes off Rendova, 8 May 1943

Sagiri 31 January 1931 Sunk by submarine K-XVI (RNN) off Kuching, Borneo, 24 December 1941

Samidare 29 January 1937 Beached, destroyed by *Batfish* at Palau, 25 August 1944

Sanae 5 November 1923 Sunk by *Bluefish* off Basilan Island, 18 November 1943

Satsuki 15 November 1925 Sunk by TF 38, Manila Bay, 21 September 1944

Sawakaze 16 March 1920 Surrendered on 2 September 1945

Sazanami 19 May 1932 Sunk by *Albacore* southeast of Yap Island, 14 January 1944

Shigure 7 September 1936 Sunk by *Blackfin* off Kota Bharu, 24 January 1945

Shikinami 24 December 1929 Sunk by *Growler* off Hong Kong, 12 September 1944

Shinonome 25 July 1928 Sunk off North Borneo, 17 December 1941

Shiokaze 29 July 1921 Surrendered on 2 September 1945

Shirakumo 28 July 1928 Sunk by *Tautog* off Hokkaido, 16 March 1944

Shiranuhi 20 December 1939 Sunk by carrier planes off Panay, 27 October 1944

Shiratsuyu 20 August 1936 Sunk in collision southeast of Surigao Strait, 15 June 1944

Shirayuki 18 December 1928 Sunk in Battle of Bismarck Sea, 3 March 1943

Suzukaze 31 August 1937 Sunk by *Skipjack* off Ponape, 26 January 1944

Tachikaze 5 December 1921 Sunk by TF 38 off Truk, 17 February 1944

Tanikaze 25 April 1941 Sunk by *Harder* off Basilan, 9 June 1944

Tokitsukaze 15 December 1940 Sunk in Battle of Bismarck Sea, 3 March 1943

Tsuga 20 July 1920 Sunk by TF 38 off Pescadores, 15 January 1945

Umikaze 31 May 1937 Sunk by *Guardfish* off Truk, 1 February 1944

Urakaze 15 December 1940 Sunk by *Sea Lion* off Taiwan, 21 November 1944

Uranami 30 June 1929 Sunk by TF 77 off Panay, 26 October 1944

Ushio 14 November 1931 Surrendered on 2 September 1945

Usugumo 26 July 1928 Sunk by *Skate* off Paramushiro, 7 July 1944

Uzuki 14 September 1926 Sunk by PT boat off Cebu, 12 December 1944

Wakaba 31 October 1934 Sunk by TG 38.4 off Panay, 24 October 1944

Wakatake 30 September 1922 Sunk by TF 38 off Palau, 30 March 1944

Yamagumo 15 January 1938 Sunk in Battle of Surigao Strait, 25 October 1944

Yamakaze 30 July 1937 Sunk by *Nautilus* off Yokosuka, 25 June 1942

Yayoi 28 August 1926 Sunk by USAAF and RAAF off Normanby Island, 11 September 1942

Yudachi 7 January 1937 Sunk in Battle off Guadalcanal, 13 November 1942

Yugiri 3 December 1930 Sunk in Battle of Cape St. George, 25 November 1943

Yugumo 5 December 1941 Sunk in Battle of Vella Lavella, 7 October 1943

Yugure 30 March 1935 Sunk by USAAF, Vella Lavella Gulf, 21 July 1943

Yukaze 24 August 1921 Surrendered on 2 September 1945

Yukikaze 20 January 1940 Surrendered on 2 September 1945
Yunagi 24 April 1925 Sunk by *Picuda* off Cape Bojeador, 25 August 1944
Yuzuki 25 July 1927 Sunk by planes off Cebu, 12 December 1944

Completed after 7 December 1941

BATTLESHIPS (BB)

Musashi 5 August 1942 Sunk in Battle of Sibuyan Sea, 24 October 1944
Yamato 16 December 1941 Sunk by TF 58 south of Nagasaki, 7 April 1945

CONVERTED TO BATTLESHIP/CARRIERS (BB/XCV)

Hyuga 30 November 1942 Sunk by TF 38 at Kure, 24 July 1945
Ise 8 October 1943 Sunk by TF 38 at Kure, 28 July 1945

CARRIERS, HEAVY (CV), LIGHT (CVL), ESCORT (CVE)

Amagi (CV) 10 August 1944 Bombed by TF 38, capsized at Kure, 24 July 1945
Chitose (CVL) 1 January 1944 (converted from seaplane tender) Sank under tow after Battle off Cape Engaño, 25 October 1944
Chiyoda (CVL) 31 October 1943 (converted from seaplane tender) Sunk in Battle off Cape Engaño, 25 October 1944
Chuyo (CVE) 25 November 1942 Sunk by *Sailfish* off Yokosuka, 4 December 1943
Hiyo (CV) 31 July 1942 Sunk by carrier planes northwest of Yap, 20 June 1944
Junyo (CV) 3 May 1942 Surrendered on 2 September 1945
Kaiyo (CVE) November 1943 Mined and sunk off Japan, 18 July 1945
Katsuragi (CV) 15 October 1944 Surrendered on 2 September 1945
Ryuho (CVL) November 1942 Surrendered on 2 September 1945
Shinano (CV) 19 November 1944 Sunk by *Archer Fish* between Tokyo and Kobe, 29 November 1944
Shinyo (CVL) 15 December 1943 Sunk by *Spadefish* off Shanghai, 17 November 1944
Taiho (CV) 7 March 1944 Sunk by *Albacore* northwest of Yap, 19 June 1944
Unryu (CV) 6 August 1944 Sunk by *Redfish* near Shanghai, 19 December 1944

Unyo (CVE) 31 May 1942 Sunk by *Barb* off Hong Kong, 16 September 1944

LIGHT CRUISERS (CL)

Agano 31 October 1942 Sunk by *Skate* near Truk, 16 February 1944
Noshiro 30 June 1943 Sunk by planes off Panay, 26 October 1944
Oyodo 28 February 1943 Sunk at Kure by TF 38, 28 July 1945
Sakawa 30 November 1944 Surrendered on 2 September 1945
Yahagi 29 December 1943 Sunk by planes in *Yamato*'s last sortie, 7 April 1945
Yashoshima 25 September 1944 Sunk by planes, Santa Cruz Bay, Luzon, 25 November 1944

DESTROYERS (DD) (an asterisk (*) indicates a small 750- to 1200-ton destroyer, which would be designated a "destroyer escort" in the U. S. Navy.)

Akishimo 11 March 1944 Sunk by TF 38 off Manila, 13 November 1944
Akizuki 13 June 1942 Sunk by TF 38, 25 October 1944
Asashimo 27 November 1943 Sunk by TF 58 south of Nagasaki, 7 April 1945
*Enoki** 31 March 1945 Mined off Japan, 26 June 1945
Fujinami 31 July 1943 Sunk by TF 38 near Ilo Ilo, 27 October 1944
Fuyuzuki 25 May 1944 Surrendered on 2 September 1945
*Hagi** 1 March 1945 Surrendered on 2 September 1945
Hamanami 15 October 1943 Sunk by TF 38 off Cebu, 11 November 1944
Hanazuki 31 January 1945 Surrendered on 2 September 1945
Haruzuki 28 December 1944 Surrendered on 2 September 1945
Hatsuume 18 June 1945 Sunk by mine off Maizuru, 26 June 1945
*Hatsuzakura** 28 May 1945 Surrendered on 2 September 1945
Hatsuzuki 29 December 1942 Sunk by gunfire, Battle off Cape Engaño, 25 October 1944
Hayanami 31 July 1943 Sunk by *Harder* off Sibutu Islands, 7 June 1944
Hayashimo 20 February 1944 Sunk by TF 38 off Mindonoro, 26 October 1944
*Hinoki** 30 September 1944 Sunk by gunfire, Manila Bay, 5 January 1945
*Kaba** 29 May 1945 Surrendered on 2 September 1945
*Kaede** 30 October 1944 Surrendered on 2 September 1945
*Kaki** 5 March 1945 Surrendered on 2 September 1945

*Kashi**   30 September 1944   Surrendered on 2 September 1945

*Kaya**   30 September 1944   Surrendered on 2 September 1945

Kazagumo   28 March 1942   Sunk by *Hake* off Mindonoro, 8 June 1944

*Keyaki**   15 December 1944   Surrendered on 2 September 1945

*Kiri**   14 August 1944   Surrendered on 2 September 1945

Kishinami   3 December 1943   Sunk by *Flasher*, Philippine Sea, 4 December 1944

Kiyonami   25 January 1943   Sunk by planes off Kolombangara, 20 July 1943

Kiyoshimo   16 May 1944   Sunk by planes and PT boats south of Manila, 26 December 1944

*Kusunoki**   28 April 1945   Surrendered on 2 September 1945

*Kuwa**   25 July 1944   Sunk by gunfire, Leyte Gulf, 3 December 1944

*Maki**   10 August 1944   Surrendered on 2 September 1945

Makigumo   14 March 1942   Mined off Savo Island, 1 February 1943

Makinami   18 August 1942   Sunk in Battle of Cape St. George, 25 November 1943

*Matsu**   28 April 1944   Damaged by planes, sunk by gunfire off Chichijima, 4 August 1944

*Momi**   7 September 1944   Sunk by TF 38 off Manila, 5 January 1945

*Momo**   10 June 1944   Sunk by *Hawkbill* off Cape Bolinao, 15 December 1944

Naganami   30 June 1942   Sunk by TF 38 off Cebu, 11 November 1944

*Nara**   26 November 1944   Surrendered on 2 September 1945

*Nashi**†   15 March 1945   Sunk by TF 38 off Kure, 28 July 1945

Natsuzuki   8 April 1945   Surrendered on 2 September 1945

Niizuki   31 March 1943   Sunk in Battle of Kula Gulf, 6 July 1943

*Nire**   31 January 1945   Surrendered on 2 September 1945

*Odake**   15 May 1945   Surrendered on 2 September 1945

Okinami   10 December 1943   Sunk by TF 38 off Manila, 13 November 1944

Onami   29 December 1942   Sunk in Battle of Cape St. George, 25 November 1943

*Sakura**   25 November 1944   Mined in Osaka Harbor, 11 July 1945

*Shii**   13 March 1945   Surrendered on 2 September 1945

Shimakaze   30 April 1943   Sunk by TF 38 off Cebu, 11 November 1944

† The destroyer *Nashi* was raised in 1955, refitted and renamed the *Wakaba*, and put in service in Japanese Maritime Self Defense Force—the only IJN ship of World War II to become part of Japan's new navy.

Shimotsuki   31 March 1944   Sunk by *Cavalla* east of Singapore, 25 November 1944

Sugi*   25 August 1944   Surrendered on 2 September 1945

Sumire*   26 March 1945   Surrendered on 2 September 1945

Suzunami   27 July 1943   Sunk by planes at Rabaul, 11 November 1943

Suzutsuki   20 December 1942   Surrendered on 2 September 1945

Tachibana*   20 January 1945   Sunk by TF 38, Hakodate Harbor, 14 July 1945

Takanami   31 August 1942   Sunk by ship gunfire off Savo Island, 1 December 1942

Take*   16 June 1944   Surrendered on 2 September 1945

Tamanami   30 March 1943   Sunk by *Mingo* off Manila, 7 July 1944

Teruzuki   31 August 1942   Sunk by PT boats near Savo Island, 11 December 1942

Tsubaki*   30 November 1944   Surrendered on 2 September 1945

Tsuta*   8 February 1945   Surrendered on 2 September 1945

Ume*   28 June 1944   Sunk by USAAF off Taiwan, 31 January 1945

Wakatsuki   31 May 1943   Sunk by TF 38 off Cebu, 11 November 1944

Yanagi*   18 January 1945   Surrendered on 2 September 1945

Yoizuki   26 December 1944   Surrendered on 2 September 1945

Appendix A compiled from information supplied by Dr. Kengo Tominaga of the Japan Defense Agency, War History Section; the Japanese Operation Monograph Series, No. 116 (JOMS); and *The Imperial Japanese Navy*, by A. J. Watts and B. G. Gordon (New York: Doubleday, 1971). In cases of contradiction, the Japanese sources and JOMS were utilized. In the ideographs for cloud, *kumo* or *gumo*, and for moon, *tsuki* or *zuki*, the correct reading was supplied by Dr. Tominaga.

APPENDIX B

Names of Imperial Japanese Navy Ships

With four exceptions, the Japanese reader can tell the type of warship by its name.

Carriers   Named after mythical flying objects or animals or large birds.

Battleships   Named after ancient provinces. However, four battle cruisers, the *Haruna*, *Kongo*, *Kirishima*, and *Hiei*, were given mountain names. The distinction between battleships and battle cruisers was later dropped and these four ships were regarded as battleships, without any change of name.

Heavy cruisers   Named after mountains.

Light cruisers   Named after rivers.

Destroyers   Given poetic reading of weather conditions: e.g., *Kawakaze* —"River Wind;" *Shigure*—"Drizzling Autumn Rain." In 1944 the Japanese Navy tried to speed up destroyer construction and save shrinking building material. It began to produce only 1,250- and 750-ton destroyers and named them after flowers, fruit, and trees.

Submarines   The Japanese language, while ideographic, can also be written phonetically—not with an alphabet but with a syllabary. There were three classes of submarines, *I*, *RO*, and *HA*, corresponding to A, B, and C.

NOTES

The following are referred to by author's last name alone
after the first entry.

Boeicho Kenshujo Senshishitsu (BKS); *Senshi sōsho*, Tokyo, Japan.

Hara, Tameichi; *Japanese Destroyer Captain*, New York: Ballantine
Books, 1961.

Joint Operational Monograph Series, No. 116 (JOMS); *The Imperial Japanese Navy in World War II. A Graphic Presentation of
the Japanese Naval Organization and List of Combatant and
Non-Combatant Vessels Lost or Destroyed in the War*, Tokyo:
U. S. Army, Far East Command, 1952.

Kirby, Major-General S. Woodburn; *The War Against Japan*, 5 vols.,
London: Her Majesty's Stationery Office, 1957–1969.

Lord, Walter; *Incredible Victory*, New York: Harper and Row, 1967.

Morison, Samuel Eliot; *History of United States Naval Operations in
World War II*, 15 vols., Boston: Little, Brown, 1947–1962.

Roskill, Stephen W.; *The War at Sea, 1939–1945*, 4 vols., London:
Her Majesty's Stationery Office, 1954–1961.

van Oosten, F. C.; *The Battle of Java Sea*, London: Ian Allan, Ltd.,
1975.

chapter 1

1 For the Japanese Imperial General Headquarters assessment of the
strength of the United States Navy and the possibility and proba-
bility of war with the United States see Boeicho Kenshujo Senshishitsu (hereafter cited as BKS), Japanese Defense Agency, War History Section, *Senshi sōsho*, Vol. 31, Pt. 1, pp. 18–48. (See
bibliographical essay on Japanese sources.)

2 James B. Crowley, "A New Asian Order: Some Notes on Prewar
Japanese Nationalism," *Japan in Crisis*, eds. Bernard S. Silberman
and H. D. Harootian. Princeton: Princeton University Press, 1974,
p. 293.

3 BKS Vol. 31, Pt. 1, pp. 24–33.

4 BKS Vol. 5, pp. 301–13. The whole of Vol. 5 deals with the planning and execution of the attack on Pearl Harbor.

5 The standard Japanese battle doctrine was for a destroyer squadron
to be led by a light cruiser (as flagship) with the destroyer squadron

commander on board. The destroyer squadron, if possible, for purposes of acting as a trained unit, remained as an entity with the same light cruiser as leader and the same destroyers. An ideal squadron had four divisions, each with four destroyers—a total of sixteen. Of course the practice could not always be followed if circumstances called for variation, and, by the beginning of 1943, was difficult to maintain.

6 BKS Vol. 5, pp. 258–60, 363–64. For details of all major IJN ships see Appendix A.

7 See BKS Vol. 5, p. 404 for route taken and p. 266 for sailing formation.

8 For data on all submarines involved see BKS Vol. 5, pp. 154–64, and Mochitsura Hashimoto, *Sunk: The Story of the Japanese Submarine Fleet*, trans., E. H. M. Colegrove. London: Cassell, 1954.

9 See BKS Vol. 5, pp. 325–46 for details of the attacks. Routes of both waves of planes are on pp. 335, 340.

10 United States Pacific Fleet, Flagship of the Commander-in-Chief, (C) "Damage Sustained by Ships as a Result of the Japanese Raid, December 7, 1941," Declassified from Secret. BKS Vol. 5, Supplement, Maps 3 and 4 show USN ships' location and damage.

11 See BKS Vol. 5, pp. 350–51.

chapter 2

1 TROMs of the destroyer *Sazanami* and *Ushio* (JD 205).

2 It was not unusual in the IJN for a minelayer instead of a light cruiser to carry the flag for a destroyer squadron. See BKS Vol. 31, Pt. 1, p. 242.

3 BKS Vol. 31, Pt. 1, pp. 258–71.

4 Data for first attack on Wake from TROMs and ARs of the cruisers *Tatsuta* and *Tenryu* (JT 1) and of the destroyers involved in the action (JD 204 and 205); Desron 6 DAR (JD 32); and BKS Vol. 31, Pt. 1, pp. 128–66. For preparation for and execution of successful second Wake invasion, microfilm reels of ships involved (JT 1 and JDs 204 and 205) and BKS Vol. 31, Pt. 1, pp. 172–220.

5 BKS Vol. 21, pp. 173–84.

6 The *Amatsukaze* was commanded by Tameichi Hara, later to become renowned as Japan's top destroyer captain. After the war, he and Fred Saito wrote a book about his career, translated by Roger Pineau, called *Japanese Destroyer Captain*, New York: Ballantine Books, 1961 (hereafter cited as Hara). BKS Vol. 21, pp. 220–24 differ from Hara's account.

7 BKS Vol. 21, pp. 205–06. TROM and AR of the light cruiser *Natori* (JT 1) and TROMs and ARs of destroyers involved (JDs 204 and 205).

8   BKS Vol. 21, p. 214. TROM of the light cruiser *Naka* (JT 1) and TROMs and ARs of destroyers involved (JDs 204 and 205).

9   BKS Vol. 21, p. 228. TROM of the light cruiser *Nagara* (JT 1) and TROMs of destroyers involved (JDs 204 and 205). Samuel Eliot Morison, in his *History of United States Naval Operations in World War II*, Boston: Little, Brown, 1947–1962 (hereafter referred to as Morison), Vol. III, p. 177, states that the 11 December minelaying group was attacked by the U.S. submarine *S-39*, but the TROM of the *Jintsu* (JT 1) shows no such attack. It does record an unsuccessful submarine and bombing attack on 19 December, with a probable sinking of a submarine.

10 BKS Vol. 21, pp. 261–68 covers the Lingayen invasion. TROM of the destroyer *Nagatsuki* (JD 205).

11 BKS Vol. 21, p. 293. TROM of the destroyer *Kuroshio* (JD 205).

chapter 3

1   Account of Malaya landings is in microfilmed IJN records and BKS Vol. 21. For the Royal Navy material, Stephen W. Roskill, *The War at Sea, 1939–1945* (hereafter cited as Roskill), 4 volumes, London: Her Majesty's Stationery Office, 1954–1961.

2   BKS Vol. 21, pp. 367–68.

3   TROM of the light cruiser *Sendai* (JT 1) and TROMs of destroyers involved (JDs 204 and 205); BKS Vol. 21, pp. 395–406.

4   BKS Vol. 21, p. 391.

5   BKS Vol. 21, pp. 435, 450–53; BKS Vol. 21, Supplement, Track Chart 7.

6   BKS Vol. 21, pp. 434, 439.

7   BKS Vol. 21, pp. 460, 463, 466, 469–70, 479.

8   The best British account of the land campaign is that of Major-General S. Woodburn Kirby, *The War Against Japan* (hereafter cited as Kirby), 5 volumes, London: Her Majesty's Stationery Office, 1957–1969.

9   BKS Vol. 21, pp. 596–99; Kirby I, p. 331 overestimates the ships involved at Endau.

10 BKS Vol. 21, pp. 590–96; TROMs and ARs of the destroyers *Amagiri, Hatsuyuki,* and *Shirayuki* (JDs 204 and 205).

11 BKS Vol. 21, pp. 521–23.

12 Kirby I, p. 223 gives the date of sinking as 19 December, and the cause as Dutch planes. *The Imperial Japanese Navy in World War II. A Graphic Presentation of the Japanese Naval Organization and List of Combatant and Non-Combatant Vessels Lost or Damaged in the War*, Tokyo: U. S. Army, Far East Command, 1952 (Joint

Operational Monograph Series, No. 116, hereafter cited as JOMS), lists cause of sinking as a mine. BKS Vol. 21, p. 523 states cause as unknown.

13 BKS Vol. 21, pp. 524, 532, 536. TROM of the destroyer *Sagiri*.

14 See F. C. van Oosten, *The Battle of the Java Sea* (hereafter cited as van Oosten), London: Ian Allan, Ltd., 1975, pp. 14–16.

15 This organization is based on BKS Vol. 21, p. 349 and cross-checked with official IJN microfilmed records (JT 1, JDs 204 and 205). There was considerable interchange of command assignments. The invasions of the Philippines, Siam, Malaya, and British Borneo were being carried out simultaneously and ships were transferred tactically to meet each new situation.

chapter 4

1 TROM and AR of the heavy cruiser *Myoko* (JT 1). Morison and David Thomas (*Battle of the Java Sea*, London: Deutsch, 1968) do not cite this incident and therefore have the *Myoko* operating in January and February with Crudiv 5 to which she was assigned. Morison in a later edition caught the error and corrected it in a footnote.

2 BKS Vol. 23, pp. 159–77; microfilmed records for ships involved (JT 1, JDs 204 and 205).

3 Morison III, p. 293 and BKS Vol. 23, p. 211.

4 BKS Vol. 23, pp. 210–15; microfilmed records for ships involved (JT 1, JDs 204 and 205). van Oosten, p. 20, says "the resistance put up by the defenders was weak."

5 BKS Vol. 23, pp. 210–15; microfilmed records for ships involved (JT 1, JDs 204 and 205).

6 BKS Vol. 23, pp. 215–66; van Oosten, p. 23.

7 BKS Vol. 23, p. 263; TROM of the destroyer *Suzukaze* (JD 205).

8 BKS Vol. 23, p. 265; TROMs of the destroyers *Kuroshio* and *Natsushio* (JD 205).

9 Compiled from BKS Vol. 23, p. 347 and microfilmed records for ships involved (JT 1, JDs 204 and 205).

10 BKS Vol. 23, p. 354 gives approach of Nagumo's force and flight diagram, and p. 349 gives table for planes launched.

11 BKS Vol. 23, p. 353.

12 BKS Vol. 23, pp. 318–42; microfilmed records for ships involved (JT 1, JDs 204 and 205); van Oosten, pp. 33–35.

13 van Oosten, p. 34, claims the *Java* hit one destroyer several times; however, the Japanese records mention no such hits.

14 The material contained in BKS Vol. 23 on the battle is interesting. A preliminary track chart on p. 329 (undoubtedly based on reports

from the *Asashio* and *Oshio*) shows that two American destroyers were sunk by gunfire, one by *Asashio* and one by *Oshio*, about 2317. The track chart issued after assessment by various and higher IJN authorities, Vol. 23, p. 338, made the correct deduction as to who was firing at whom.

15 Morison III, p. 329 claims that there was a total of only five MTBs.

16 IJN battle data comes from track charts on pp. 338 and 341 of BKS Vol. 23, and fns. 33, 34, and 35, p. 690, and narrative pp. 337–42; TROMs and ARs of IJN destroyers involved (JDs 204 and 205).

17 See van Oosten, p. 35 for an assessment of the poor performance of the ABDA ships.

18 Table in Hara converted from metric system.

19 BKS Vol. 23, pp. 355–70; microfilmed records for ships involved (JT 1, JDs 204 and 205).

20 The occupation of Tarakan is in BKS Vol. 23, pp. 136–59.

21 BKS Vol. 23, p. 202. JOMS reports the *Nana Maru* was not sunk as reported by van Oosten, p. 18. BKS also claims the Dutch submarine *K-XIV* was at the Balikpapan harbor.

22 van Oosten, p. 19, lists the Japanese *P-37* as damaged; JOMS also says it was damaged.

23 van Oosten, p. 19.

24 The occupation of Balikpapan and Bandjarmasin is in BKS Vol. 23, pp. 193–210, 268–318.

25 Kirby I, pp. 417–19, gives a graphic description of this debacle.

26 BKS Vol. 23, pp. 292–318 covers the fall of Singapore, the confusion at Bangka Strait, and the capture of southeast Sumatra.

27 The Table of Organization (cited above) of the Imperial Japanese Navy for the conquest of the Netherlands East Indies (excluding Java) is from BKS Vol. 23, Supplement, Diagram 1. This Table of Organization differs considerably from those of Western naval historians. van Oosten scores best, having only a few differences from the table above. This Table of Organization, as are others in this book, is based on the revelant BKS volumes and checked with the microfilmed official Japanese Navy records of involved ships. The following references are all from BKS Vol. 23: Bangka Roads, Kema, Menado-Celebes, pp. 159–77; Kendari-Celebes, pp. 210–15; Ambon Islands, pp. 224–40—the BKS does not put the destroyer *Ikazuki* in the Eastern Distant Support Force but her TROM (JD 204) does; Makassar Town–Celebes, pp. 257–67; Bali-Lombok, pp. 318–42; Timor, pp. 359–60; Tarakan–Dutch Borneo, pp. 136–59; Balikpapan–Dutch Borneo, pp. 193–210; fall of Singapore and Bangka Island, pp. 292–318 and microfilmed official Japanese records for ships involved (JT 1, JDs 204 and 205).

28 van Oosten, pp. 27 and 108; Morison III, p. 273.

chapter 5

1   van Oosten, p. 29.
2   van Oosten, pp. 63–64; TROM and AR of the destroyer *Shirakumo* (JD 205).
3   Hara, p. 73. Hara consistently disagreed with higher naval officers.
4   Battle of the Java Sea is reconstructed from the track charts in BKS Vol. 23, Supplement. van Oosten's track chart differs entirely from the track charts published up until now but shows surprisingly little difference from the Japanese reconstruction. The narrative is in BKS Vol. 23, pp. 448–78. The Strike Force narrative material is from van Oosten, pp. 46–55.
5   Desron 2 WD and DAR (JD 25).
6   Desron 4 WD and DAR (JD 29) not available from U. S. Naval Historical Center. The cruiser *Naka*'s part in the battle from track charts, *Naka*'s TROM and AR (JT 1) and from Desron 4's destroyers' ARs and TROMs (JDs 204 and 205).
7   Morison has the distance at 4,400 yards but the BKS Vol. 23, Supplement track chart shows the greater distance. At a range of 4,400 yards it was likely that shell hits would have been made by both sides.
8   TROM of the destroyer *Asagumo* (JD 204).
9   Morison III, especially pages 351–53, credits U. S. Destroyer Division 58 with feats of daring-do (including possibly hitting the *Asagumo*), but van Oosten and Japanese records do not support him.
10 TROMs and ARs of ships involved in the sixth phase of the battle. Morison claims that six dive bombers from the light carrier *Ryujo* sank the *Pope*. Kirby does not mention planes, claiming the sinking was caused by the naval battle.
11 Morison and van Oosten describe a brief fire fight, but this is not confirmed by the Japanese records of the ships concerned.
12 Battle of Sunda Strait is reconstructed from BKS Vol. 23, Supplement, Map 7. The narrative on the Japanese side is from BKS Vol. 23, pp. 482–526; for the ABDA side from van Oosten, pp. 55–60.
13 The Table of Organization for all IJN forces directly or indirectly involved in the invasion of Java is from BKS Vol. 23, pp. 398–99, and the microfilmed TROMs (JDs 204 and 205) of ships involved. The BKS Table of Organization omits the light carrier *Ryujo* but WDC 160677, Group 100, Item A-101 in the *Japanese Microfilm Index*, which has a condensed version of the log of the *Ryujo*, puts her in the western invasion. The IJN Table of Organization given here differs considerably from Morison III, pp. 331–32 and Kirby I, pp. 537–38, who also differ from one another.
14 van Oosten, p. 42.

1 BKS Vol. 31, Pt. 1, pp. 301–421 covers the Imperial General Headquarters' planning for the Marshalls.
2 BKS Vol. 31, Pt. 1, pp. 281–82; 290–91.
3 BKS Vol. 31, Pt. 1, pp. 292–93.
4 Translation from BKS Vol. 39, Pt. 1, p. 27.
5 BKS Vol. 39, Pt. 1, pp. 118–20.
6 BKS Vol. 39, Pt. 1, pp. 110–12.
7 TROMs and ARs of convoy warships involved (JT 1, JDs 204 and
205). Strangely, Kirby downgrades the raid as achieving little, and
Morison also tends to discount the damage. The disparity between
the works of English-language historians of high repute and the Japanese official records underlines the necessity for the latter to be
used. The Japanese record of damages and casualties is much higher
than Kirby and Morison, an indication of the Japanese record's im-
partiality and accuracy.
8 BKS Vol. 39, Pt. 1, pp. 130–34.
9 Composition based on BKS Vol. 39, Pt. 1, pp. 48–49 and microfilmed official records of Japanese ships involved.

1 Table of Organization from TROMs of IJN records of ships involved. BKS Vol. 23, pp. 613–22 gives the narrative.
2 TROM of the light cruiser *Naka* (JT 1).
3 For Nagumo's track chart, see BKS Vol. 23, p. 635 (map).
4 BKS Vol. 23, p. 643. Japanese plane terminology, as reflected in
official records, changed at this time. They kept the terms "fighter,"
"bomber" (meaning high-altitude bomber), and "dive bomber."
They replaced the designation "torpedo plane" with the more general "attack plane," indicating that the planes could carry either torpedoes or bombs.
5 Kirby II, pp. 119–20; BKS Vol. 23, pp. 642–44.
6 For chart of bomb hits on the *Dorsetshire* see BKS Vol. 23, p.
648.
7 BKS Vol. 23, Supplement, Diagram 9.
8 BKS Vol. 23, p. 651.
9 BKS Vol. 23, p. 654.
10 For chart of bomb hits on the *Hermes* see BKS Vol. 23, p. 656.
11 For track chart of the Soex Fleet's raid on India's east coast see BKS
Vol. 23, Supplement, Track Chart 10. For the narrative, BKS Vol.
23, pp. 661–68.
12 Roskill II, p. 28.

13 Table of Organization constructed from BKS Vol. 23, p. 636 and microfilmed official IJN records of ships involved.

14 Kirby II, Appendix 9, pp. 448–49.

chapter 8

1 BKS Vol. 39, Pt. 1, pp. 238–39.

2 BKS Vol. 39, Pt. 1, Supplement, Diagram 2 gives track charts of all the IJN forces.

3 U. S. Navy material is from Morison IV, pp. 13–16; 21–64.

4 TROM of the destroyer *Kikuzuki*.

5 Desron 6 DAR (JD 33). Again, the Japanese records give more battle damage than Morison does.

6 BKS Vol. 39, Pt. 1, pp. 239–40.

7 See Morison IV, pp. 8–9.

8 BKS Vol. 39, Pt. 1, pp. 244–45; 269.

9 BKS Vol. 39, Pt. 1, Supplement, Diagram 4; BKS Vol. 39, Pt. 1, p. 275.

10 Diagram of hits on the *Shoho* is in BKS Vol. 39, Pt. 1, p. 285.

11 For IJN operations on 8 May see BKS Vol. 39, Pt. 1, Supplement, Diagram 4; and BKS Vol. 39, Pt. 1, pp. 274–77. The Japanese estimates of TF 17's operations on 7 May are on pp. 281–82.

12 Time becomes a problem at this point. Both the IJN carriers and TF 17 were straddling East longitude 157° 30'. To the west was Time Zone −10; to the east was Time Zone −11. Most of the battle was fought in Time Zone −10, and the text and BKS track chart as modified use exclusively Time Zone −10 time to prevent confusion.

13 BKS Vol. 39, Pt. 1, pp. 267–327 and especially pp. 267–68 and microfilmed official IJN records of ships and units involved. In the Port Moresby Attack Force, BKS Vol. 39, Pt. 1, p. 268, the T.O. has a typographical error. It lists *Asakaze* for *Asanagi*. See TROMs for both destroyers, which place the *Asanagi*, not the *Asakaze*, in the chart. Morison IV, p. 17 correctly identifies *Asanagi* and correctly adds the destroyer *Uzuki*. The TROM of the *Uzuki* places her in the Attack Group contrary to the table in BKS Vol. 39, p. 268. Morison IV, p. 18 places the minelayer *Tsugaru* with the Transport Force, but the BKS identifies her as attached to the Attack Group.

14 USN data based on Morison IV, pp. 18–20.

chapter 9

1 BKS Vol. 34, pp. 29–30.

2 BKS Vol. 34, pp. 22–23.

3 BKS Vol. 34, pp. 92–95.

4 The story of the JN-25 code-breaking by Captain Joseph J. Rochefort is told in Walter Lord, *Incredible Victory*, New York: Harper
and Row, 1967 (hereafter cited as Lord), pp. 17–42. Code-breaking
has often been misunderstood. It does not mean the code-breaker
can read a message in the clear—perhaps he can grasp only 10 to 15
percent of it. So a code-breaker must be not only an excellent cryp-
tographer but an excellent analyst. "Joe" Rochefort was a genius in
his field.

5 Morison IV, p. 81.

6 For the Japanese explanation of K Operation, see BKS Vol. 34, pp.
220–22, 240.

7 BKS Vol. 34, p. 249; TROM of the light cruiser *Jintsu* (JT 1).

8 BKS Vol. 34, pp. 1–647 is devoted entirely to the Battle of Midway,
as is much of microfilm reel JD 1.

9 The IJN Table of Organization of the Battle of Midway is in BKS
Vol. 34, pp. 137, 171–73, 191–92.

10 For number and types of planes on Nagumo's four fleet carriers, see
BKS Vol. 34, p. 136. For technical plane data, pp. 147–60.

11 For the IJN Table of Organization for the Aleutians Operation, see
BKS Vol. 34, pp. 234–35.

12 For the U. S. Navy Tables of Organization for the Battle of Midway and the number of planes on the three fleet carriers, see
Morison IV, pp. 90–93.

13 For the U. S. Navy Table of Organization for the Aleutians Operation, see Morison IV, pp. 173–74.

chapter 10

1 Time again is a problem. This account makes use of the World
Time Zone map, which places Midway in Time Zone −12. Time
Zone −12 is used for all elements in the battle (even though the
Japanese forces were in Time Zone −11). By doing this, true
elapsed ·time between Japanese and American forces is maintained.
To complicate matters, Midway is just east of the International
Date Line; thus Japanese planes were launched on 5 June and U.S.
planes on 4 June.

2 BKS Vol. 34, pp. 294–97. For all phases of the battle see also MI
Operation on JD 1.

3 For the official Japanese version of the attack, see BKS Vol. 34, pp.
298–301. For the American version, Morison IV, pp. 104–05; Lord,
pp. 92–110.

4 BKS Vol. 34, pp. 281–84.

5 BKS Vol. 34, pp. 281–82.

6 BKS Vol. 34, pp. 281–84, from records kept on the *Akagi*.

7   The *Hiryu*'s ring defense at Midway, BKS Vol. 34, p. 353.

8   Morison IV, pp. 116–21.

9   BKS Vol. 34, p. 282.

10 IJN records do not mention an attack by a submarine at this time. The official records of the Air Fleet do mention a three-torpedo attack by a submarine on the *Kaga*. The BKS Vol. 34, Supplement, Track Chart 3 indicates a USN submarine in the battle area at 0920.

11 Morison IV, pp. 111–12, 122; Morison's times have been altered to World Time Zone hours.

12 Attack and sinking data of the *Soryu* taken from BKS Vol. 34, pp. 377–89. The BKS volume reproduces the microfilm reel JD 1, First Air Fleet War Diary material with notes by personnel on board. Morison IV, p. 123 and footnote 51, on the basis of evidence from the captain of the *Chikuma*, credits the submarine USS *Nautilus* (SS 168) with sinking the *Soryu* around 1410 with three torpedoes. Morison admits, however, that Commander Amagai raises doubt that the *Nautilus* torpedoed the *Soryu*—but rather the *Kaga*. The BKS Vol. 34, p. 377 records "an enemy submarine" fired three torpedoes about this time at the *Kaga* but none hit.

13 Translation from First Fleet War Diary (JD 1).

14 Attack and sinking data of *Akagi* taken from BKS Vol. 34, pp. 372–78 which includes quotations from the War Diary, First Air Fleet, June 1942.

15 BKS Vol. 34, p. 377; Morison IV, pp. 126–27. Morison, quoting an interview with Commander Amagai, has him in the water seeing a submarine's periscope. There is no evidence in the official Japanese sources of his ever being in the water. They record that he was transferred to a destroyer.

16 Attack and sinking data of the *Kaga* taken from BKS Vol. 34, pp. 376–77 written by the surviving senior officer, Commander Amagai, and from the War Diary, First Fleet, June 1942.

chapter 11

1   Attacks from and on the *Hiryu* from BKS Vol. 34, pp. 335–67, 379–81 and the War Diary, First Air Fleet, June 1942 (JD 1).

2   Material on the *Yorktown* from Morison IV, pp. 132–36, 153–56 and from BKS cited in footnote 1.

3   The discussion of future action by Yamamoto and his officers leading to the termination of MI Operation is in BKS Vol. 34, p. 489. BKS Vol. 34, pp. 445–46 reproduces this order. It differs from the order quoted in *ONI Review*, May 1947, p. 37, which is quoted in Morison IV, pp. 138–39, footnote 72. The latter source does not

contain item 4 cited in the BKS and the latitude/longitude for rendezvous are at variance.

4 BKS Vol. 34, pp. 444–46.

5 BKS Vol. 34, pp. 468–69.

6 BKS Vol. 34, pp. 464–74 gives the complete story of Yamamoto's efforts to extricate himself from his predicament and to fight a "decisive" night battle.

7 BKS Vol. 34, pp. 473, 475–77, 485–92, 496, 499–505, and TROMs and ARs of ships involved (JT 1, JDs 204 and 205); also from JD 1.

8 BKS Vol. 34, p. 484.

9 BKS Vol. 34, p. 429; TROM of destroyer *Tanikaze* (JD 205).

10 TROM of the heavy cruiser *Mogami* (JT 1).

11 BKS Vol. 34, p. 489. Morison IV, p. 150 states that in the third attack a bomb also struck the destroyer *Arashio*, killing most of the *Mikuma*'s crew that had been rescued. No mention is made of this in any official IJN records consulted for either the *Arashio* or the *Mikuma*. The *Arashio* was fully functional the next day when sent back to check on the *Mikuma*.

12 Morison IV, p. 150, fn. 13 quotes a survivor as saying more than 1,000 men lost their lives on the *Mikuma*. This is 122 men over her normal complement plus the 240 saved. This survivor was also responsible for the story that the *Arashio* was bombed. (See fn. 11 above).

13 BKS Vol. 34, p. 489.

14 BKS Vol. 34, p. 530.

15 Maruyama's thesis is explained in a review of his "Rekishi Ishiki No Koso" (The Deep Layer of Historical Consciousness), *Rekishi Shisoshu (Japanese Views of History)* in *Nihon no Shiso* VI, 1972. The reviewer is Shinichiro Nakamura, "The Unending Nightmare" in *The Japan Interpreter*, VIII, No. 8, 1974, pp. 525–31.

16 For Dutch Harbor raids see BKS Vol. 34, pp. 279–80. For USN reaction see Morison IV, pp. 176–77.

chapter 12

1 Kirby II, p. 278.

2 BKS Vol. 39, Pt. 1, pp. 593–643 covers the Papuan campaign.

3 TROM of the destroyer *Urakaze* (JD 205).

4 The sinking of the *Yayoi*, the rescue of her survivors and the remnants of the Tsukioka Unit is in BKS Vol. 39, Pt. 1, pp. 633–39. A good map showing the wanderings of the Tsukioka Unit is on p. 635. Additional details are from TROM of the destroyer *Isokaze*. See TROM of the *Tenryu* (JT 1) for account of final rescue. Morison VI, p. 40 states all the unit was rescued by submarine but the records of the *Tenryu* disprove it.

5 See TROMs of ships involved (JDs 204 and 205).
6 See TROMs and ARs of ships involved (JDs 204 and 205).
7 Kirby II, p. 289.
8 Morison V, p. 12.
9 BKS Vol. 13, Pt. 2, p. 7.
10 BKS Vol. 39, Pt. 1, p. 442. Morison IV, p. 18 has six transports in the convoy; Eighth Fleet records to not correspond with this. Morison also states the convoy was recalled after the sinking, but Eighth Fleet records state the recall was more than eight hours before.
11 BKS Vol. 39, Pt. 1, pp. 439–42.
12 Morison V, p. 16.
13 BKS Vol. 39, Pt. 1, pp. 464–65; DAR Crudiv 6, August 7–10, 1942 (JD 15).
14 See Admiral George Carroll Dyer, *The Amphibians Came to Conquer: The Story of Admiral Richmond Kelly Turner*, Washington: Government Printing Office, 1972, pp. 355–401 for a thorough analysis of what led to the USN debacle at the Battle of Savo Island. A painstaking USN official investigation—the Hepburn Investigation—cleared Turner of the accusations made against him and repeated by most subsequent naval historians. The actions of the Australian pilot who made first sighting defy description. Standing regulations ordered him to keep a discovered Japanese force in sight as long as he could. He did not. Nor did he break radio silence to make a report of his sighting. He returned to Milne Bay, had tea, and then made his report; meanwhile, five precious hours were wasted.

chapter 13

1 Morison V, p. 39, states that it was the *Chicago* dueling with the destroyer *Yunagi*; but the official Japanese track chart indicates that the *Yunagi* was probably firing at the *Jarvis*.
2 Back at Rabaul, the Outer South Seas Force also feared that task forces of both Sherman and Halsey might be in the vicinity; see BKS Vol. 39, Pt. 1, p. 493.
3 Morison V, p. 63.
4 ARs of ships involved (JT 1).
5 AR of the cruiser *Chokai* (JT 1).
6 Details of the battle are from BKS Vol. 39, Pt. 1, pp. 477–79. The battle reconstruction is taken from the track chart in the same volume, pp. 478–79. The U. S. Navy details not given in the Japanese sources are from Morison V, pp. 17–64.
7 AR of the cruiser *Kako* (JT 1).
8 The P-400s could not get up to a high enough altitude to be fighter planes, but they were excellent in cooperation with ground troops.

9 The Japanese Army often abandoned the practice of naming its
   units as companies, regiments, etc., but instead used the commander's name, and *tai* or *butai*. Thus, this would be called the *Ikki
   butai*, with no indication made of its strength or size. "*Butai*" used
   thus will be translated "unit."

10 BKS Vol. 39, Pt. 1, p. 519, and TROMs of destroyers involved
    (JDs 204 and 205).

11 BKS Vol. 39, Pt. 1, p. 534, and TROMs of ships involved.

12 See BKS Vol. 39, Pt. 1, pp. 521–23, for details of the planned oper-
    ation. The total campaign to recapture Guadalcanal was code-
    named KA.

13 BKS Vol. 39, Pt. 1, pp. 550–52.

14 BKS Vol. 39, Pt. 1, p. 552 gives account and track chart of the en-
    gagement of the destroyers *Kawakaze* and *Blue*.

chapter 14

1 BKS Vol. 39, Pt. 1, p. 564.

2 Hara was extremely critical of the operation of the *Ryujo*
   specifically, and Yamamoto's forces generally.

3 BKS Vol. 39, Pt. 1, p. 564.

4 Morison V, p. 90 differs from this. He claims the *Ryujo* was hit by
   four to ten bombs and one torpedo.

5 Hara, pp. 106–12 gives a graphic description of the battle. BKS Vol.
   39, Pt. 1, pp. 564–66.

6 BKS Vol. 39, Pt. 1, pp. 575–76.

7 BKS Vol. 39, Pt. 1, p. 586; ARs of the *Kinugasa* and *Chokai* (JT
   1).

8 Morison V, p. 84 has the destroyer *Sazanami* with Yamamoto's
   Combined Fleet. The *Sazanami* was not in Truk at the time (JD
   205).

9 Reconstructed from BKS Vol. 39, Pt. 1, pp. 542–43. The BKS table
   is in error by having Desdiv 18 which was disbanded before mid-
   August 1942. It was replaced by Desdiv 15 as shown in the table
   contained herein. The TO was also reconstructed and the above
   error corrected from reference to microfilmed official IJN records of
   ships involved. See also Eighth Fleet WD (JD 8); Crudiv 5 WD
   (JD 15) and Desron 2 WD (JD 26) for maneuver and battle details.

10 USN data from Morison V, pp. 86–87.

11 BKS Vol. 39, Pt. 1, pp. 577–80.

1 At the time of this writing the Japanese have not published a volume on the IJN for this period. There is, however, a BKS volume on the IJA (Vol. 13) which gives some IJN material. The major source for this chapter is the microfilmed official IJN records. For movement and losses of destroyers, see TROMs of destroyers involved (JDs 204 and 205). See also WD Desron 2 (JD 26).

2 BKS Vol. 13, Pt. 2, pp. 20–22.

3 The destroyer *Yudachi* laconically reported, "*Yudachi* sank two enemy ships." WD Desron 2 (JD 26).

4 BKS Vol. 13, Pt. 2, pp. 10, 12.

5 Potter, Elmer B. and Chester W. Nimitz, editors, *Triumph in the Pacific: The Navy's Struggle Against Japan*. Englewood Cliffs, New Jersey: Prentice-Hall, 1965 (hereafter cited as Potter and Nimitz), p. 28.

6 USN details from Morison V, pp. 130–38.

7 ARs and TROMs of cruisers and destroyers involved (JT 1); JOMS. The TROM and AR records of the destroyers *Minegumo* and *Murasame* are missing from JD 205. See DAR Desron 4 (JD 30). For a full account of the IJN's cooperation with the IJA in the decisive Guadalcanal campaign, see BKS Vol. 13, Pt. 2, pp. 7–77; and WD Eighth Fleet (JD 8).

8 BKS Vol. 39, Pt. 1, p. 542 shows the IJN Table of Organization for the reinforcement operation. The eleven destroyers were the *Kazagumo, Yugumo, Makigumo, Akigumo, Tokitsukaze, Amatsukaze, Hatsukaze, Akikaze, Uranami, Shikinami,* and *Ayanami*. Battle narrative from BKS Vol. 13, Pt. 2, pp. 77–79; TROMs and ARs of light cruisers *Tatsuta, Sendai, Yura* (JT 1).

9 TROMs and ARs for the heavy cruisers *Aoba, Kinugasa, Furutaka* (JT 1) and destroyers (JD 204).

10 DAR Desron 4 (JD 30); TROM of the destroyer *Natsugumo* (JD 205).

11 For USN data of situation of Guadalcanal and Esperance, Morison V, pp. 147–71. IJN data from BKS Vol. 13, Pt. 2, pp. 77–78 and DAR Crudiv 5 (JD 15), which gives track chart for the battle.

12 IJN TO for Battle of Cape Esperance from DAR Crudiv 5 (JD 15).

13 USN TO for Battle of Cape Esperance from Morison V, pp. 150–51.

chapter 16

1 USN data from Morison V, pp. 172–82.

2 BKS Vol. 13, Pt. 2, p. 82.

3 ARs of battleships and light cruiser involved in bombardment (JT
   1); DAR Desron 2 (JD 26); DAR Desron 4 (JD 30); WD Desron
   4 (JD 31).
4 BKS Vol. 13, Pt. 2, pp. 80–83 gives the story of the transport convoy. See ARs and TROMs of destroyers involved (JDs 204 and
   205), WD Desron 4 (JD 31).
5 See ARs of the cruisers (JT 1) and destroyers (JDs 204 and 205)
   involved in the bombardment.
6 ARs of the heavy cruisers (JT 1) and ARs and TROMs of destroyers (JDs 204 and 205) involved in the bombardment; Desron 2
   WD and DAR (JD 26).
7 For the whole range of American strategy in the war against Japan
   as part of World War II, see the now-declassified secret document:
   *The History of the Joint Chiefs of Staff in World War II: The War
   Against Japan,* by Lieutenant Grace P. Hayes, USN, on microfilm at
   the USN Historical Document Center, Washington, D. C.
8 President Roosevelt's quotation is *ibid.,* Vol. 1, p. 271; Halsey's ap-
   pointment on p. 266.
9 For the IJA record of the land battle, see BKS Vol. 13, Pt. 2, pp.
   83–163.
10 WD Desron 4 (JD 31).
11 WD Desron 4 (JD 31).
12 BKS Vol. 13, Pt. 2, pp. 165–69 gives battle narrative. For USN account of battle not in Japanese sources, see Morison V, pp.
   207–24.
13 The 207 Japanese carrier planes were coordinated with Air Flotilla
   11 at Rabaul, with 220 land-based planes.
14 Japanese Table of Organization based on BKS Vol. 13, Pt. 2, p.
   165; WD Destroyer Squadron 2 (JD 26); DAR Destroyer Squadron
   4 (JD 30).
15 The USN Table of Organization is based primarily on Morison V,
   pp. 204–06.

chapter 17

1 Potter and Nimitz, p. 28.
2 TROMs of the destroyers *Naganami* and *Takanami* (JD 205).
3 Morison states that Abe's ships were in single column for bombardment and that Abe was totally surprised by the presence of U.S.
   ships. Morison, however, gives only three fragmented track charts
   for Abe's formation. On the other hand, Captain Hara, who was in
   the battle, and whose book contains a simplified track chart, disa-
   grees. He categorically states that Abe's Bombardment Force expected a battle and was in battle formation with destroyers placed
   to use their torpedoes to maximum advantage. Hara's narrative and

track chart show no single column. The official track chart, illegible as it is, tends to agree with Hara and the battle account is based on the IJN version.

4   The word "horrendous" is not used lightly. Battle narrative from Hara sustains its use here. Battle narrative also from microfilmed official IJN records, especially Eighth Fleet WD (JD 8) and TROMs of involved ships also make the word applicable. It was the biggest surface ship to surface ship battle since Jutland.

5   The destroyers *Shigure*, *Shiratsuyu*, and *Yugure* were also designated Volunteer Attack Force.

6   ARs of the cruisers *Chokai*, *Kinugasa*; TROMs of the cruisers *Isuzu* and *Maya* (JT 1). (The battleship *Hiei*'s records are missing in JT 1.)

7   An official IJN track chart for this battle cannot be provided here at this time. The part of the battle west of Savo Island is on a track chart of Desron 4 War Diary (JD 31), but the track chart of the ships east of Savo Island is in JD 29, and reel 29 is not available. There is no BKS volume at this time for this battle. The narrative of the battle was taken from the TROMs and ARs of Japanese ships involved. The best unofficial track charts are in Potter and Nimitz, p. 30, and Hara, p. 145.

8   ARs of the battleship *Kirishima* and the cruisers *Takao* and *Nagara*; TROMs of the cruiser *Atago* (JT 1), the destroyers *Asagumo* (JD 204) *Samidare*, and *Teruzuki* (JD 205).

9   BKS Vol. 13, Pt. 2, pp. 233–36; WD Desron 2 (JD 27).

10 For use of terms, see BKS Vol. 13, Pt. 2, p. 231. The first Japanese reinforcements sent to Guadalcanal in August, a small detachment of Colonel Ikki's troops, used the term.

11 Morison V, p. 234, places the converted carrier *Hiyo* with the *Junyo*; Andrieu d'Albas, *Death of a Navy*, p. 211, has only the *Hiyo*. *Records of Activities of Japanese CVs: Extract from Various Ships' Records* (WDC 160 377, Group 100, Item A-101: JT 1) categorically places the *Hiyo* at Truk with engine trouble all of November. The BKS Vol. 13, Pt. 2, p. 232 confirms this.

12 Reconstructed from microfilmed official Imperial Japanese Navy records. There is as yet no BKS volume on this naval battle. It is dealt with in part in BKS Vol. 13, Pt. 2, which deals primarily with land forces.

13 This organization based on Morison V, pp. 231–33. USN battle data is partially from Morison V, pp. 235–87.

chapter 18

1   The struggle between the Japanese Navy and Army over this decision is in BKS Vol. 13, Pt. 2, pp. 419 ff.

2   DAR Desron 2 (JD 27).

3   Battle narrative for the Japanese can be found in DAR Desron 2 (JD 27) and the TROMs (JDs 204 and 205) for the eight destroyers involved. See also BKS Vol. 13, Pt. 2, pp. 412–14. For the U. S. Navy side, see Morison V, pp. 296–313.

4   Morison V, p. 299 states that they taxied on the water one and one-half hours before becoming airborne. The TROM of the *Oyashio* does not confirm this. She recorded enemy planes dropping parachute flares at 2324, three minutes before the cruiser *Minneapolis* was first hit.

5   BKS Vol. 13, Pt. 2, pp. 414–15.

6   For sinkings, see JOMS.

7   Material for activities of Tanaka's ships from TROMs of the destroyers involved (JDs 204 and 205); JOMS.

8   Table of Organization for KE Operation is in BKS Vol. 13, Pt. 2, pp. 565–67.

9   BKS Vol. 13, Pt. 2, p. 600.

10   BKS Vol. 25, pp. 199–673 gives the account of the Japanese on Attu and Kiska and the American attempt to dislodge them.

11   Battle on Japanese side reconstructed from track chart in BKS Vol. 25, pp. 477–502 and Supplement, Diagram 6 (track chart). Morison VII, pp. 22–34 gives U.S. track charts and battle narrative. Morison's track chart and narrative differ from World Time Zone time given in this book.

12   For table of Japanese ships' ammunition expended, see BKS Vol. 25, p. 500.

13   BKS Vol. 25, pp. 529–31, 549–50, 561–65.

14   BKS Vol. 25, pp. 629–46.

chapter 19

1   See Hara, pp. 174–75 for a destroyer captain's dread of skip-bombing. See TROMs and ARs for destroyers in this battle (JDs 204 and 205).

2   WD Desron 4 (JD 31) and DAR Desron 4 (JD 30).

3   BKS Vol. 9, Pt. 6, pp. 367–69.

4   BKS Vol. 9, Pt. 6, p. 371.

5   JOMS; WD Desron 2 (JD 26).

6   JOMS; TROMs of destroyers involved (JDs 204 and 205).

7   TROM of the destroyer *Niizuki* (JD 205).

8   The battles up the Slot have not been published as yet by the Japan Defense Agency, BKS series. The author has used the various microfilmed official Japanese records which are explained in the bibliographical essay. U. S. Navy data from Morison VI, pp. 163–74.

For Battle of Kula Gulf see TROMs and ARs of destroyers involved (JDs 204 and 205); BKS Vol. 9, Pt. 7, p. 30. For Battle of Kolombangara see TROM and AR of the *Jintsu* (JT 1) and her five destroyers (JDs 204 and 205).

9 TROMs and ARs of cruisers and destroyers involved (JT 1, JDs 204 and 205).

10 TROMs and ARs of the destroyers involved (JDs 204 and 205); JOMS; and Hara, pp. 187–90. U. S. Navy data from Morison VI, pp. 212–20.

chapter 20

1 Reel JD 29, which has records of Desron 3 for this battle, is missing from the U. S. Navy Historical Center. Therefore, the battle is reconstructed from TROMs and ARs of destroyers involved (JDs 204 and 205); Hara, pp. 195–202. U. S. Navy data from Morison VI, pp. 234–36.

2 TROMs and ARs of destroyers involved (JDs 204 and 205). A peculiarity, unresolved, is that the TROMs of the destroyers *Isokaze* and *Hamakaze* record that the light cruiser *Sendai* was with this group, but the TROM of the *Sendai* places her with a group in the Santa Cruz Islands Operation (JT 1). For U. S. Navy data, Morison VI, pp. 243–52.

3 BKS Vol. 9, Pt. 7, pp. 50–54.

4 For a detailed account of Imperial General Headquarters' 1943 plans to hold all of the defense perimeter from the Gilberts to Burma, see all of BKS Vol. 9, Pt. 7.

5 From TROMs and ARs of cruisers (JT 1) and destroyers involved (JDs 204 and 205); BKS Vol. 9, Pt. 7, pp. 418–19; Hara, pp. 244–45.

6 BKS Vol. 9, Pt. 7, p. 431.

7 Morison VI, p. 332, states that the *Agano* was hit by a torpedo, but her records do not indicate any torpedo hits. See AR of the cruiser *Agano* (JT 1) and TROMs of the destroyers (JD 205); JOMS. U. S. Navy data taken partly from Morison VI, pp. 330–36.

8 The records of the *Yugiri* and the *Makinami* were lost, but TROMs and ARs of the *Amagiri*, *Uzuki*, and *Onami* were not. U. S. Navy data from Morison VI, pp. 253–58.

9 DAR Crudiv 5 (JD 15) has a poorly microfilmed official Japanese track chart. It does not show all of the battle or the U.S. ship dispositions. Therefore, Hara, p. 234 was consulted for this account. The Japanese formations differ partially from Morison's track chart (Vol. VI, p. 311), which was also used to determine U.S. ship dispositions.

chapter 21

1   Tabulated from JOMS.
2   JOMS.
3   BKS Vol. 12, pp. 55–66.
4   JOMS.
5   BKS Vol. 12, pp. 493–94.
6   BKS Vol. 12, p. 496. There are excellent microfilmed official Japanese records for this operation: WD Desdiv 27 (JD 36).
7   BKS Vol. 12, p. 579.
8   See BKS Vol. 12, p. 587 for slightly different version.
9   BKS Vol. 12, pp. 567–87. This battle is covered in detail in a separate microfilm reel (JD 1). U. S. Navy data from Morison, VIII, pp. 211–321. BKS Vol. 12, p. 566 gives the number of Japanese planes as 450, plus land-based plane cooperation. For the land-based plane situation see BKS Vol. 12, pp. 548–51. See Morison V, pp. 412–16 for USN TOs. Morison VIII, p. 416, has the destroyer *Naganami* in the Mobile Force, Vanguard Screen, but her records show that she was at Kure.

chapter 22

1   BKS Vol. 30, Pt. 2, p. 24. The material from which these battles are reconstructed comes primarily from four microfilmed reels, JDs 1 through 4. The last part of JD 1 and all of JDs 2, 3, and 4 are devoted entirely to SHO 1, operational orders and movements. (See microfilm bibliography.) The battles are also covered in detail in BKS Vol. 30, Pt. 2, pp. 1–498. Battle off Samar reconstruction also comes from the track charts of these battles in the volumes' Supplement: Diagrams 4, 5, and 6. For U. S. Navy data, see Morison XII; Charles A. Lockwood and Hans C. Adamson, *Battles of the Philippine Sea.* New York: Crowell, 1967.
2   BKS Vol. 30, Pt. 2, p. 138 gives approach routes. See also JD 3.
3   BKS Vol. 30, Pt. 2, pp. 141–46. See also JD 3.
4   BKS Vol. 30, Pt. 2, pp. 165–83 describes the raids. See also JD 2. Figures compiled from table in BKS Vol. 30, Pt. 2, p. 197; and from JD 2.
5   BKS Vol. 30, Pt. 2, p. 261.
6   BKS Vol. 30, Pt. 2, pp. 266–68. Track chart on pp. 265 and 269. See also JD 4.
7   BKS Vol. 30, Pt. 2, p. 270. Records of all ships sunk in Nishimura's force were lost. The account of the surviving ship, the destroyer *Shigure*, is in JD 4.
8   BKS Vol. 30, Pt. 2. Time on track chart, p. 273 and text, p. 274.

9   See BKS Vol. 30, Pt. 2, pp. 274–80, 283 for the story of the *Mogami*.

10 See BKS Vol. 30, Pt. 2, pp. 281–82 for additional details of the *Shigure*; see also pp. 289–96 for the story of Force C. Morison XII, p. 240, claims that this battle was the last strictly surface battle; that distinction, however, belongs to the battle fought on 16 May 1945, between the Japanese heavy cruiser *Haguro* and the destroyer *Kamikaze*, and five RN destroyers, off Penang.

11 JDs 3 and 4.

12 JD 4.

13 For a full description of the battle, see JDs 2, 3, and 4.

14 From table in Ito Masanori, *The End of the Imperial Japanese Navy*, New York: Norton, 1962, p. 144.

15 BKS Vol. 30, Pt. 2, pp. 431–42.

16 BKS Vol. 30, Pt. 2, p. 433.

17 The IJN and USN counted the raids differently: the Japanese listed four, the Americans six.

18 For a full description of the battle, see JDs 1–4, especially JD 1.

19 JOMS.

20 BKS Vol. 30, Pt. 2, pp. 581–95. The only official record of this force is in the TROM of the destroyer *Sugi* (JD 205). By late 1944, most ship and unit records are not on the JD reels, for reasons unknown.

21 This battle took place after the *Yamato*'s last mission, but it is placed here, out of chronological order, for the obvious reason that the sinking of the *Yamato* was the real end of the IJN. Allied data from conversations with Rear Admiral D. H. F. Hetherington, RN (Retired); Roskill III, Pt. 2, pp. 319–20.

22 Battle reconstructed primarily from Hara, pp. 284–304. Hara was then captain of the light cruiser *Yahagi*. The last mission of the battleship *Yamato* is in JD 4A. Also see Hara, pp. 284–304.

BIBLIOGRAPHY

Japanese Language Sources

Original Japanese Sources

At war's end the United States government seized 30,000 volumes of Japanese military records, handwritten, often almost illegible and mostly unpaginated, and sent them to the Washington Document Center in Washington, D. C., where they were roughly categorized. Various sections were separated and some order was given them by an identification label, e.g., WDC 132564. The records were then sent to the Central Intelligence Agency for scrutiny and then to the National Archives, where they were further organized and given a second identification number, e.g., NA 51467. Finally they were sent to the United States Naval Historical Center. Some 260 microfilm reels were made, under the direction of Samuel E. Morison, ordered in logical categories, and given classification numbers, e.g., JD 4, before the documents were returned to the Japan Defense Agency in 1958. (A partial history of the seized documents is to be found in an article by Professor James William Morley, "Checklist of Seized Japanese Records in the National Archives," *Far Eastern Quarterly*, Vol. IX, No. 3 (May 1950), pp. 306–33.) The contents of the pertinent microfilm reels form the corpus of this book.

The microfilm reels utilized are divided into five categories:

1 *Tabular Records of Movement* (TROMs) These are day-to-day records (similar to ships' logs) of each individual ship, arranged according to the English alphabet. The record gives the name of the ship, its administrative and tactical designation, its day-by-day duty, its movements, and, if in battle, the narrative, the amount and kind of ammunition expended, any damage to the ship, casualties, and damage inflicted on enemy ships. (As in all navies, because of the nature of naval battles, especially at night, this last item is often unreliable.) The author used these records for all ships from carriers down through destroyers.

There is one reel: "Tabular Records of Battleships and Cruisers" (not a JD number but JT 1) which is translated into English. It contains the TROMs and ARs of all battleships and cruisers, with the exception of three that have been lost.

2 *Action Reports* (ARs) These are more detailed accounts of each ship's battle action.

3 *War Diaries* (WDs) These are concerned with a fleet, or with a carrier, battleship, cruiser, or destroyer squadron or division. Occa-

sionally the microfilm will yield the War Diary or Detailed Action Report of a single ship for a certain action. The name describes the contents: a daily record of the unit.

4 *Detailed Action Reports* (DARs)   These are concerned with the same administrative categories as the War Diaries. The word "action" does not necessarily mean "in battle." The DAR is a much more detailed account of an administrative unit's activities, including its track chart, original orders, and battle activity.

5 Five special battle operations were chosen for microfilming of a meticulously detailed account of the actions, including fragmentary orders. The operations chosen were: (1) Midway and the Aleutians (MI and AL operations); (2) Battle off the Marianas (A-GO Operation); (3) the battles near Leyte (SHO 1 Operation); (4) the last sortie of the battleship *Yamato* (TEN GO); and (5) the *Kikusui* (Kamikaze) operations. (The last was not used here.)

Because of the confusion in Japan at the end of the war and the repeated transfers of a voluminous amount of material from one agency to another in the United States, some of the documents have been irretrievably lost. Fortunately, if there is a missing Tabular Records of Movement for a certain ship, its squadron, division, and fleet record can be found, and, by searching, almost all ships' records can be pieced together. Finally, the records are often written in execrable Japanese and are extremely difficult to read, and the War Diaries and Detailed Action Reports are sometimes out of chronological order and are not paginated, nor are the tens of thousands of frames numbered. But the whole story is there, if it can be found.

In addition to the above microfilm reels in Japanese there is an unnumbered reel (in English): *Japanese Microfilm Index*; and there is a semioriginal source, reel NRS432 (in English): *The Imperial Japanese Navy in World War II. A Graphic Presentation of the Japanese Naval Organization and List of Combatant and Non-Combatant Vessels Lost or Damaged in the War*, Japanese Operational Monograph Series No. 116 (JOMS), prepared by the Military History Section, Special Staff, General Headquarters, U. S. Army Far East Command. (This has also been published as a book; see works in English below.) It is arranged in two parts: (1) a monthly report of the location of IJN warships and Japanese non-combatant vessels sunk or damaged, superimposed on a map, and the name of each ship, chronologically, lost or damaged and by what means; (2) an alphabetically and monthly arranged table of organization of the above ships.

The remainder of the 260 reels are concerned with other than IJN warship data.

AN INVENTORY OF MICROFILMED JAPANESE RECORDS USED

JT 1   TROMs and ARs (in English) of battleships and cruisers.

JDs 1   through 4A contain special reports of four operations (counting the battles for Leyte as one). Unfortunately, the reels were not put together by fleets or in chronological order.

JD 1 (a).   Operational orders and records for Battle of Midway June 1942.

CVs *Akagi, Kaga, Soryu, Hiryu*.

Desron 10.

DAR CV *Kaga*, 5 June; DAR CV *Soryu*, 27 May–9 June (sic); DAR CV *Hiryu*, 27 May–6 June (*Akagi* not included).

DAR First Air Fleet, 27 May–9 June.

JD 1 (b).   Operational orders and records for Battle off the Marianas, June 1944 (A-GO Operation). Land plane units and subsidiary ships' records omitted by author.

DAR First Mobile Fleet, 13–22 June 1944.

WD Crudiv 5, 1–30 June; WD Batdiv 1, 1–30 June; WD Desron 10, 1–30 June; WD 22nd Airflot, 1–30 June; DAR CL *Yahagi*; DAR CVL *Chiyoda*, 15–22 June; DAR CVL *Chitose*, 15–22 June; DAR CV *Shokaku*, 15–20 June. No designation of WD or DAR for Desrons 1, 2, 3. DAR Desdiv 61, 20 June.

JD 1 (c).   Battle off Cape Engaño.

DAR CV *Zuikaku*, 20–25 October 1944.

DAR CVL *Zuiho*, 20–25 October 1944.

DAR Mobile Force, 20–25 October 1944.

JD 2   Operational orders and records for most but not all ships and units involved in SHO 1 (Battles off Leyte). Author omitted land plane records.

DAR Cardiv 4, 24–25 October 1944.

DAR BB/XCV *Ise*, 20–25 October.

DAR BB/XCV *Hyuga*, 20–29 October.

DAR First Strike Force, 16–28 October.

DAR BB *Yamato*, 24 October; DAR BB *Musashi*, 24 October; DAR BB *Nagato*, 24 October; DARs BBs *Haruna* and *Kongo*, 22–28 October; DARs Batdiv 1, Crudiv 7, Desron 10, Crudiv 16, 20–29 October; DAR Batdiv 1, 18–28 October; DAR Desron 10, 17–31 October; DAR Crudiv 16, 17–27 October.

JD 3   For SHO 1, WDs of Batdiv 1, Crudiv 5, Crudiv 7, Desron 1, Desron 10, CVLs, *Zuiho, Chitose*, CV *Zuikaku*, BB/XCV *Hyuga*, CL *Oyodo*, CAs *Suzuya, Nachi*, 1–25 October; CL *Isuzu*, 1–31 October; CA *Myoko*, 1–31 October; CL *Abukuma*, 1–26 October; DD *Kiyoshima*, DD *Akishimo*, 1–31 October; BB *Musashi*, 1–24 October; CL *Noshiro*, 1–26 October; DARs CA

Myoko, 24 October; CA *Haguro*, 25–26 October; CA *Tone*, 24–26 October; CA *Maya*, 22–25 October; CA *Suzuya*, 18–25 October; CA *Atago*, 23 October; CA *Aoba*, 23 October.

JD 4 DARs CLs *Oyodo*, 20–28 October; *Yahagi*, 22–28 October; *Noshiro*, 23–26 October; *Abukuma*, 24–26 October; *Isuzu*, 20–29 October; *Kinu*, 18–26 October; DAR DD *Uranami*, 18–26 October; WD DD *Ushio*, DARs DDs *Akishimo*, 22–28 October; *Shigure*, 23–27 October; *Kiyoshimo*, 24 October; *Ushio*, 25 October; *Kuwa*, 25 October; *Kasumi*, 24–25 October; *Kishinami*, 24–26 October; *Shimotsuki*, 25 October; *Kasumi*, 29 October–13 November.

JD 4A TEN GO Operation and *Kikusui* Operation (the latter not utilized in this book). TEN GO Operation includes the operational orders and records for the last sortie of the *Yamato*.

JD 7 WD 4th Fleet, December 1941–August 1944, less September 1943.
WD 5th Fleet, December 1941–June 1944.

JD 8 WD 5th Fleet, November 1944–5 February 1945.
WD 7th Fleet, April–June 1945.
WD 8th Fleet, 14 August 1942–March 1943.
DAR 8th Fleet, 16 September–15 December 1942; 15 March–20 April 1943; 30 June–15 August 1943.

JD 15 WD Crudiv 5, June–November 1942.
DAR Crudiv 6, 7–10 August 1942.

JD 16 DAR Crudiv 7, 13–14 November 1942.

JD 22 WD Desron 1, January–March; May–November 1942.
DAR Desron 1, 29 May–10 June; 26 October–1 November; 20–28 November 1942.

JD 23 WD Desron 1, December 1942–August 1944.
DAR Desron 1, 30 November–7 December 1942; 23–28 March 1943; 22 July–1 August 1943.

JD 24 WD Desron 1, September; November 1944.
DAR Desron 1, 31 October–4 November 1944.
WD Desron 2, December 1944. Partially missing and scrambled.
DAR Desron 2, 6 December 1941–17 January 1942.

JD 25 WD Desron 2, January–February 1942.
DAR Desron 2, 18 January–11 March 1942.

JD 26 WD Desron 2, March–October 1942.
DAR Desron 2, 19–22 April; 20 May–7 August; 13–21 August; 9–23 September; 11–30 October 1942.

JD 27 WD Desron 2, November 1942–May 1943; August 1943–February 1944.
DAR Desron 2, 3–15 November; 29 November–1 December; 3–12 December; 15–28 December 1942; 2–3 January; 10–11 January; 14–19 June; 11 November; 30 December 1943; 4 January 1944.

JD 28   Greater part of document missing.

WD Desron 2, November 1944–20 April 1945.

DAR Desron 2, 20–30 December 1944; 6–8 April 1945.

WD Desron 3, January–June 1942.

DAR Desron 3, 4–11 December; 13–21 December 1941; 20–30 January; 9–27 February; 3–14 March; 20–31 March; 1–10 April 1942.

JD 29   Not available from U. S. Naval Historical Center.

JD 30   WD Desron 4, February–June 1942.

DAR Desron 4, 8 February–10 March; 29 March–1 April; 26 September–9 November; 12–18 October; 20–30 October 1942.

JD 31   WD Desron 4, October 1942–19 July 1943.

DAR Desron 4, 31 October–3 November 1942; 7–19 July 1943.

JD 32   First three charts are duplicates of DAR Desron 2, December 1941 (JD 24).

WD Desron 5, December 1941–March 1942.

DAR Desron 5, 30 November–13 December; 17–26 December; 28 December 1941–12 January 1942; 25 January–19 March 1942.

WD Desron 6, December 1941.

DAR Desron 6, 8–13 December; 21–23 December 1941.

JD 33   WD Desron 6, January–April 1942.

DAR Desron 6, 5–31 January; 25–27 January; 1–15 February; 19–22 February; 20 February–17 March; 23 April–12 May 1942.

JD 34   WD Desron 6, May–July 1942.

DAR Desron 6, 15–16 May; 24 June–10 July 1942.

WD Desron 10, December 1943–May 1944; 15 July–1 November 1944 (less October).

WD Desron 11, December 1943–July 1945 (less February and July 1944).

DAR Desron 11, 4 March–1 April 1944.

JD 35   WD Desdiv 2, December 1944–January 1945.

DAR Desdiv 2, 26–27 December 1944.

WD Desdiv 4 (Destroyer *Yamagumo*), December 1943; March–April 1944; July 1944.

DAR Desdiv 4 (Destroyer *Yamagumo*), 1 January 1943; 5 December 1943.

WD Desdiv 4 (Destroyer *Nowaki*), April; June; July 1944.

WD Desdiv 4 (Unit (*sic*) and DD *Michishio*), April; July 1944.

WD Desdiv 17, September–December 1944; February–May 1945.

WD Desdiv 17 (DD *Yukikaze*), August 1944; January 1945.

WD Desdiv 17 (DD *Urakaze*), August 1944.

WD Desdiv 17 (DD *Hamakaze*), January 1945.

WD Desdiv 17 (DD *Isokaze*), January 1945.

DAR Desdiv 17, 1–8 February 1943.

DAR Desdiv 17, 15 January 1945.

JD 36   WD Desdiv 27 (DD *Shigure*), June–September 1944.

  DAR Desdiv 27 (DD *Shigure*), 8–9 June; 20 June; 15–26 August 1944; 24 January 1945.

  WD Desdiv 27 (DD *Shiratsuyu*), 1–15 June 1944.

  DAR Desdiv 27 (DD *Samidare*), 8–9 June; 18–26 August 1944.

  WD Desdiv 20, October–December 1944.

  DAR Desdiv 20, 3–4 November 1944.

  WD Desdiv 20 (DD *Akikaze*), May–September 1944.

  DAR Desdiv 30 (DD *Akikaze*), 25 September 1944.

  WD Desdiv 30 (DD *Yuzuki*), July–September 1944.

  DAR Desdiv 30, 11 September 1944.

  WD Desdiv 30 (DD *Satsuki*), 31 August–September 1944.

  DAR Desdiv 30 (DD *Satsuki*), 21 September 1944.

  WD Desdiv 30 (DD *Uzuki*), June–September 1944.

  DAR Desdiv 30 (DD *Uzuki*), 20 June 1944.

  DAR Desdiv 30 (DD *Yunagi*), 21–25 August 1944.

  DAR 9th Transport Force (DD *Yuzuki, Utsuki, Kiri*), 9–13 December 1944.

  WD Desdiv 31 (DD *Kishinami*), October 1944.

  DAR Desdiv 31 (DD *Okinami*), 25–26 October 1944.

JD 201   TROMs of carriers so poorly processed onto the microfilm as to be unreadable.

JD 204   TROMs and ARs of destroyers alphabetically (*Akatsuki–Kasumi*).

JD 205   TROMs and ARs of destroyers alphabetically (*Kawakaze–Uzuki*).

The most serious loss of apparently irretrievable documents occurs here. Some 33 destroyers' records are missing, being neither in the United States Library of Congress, National Archives, or Naval Historical Center, nor in the Japan Defense Agency. This loss is inconvenient, but destroyers' battle activities can be extrapolated from their Desron War Diaries and Detailed Action Reports.

Official Japanese War History

The Japan Defense Agency, War History Section (Boeicho Kenshujo Senshishitsu, abbreviated in the text to BKS) has been engaged in a massive history of the war in all its aspects. The entire series is entitled *Senshi sōsho*. Included are: (1). Imperial General Headquarters' records of discussions, decisions, and orders; (2). Material that concerns the IJA mainly, although some of the IJN activities are recorded; (3). Volumes devoted solely to the IJN. The material in the *Senshi sōsho* is based primarily on the original sources returned to Japan, but foreign sources are also used and footnoted. Some ninety volumes have already been published. Each volume contains about 600 pages and has a supplement with tables of organization and search and track charts. The work is in a Germanic style of history, as to detail. No bias is observable. Any Western library that has an Orientalia collection will have these volumes. (Unfortunately, the American system of classification does not always follow the Japanese distribution numbering, e.g., American classification: Vol. 4, Pt. 2; Japanese classification, Vol. 30.) The BKS volumes have been particularly useful in providing a fuller story, and most furnish excellent large track charts.

Volumes used from Boeicho Kenshujo Senshishitsu, *Senshi sōsho*, Tokyo, Japan

Title of Volume	American Library Classification	Japanese Publisher Distribution Numbering
Hawai Sakusen	Vol. 5	10
Daihon'ei rikugunbu	Vol. 9, Pt. 6	66
	Vol. 9, Pt. 7	67
Mariana oki kaisen	Vol. 12	12
Minami Taiheiyō rikugun sakusen Gadarukanaru	Vol. 13, Pt. 2	28
Hitō Marē hōmen kaigun shinkō sakusen	Vol. 21	24
Ran'in Bengaru wan hōmen kaigun shinkō sakusen	Vol. 23	26
Hokutō hōmen kaigun sakusen	Vol. 25	29
Kaigun shōgō sakusen Fuirippin oki kaisen	Vol. 30, Pt. 2	56
Chūbu Taiheiyō hōmen kaigun sakusen	Vol. 31, Pt. 1	38
Middowē kaisen	Vol. 34	43
Nantō hōmen kaigun sakusen	Vol. 39, Pt. 1	49

In addition to official sources, the following source in Japanese was consulted.

Sena, Takashiko, *Junyokan D. Roiteru to sono saigo* in the series *Ships of the World*, February 1976, Vol. 223, edited by Koji Ishiwata. This article is the history of the RNN cruiser *De Ruyter*; there is also brief mention of the RNN cruiser *Tromp*, and the article includes the Battle of the Java Sea. A track chart is given of that phase of the battle in which the *De Ruyter* was sunk.

Sources of Track Charts

Most of the track charts were drawn from those in a BKS volume or its supplement. The few that were not were constructed from photographs of Japanese track charts on microfilm. The latter do not always show USN ships' names or formations. For these battles Mr. Donald Hoegsberg has drawn a composite track chart using the microfilm sources and *History of U. S. Naval Operations in World War II*, by S. E. Morison.

English Language Annotated Bibliography

Inasmuch as this book is concerned with the battles in which the IJN was engaged and is based on the IJN's documents and the Japan Defense Agency's voluminous history of the war, books in English were utilized primarily for Allied strategy, tables of organization, battle formations, and battle details unknown to the Japanese. The bibliography below is selective.

Original English Language Sources

Commander-in-Chief, United States Pacific Fleet, to the Secretary of the Navy, *Report of Japanese Raid on Pearl Harbor*, 7 December 1941. 15 February 1942. Declassified from Secret.

Hayes, Grace P., Lt., USN. *The History of the Joint Chiefs of Staff in World War II: The War Against Japan. Vol. I, Pearl Harbor Through Trident*. Historical Section, Joint Chiefs of Staff, 1953. Declassified from Secret. On microfilm in U. S. Naval Historical Center, Washington Navy Yard, Washington, D. C. It includes the official record of the meetings of the Joint Chiefs of Staff plus the author's excellent interpretative analysis.

United States Navy Department Bureau of Ships. *Ships' Data, U. S. Naval Vessels*, Vol. I, Washington: GPO, April 15, 1945. Declassified.

Secondary English Language Sources (and foreign works in translation)

Barbey, Daniel E. *MacArthur's Amphibious Navy; Seventh Amphibious Force Operations, 1943–1945*. Annapolis: U. S. Naval Institute Press, 1969. An excellent book on a little-known aspect of the war—the USN's role in the breakthrough from New Guinea, Bismarck Barrier to the Philippines.

Belote, James H. and William M. *The Titans of the Seas: the Development and Operations of Japanese and American Carrier Task Forces during World War II*. New York: Harper and Row, 1975. This book supplies a contrast between USN and IJN carriers and carrier doctrine.

Blair, Clay, Jr. *The Silent Victory: the U. S. Submarine War Against Japan*. Philadelphia: Lippincott, 1975. An account of the improvement and use of USN submarines which decimated both IJN ships and Japanese freighters during the war. USN submarines were to a great extent responsible in isolating Japan from her newly-gained empire.

Brown, David. *Carrier Operations in World War II*. Revised edition, Volume I, *The Royal Navy*. Annapolis: U. S. Naval Institute Press. An accurate account of the British carrier war against Japan.

Butow, Robert J. C. *Japan's Decision to Surrender*. Stanford: Stanford University Press, 1954. An excellent account of the forces that led to the decision to surrender.

Butow, Robert J. C. *Tojo and the Coming of the War*. Princeton: Princeton University Press, 1961. A scholarly analysis using Japanese sources.

Cook, Charles. *The Battle of Cape Esperance; Strategic Encounter at Guadalcanal*. New York: Crowell, 1968. A popular account of the Battle of Cape Esperance, told from the USN data.

Crowley, James B. "A New Asian Order: Some Notes on Prewar Japanese Nationalism," in *Japan in Crisis: Essays on Taisho Democracy*, Bernard S. Silberman and H. D. Harootian, editors. Princeton: Princeton University Press, 1974. An excellent analysis of the forces that led Japan into World War II.

Dyer, George C. *The Amphibians Came to Conquer: The Story of Admiral Richmond Kelly Turner*. Washington: GPO, 1972. Two volumes. A meticulous (and "salty") story of Admiral Turner's command, and the U. S. Pacific Fleet's logistical problems and solutions.

Fuchida, Mitsuo and Masatake Okumiya. *Midway, the Battle that Doomed Japan; The Japanese Navy's Story*. Annapolis: U. S. Naval Institute Press, 1955. The narrative of the Battle of Midway as seen by one of Japan's top airmen (Fuchida). Occasionally differs from the official IJN documents, but valuable.

Hara, Tameichi; with Fred Saito and Roger Pineau. *Japanese Destroyer Captain*. New York: Ballantine Books, 1961. Written by one of Japan's top destroyer captains. Valuable for atmosphere and personal accounts of Hara's battle experiences; very critical of Japan's military leadership, especially the IJN.

Hashimoto, Mochitsura. *Sunk; The Story of the Japanese Submarine Fleet*. Translated by E. H. M. Colegrave. London: Cassell, 1954. At times unreliable, but properly critical of the disastrous IJN submarine operations.

Hydrographic Office (under authority of the Secretary of the Navy).

Standard Time Chart of the World. 5192. Washington: 12th edition, January 1940. The chart upon which this book bases its time.

Ito, Masanori. *The End of the Imperial Japanese Navy,* translated by Andrew Y. Kuroda and Roger Pineau. New York: Norton, 1962. Written by a Japanese war reporter, it is valuable for Ito's conversations with Admiral Kurita and for the Battle off Cape Engaño. The author, however, utilized the United States Strategic Bombing Survey, *Interrogation of Japanese Officials,* and repeats many of the errors in the USSBS.

Jones, Francis Clifford. *Japan's New Order in East Asia, its Rise and Fall, 1937–1945.* London, New York: Oxford University Press, 1954. A scholarly description of the establishment and rule of the Greater East Asia Co-Prosperity Sphere.

Kahn, David. *The Codebreakers; the Story of Secret Writing.* New York: Macmillan, 1967. Among other things, an excellent description of how the United States had broken the Japanese code before Pearl Harbor and the codebreaking that led USN fleet carriers to protect Midway against the Japanese invasion forces in June 1942.

Kase, Toshikazu. *Journey to the Missouri.* New Haven: Yale University Press, 1950. A balanced account of how and why Japan lost World War II, written by a leading Japanese diplomat.

Kato, Masuo. *The Lost War.* New York: Alfred A. Knopf, 1946. A journalist's account of the internal struggles in Japan among industry, the Army, and the Navy in World War II.

Kirby, Stanley Woodburn (with C. T. Attis and others). *The War Against Japan.* London: HMSO, 1957–69. Volumes 1–5 of *History of the Second World War: United Kingdom Military Series.* The definitive official British military history of the war. Although primarily concerned with the British war against the IJA, it gives valuable (and accurate) information in capsule form on most of the IJN operations. Derived from Japanese sources, it corrects some errors made by Samuel Eliot Morison and Stephen W. Roskill. A meticulously researched work. The maps are excellent.

Lockwood, Charles A. and Hans C. Adamson. *Battles of the Philippine Sea.* New York: Crowell, 1967. Although, properly speaking, there was only one Battle of the Philippine Sea (off Saipan) and this volume is primarily concerned with the battles caused by the Leyte invasion, the ambiguous title does not detract from an excellent book, probably the best account of the battles caused by the Leyte invasion. The authors use to great advantage Admiral Kurita's radiograms to the other participating forces and to the CINC, Admiral Toyoda, in Tokyo, and his answers.

Lord, Walter. *Incredible Victory.* New York: Harper and Row, 1967. A popularly written book. A generally accurate account of the Battle of Midway. Gives a long description, not found elsewhere, of K Operation and the breaking of the Japanese code.

Morison, Samuel Eliot. *History of United States Naval Operations in World War II.* Boston: Little, Brown, 1947–1962. (Now published by Atlantic Monthly Press.) —— 15 volumes.

III   *The Rising Sun in the Pacific, 1931–April 1942.*

IV   *Coral Sea, Midway and Submarine Actions, May 1942–August 1942.*

V   *The Struggle for Guadalcanal, August 1942–February 1943.*

VI   *Breaking the Bismarck Barrier, 22 July 1942–1 May 1944.*

VII   *Aleutians, Gilberts and Marshalls, June 1942–April 1944.*

VIII   *New Guinea and the Marianas, March 1944–August 1944.*

XII   *Leyte, June 1944–January 1945.*

XIII   *The Liberation of the Philippines: Luzon, Mindanao, the Visayas, 1944–1945.*

XIV   *Victory in the Pacific, 1945.*

XV   *Supplement and General Index* (and errata).

Samuel Eliot Morison, a Harvard professor, was appointed by President Roosevelt to be the U. S. Navy historian for World War II. He participated in eight naval battles. His prose is at times magnificent. The matter of frequent reprints creates problems, however. Most libraries and many private purchasers acquired his first editions, as they were released. At that time he had very little access to IJN records, then in disarray in Washington, D. C., and his volumes contained a goodly number of errors on the IJN side. (See author's note in Preface.) Although new editions corrected some, but by no means all, of these errors, the new editions generally did not replace the original acquisitions in most libraries. Criticism of some errors, then, depends on which edition the reader is using. The author's policy in pointing out errors has been to use the first edition, on the premise that this would present the corrections for those libraries and private purchasers still using the first edition. There still remain, however, a number of errors in the new editions because the corpus of primary IJN documents has still not been incorporated in them. There is, perhaps, also a bit of chauvinism in all the editions. (The Office of Naval History has a set with penned corrections entered, which must be considered the definitive copy.)

    With this criticism, written reluctantly, there can be no doubt that on the USN side Morison will always remain the doyen of naval historians of World War II. We all owe him a debt of gratitude for the monumental work that he produced. To understand World War II's naval aspects, one must start with Morison.

The Two-Ocean War; A Short History of the United States Navy in the Second World War. Boston: Little, Brown, 1963. An original

but shorter version of his 15-volume history. It deserves the same
plus and minus marks.

Morton, Louis. "Japan's Decision for War" in Greenfield, K. R., *Command Decisions.* Washington: Office of the Chief of Military History, Department of the Army, 1960. An excellent analysis of the events and debates that led Japan into World War II. It depicts the IJA-dominated decision.

Nakamura, Shinichiro. "The Unending Nightmare" in English in *The Japan Interpreter,* VIII, No. 4 (Winter, 1972), pp. 525–31. This is a review article based on Masao Maruyama's "Rekishi ishiki no koso" (The Deep Layer of Historical Consciousness), part of his book, *Rekishi shisoshu* in the *Nihon no shiso* series. VI. Tokyo: Chikuma Shobo, 1972. A penetrating study of the psychological reasons for Japan's participation in the war. Maruyama is considered one of Japan's best political scientists.

Potter, Elmer B. and Chester W. Nimitz, editors. *The Great Sea War; The Story of Naval Action in World War II.* Englewood Cliffs, New Jersey: Prentice-Hall, 1960. This is an excellent adaptation of the authors' *Sea Power.*

Potter, Elmer B. and Chester W. Nimitz, editors. *Triumph in the Pacific: The Navy's Struggle Against Japan.* Englewood Cliffs, New Jersey: Prentice-Hall, 1965. A useful smaller book by these editors.

Potter, John Deane. *Admiral of the Pacific: the Life of Yamamoto.* London: William Heinman, Ltd., 1960. An English reporter's biography of Admiral Isoroku Yamamoto. In places where he utilizes Yamamoto's yeoman's diary, gives some valuable insights into Admiral Yamamoto's character and decisions. Otherwise an inaccurate history.

Reynolds, Clark G. *The Fast Carriers; the Forging of an Air Navy.* New York: McGraw-Hill, 1968. A good account of the way in which, with the construction of more than two dozen fast carriers by 1944, the USN was able to use the new fleet tactics of crippling carrier raids throughout most of Japan's dwindling empire. Together with submarine interdiction these mortally injured the IJN and its bases, and cut Japan off from the resources of her empire.

Roskill, Stephen W. *The War at Sea, 1939–1945,* Vols. I, II, IIIA, IIIB. London: HMSO, 1954–61. Three volumes in four. The official Royal Naval history of World War II. In discussing USN action in the Pacific, Roskill seems to follow Morison's volumes exactly.

Thomas, David A. *Battle of the Java Sea.* London: Deutsch, 1968. A popular and generally accurate account. Dutch sources apparently were not consulted.

Toland, John. *But Not in Shame; the Six Months after Pearl Harbor.*

New York: Random House, 1961. A well-researched account of the operations of the American forces from Pearl Harbor to the Battle of the Coral Sea.

Tuleja, Thaddeus V. *Climax at Midway*. New York: Norton, 1960. A solid account of the crucial battle, from American sources.

U. S. Army Far East Command. *The Imperial Japanese Navy in World War II; A Graphic Presentation of the Japanese Naval Organization and List of Combatant and Non-Combatant Vessels Lost or Damaged in the War*. Tokyo: Military History Section, Special Staff, General Headquarters, Far East Command, 1952. (Japanese Operational Monograph Series No. 116 (JOMS).) See microfilm bibliography.

U. S. Congress, Joint Committee on the Investigation of the Pearl Harbor Attack. *Pearl Harbor Attack*. Washington: GPO, 1946. 19 volumes. (79th Congress, First and Second Sessions. Reprinted 1972 by AMS Press.) Hearings before the committee.

U. S. Strategic Bombing Survey. *Interrogations of Japanese Officials*. Washington: GPO, 1947. 2 volumes. These volumes give valuable material otherwise unavailable, but must be cross-checked with the original records because there are glaring errors. For example, the account of the Battle of Surigao Strait is completely inaccurate.

van Oosten, F. C. *The Battle of the Java Sea*. London: Ian Allan, Ltd., 1975. The best account of the Battle of the Java Sea including Dutch and Japanese sources. The text is short but the 17 appendices contain valuable statistical material.

INDEX

V32

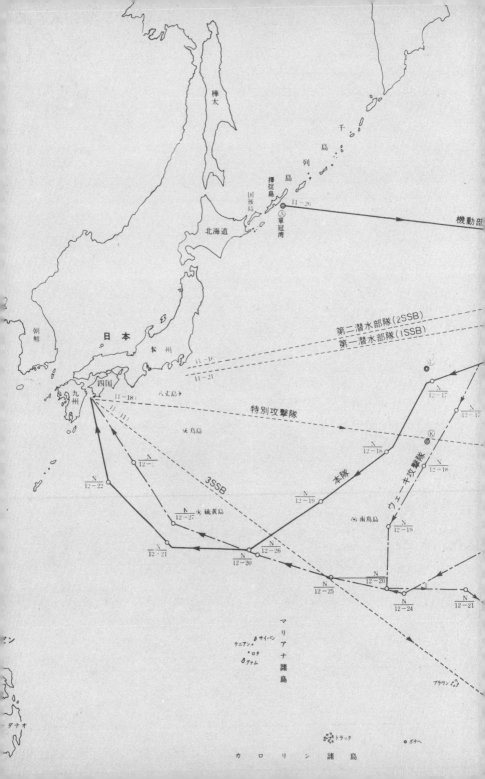

樺太

千
島
列
島

擇捉島
国後島
11-26
Ⓐ 單冠湾

機動部

北海道

第二潜水部隊(2SSB)
第一潜水部隊(1SSB)

日 本

11-19
11-21

本 州

Ⓛ

四国

11-18
八丈島

11-11

特別攻撃隊

N
12-17

N
12-17

N
12-1

鳥島

Ⓚ

N
12-18

N
12-22

3SSB

本隊

N
12-19

ウ
ェ
ー
キ
攻
撃
隊

N
12-18

N
12-27
硫黄島

N
12-21

N
12-20

N
12-19

南鳥島

N
12-26

N
12-20

N
12-25

N
12-24

N
12-21

マ
リ
ア
ナ
諸
島

サイパン

テニアン
ロタ
グァム

ブラウン

トラック
ポナペ

カ ロ リ ン 諸 島

剣鮮

ン

ダナオ